Adventuring
in the Andes

The Sierra Club Adventure Travel Guides

by Charles Frazier
with Donald Secreast

Adventuring
in the **Andes**

The Sierra Club Travel Guide
to Ecuador, Peru, Bolivia,
the Amazon Basin, and the Galapagos Islands

Sierra Club Books   San Francisco

The Sierra Club, founded in 1892 by John Muir, has devoted itself to the study and protection of the earth's scenic and ecological resources—mountains, wetlands, woodlands, wild shores and rivers, deserts and plains. The publishing program of the Sierra Club offers books to the public as a nonprofit educational service in the hope that they may enlarge the public's understanding of the Club's basic concerns. The point of view expressed in each book, however, does not necessarily represent that of the Club. The Sierra Club has some fifty chapters coast to coast, in Canada, Hawaii, and Alaska. For information about how you may participate in its programs to preserve wilderness and the quality of life, please address inquiries to Sierra Club, 730 Polk Street, San Francisco, CA 94109.

Copyright © 1985 by Charles Frazier

Library of Congress Cataloging in Publication Data

Frazier, Charles, 1950-
   Adventuring in the Andes.

   Bibliography: p. 255
   Includes index.
   1. Hiking—Andes—Guide-books. 2. Andes—Description and travel—Guide-books. I. Secreast, Donald. II. Sierra Club. III. Title.
GV199.44.A5F73   1985   918   84-22219
ISBN   0-87156-833-0

Cover design by Bonnie Smetts
Book design by Paul Quin
Illustrations by Nancy Warner
Printed in the United States of America

10 9 8 7 6 5 4 3

Contents

Preface   vii

CHAPTER 1   **Human and Natural History**   1

CHAPTER 2   **Planning an Outdoor Trip to the Andes**   19

CHAPTER 3   **Getting Along in the Andes**   39

CHAPTER 4   **Ecuador**   70

CHAPTER 5   **Peru**   105

CHAPTER 6   **Bolivia**   214

CHAPTER 7   **The Amazon Basin**   232

APPENDIX I   **Spanish Glossary**   246

APPENDIX II   **Quechua Glossary**   250

Annotated Bibliography   255

Index   259

Preface

The Incas called their empire Tawantinsuyo—the four corners of the world. The title to this book might just as well have been *Adventuring in Tawantinsuyo,* for we have taken as our scope the primary boundaries of the Inca empire from northern Ecuador through Peru and into northern Bolivia. Often called the Andean countries (though of course the great Andes chain is not limited to just these three nations), Ecuador, Peru, and Bolivia with their spectacular landscapes and high percentage of Indian inhabitants form a coherent geographical and cultural unit. Within the boundaries of Tawantinsuyo the adventure traveler will find an amazing spectrum of outdoor activities. Thus, we have by no means confined our attention only to mountain trekking.

Of course, the backpacking/trekking in Tawantinsuyo is among the most spectacular in the world, and Chapters 4, 5, and 6 provide information on a wide range of hiking and trekking routes—everything from easy day hikes that beginners can make from their hotel rooms to long treks crossing passes above glacier level for seasoned veterans of the backcountry. Virtually everyone has heard of the justly famous Inca Trail, but most people are unaware that between the volcanoes of Ecuador and the ragged peaks of the Cordillera Real in Bolivia thousands of miles of mountain trails—most of them in use *before* the Incas —crisscross the high passes and *quebradas* (canyons) of the mountains. Used by the Quechua Indians of the highlands to travel among pastures and roadless villages, these trails take you into some of the most remote regions of one of the world's great mountain ranges.

A word of caution: though we have gone to great lengths to obtain firsthand information on all the treks and excursions described in this guide, remember that nothing remains stable in the Andes—new roads disrupt centuries-old trails, landslides obliterate normally clear routes, footbridges collapse. We strongly advise that you seek local information on trail conditions before setting out on any of the more remote of the routes listed here.

On these ancient trails you'll see not only magnificent alpine scenery but also the way of life of the Quechuas that, while changing rapidly, still remains firmly rooted in the deep past of the Incas and their predecessors. Whether celebrating with abandon at a local fiesta or working hard harvesting crops, these people of the high Andes are constantly fascinating (referring to these people as *Quechuas*, by the way, does not denote a particular tribe; rather it is simply a convenient term for the highlanders, most of whom still speak the language of the Incas—Quechua). Because you'll walk through the homeland of *campesinos* (mountain or country people) on every trail that we list, it is our purpose to give you the information not only to find your way among the mountains but also to adapt to Andean culture and travel among the mountain people with as little disruption and as much grace as possible. Chapter 3, therefore, provides information on coping with the many cultural differences you'll experience in the Andes.

Nearly as fascinating as the mountains and the people is the staggering historical wealth of Tawantinsuyo. Though the mysterious and much-photographed ruins of Machu Picchu are well known, fewer travelers are aware that in Peru especially the architectural remains of the myriad pre-Columbian civilizations that flourished there dot the coastal and mountain landscape. Many of the treks, day hikes, and excursions covered here have as their destinations some of the most important of these ancient sites.

Equally interesting are the highland towns and villages where the wonderful culture of the Quechua Indians—a product of the clash between ancient ways of life, the devastation of Spanish conquest, and the modern world—is evident at every turn. Whether shopping for typical Andean crafts in a colorful market or simply walking the streets taking in the sights, most outdoor travelers make the towns and cities

Otavalo Indian

of the Andean countries an important part of their visits. We have, therefore, provided considerable information on entry cities, principal market towns, trailhead towns, etc.; included in city/town descriptions are Resources sections, which give you the information you'll need to find hotels, restaurants, transportation, etc., as you move through the Andes.

For travelers especially interested in wildlife observation and in visiting one of the world's unique, isolated ecosystems, we have included information on traveling among Ecuador's Galapagos Islands.

Just east of the snow mountains of the Andes lies the world's largest tropical rain forest, the basin of the great Amazon River and its tributaries. For those wishing to visit the Amazon as a sidelight to mountain travel, Chapter 7 introduces information on jungle and river travel.

Other sections cover preparing for travel in the Andes, basic communication in Spanish and Quechua, and sources for further reading.

In short, we've tried to give you a wide range of information to match the wide range of outdoor travel experiences available in Tawantinsuyo.

One final word of caution: though we feel safer traveling in the Andes than in most major metropolitan areas of the United States or Europe, we strongly suggest that visitors to Peru avoid the Ayacucho area, where in 1983 and 1984 random violence by a small band of guerillas and a large contingent of Peruvian military made travel, especially in the surrounding mountains, dangerous.

1
Human and Natural History

Though it is possible to be a successful *tourist* while knowing almost nothing about the historical context of the land one intends to visit, it is impossible to be a successful *traveler* without at least a little bit of knowledge. The purpose of this chapter is to acquaint you with at least a rudimentary understanding of the natural and human history of the Andes. Though a comprehensive treatment of these subjects is outside the scope of this book, the Annotated Bibliography provides direction for those who wish more in-depth information.

Human History of the Andean Countries

PRE-INCA CIVILIZATIONS

One of the difficulties in constructing a coherent and accurate picture of the diverse cultures that flourished along the coastline and in the highlands of the Andean countries for centuries before the Spanish arrived in Peru in 1532 is that none of these cultures developed a written language. Though the Incas kept historical records on bundles of knotted string called a *quipu* and the Moche people developed a similar form of record keeping by inscribing lima beans, both of these forms of information storage seem to have been mnemonic devices rather than translatable forms of writing. For historical information, therefore, we must rely on archaeology (primarily the development of ceramics) and oral tradition.

What appears certain from the evidence available is that the Pacific coast has been inhabited for at least 20,000 years. The caves at Lauricocha in northern Peru, for example, provide evidence of human occupation as early as 8000 B.C. Farther south in Chile, recent work has pushed back the date of first human habitation to nearly 18,000 B.C. These early Andeans lived largely by hunting, fishing, and gathering.

By 2500 B.C. inhabitants of the region began to develop agriculture, at first domesticating squash, beans, cotton, and, later, maize.

They also developed pottery (the most important form of information because of its longevity in damp climates) and settled, organized villages. The first culture to distinguish itself through a clearly distinct art style was the Chavín cult, which apparently was centered at the Chavín de Huantar site on the eastern side of the Cordillera Blanca in Peru. Though probably an artistic and religious influence rather than a governmental force, the Chavín cult dominated the art styles of northern and central Peru as well as the south coast for several centuries beginning approximately in the eighth century B.C. One characteristic feature of Chavín textiles, pottery, and stone carvings is the stylized depiction of a jaguar.

Another culture that developed shortly after the Chavín was located near present-day Paracas in Peru. Its pottery indicates strong Chavín influence, but more characteristic of the culture are the tightly woven Paracas textiles, which surpass anything produced in the New World. Though the Paracas culture lasted somewhat longer than the Chavín, by 400 B.C. the pottery suggests influence by the newer Nazca culture, which had begun to develop (or perhaps just evolve from the Paracas culture) in the fertile valleys of Pisco, Ica, Nazca, and Acari along south Peru's coast. Though the Nazcas developed fine pottery and textiles, it is primarily for the strange lines and figures they cut into the desert floor at Pampa San Jose that they are known today.

As the Nazcas were spreading along the south coast, the Moche culture was growing on the north coast. An aggressive and highly stratified civilization ruled by a small group of aristocrats (represented in many surviving pottery figurines), the Moche are responsible for the construction of several huge temples and fortifications, which still stand in Peru's northern desert.

By A.D. 600 the Tiahuanaco culture, with its center at the great ceremonial complex near Lake Titicaca in Peru, had begun to bring together the lives and art of people from the Titicaca basin all the way to the coast of Chile. At the same time, the Huari people of the present-day Ayacucho region—heavily influenced by the Tiahuanaco —began to exert their own cultural and political authority. The two related art styles have become known as the Huari-Tiahuanaco horizon, and its characteristic geometrical pumas and condors are a pervasive influence in textiles, pottery, and carvings throughout northern Bolivia, Peru, and southern Ecuador. For unknown reasons, by A.D. 800 both Huari and Tiahuanaco had collapsed from internal problems rather than from external invasion. Both sites were left empty.

No strong unifying culture developed until roughly 1350 when Emperor Ñancen Pinco began to direct the political course of the north coast Chimu culture, descendants of the Moche. Like their predecessors, the Chimu were both highly aggressive and highly organized, but their empire enjoyed only ten rulers before the rapidly expanding Inca empire conquered them in 1460. The last Chimu ruler, Minchancaman, was taken to Cuzco by Topa Inca, the great commander who was largely responsible for sudden rapid expansion of the Inca empire during the reign of his father, Pachacuti. Topa evidently learned much about the organization of an empire from his captive, for much of the eventual structure of the Inca political system is based on Chimu models.

THE INCA EMPIRE

During its brief life, the Inca empire was one of the most controlled societies in our planet's history. The political organization of the empire could fairly accurately be called aristocratic socialism since the state owned virtually everything, and the Inca emperor *was* the state. Considered a direct descendant of the sun, the center of the Inca religion, the Inca was himself worshipped as a deity. Though the word *Inca* has come to denote the entire culture and population of the empire, in strict practice the term referred only to this divine ruler, the Sapa Inca. In looser application, it could also refer to the ruler's family, and it could be earned, too, by bravery in battle or by useful service to the ruler.

In a sense, this small group of Incas was the central nervous system of the empire's social order. They were administrators as well as generals, entrepreneurs as well as priests. Beneath them existed a complex body of lesser administrators and governors, principal of which were the masters (*apus*) of the empire's four districts: Chincha-suyu, Anti-suyu, Colla-suyu, and Conti-suyu. This administrative network descended in area of control all the way to the local level. There an official called the *curaca* was responsible for overseeing a unit of 10,000 workers through yet another hierarchy of supervisors and foremen. This hierarchy was so rigid and dependent on control from above that when the conquistadores captured and executed the Incas, putting themselves at the head of the hierarchy, the system beneath them continued to function for quite some time on its own momentum.

The commoners ruled by the Inca and his subordinate administrators were called *runa-simi,* and although the power of the Incas was absolute, they also recognized that the welfare of the *runa-simi* was one of their most important responsibilities. Since agriculture was the basis for the empire's economy, one significant concern for the Incas was ensuring adequate food supplies for the *runa-simi* during times of poor harvests. To accomplish this, the Incas effected the construction of food storehouses in most towns of the realm, and during times of crop failure, these were open to everyone.

The basic social unit of the *runa-simi* was the *ayllu* (tribe), a community of mutually dependent workers and taxpayers. Even today, some of the more traditional mountain communities remain similar in many ways to the Inca *ayllu.* In theory, the community was composed of a variable but even number of able-bodied males who could be counted on as taxpayers. The tax required of an *ayllu* was determined by the size of its population and the fertility of its land (*marka*). Tax payments were usually made in the form of craft or agricultural products. The *ayllu*'s land was divided by the administrators into three parts: a third was allotted to the sun (the state religion), another third to the Inca, and the final third to the *ayllu.* The workers who tilled all the land received produce only from their third, and they were allowed only a few personal possessions, usually little more than a house, a few small animals (the Inca officially owned most of the empire's llamas), and a few essential utensils and tools. In addition, most able-bodied workers were required to perform yearly public works service. Called *mita,* this service allowed for the construction and maintenance of roads, irrigation projects, and public buildings.

Perhaps the greatest accomplishment of Inca engineers and *mita* workers was the empire's vast system of highways. Anyone who walks any of the surviving paved portions of Inca roads cannot help but be impressed with the extreme difficulty their construction involved and with the important contribution such a system of roads must have made to controlling a far-flung empire. Certainly Pizarro and his men did not underestimate the Inca's achievement in this regard. Except for gold, nothing in the Inca empire impressed the conquering Spaniards more than the extensive road system. So efficient was this highway that one Spanish conquistador remarked: "After God, it was the Inca's roads that gave us victory." The first systematic chronicler of the Inca highway was Pedro de Cieza de Leon, a sort of soldier-journalist of the sixteenth century. He began his description of the road by comparing it to the Roman road that connected Seville to Triana. The comparison was apt because not since the Romans had Europeans seen roads to match what the Incas had built in their relatively short imperial span.

The Incas themselves were justifiably proud of this engineering feat, which bound their territory together and even allowed the Inca to enjoy the luxury of fresh fish—delivered by *chasquis* (relay runners) via the highway from the Pacific to Cuzco. The Incas called their highway system *Capac Nañ* (beautiful road). The highways began at the empire's navel, in Cuzco, and from there they radiated to the four *suyos* (quarters). One major artery ran west to Vilcashuaman where it forked. The northern branch reached all the way to Quito in Ecuador. The other branch continued west to the city of Ica where it forked again, running north and south to connect the important coastal towns from Tumbes in northern Peru to Talca in Chile. Another major route traveled south from Cuzco, looping around Lake Titicaca, crossing the Bolivian *altiplano* (high plain), descending into the jungle, and recrossing the Andes to join the coastal road in Chile. All in all, the road covered nearly 5,000 miles of the most difficult terrain imaginable, crossing the world's driest desert and traversing some of the Western hemisphere's highest mountains.

One of the most serious engineering obstacles facing the Inca road builders was moving huge masses of rock to form the roadbed. As did the Romans, the Incas first searched for cracks in the stone. Holes were drilled into the cracks, and then wooden pegs were driven into the holes. When soaked with water, the pegs expanded, further cracking the stone. When necessary, workers helped the splitting by using bronze crowbars. Another method used by the Inca road builders to split stone was to build huge fires close to the obstructing rock. When the rock became white hot, the builders would dash cold water on it to create cracks.

Naturally, the Inca road builders had stream and canyon crossings to contend with, so in addition to the engineering problems connected with building a paved highway often as much as twenty-four feet wide, they also had to construct approximately a thousand bridges to complete their road system. The most dramatic example of Inca bridge building was found outside Curahuasi where the road had to cross the gorge of the Rio Apurimac. The 150-foot bridge was constructed of five cables—two suspension cables (supported by stone towers) and three floor cables. Woven from the fibers of aloelike *fourcroya* and *cabuya* plants, each cable would have been able to support up to 50,000 pounds. The cables were roughly twenty-five inches in circumference and may have weighed as much as 5,000 pounds.

As spectacular as the achievement of the Inca engineers was, it must be remembered that the main function of the highway system was purely practical—to move people, messages, and products from one part of the empire to another as quickly as possible. As the head of a very centralized government, the Sapa Inca needed a transportation system that would guarantee that he receive information from the far reaches of his kingdom with great speed. From this need the Inca couriers were born. These *chasquis* were raised from childhood to run the *Capac Nañ*. Running in relay, *chasquis* routinely covered the distance from Cuzco to Quito (over 1,200 miles) in five days, with most of the running done at elevations between 8,000 and 12,000 feet.

Less rapid travelers along the Inca highway could judge their progress in two ways. First, at regular intervals of twelve to fifteen miles, the Incas built *tambos*—roadside inns for food and shelter. *Tambos* were situated a comfortable day's walk apart. Second, travelers could note their progress by watching for smaller shelters called *o'klas,* small houses where usually two *chasquis* lived with their families. These shelters were normally situated about 1.5 miles apart.

By the time of the Spanish conquest, the Inca empire extended from northern Ecuador to central Chile, approximately the distance from New York City to Los Angeles. When the empire was at its peak, the Incas held sway over one hundred different cultures, which comprised at least 12 million people. Today it might be hard for travelers to imagine such a thriving empire taking shape in the severe landscape of the Andes. It must be remembered, however, that the Incas represent an extraordinarily high degree of human adaptability. Their religious, political, and social systems were an organic outgrowth of the land they inhabited.

Within the Inca civilization, historical records were quite detailed, despite the absence of a written language. Official oral historians were taught all the Inca traditions and legends. They, in turn, passed the lore down to the next generation. To aid them in their accountings, the Incas used the previously mentioned *quipu,* a rather beautiful device that to modern eyes appears more decorative than functional, but it was the basic record-keeping method for a complex society. The *quipu* is composed of cord from which hang numerous smaller strings of various colors. The smaller strings were knotted by the *quipucamayoc* —the *quipu* master—to represent some significant event or to record tax payments or other accounting matters. The nature of the information, whether historical, political, religious, or economic, determined the color of the string to be knotted. However, we cannot today "read" an Inca *quipu* in the sense that Mayan or Egyptian heiroglyphics can be read and understood. And it is unlikely that we ever will because the method of encoding information onto them was probably more idiosyncratic than systematic, varying widely among *quipucamayocs*. Fortunately, though, much of the history presumably incorporated into the *quipu* survived in oral form and was recorded by the early chroniclers. Inca oral history, though, was "official history"; that is, only those events that the Sapa Inca wanted memorized were passed down to subsequent *quipucamayocs*. Also, the early stages of Inca history are probably at least as much legend as fact. Only with the reign of Pachacuti does Inca history become reasonably verifiable.

According to Inca tradition, their race began when Manco Capac and his sister/wife Mama Ocllo emerged from Lake Titicaca and traveled north to found Cuzco. An alternate legend claims that Manco, along with his brothers and sisters and ten *ayllus*, emerged from holes in the ground at Paccari Tampui, just south of Cuzco.

At any rate, the Incas prospered in Cuzco, and soon they were busy interfering in the lives of neighboring tribes, demanding tribute and water rights from them in return for freedom from harassment. By the time of the fourth Inca, Mayta Capac, the domain begin to expand significantly. During his reign in the fourteenth century, the Incas conquered tribes in the nearby Cuzco valley as a sort of prelude to what was to follow under later rulers. After modest expansions of territory under the subsequent rules of Capac Yupanqui, Inca Roca, and Yahuar Huacac, Inca domination became much more aggressive and systematic during the early decades of the fifteenth century under Inca Viracocha. Aided by his two uncles, Vicaquirao and Apo Mayta, Viracocha set his expansionist sights on the Urubamba valley, and he developed a style of warfare and domination that became standard operating procedure in subsequent Inca conquests. Attacking on two fronts simultaneously, the Inca forces defeated the Ayarmacas, and then Viracocha instituted his new practice of incorporating conquered peoples into the Inca system of government rather than just exacting tribute and moving on.

While Viracocha was busy establishing permanent Inca settlements in the Urubamba valley and on toward Lake Titicaca, another group, the Chancas, was expanding to the west. The clashes between these two aggressive groups precipitated the first of the Inca civil wars. Viracocha had picked Inca Urcon to be the next Sapa Inca, but Vicaquirao and Apo Mayta were not happy with his choice. They supported another of Viracocha's sons, Cusi Inca Yupanqui. When a strong Chanca force attacked Cuzco, Viracocha and Urcon retreated to Calca, leaving Cusi and his old warrior uncles with the seemingly impossible task of holding Cuzco. But hold it they did, saying later that they were so outnumbered that the stones of the city must have been transformed into soldiers to aid in their defense. Some of these stones were set up in Cuzco's temples as sacred *huacas*. After driving back the Chancas and unsuccessfully attempting a reconciliation with his father, Cusi declared himself Sapa Inca and took the name Pachacuti, thus establishing two Inca kingdoms—his own in Cuzco and his father's in Calca.

Thus Pachacuti found himself with two very real enemies—the Chancas, who had been defeated but not conquered, and his father and brother, who also had an army to back their desire to be sole rulers of the kingdom. To solve these problems, Pachacuti first formed a shaky alliance with the Chancas and then surrounded Calca. When Viracocha died of natural causes and Urcon was killed in battle, the empire was again united.

Pachacuti, who reigned from about 1438 to 1471, became the greatest of the Inca emperors, building Cuzco into the finest city in the Western hemisphere and conquering new lands. Under Pachacuti, the empire expanded incredibly. During his reign, one of the most amazing journeys of conquest in history was undertaken by his son, Topa Inca. Setting out north from Cuzco, Topa subjugated the mountain tribes as far north as Quito in Ecuador. Turning south, he then attacked the powerful Chimu civilization from both the desert and the mountains, sweeping over them on two fronts as his grandfather, Viracocha, had done with the Ayarmacas. Continuing down the coast to the area of present-day Lima, Topa conquered the huge ceremonial city of Pachacamac. By the time he returned home to Cuzco, Topa had brought a vast area—most of Peru and Ecuador—under Inca control. One would have to go to Alexander or Napoleon to find a proper comparison to Topa's accomplishment.

Finding himself suddenly the ruler of a huge empire, Pachacuti was faced with major administrative problems, which he solved brilliantly. First, in a decision of surprising tolerance, he allowed the newly conquered peoples to keep their previous religion so long as they added the Inca creator-god Viracocha to their pantheon of gods. Second, to help unite the empire, he established Quechua as the state language. Third, he established the practice of *mitma*, a resettlement program. Under this system, conquered people were uprooted from their homeland and replaced by a group loyal to Inca rule. The uprooted people were brought to settlements deeper inside the Inca domain where they could be controlled more easily and taught to be grateful for Inca domination.

After Pachacuti abdicated in favor of Topa to ensure an unchallenged succession, Topa turned to the south, conquering tribes throughout highland Bolivia, northern Chile, and northwestern Argentina. With these campaigns, the Inca empire reached its maximum extent. The remainder of Topa's reign was spent organizing administrative procedures to govern the enormous empire he and his father had conquered. He is credited with establishing a census, with organizing the Chosen Women (both nuns and concubines to Inca royalty), and with setting up the decimal system of administration under which male workers were divided into pyramidal groups of 100, 500, 1,000, 5,000, and 10,000 members, each level having its own administrator, the *curaca.*

When Topa Inca died in 1493, his son, Huayna Capac, became the ruler. His long reign was occupied primarily with the complex administrative problems of the empire. In 1525, during an epidemic, Huayna Capac died in Quito, giving rise to a second civil war to decide succession to the throne. His son Huascar was appointed Sapa Inca by a priest, but another faction preferred that another son, Atahuallpa, take control of the empire. The civil war that ensued lasted nearly seven years, but as the struggle between Atahuallpa and Huascar was drawing to a close in 1532, the empire's real enemy had already set foot in Tumbes in northern Peru—the Spanish conquistadores under the command of Francisco Pizarro. Pizarro was to manipulate the civil war for his own benefit. Adapting the methods that his mentor, Cortez, had perfected in the conquest of Mexico, Pizarro planned to capture Atahuallpa. Not quite understanding what the Spaniards were promising or asking of him, Atahuallpa—after defeating Huascar—met the Spaniards in Cajamarca. On November 16, 1532, the last true Sapa Inca was taken captive.

THE SPANISH CONQUEST

In light of the fact that Pizarro began his conquest of the vast Inca empire with only 180 men, it is tempting to attribute the Inca defeat either to cowardice or to a military inept beyond belief. Neither is the case. The Inca forces had proven their courage and prowess many times against numerically superior but similarly armed enemies. They were defeated by a combination of the political chaos that followed the civil war, the Inca's initial confusion of the Spanish with the prophesied return of the god Viracocha, and the advanced military technology of the conquistadores. The Spanish were simply incredibly lucky. The civil war left the empire ripe for the picking, and the old legend of the white-skinned, bearded god Viracocha and his followers vowing to return from their sea journey across the Pacific only compounded the luck. But the last of these factors—technology—is the least often discussed and most often misunderstood.

The advanced technologies the Spanish possessed were horses, metal armor, long-handled lances, and swords made from the best steel in the world. The combination of these weapons proved virtually invincible, and the Inca military never found a way to combat them. To the Incas who had never seen them before, the horses were both immensely powerful and frightening. They gave their riders devastating mobility during battle and lifted them above easy range of the battle clubs and short brittle swords that made up most of the Inca armory. The metal armor offered almost complete protection from these simple weapons, and the Incas never developed a projectile capable of penetrating the armor. The long-handled lances enabled the mounted conquistador to kill at arm's length, seldom allowing the Inca foot soldiers within striking distance. The fine Toledo-steel swords of the Spanish were deadly efficient works of military art—strong, light, sharp, and supple. Against trained fighting men so well equipped, the armorless, club-wielding Inca foot soldier hadn't a chance. According to the chronicles, the conquistadores slaughtered them by the thousands.

The slaughter began with several hundred men, women, and children during the capture of Atahuallpa in Cajamarca. According to those who participated, the bodies of the dead accumulated so quickly and in such huge piles that some Indians caught in the struggle simply smothered to death beneath them. Following this massacre, Atahualpa tried to buy his freedom. In the room where he was being confined, he made a mark on the wall—about eight feet high according to legend (the present mark on the wall in Cajamarca is a recent addition). He promised Pizarro that if he were freed, he would fill the room to that mark once with gold and twice with silver.

Since wealth was what Pizarro had come for, he agreed, promising in return not to shed one drop of Atahuallpa's blood. Atahuallpa kept his word; gold and silver was brought from all over the empire to fill the chamber. And in his own way, Pizarro kept his word as well; after the ransom was collected he had Atahualpa taken to the central plaza and bloodlessly garroted.

To quiet the unrest caused by this execution, Pizarro, upon reaching Cuzco, set up Manco Inca as the new Sapa Inca. By using Manco, the dead Huascar's brother, Pizarro hoped to gain favor with those Cuzqueñas who had supported Huascar in the recent civil war. And for a few years Manco Inca played his puppet role without outward complaint, not a particularly auspicious start for the man who would become a great guerrilla leader.

Over time, however, Manco came to realize that the Spaniards were insatiable. He watched as they stripped the palaces of their treasures, and after nothing was left there, they stripped the temples, tossing out the sacred mummies of former Sapa Incas in the process. By 1536, Manco had had enough. Somehow he convinced Hernando Pizarro to let him leave Cuzco and go to the Yucay valley, a pilgrimage he promised to return from, bringing with him a statute of Huayna Capac—a life-sized, solid-gold statute, he must have been careful to add. Apparently this was all Hernando Pizarro needed to hear, and ignoring the objections raised by his own men and some of the Indians who had joined the Spaniards, he granted Manco's request.

Manco, of course, did not return with the statue. Instead, he began putting together an army, which soon numbered 100,000 men. This was the beginning of the final Inca resistance, which lasted from 1536 until 1572. Manco began his campaign by attacking Cuzco and burning much of the thatch-roofed city. He failed to take the city, however, and after a major defeat at Sacsayhuaman, the huge *pucara* (fortress) overlooking Cuzco, he withdrew to Ollantaytambo, another massive fortification. Soon the Spaniards had regrouped their forces and attacked Ollantaytambo, but Manco was able to repulse them. Instead of pursuing the Spaniards, though, he decided to withdraw further north to Vitcos where he hoped the Spaniards and their Indian allies would not be able to find them.

Unfortunately, the Spanish forces pursued Manco and his followers to Vitcos and attacked him there, taking the town. Manco managed to escape, probably while the Spanish had their attentions concentrated on looting the town. The loss of Vitcos was a devastating blow to Manco. The Spanish took about 20,000 prisoners and 50,000 llamas and alpacas. Matters might have been worse, though. Rather than pursuing Manco Inca, Orgoñez took his prisoners and booty back to Cuzco, thinking that the Inca guerrillas had finally been crushed.

They had not. Retreating far into the remote region of Vilcabamba, Manco and his followers soon began directing a successful series of small-scale guerrilla attacks upon the Spanish from their stronghold in the jungles. By 1541 the resistance had strengthened its position enough to return to Vitcos, and in that year Manco received good news. Francisco Pizarro, while sleeping in his palace in Lima, had been chopped to pieces by a group of unhappy soldiers. In a twist of events strange and ironic enough to be fiction, seven of these soldiers found their way to Vitcos where they were welcomed as friends of the Inca ruler. At first the renegades were helpful to Manco, teaching him and his men to use a harquebus (the earliest form of portable firearm) and to ride horses. But later they began to scheme. News had come to them that a new viceroy sent from Spain was having trouble dealing with the remaining Pizarro brothers. Conditions seemed right to the seven Spaniards for a daring move. They reasoned that if they could kill Manco, they could return to Lima as heroes. Thus, during a game of horseshoes with the Inca, these same seven men who had killed Pizarro also stabbed Manco Inca to death. Before they could escape, however, Manco's men killed them.

Manco's son, Sayri Tupac, thus assumed leadership of the Inca resistance in 1544. Under Sayri Tupac, the Incas were able to hold their positions in the higher, rougher sections of their former kingdom. In 1558, though, after an offer of amnesty from the king of Spain, Sayri Tupac surrendered and traveled to Lima. The peace that followed the surrender was brief. Sayri Tupac died in 1560, and another of Manco's sons, Titu Cusi, resumed the war with the Spanish from a stronghold in Vilcabamba.

Upon Titu Cusi's death in 1571, a third of Manco's sons, Tupac Amaru, became ruler and escalated the fighting. This provoked the Spanish into an all-out attack on Vilcabamba, and in 1572, Tupac Amaru was captured, taken to Cuzco, quickly converted to Christianity, and beheaded. This final execution brought to an end the line of Inca rulers and established the Spaniards as the absolute power in the Andes. Under their rule the magnificent fortresses, palaces, and temples were demolished; the highway system with its *tambos* and *chasquis* was destroyed in large stretches; and what little Inca art of gold and silver that remained was melted down, and most of the rest was burned, or broken.

The cultural, historical loss was immense, but the greatest loss must be measured in terms of lives. Indians who had been hard-working and self-sufficient were subjugated virtually to the status of slaves and put to work for the conquerors in mines and on *encomiendas* (plantations) where the death toll was staggering. To add to the toll, European diseases such as smallpox and measles, to which Andeans had developed no immunities, wiped out huge sections of the population. Perhaps the most telling comment on the Spanish occupation is a simple statistic: when the conquistadores first landed, the Inca empire controlled the lives of 12 million people; after only fifty years of Spanish civilizing and Christianizing, the Indian population of the former empire had been reduced to 2 million.

TODAY'S CAMPESINOS

Given the devastating effect of the conquest on the highlanders, it is remarkable that any of the indigenous culture survived. It is a tribute to the *campesinos'* tenacity that such a distinctive culture remains in the Andes. Though it cannot be said that the contemporary *campesinos* have prevailed, they have at least survived. Their survival is largely because they are fitted mentally, physiologically, and culturally to make their lives in the hard world of the high Andes. Today, between 15 and 20 million *campesinos* live in the cold high *puna* above 10,000 feet, and there are even a few permanent settlements near the

Machu Picchu

16,000-foot level. At these elevations whatever lives must become tough or die, and like the vicuña or the *queñoa* tree, both of which flourish almost at snowline, the Quechuas have over the centuries become remarkably adapted to high-altitude conditions.

You will notice that the *campesinos* are rather cylindrical people with thick, short-waisted torsos set on short legs. This reduces skin surface in relation to body bulk, holding in crucial body heat by providing less radiating surface and promoting faster circulation of blood from the colder extremities to the warmer core. Less noticeable is the fact that their basal metabolic rate is high, enabling them to maintain a somewhat elevated internal temperature to combat the mountain cold. Their hearts beat almost as slowly as a marathon runner's and are up to one-fifth larger than the hearts of similarly sized sea-level dwellers. And their bodies contain one-fifth more blood, which is, additionally, more than 50 percent higher in crucial oxygen-absorbing hemoglobin than the average sea-level dweller's.

But no matter how well suited they are for their environment, life for the mountain people is not easy. Like most indigenous mountain dwellers of the world, they are by Western standards dirt poor. They scratch a subsistence living from a difficult land. Their fields are often irrigated by the same systems built centuries ago by the Incas, and their small crops of wheat, barley, and corn often grow on hills terraced by the Incas. There is no mechanized farming. In the matter of dress, very little has changed since the Spaniards settled among the Indians. Medical services are extremely limited, and in some areas life expectancy can be as low as forty years.

People who pass quickly through only the larger Andean cities usually come away with a memory of ragged, filthy, displaced *campesinos* wandering the poorer sections of the cities, begging or drinking or completely oblivious to the world around them. Such scenes are everyday facts of Andean life. The shanty towns that continue to grow around the outskirts of Lima and La Paz are an unnerving and unforgettable sight: people without a future living in cardboard shacks stacked like drunken honeycombs on bone-dry hills where nothing has ever grown. Help for these displaced people is slow in coming, given the economic difficulties of the Andean countries and the present dominant attitude that the *campesino* is a shiftless, hopeless weight on society.

But there is also another side of *campesino* life that can be seen only in the traditional communities of the mountains. There the *campesino* remains close to the kind of self-sufficiency so valued by the Incas. The lives of mountain *campesinos* are too hard to romanticize, but these people do have something valuable—a very distinct awareness of the beauty of their land, their language, and their history. They are proud of their land and heritage. If you make the effort to communicate with them, once you get past the initial shyness and stolidity, you find this pride, and you also find a considerable sense of humor and a desire to find something in life to celebrate. You see this sense of celebration expressed in even the smallest ways, for example, an old man sitting on the lip of a collapsed volcano crater in Ecuador playing a few shaky notes on a wooden flute as if in tribute to the landscape.

Something undefinable is there. And even in cities, if you look hard enough, you observe brief flashes of it in the sense of play underlying the serious business of earning a living that street vendors bring to their salesmanship. They are delighted when you buy, but you also sense that the purchase is part of their entertainment. You are the source of amusement. Tomorrow you will be gone. They will still be there with their mountains and their pride—which some sociologists consider their real problem—in being who they are.

Natural History

GEOLOGY

If, on a relief map of South America, you trace your index finger south from Colombia to near the tip of the continent, the uninterrupted string of tiny bumps you feel represents the longest continuous mountain range in the world, stretching 4,500 miles in a long, thin band usually less than 300 miles wide. It is also among the youngest mountains in the world. In comparison with an ancient range like the Appalachians whose age is measured in hundreds of millions of years, the Andes are brash upstarts, so young, in fact, that the geologic forces of mountain building that lifted the peaks into the sky have not yet completely given way to the forces of erosion.

One of the keys to understanding the ongoing process that has formed the spectacular terrain of the Andes is realizing that the complex geological structure of the range includes not only the overwhelmingly evident mountains but also the nearby but hidden Peru-Chile trench. In this trench, just off the Pacific coast, the ocean floor reaches a depth of up to 25,000 feet below sea level. In other words, in less than 100 horizontal miles from the top of a mountain like Nevado Huascarán, the earth plunges an incredible nine vertical miles.

To understand the intimate relationship between the Andes and the Peru-Chile trench, it is necessary to discuss plate tectonics—the relative movements of the six huge, interlocking, sixty-mile-thick plates that make up the earth's surface. At certain boundaries of these plates, along great submerged mountain ranges in the mid-Pacific and mid-Atlantic, earth is, in a sense, being formed. Magma rising from deep within the planet spreads the sea floor, pushing it away from the plate junctures to both the east and the west. Along other boundaries, earth is in a sense being consumed as one plate plunges beneath an overriding plate. The South American plate, part of which is occupied by the continental land mass, is generated in the mid-Atlantic and moves westward; the Nazca plate, all of which is occupied by ocean floor, is generated in the mid-Pacific and moves eastward. The meeting point of these two gigantic pieces of the earth's simple six-piece jigsaw puzzle is the Peru-Chile trench just off the Pacific coast. There the Nazca plate subsides beneath the South American plate at the rate of nearly three inches per year. At this juncture the Andes formed.

Though some modest mountain building occurred along South America's west coast around the time of the continent's separation from Africa some 200 million years ago, the Andes began to be thrust upward in earnest only 15 million years ago. At that time a long line of massive volcanoes erupted along the boundary between the Nazca and South American plates. Vast amounts of magma (probably the result of underground heating of the rock from the Nazca plate descending beneath the South American plate) rose from deep within the earth to form not only the volcanoes but also gigantic bulges and folds in the earth's crust. Since that time, the work of rivers, glaciers, and earthquakes has sculpted these four-mile-high bulges and folds into the forms the Andes take today.

ANDEAN FLORA

The astonishing variety of Andean plant life and habitat will become clear if you walk a trail with extreme altitude variation like the Le Cumbre-to-Corioco trail in Bolivia or the Mollepata-to-Santa Teresa trail in Peru. On trails of this sort, you get a first-hand lesson in the effects of rainfall, temperature, and altitude on the region's flora as you descend in only a day or two from a glacier-level, 16,000-foot pass, through high alpine meadows, and into the high jungle where banana, orange, and rubber trees grow in profusion.

Just below the lifeless high rocky peaks and the tongues of glacial moraines, the *puna* region begins (in Ecuador the corresponding but much damper high-altitude region is called the *paramos*). These open, almost tundralike grassy hillsides and plains extend from snowline down to about 12,000 feet and are dominated by the yellow-beige of *ichu* grass. This most common and important plant of the *puna* grows in tussocks sometimes three feet high and a foot thick. Besides being a favorite grazing food for llamas and alpacas, *ichu* grass is used as roof thatch by the highlanders. Smaller plants such as gentians, valerians, madders, lupines, and violas often grow inside these *ichu* tussocks. Among the high mountains, valley floors too boggy for *ichu* are often intermittently carpeted with *distichia,* a grassy-mossy cushion of vegetation. The clumps of *distichia* are solid enough to stand on, but between the clumps you can easily sink to your knees in the bog.

This high Andean plateau appears, at first glance, rather barren, a vast landscape of burned yellow, making the few flashes of color provided by the wild plant life of the region all the more welcome. One source of color is the *iochroma grandiflora,* a shrub with lush purplish flowers that you find dotting the floors of high *quebradas.* Another source of color in the mountains is a type of elderberry, the *sambucus peruviana,* which sometimes glitters with white blooms. You also find growing among hedges the passion flower, called *ccoto-ccoto* in Quechua, with its large red petals and a deep purple edge. Also colorful are the *bejaria,* a pink-blossomed, azalealike shrub, and the *erythrina* or *puru-puru,* the deep red beans of which are used as jewelry by the mountain people. Less appealing to the eye but more functional is the *dodonaea viscosa,* the leaves of which are used by the Indians for mattresses. The leaves are mildly sticky, enough so that when pressed together to make a bed, they can be picked up and carried as if sewn together. Another functional shrub is the *tola,* used in treeless higher altitudes for cooking fires.

In the mountains you occasionally come upon lovely groves of the gnarled *queñoa* tree and the silvery-leafed *quisuar* tree, which sometimes grow in sheltered valleys at elevations as high as 15,000 feet. But the tree that constantly attracts your attention in the highland towns and lining lanes and roads in the countryside is the eucalyptus, fairly recently introduced to the Andes. The landscape would certainly look barren if not for the graceful silhouettes of these beautiful trees. Eucalyptus is a primary source of firewood, and its spicy-sweet smoke scents the evening air in most highland towns.

Also in the vicinity of inhabited regions you find several large varieties of aloe and agave, including a monstrous relative, the *fourcroya* plant. In Inca times, the huge, hard leaves of the *fourcroya* were dried and the tough fibers used in construction of the famous Inca suspension bridges. Highlanders today still use fibers from this plant and the similar *cabuya* for mats and sandals. Bromeliads are also common, ranging in size from tennis-ball-sized plants growing on the faces of cliffs to the gigantic *puyas,* one variety of which, the *puya raimondi* of the Cordillera Blanca, has the largest flower stalk of any plant in the world.

Since more and more of the Andean countryside is coming under cultivation, some of the most common crops in the highlands are barley, alfalfa, corn, beans, sweet potatoes, yuca, peppers, tomatoes, and the ubiquitous potato. Called *pusasuaylla* in Quechua, the potato was first domesticated in the Andes, and it would be more accurate, therefore, to call the Irish potato the Peruvian potato. The potato remains the staple of the highlanders' diet, and if you visit the produce section of any market you find an amazing variety of these tubers, the smallest and gnarliest of which have been adapted over the centuries for growth at high altitudes.

As you descend from the high *cordilleras* (mountain ranges) along the eastern slope of the Andes, you enter the cloud forest, a wonderfully green and misty region. This large ecological system, part of which is called the *ceja de la montaña* (eyebrow of the jungle), extends from about 11,000 to 3,000 feet. Created by condensation resulting from the collision of warm moist air rising from the Amazon basin with the cold dry mountain air, the cloud forests are seldom free of rain, clouds, and fog. In this wet climate, plant life flourishes, and a list of typical cloud forest vegetation reads like the inventory of a tropical plant store— ferns, orchids, bromeliads, monstera, philodendron, diffenbachia, xanthosoma. Also common, especially near streams, is the *chusquea,* a bamboolike plant with sharp, cutting leaves. You also enjoy the spots of brilliant color provided by the profusion of *fuchsia*, the burning scarlet of *aphelandra*, the blue vines of *cobaea*, and the orange flowers of the *bomarea*.

The largest plants in the cloud forest are the South American conifers such as the *podocarpus utilior* (*uncumanu* in Quechua) and the *podocarpus glomeratus* (*piña* or *intimpa*). Rather than taking the shape of needles, the leaves of these conifers grow stiff and thick, sometimes reaching the width of a quarter of an inch. One of the most important of the larger cloud-forest plants for the *campesinos* is the *tuna* or *opuntia*, a prickly pear that provides food and a source of income.

The plant that outsiders most associate with the Andes is, of course, the *erythroxylon coca*, domesticated since long before the Incas. It grows in the *ceja de la montaña* at elevations up to 8,000 feet. Economically important now because it is the raw material for cocaine, the coca plant has been considered sacred by Andeans for centuries. Perfectly formed coca leaves were burned by the Incas (and in some remote areas still are) in a ceremony of sacrifice and offering. In Inca times, the use of coca was strictly limited to royalty. But the Spaniards encouraged the chewing of coca when they discovered that its numbing and hunger- and pain-reducing effects enabled their Indian workers to put in longer hours under harsh conditions in mines and on plantations.

Today, coca chewing remains widespread. You find clear plastic bags of the small laurellike leaves for sale in any market in Peru and Bolivia (they are illegal in Ecuador). Many travelers like to try coca chewing, especially in the way many Quechuas use it—to help in the hard climbs to high passes. There is no big trick to coca chewing; just fold a few leaves together and put them between your gum and your cheek. You also need to rub a little potash or lime onto the quid in order to release the alkaloids that produce the very mildly euphoric feeling coca chewers experience (sticks of lime are usually sold along with the coca leaves). Chewing, however, is not really descriptive of what one actually does to a coca quid. Once it is in your mouth, just let it sit there releasing the alkaloids. Don't expect a dramatic rush of sensation, just a slight feeling of contentment and energy not particularly more pronounced (just more soothing) than what you'd get from a strong cup of coffee. A word of warning: though coca leaves are perfectly legal in Peru and Bolivia, cocaine laws are very strictly enforced. (See Chapter 2 for further information on this subject.)

Perhaps the strangest plant ecosystem in the Andean countries is along Peru's dry Pacific coast. Most of this desert is virtually rainless, but in a few spots, coastal fogs are heavy enough to support plant life for a brief period during the year. The small, temporary meadows that the fog allows to grow are called *lomas*. Most common in September, *lomas* are usually made up of blooming *Oxalis, Cryptantha, Plantago,* and *Drymaria*, all just a few inches high. More common in the desert is the *Tillandsia stramenea*, a tough, silvery plant related to the pineapple and Spanish moss. Having practically no root system, it depends on the fogs for water as well, pulling what moisture it can from the air. *Tillandsia* also serves a unique social service. It is the practice in the Andean countries to erect a wooden cross to mark the spot along the roadway where a traveler has died. But in treeless desert areas mourners sometimes spell out the victim's name in the sand with *Tillandsia.*

ANDEAN FAUNA

Even after several trips into the Andean backcountry, you may be convinced that the mountains are devoid of wild animals. Though this is not really the case, the Andes simply do not overwhelm the visitor with animal life in the way that, say, the southern Appalachians in the United States do. Larger animals are fairly scarce because the habitat has been severely reduced by human population, and until recently hunting, even of rare species, was largely unrestricted. The animals are there, though, but you must keep your eyes open in order to see them. We've found that traveling with *arrieros* (mule or horse drivers) helps in animal observation; local people know where the animals are likely to be and their eyes are much sharper than ours.

Certainly the animal most characteristic of the Andes is the giant condor, the largest flying bird on earth. Condors are carrion feeders, and in the mountains they sweep the open slopes looking for food. They ride the thermals with seldom a flap of their great wings (up to a ten-foot span), cruising effortlessly for hours and attaining altitudes well above 20,000 feet. In some remote Peruvian villages (notably Huaylas in the Cordillera Blanca), condors are still caught and killed in a brutal ritual. Tied either to the back of a bull or to a wooden scaffold, the condor is pummeled by the participants in the ceremony until, near death, its tongue is bitten out by the "bravest" man in attendance. Though cruel, the practice (called *condorachi*) is less a threat to the continued existence of the species than the casual shooting of the great birds by highland herders and coastal *guano* companies. Though usually considered a mountain dweller, the condor is also frequently seen along the coast, particularly at the Paracas peninsula during calving season for the seal and sea lion colonies there.

Other birds of the Andes include several varieties of hawk. Called *huaman* in Quechua, hawks are easy to observe in the mountains where they often soar in pairs using the thermals along cliffs to lift themselves almost effortlessly high into the sky. Closer to earth is the almost flightless *tinamou.* This mottled brown bird somewhat resembles the summer plumage phase of the North American ptarmigan. It inhabits the grasslands of the *puna.* More common in the highlands is a type of woodpecker called *Yaco-yaco* in Aymara. In the almost treeless *puna* (high plains), though, this woodpecker has adapted itself to find its food and shelter in underground burrows. Around mountain lakes, bird life abounds. Ducks, geese, grebes, teals, coots, cormorants, and even flamingos frequent the cold waters of Andean lakes and ponds.

Surprisingly for such a cold climate, several varieties of hummingbird inhabit the Andes all the way up to the 16,000-foot level. In an environment where flowers are rare, Andean hummingbirds eat mostly insects. The most notable variety is the giant hummingbird. Although as large as a robin, the giant hummingbird, nevertheless, shares with its smaller relatives the characteristic figure-eight wing stroke, giving it the ability to hold itself almost stationary in the air.

Though you certainly see the squirrellike *viscachas* scurrying among the rocks in boulder fields, most of the larger wild mammals of the Andes are very seldom observed. The *taruka* or Andean stag is rare indeed. Hunted vigorously by the *campesinos*, the *taruka* survives only in the highest, most remote regions of the Andes. Keep an eye out for *taruka* along rock ledges in the Cordillera Vilcanota and northern Cordillera Real. Another very rare, large mammal is the spectacled bear, called *ucumari* in Quechua. Black but for white rings around its eyes, this bear inhabits the *paramos* region of Ecuador and the margin between the *puna* and the cloud forest in Peru and Bolivia. An unusual resident of the Ecuadorian *paramos* (another term for the high, grassy Andean plains) is the mountain tapir. It has been found as high as 14,000 feet where it feeds on grasses and the fruits of *puya* plants. Also rare is the mountain lion.

Characteristic of the Andes are the various members of the camelidae family—the vicuña, guanaco, llama, and alpaca. Despite its relationship to the ungainly camel, for grace and delicacy of form, few creatures can match the lovely vicuña. If you're lucky enough to observe a herd of these elegant, slender-necked animals making their way across a scree slope below a glacier-covered peak, you'll never forget it. The vicuña lives in the cold altitudes between 13,000 and 16,000 feet, and its silky fleece has been valued since long before the Inca royalty claimed it for their exclusive use. Threatened by both intense hunting and severe habitat reduction, the vicuña is now a protected species (though poaching is quite common). Vicuñas are easiest to observe at the Pamapa Galeria preserve east of Nazca and the Aguada Blanca preserve outside Arequipa. However, we've also been lucky enough to see vicuña many times in the Cordilleras Blanca and Vilcanota. The guanaco is a much larger camelidae, over twice the size of the slight, 100-pound vicuña. Resembling a small llama, the guanaco inhabits both highland and coastal lowland areas in Peru and Bolivia.

The llama and alpaca, domesticated relatives of the vicuña, are common throughout the mountains of the Andean countries. Llamas are used primarily as beasts of burden and for meat. Particularly in Bolivia, llamas are ritually important; among other things, a llama fetus is always placed under the foundations of a new house to bring its occupants good luck. Alpacas are raised primarily for their high-quality wool and are distinguishable from llamas by their heavy coats and broad, flat tails.

2
Planning an Outdoor Trip to the Andes

Many people dream of traveling in the Andean countries, of walking through one of the world's great mountain ranges to arrive at the mysterious abandoned city of Machu Picchu or of floating down the Amazon on a boat that looks a little like *The African Queen.* For a few of these would-be travelers, there comes one great moment of decision when simply dreaming about travel becomes transformed into the firm determination to go. However, when you make this decision, dreams have to give way to the reality of careful, concrete planning. It is the purpose of this chapter to provide you with the kinds of information you'll need to prepare yourself for the reality of traveling in the Andes.

Trip Style

Perhaps the first major decision you need to make is *how* you want to travel—with an agency-led group or on your own. Ask yourself a few questions. Do you have plenty of time but little money? Or vice versa? Does the idea of having to arrange every single transaction involving accommodations, meals, and transportation in a foreign language and an unfamiliar culture set your nerves on edge? Or does the thought of having a rigid schedule and having to submit to the will of a group of people leave you feeling claustrophobic? The answers to these questions and the trip style that suits you are matters of personal taste, but the kinds of travel experiences you'll have in the Andes very much depend on the decisions you make.

AGENCY TOURS

The adventure travel business has grown dramatically in the past decade. People of all sorts are ready and willing to spend their vacation dollars on exotic, often once-in-a-lifetime adventure trips to exotic destinations. To accommodate this new segment of the travel market, literally dozens of adventure travel outfitters and agencies have sprung up, offering an incredible choice of possible trips—everything from standard treks on the Inca Trail to mountain bike trips in the Cordillera

Vilcabamba to cross-country skiing on the glaciers of Ausangate. Chances are that some outfitter already provides whatever kind of Andean adventure you're interested in experiencing.

Much of what you pay an agency for is convenience, both before and during the trip. Planning an independent trip to the Andes takes a considerable investment in time, more time than some people are willing or able to devote to it. Outfitters take care of most of that for you. They do the preplanning, make the necessary reservations, assemble the camping gear, buy the food, select the route, and hire the porters, saving you all the time and trouble of making those arrangements for yourself. During the trip, the group leader copes with the inevitable difficulties that crop up on any such trip, saving you from the frustration of dealing with them yourself. And, of course, on an agency-led trip, you will have the luxury of having your gear carried for you, of having most camp chores done for you, and of having good meals (usually not freeze-dried) cooked for you. An agency-led trip can also, if you're lucky, provide you, in the person of your group leader, with a source of considerable information about the land and the people of the Andes. Finally, many people enjoy group treks for the opportunity to meet and get to know on an intimate day-to-day basis an assortment of interesting fellow trekkers. In short, a good outfitter offers you as much certainty and convenience as is possible under typical Andean conditions.

On the other hand, you pay a price for all this certainty and convenience in the loss of independence and flexibility. By committing yourself to the group, you commit yourself to the group's schedule. Every day is carefully planned, so if, for example, you fall in love with Cuzco and want to spend an extra day or two there before beginning a trek, you can't. If you want to spend an unplanned rest day camping at a beautiful alpine lake surrounded by 20,000-foot peaks, you can't. If flexibility and independence are of major importance to you, then you'll probably be happier traveling on your own, and this book should give you the information to do that with confidence.

For most travelers, choosing an outfitter represents a major financial decision, since their services are far from cheap, usually averaging about $100 per day for ground costs alone. In our travels through the Andes, we've encountered many agency-led groups and have talked to many of their members. We've met many ecstatic trekkers thrilled with their trip and with the services of their outfitter. And we've also met a few irritable, angry groups who've felt that they were not getting their money's worth. By doing some homework before you select your outfitter, you can dramatically increase your chances of having an enjoyable travel experience rather than returning home feeling disappointed.

If at all possible, try to work with a reliable travel agent who has booked adventure vacations before. He or she may be familiar with the reputations of several adventure travel outfitters and may even be able to put you in contact with someone in your area who has used the services of the outfitter you are considering.

Even if you are using a travel agent, you should also do some of the homework yourself in selecting an outfitter. To get a clear idea of what kinds of trips are available, send for a selection of brochures from a wide range of outfitters (most of them advertise in the back pages of *Outside* magazine). After you've assembled the brochures from the outfitters, do a little comparison shopping. See what you're getting for your money. Look especially closely at the off-trail services: hotel accommodations, meals, and especially air and surface transportation. These types of services can vary greatly from agency to agency. Look closely also at the degree of difficulty involved in the trips you're considering. If you sign up for a trip for which you're not physically prepared, you'll slow everyone else down and probably be miserable. Conversely, if you want to walk fifteen miles a day and you're on a trip with a slow easy pace of only a few miles a day, you'll feel frustratingly restrained.

ON YOUR OWN IN THE ANDES

If you have neither the money nor the inclination to travel with one of the agencies, on-your-own travel in the Andes can be one of the most exciting experiences of your life. And you'll almost inevitably develop a more intimate feel for the land and the people of the Andes than an agency-led traveler ever could because you'll have no group leader acting as intermediary between you and the experiences of travel. If you are ultimately responsible for keeping your bearings on the trail, for essential communication with the *campesinos,* for handling all the small but crucial details of moving yourself around in a strange environment, you're simply forced to take more careful notice of the terrain and the people around you. Developing this kind of knowledge and travel skill is a tangible reward denied to the group traveler.

On the other hand, on one of the unavoidable days when you can't find a decent meal or a clean hotel, when every bus going to your destination has been booked for days, when your trail disappears in a complex web of llama tracks, you may be glad to trade some of the rewards of independent travel for a little certainty. If you can cope with large doses of uncertainty, though, independent travel may be for you.

You don't have to pay outfitters' prices or travel with a group to enjoy the luxury of shedding your pack. In most areas of the Andes, especially the Ecuadorian volcanoes, the Cordillera Blanca, and the Cordilleras Vilcabamba and Vilcanota, it is quite easy to hire local porters, guides, and *arrieros* at reasonable rates. With a little extra trouble, you can enjoy some of the benefits of an organized tour without having to give up the freedom and flexibility of the independent traveler.

Passports and Other Documents

Ecuador, Peru, and Bolivia do not require entry visas for citizens of the United States. All you need to enter these countries is a valid passport and, in some cases, proof of a return ticket (more on this later). You need your passport for entering and leaving the various countries along your route, but in South America, you also need it almost every time you conduct even the simplest of transactions: registering in hotels; buying plane, train, bus, and even truck tickets; cashing travelers checks; making credit card purchases; and receiving mail. Some small-town policemen will also ask for your passport just out of curiosity. Therefore, *always* carry your passport with you anytime you leave your hotel room.

If you don't have a passport, by all means don't underestimate the amount of time it will take to assemble and process the paper work necessary to obtain one. Most passport requests are filled within a month, but unexpected paper work hassles can always crop up at the most inconvenient times. So allow at least three months for the application process to be completed, especially if you are applying in the spring when passport offices are very busy because of the heavy volume of applications from travelers preparing for summer vacations.

When you enter Ecuador, Peru, and Bolivia, you'll be issued a Tourist Card with the length of visit permitted stamped on it. Especially if you're on a long, loosely planned trip, make sure to have your card stamped with the maximum number of days, usually sixty to ninety. Some immigration officials will try to issue cards with very short maximum visits, requiring a time-consuming application for extension if you stay longer. Keep your Tourist Card with your passport, and carry both documents with you at all times.

Officially, the Andean countries require proof of an ongoing or return ticket before entry. Only a few years ago, this rule was fairly strictly enforced and often led to difficulties and even rip-offs. If, for example, your round-trip air ticket was for Miami-Cuzco-Miami and you wanted to drop down for a week or so to Bolivia, you had to show a prepurchased exit ticket before you could enter Bolivia. This situation led to the sale of unnecessary and sometimes outright bogus "miscellaneous charges" tickets, which could, in theory, be exchanged later for a bus ticket out of the country. Luckily for travelers, this requirement is largely ignored these days in the Andean countries, though selective enforcement may still occur, especially if travelers look in any way "undesirable."

The International Certificate of Vaccination is no longer required for entry into the Andean countries. It is probably still a good idea to carry one on the off chance that you should, for example, find yourself in the midst of a yellow fever outbreak and need proof of innoculation.

A few other documents may help solve problems that could crop up. If car rental is part of your travel plans, get an International Driver's Permit. These are used in conjunction with your regular driver's license and are available through most travel agents and automobile clubs. If you qualify for a Student Card, take one. It might get you considerable discounts on tickets to ruins, museums, and the like. However, because of flagrant abuses of student card privileges (encouraged by some travel guides), fewer and fewer museums and other attractions will honor them. Include with your documents proof of insurance, both medical and baggage, and copies of prescriptions for eyeglasses and any necessary medicine.

Money

If possible, get a small amount of currency of the countries you plan to visit before you leave home. Many flights from the United States to South America arrive at the most inconvenient times—often in the middle of the night. Having a little local currency can ease problems with paying for taxi rides into town and getting something to eat before the banks and money exchanges open in the morning. Given enough time, your local bank can probably obtain the currencies you need. (Currencies for the Andean countries are the Ecuadorian *sucre,* the Peruvian *sol,* and the Bolivian *peso.*) Don't however, buy very much foreign money since the exchange rate will usually be much more favorable in South America.

Plan to take most of your funds for the trip in the form of traveler's checks. American Express and Thomas Cook checks are the most widely recognized and accepted in small-town banks, though banks in larger cities will usually cash traveler's checks from any established company. Don't however, let experience in traveling in the United States or Europe lull you into thinking that if your traveler's checks are lost or stolen in South America, you can get an immediate refund. The process will probably be long and frustratingly slow, and you'll normally have to return to the capital city to get your checks replaced. Also, considering how many times we've been stuck in a bank line behind a tourist cashing $300 worth of $10-denomination traveler's checks, it's apparent that many first-time visitors to the Andean countries think they should get all their traveler's checks in small denominations in order to be able to cash them more easily in out-of-the-way places. Though this reasoning may have a certain theoretical appeal, in practice it makes no sense whatsoever. Most budget hotels, restaurants, and shops will not cash a traveler's check. That means you'll cash virtually all your checks in banks where they're quite used to dealing with $50 or $100 denominations, which will speed things up for you and those in line behind you.

Some of your funds, however, should be in dollars. You'll inevitably find yourself in a situation where you need to change money but all the banks are closed for unexpected holidays. Don't worry; U.S. currency is in high demand in Latin America, and in some countries there is virtually a secondary economy based on the dollar. You'll normally have no trouble finding someone who'll be glad to exchange local currency for your dollars. Don't take more cash than you can afford to lose.

When the dollar is strong, the Latin American black market money exchange thrives. At these times, some travelers carry much of their money in cash, hoping to take advantage of favorable black market exchange rates. Though we sometimes do a bit of black market trading to stretch our funds a little, we find that the risks involved in carrying large amounts of cash far outweigh the usually small savings of black market exchange.

You'll probably also want to take a credit card with you to use as an emergency backup. With a credit card, even if you lose all your cash and checks, you'll at least be able to stay in most first-class hotels or buy a plane ticket. American Express cards are the most widely accepted, though more and more tourist-oriented businesses now accept Visa and MasterCard as well. But even in cities, credit cards are seldom accepted in average- or low-priced hotels and restaurants, and in almost all cases, once you're out of major cities and tourist areas, credit cards are virtually worthless.

Physical Conditioning

Trekking in the Andes demands at least a degree of high-level fitness. Even a much-frequented route like the Inca Trail to Machu Picchu involves long climbs at altitudes considerably higher than most backpackers are accustomed to. Therefore, you need to plan carefully to get (or stay) in shape before your trip begins. Trekking is, of course, an aerobic exercise, one that works the cardiovascular system hard. It also makes special demands on the large muscles of the legs and buttocks. Brisk walking, running, biking, and cross-country skiing are excellent conditioning activities to help prepare for Andean treks. Remember, though, that to receive any meaningful benefit from these aerobic exercises, you cannot simply put in a hard day every weekend. Building even a minimal aerobic base requires an hour of exercise *at least* three times a week. And, of course, the amount of time needed to get into adequate shape will depend on your level of fitness when you began your conditioning period. Whatever your level of fitness, though, you should begin to plan your conditioning schedule as soon as you start planning your trip. Remember, when you're on the trail in the Andes, you'll probably be walking six to eight hours per day over very difficult terrain at very high altitudes. Being physically unprepared for those conditions can ruin your trip either by severely limiting the routes you're capable of handling or even by forcing you to abort what could be a wonderful trek because of fatigue or muscle soreness.

Language Preparation

Native English-speakers sometimes have the feeling that ours is an international language, that wherever we go someone will surely speak English well enough to communicate with us. Though that is often the case in industrialized, developed nations, it is certainly *not* the case in the Andean countries. Though you'll find quite a few English speakers in the major cities, elsewhere you'll have to deal almost exclusively in Spanish. That means that if you're traveling independent of agencies and outfitters, virtually everything you do will involve a foreign language transaction. Unless you're fairly fluent in Spanish (Latin Americans usually call it *castellino*), this can become an unexpected strain on your nerves. Over and over on our South American trips, we've observed travelers become illogically but nevertheless thoroughly irritated at the inability of the locals to understand either their loudly spoken English or their poorly pronounced Spanish. These unsuccessful language transactions fray nerves on both sides. But they can easily be avoided with a little advance preparation.

Obviously the best way to overcome a language deficiency before your trip is to take a class in conversational Spanish. These can be arranged quite easily and inexpensively if you live near a university or a community college. You could also study the language yourself through books, tapes, or even home computer language programs. If you know little Spanish and have a limited amount of time to devote to it, remember that you can successfully carry on most necessary transactions with only a fairly limited knowledge of Spanish grammar and a vocabulary of a couple of hundred words. You won't be able to enter into real conversations, but you'll be amazed at how easily you can make the necessary daily arrangements for transportation, food, and lodging.

Attitude is almost as important to communication as grammar and vocabulary. If you enter into every language transaction with the attitude that you're going to have a hard time making yourself understood, you're handicapping your communicating ability from the start. You'll be tentative, halting, and uncertain. Try to sail into the conversation with confidence and, above all, friendliness. Since most Latin Americans you'll run into outside major tourist areas seldom encounter foreign tourists, they'll usually be curious, attentive, and quite patient with even the most awkward attempts to communicate with them in their own language. Keep your sense of humor when your Spanish is not up to the situation. Be inventive. Remember, language is not a mathematical formula; it is a creative act. If you use all the resources at your disposal—a bit of Spanish, sign language, etc.—you'll almost always be able to get your message across.

Though most *campesinos* are bilingual, in remote areas of the Andes you may occasionally encounter someone who speaks only Quechua, the modern variant of the Inca language. Quechua—a throaty, glottal-stopped language—is difficult for most English speakers to learn to pronounce. But knowing even a few words of Quechua—greetings, place names, simple questions and answers—can enrich your interaction with the mountain people immeasurably and should be considered an essential courtesy for anyone traveling through their homeland. For help in dealing with both Spanish and Quechua, see the Appendices.

Medical Preparation

To get the kinds of innoculations and prescription drugs you need for a trip to the Andes, you should visit your doctor. Don't assume, however, that she will know exactly how to help you prepare to stay healthy in South America, particularly if she isn't used to dealing with the unique medical problems of adventure travel. It's simply unreasonable to expect U.S.-trained doctors to be familiar with the conditions you'll encounter on a rough trip to the Andes or the Amazon. We've had doctors, for example, quite innocently tell us that for a boat trip on one of the upper tributaries of the Amazon, we should be very careful to treat our drinking water with halazone. This kind of misinformation might only cost you a few miserable days of gastrointestinal malfunction; it could, however, just as well result in a serious case of amoebic dysentery since halazone, unlike iodine or thorough boiling, *will not* ensure that no amoebic cysts remain alive and dangerous in your water. With luck, though, you'll have a doctor who will take an interest in your adventure and be willing to take the time to find the correct answers to your medical questions.

And time is what you need to give your physician even if she happens to be an expert in travel medicine. Make your first appointment at least six to eight weeks before you plan to begin your trip. This lead time may be needed for several reasons. For example, people who are "immune-compromised"—who suffer immune deficiencies—or who are taking steroids must be very careful about receiving live virus vaccines, several of which are recommended for South American travel. Even if you are not immune-compromised, if you live in a small town, you may have to give your doctor time to obtain the vaccines you will need. Especially in smaller towns, doctors may not keep, say, typhoid fever vaccine on hand. And to compound the time problems, typhoid fever vaccine requires two injections, a month apart. Furthermore, some of the more "exotic" prescription drugs you may need to take—malaria pills, for example—may not be in stock in all small-town drugstores.

INOCULATIONS

Have your inoculations recorded on an International Certificate of Vaccination (ICV). Though no longer required for travel to the Andean countries, the ICV is a convenient way to carry pertinent medical information. Along with a list of vaccinations, the ICV has spaces for recording personal health history, for listing blood type, and for noting special medical treatments and allergies, as well as ophthalmic information—all of which you need to have with you on your trip.

Inoculations strongly recommended for travel in the Andean countries are the following.

■ **Yellow Fever** Since yellow fever is endemic in much of South America, this is an extremely important inoculation, normally given only in special yellow fever vaccination clinics. Your doctor or local health clinic can give you the location in your area. Plan well in advance for this shot since many clinics administer yellow fever vaccinations only a couple of days a week; also, you should have the inoculation at least two weeks before leaving for South America since that is the minimum time for developing immunity. Immunity lasts ten years. People with allergies to raw eggs or who are immune-compromised should consult with their doctor before being vaccinated since reactions can be severe.

■ **Tetanus** Before heading off to the mountains or jungles, you should definitely have a tetanus shot. If you realize that in 1982 50 percent of those who contracted tetanus in the United States died, you'll handle your pocketknife with a lighter heart if you get the vaccination.

■ **Typhoid** Since typhoid fever is transmitted by poor food and water sanitation, those visiting only major cities, staying in first-class hotels, and eating in tourist restaurants may be able to get by without a typhoid innoculation. But if you are going to be in villages and small towns, you should certainly take the primary series—two shots, one month apart. Reaction to the typhoid shot—especially the first one— can be unpleasant; chills, fever, and nausea are fairly common after-shocks of a typhoid shot.

■ **Polio** Unless you've had one recently, take an oral polio booster.

■ **Gamma Globulin** Though it doesn't provide absolute immunity to hepatitis, gamma globulin does provide some protection. Considering that hepatitis is endemic in the Andes and that recovery from hepatitis can take from six weeks to a year or more, some protection is probably wise, especially if you are traveling off the beaten path and/or plan to stay for several months. Since hepatitis is spread by contaminated water and food—what medical people call the fecal-oral route—your best protection is to be scrupulous in matters of sanitation. Even under the roughest conditions, you can help protect yourself by pouring iodine-treated water over your hands before eating. Though this can become tedious, it won't make you nearly as uncomfortable as one trekker we met who contracted hepatitis on the trail and had to face a full day's hike and an eight-hour truck ride to get to the nearest hospital.

Even with a gamma globulin shot and careful hygenic practices, you could still contract hepatitis. Watch for the following symptoms: nausea, fever, weakness, loss of appetite, sudden distaste for tobacco smoke, and jaundice. Contrary to popular belief, though, jaundice (yellowish eye and skin color) is not always present in hepatitis victims; in milder cases it may not appear. We understand that new and more effective vaccines designed specifically for the various types of hepatitis (travelers are primarily at risk from type A) are currently under development; ask your doctor about these.

Innoculations for smallpox, cholera, and typhus are no longer required unless outbreaks have been declared. Your doctor or health clinic should be able to provide you with current information on the status of these diseases in South America.

Pregnant women should consult with their doctors before receiving any of the innoculations or prescription drugs mentioned in this chapter.

The most detailed and accessible source of further information concerning immunization is a government publication entitled *Health Information for International Travel* (HHS Publication No. [CDC] 82–8280).

MEDICAL KIT

When you discuss prescription drugs and the preparation of a medical kit with your doctor, make sure she understands the kind of trip you're going to be making. If your travel plans include only major tourist destinations, no jungle travel, and little backpacking, you'll need only a very small medical kit. If, however, you'll be away from towns and cities for days at at time, inaccessible to hospitals and doctors, you'll need a more extensive first-aid kit, one that you can assemble only with the help and advice of your doctor. The following items comprise the minimal medical kit we normally take with us to the Andes.

■ **Malaria Pills** Only a few years ago, scientists thought that malaria would soon be eradicated. They had not, however, counted on the development of highly resistant strains of this adaptive intracellular parasite, and today malaria is again on the increase in many areas of the world, including South America. Some strains of malaria plasmodium (vivax and ovale), though seldom fatal, are difficult to cure because they first infect the liver, then enter the bloodstream, and finally reinfect the liver. The really nasty falciparum plasmodium can be fatal. It infects not only the liver and the blood, but also the brain. So if you are going to visit a malaria-risk area, you'll certainly want to protect yourself against this disease by taking chloroquine. In addition, if you're going to an area where chloroquine-resistant strains of malaria may be present, you should also take Fansidar in conjunction with chloroquine (never as a substitute). Pregnant women are advised not to take Fansidar and, therefore, should avoid areas where resistant strains have been reported.

In Ecuador, you will need to take chloroquine unless you confine your travel to Quito, surrounding high-altitude areas, and the Galapagos Islands. If you plan to travel to the northern provinces of Ecuador, plan to take Fansidar as well as chloroquine since resistant falciparum cases have been reported there. In both Peru and Bolivia, urban areas are virtually risk-free, as is the coastal region of Peru south of Lima. Outside these locations, though, malaria risk exists all months of the year in all areas below 5,000 feet. Chloroquine-resistant falciparum have not been reported in either Peru or Bolivia; however, you should check with your doctor for current information on the spread of resistant strains.

To receive maximum benefit from your malaria drugs, you should start taking them a week before you enter the endemic zones. The normal dosage for chloroquine as well as Fansidar is one tablet each week for the duration of the trip. With chloroquine, you *must* continue to take the drug once a week for six weeks after you return home to avoid a delayed attack from vivax or ovale. So your prescription for chloroquine should include pills for the pre- and post-trip dosages as well as for the weeks you'll be in the endemic zone.

■ **Antibiotics** Include in your medical kit a broad-spectrum antibiotic such as tetracycline or penicillin for infections and dysentery.

■   **Antihistamine**   For relief from congestion of colds or hay fever. Even mild congestion becomes bothersome at altitudes where breathing is already difficult.

■   **Valium**   We reserve it for those inevitable times when the only way to get from point A to point B is an all-night truck or bus ride over a rough mountain road.

■   **Gastrointestinal Medicine**   Along with a nonprescription medicine for diarrhea (i.e., Pepto-Bismol) we also carry Lomotil for real emergencies but have never used it. See the section "Staying Healthy" in Chapter 3 for further advice on digestive disorders.

■   **Aspirin or Acetaminophen**   For muscle and joint aches after long walks, colds, *soroche* (altitude sickness), headaches, etc.

■   **Bandages**   Take an assortment of small adhesive bandages along with adhesive tape and gauze for larger cuts and a few butterfly bandages for deeper cuts. Take along an elastic bandage to support sprained ankles or sore knee joints.

■   **Antibiotic Ointment**   For cuts and abrasions.

■   **Other Medicine**   Include in your medical kit adequate amounts of any medicine you normally take.

Equipment

Though we once met an obliviously happy wanderer walking the Inca Trail carrying only a sweater tied around his waist, three cans of tuna in a brown paper bag, and a mandolin slung over his shoulder, your list of essential equipment *will* certainly be longer than his. And it *should* certainly be shorter than that of a couple we met on the same trip who had hired eleven porters to carry the movable village that their bundle after bundle of gear became when set up in the evening. Somewhere between those two extremes you should be able to arrive at an equipment list that includes everything that is essential and little that is superfluous.

Virtually every backpacking guide in existence warns its readers to pack light. This will be no exception. A heavy, bulky pack loading you down with unnecessary weight can turn a 15,000-foot pass into pure agony. Most people have enough trouble, especially early in a trip to the Andes, simply acclimatizing to the extra physical demands of high altitude. An unnecessary ten or twenty pounds in those circumstances can be all the difference between enjoying the trip you've planned or wondering, as you look up at a mile of steep trail between you and the next pass, why you ever wanted to make this trip to begin with. And not only do those extra pounds make themselves felt on the trail; extra weight and bulk can also limit your mobility in *getting to* trailheads. Loading a fifty- or sixty-pound expeditionary pack into the back seats of VW taxis, the rooftops of buses, the high beds of large passenger-carrying trucks, and especially the narrow overhead luggage racks on trains can become a comic nightmare of flailing shoulder straps and waist bands. And that's assuming you'll even *find* a spot to put your pack. Public transportation in the Andean countries is usually crowded at best. At worst, you may end up riding with your feet on a crate of chickens, a friendly goat nuzzling your shoulder, and your massive, overloaded pack in your lap.

Dealing with a huge, heavy mound of gear day in and day out over the course of a long trip can become an ordeal. On the other hand, many backpackers develop a real sense of joy in the freedom and self-sufficiency inherent in an efficient, comfortably light, and compact load. So though you may not be able to travel with only a sweater, tinned tuna, and a mandolin, you should, as you begin to accumulate the equipment for your trip, think constantly of weight and bulk. Pare away relentlessly at the superfluous, and you'll leave on your trip with everything you *really* need to propel yourself safely and perhaps even with a modicum of comfort through the spectacular landscape of the Andes.

EQUIPMENT FOR TREKKING

Most trekking agencies provide all camping equipment. That is, they provide food, cooking gear, and tents. Other group equipment varies somewhat from agency to agency. However, dining tables and stools, lanterns, toilet tents, and other luxuries are also usually provided. During the process of selecting an agency for an Andean trek, be sure to find out exactly what group equipment each of the agencies you are considering will provide.

You will, of course, be required to bring all personal items, clothing, and usually your own sleeping bag. Trekking agencies should provide you with a list of personal equipment that, from past experience on similar trips, they consider necessary. The following list of clothing and personal items is applicable to both agency-led and independent trekkers.

■ **Clothing** As in any mountain range, the climate in the Andes varies considerably in relation to altitude. But an even more important determinant is the sun. Even at 15,000 feet, a sunny day in the Andes will often be warm enough for shorts and a T-shirt. However, as soon as the sun disappears behind the high peaks in the afternoon, the temperature plunges. Evenings are often quite cool and early mornings can be frigid. To be prepared for the wide range of temperatures you will be certain to encounter, plan to take several layers of lighter clothing; layering makes a more versatile outdoor wardrobe than does a single heavy parka. The following clothing recommendations assume a layering approach to warmth.

Of course, not all the listed items are applicable to every conceivable trip. For example, a visitor to Peru planning to walk only the Inca Trail would need considerably less body insulation than would be necessary for travel in higher altitude areas such as Peru's Cordillera Vilcanota or Bolivia's Cordillera Real. Remember, though, that the nights are chilly throughout the Andes.

Underwear. Take three or four changes. Nylon is easiest to wash.

Long Underwear. These are essential if you're going into the high *cordilleras.* Kept clean and dry in a plastic bag, long underwear make comfortable, warm pajamas as well as providing insurance against colder-than-anticipated temperatures. Cotton long johns are comfortable but lose much of their insulating value when damp. Polypropylene long underwear is lighter, more compact, and absorbs virtually no moisture. It is also quite easy to wash and dry under trail conditions.

Swimsuit. The Andes are dotted with hot springs and Inca baths. These can be quite refreshing after a hard day's walk. At hot baths located near towns, you may risk arrest for nude bathing; in more remote but inhabited areas you should respect the *campesinos'* sense of modesty by wearing a swimsuit.

Socks. Take at least two pairs of good-quality wool socks, more if you're doing a lot of trekking or staying in the Andes for a long period of time. Socks are easy to lose, but good wool socks are virtually impossible to replace in South America. If you're taking a pair of hiking boots and a pair of running shoes, include a couple of pairs of light-weight socks for the running shoes; these can double as liner socks for the hiking-boot and wool-sock combination.

T-Shirts/Polo Shirts. Take a couple. Dark colors don't get grubby-looking as quickly as lighter colors.

Medium-Weight Shirt. A wool, chamois, or canvas long-sleeved shirt or a long-sleeved rugby-type shirt is a good everyday garment for cool mornings and afternoons.

Walking Shorts. One pair, for trail wear only. People in most Latin American countries have a general prejudice against short pants, so avoid wearing them in towns. On popular trekking routes, though, *campesinos* seem to have gotten used to them.

Pants. Two pairs. The big question is whether or not to take jeans. The arguments against jeans as suitable for trekking are numerous: they are relatively heavy and bulky; they are not, considering their weight, particularly warm; they are hard to hand wash in a hotel sink or mountain stream; and they take forever to dry in anything but the most ideal conditions. On the other hand, jeans are tough and hard to get dirty-looking, not to mention that many people just don't feel comfortable on the trail without them. If you're one of those people, a good compromise is to take a pair of jeans and a pair of warm wool or corduroy pants. One very comfortable and functional alternative is to substitute a pair of running-suit pants and polypro underwear bottoms for one pair of pants.

Sweaters. Nothing feels better when the temperature drops a bit than a comfortable sweater. Virtually every traveler to the Andean countries buys an alpaca sweater as a souvenir, so unless you plan to be the rare exception, don't take a sweater with you; just wear the one you buy.

Jacket. There are several functional options here depending on the warmth of your inner layers. In general, though, for most mountain travel, you will need a wind-resistant shell with either a down vest, light down jacket, pile jacket, or bunting jacket. One of the most versatile combinations we've used is a light turtleneck shirt, a wool sweater, a bunting jacket, and a 60/40 shell garment. Worn all at the same time, these provide remarkable warmth. In various other combinations, they allow for a great degree of fine tuning of insulation depending on wind, temperature, and activity levels. The drawback is that these four items are considerably more bulky than a down jacket. Synthetic insulators such as bunting, pile, and polypropylene jackets have recently become quite popular—and with good reason. They are quite warm for their weight, are much less fragile than down jackets, work well in layering combinations, and retain most of their warmth when wet. Again, though, they are bulkier than down.

Boots. You'll see *campesinos* wearing only tire-tread sandals jogging along rough trails with huge blanket-wrapped loads across their shoulders. And you'll probably see *turistas* trying to emulate them. A good-quality pair of lightweight trail boots should, however, be considered essential equipment for anyone planning to walk Andean trails. Though many trails are wide and relatively smooth, and some stretches, as on the Inca and Takesi trails, are even paved with Inca stonework, you will be certain to encounter some unbelievably steep, rocky, ankle-twisting descents for which boots are a necessity. The new lightweight hiking boots are ideal for below-snowline walking. If you opt for one of the Gore-Tex upper boots, be sure it is of the "sock-liner" type of construction. They are more waterproof than sewn-through boots, an important consideration on many Andean trails, which frequently wind through wet, marshy alpine meadows and cross many bridgeless streams. All-leather boots should, of course, be carefully waterproofed before leaving home. Whatever type of boots you take, be sure to evaluate their quality with a hard eye. The third day out on a ten-day trek is no time to have boots that seemed like such a savings back home suddenly self-destruct on you. And, as is the case with most backpacking gear, finding quality replacement boots in South America will be very difficult. If you buy new boots for your trip, be sure to break them in thoroughly. Buy them well in advance of your departure date, and wear them on several conditioning hikes. Plan to walk at least twenty-five miles in new boots before beginning an extended trek.

Other Shoes. Most people take a pair of running, tennis, or boat shoes for wearing when lightness and comfort are more important than protection and support—in towns, in camp, for packless walking, etc.

Gloves. Unless you're going into the snow or have very cold hands, down mittens probably aren't necessary. Lightweight wool gloves are usually adequate for below-glacier conditions.

Headgear. You'll need two kinds of head protection: a toboggan for warmth, and a wide-brimmed hat or long-billed cap to keep the sun off your head. The sun's burning rays are much more intense at high altitudes than nearer sea level. We've learned from painful experience not to trust all our sunburn protection to screening lotions.

Rain gear. Gore-Tex is the material of choice in rain gear these days, and it is great—*if* you can afford the high price. If not, remember that outdoorsmen got along without it for centuries, and take along a nylon poncho, cagule, or the like.

Bandannas. Take a couple. These are truly multipurpose items. Use them as neck warmers on cold nights. Carry small objects in them. Use them as pot holders. They're particularly indispensable when riding to trailheads in the beds of passenger trucks. The fine dust boils up off the dirt roads in dark, thick clouds, coating everything on the truck, including you. A bandanna worn over the nose and mouth train-robber style helps keep out at least some of that dust.

Moneybelt. Many backpacking shops now sell lightweight nylon pouches on a thin nylon belt for carrying money, passport, traveler's checks, innoculation records, etc., comfortably beneath your clothes. Theft, especially pick-pocketing, is always a possibility in South America. Replacing a lost passport or traveler's checks is a costly and time-consuming process, usually involving a trip back to the capital city of the country. So you'll want to take every precaution not to lose those important items. A moneybelt can provide a measure of protection. For further tips on theft prevention, see the "Theft" section in Chapter 3.

■ **Camping Equipment**

Backpack. Your choice here will very much depend on what kind of trip you're taking. If you are going with an agency, you'll probably need only a duffel bag for porter-carried items and a small day pack for your camera, sweater, snacks, etc. If you're on your own, you'll need a full-sized backpack. The current trend is toward internal frame models. These have one significant advantage over external frame packs for the type of traveling most people do in the Andes: an internal frame pack is much less vulnerable to damage by the extremely rough handling it will receive on public transportation. If you're buying a new pack before the trip, take a look at the new "travel packs." These are internal frame packs with a zippered or snapped panel that encloses and protects the suspension system, allowing the pack to be carried by a handle like a suitcase or duffel bag. Not only is the suspension system protected, but it is also kept out of the way, solving the problem of flapping straps and belts at times when you don't want them.

One word of caution in purchasing a travel pack: the suspension system is the most important aspect of any pack, and the quality of suspension varies widely among travel packs. Examine shoulder straps and waist belts very closely, and compare them with similarly priced standard packs. In purchasing a pack, don't become overly ambitious in size. Very few people need huge expeditionary models, whose vast capacity will simply encourage taking too much gear. Unless you plan to be on the trail for extended periods of time (a couple of weeks or so), you should be able to get along comfortably with a 4,000-to-5,000-cubic-inch pack. Not too long ago, there was a widespread South American prejudice against travelers with backpacks. The increase in adventure travel, though, has made backpacks commonplace and much more accepted.

Sleeping Bag. As with backpacks, avoid the expeditionary models:

they are too warm. Unless you're a very "cold" sleeper, a bag rated between 0 and 10 degrees should keep you warm even on the coldest treks covered in this book. The big choice, if you're buying a new bag, is whether to buy down or synthetics. Down is, of course, the ultimate in the weight/warmth relationship. A down bag will also compress into a much more compact bundle than would a synthetic bag of equal loft. A good down bag, however, is expensive and has the added drawback of losing much of its insulation value when wet. Good quality synthetic bags, on the other hand, though heavier and bulkier than down, are less expensive and retain considerable insulation value even when wet. The choice is yours, but whichever you decide, buy the best-quality bag you can possibly afford. As with boots, a sleeping bag is no place to cut corners on quality and performance.

Sleeping Pad. Closed cell foam (ensolite or the like) provides the best insulation from ground cold. Half-inch foam is a standard size.

Tent. Again, buy all the quality you can afford. At today's prices, a good, lightweight backpacking tent is, for most people, a major purchase. But properly cared for, it should last for many years. Therefore, shop around. Look at as many major brands as possible, and decide what trade-offs in size, weight, strength, etc., best fit the kinds of camping you do.

■ **Cooking Gear**   Though most camping gear is very hard to find in the Andean countries, usable cooking equipment is readily available. You could supply yourself with a complete cooking outfit in a matter of minutes in almost any outdoor market in the Andes. However, the kerosene primus stoves, pots, pans, and utensils that you would find there are considerably heavier and bulkier than normal backpacking equipment. Therefore, you should take cooking gear with you.

Stove. Take one. Don't plan on cooking over fires; wood is scarce, and *campesinos* need it more than you do. White gas for the popular Svea, Optimus, and Coleman stoves is very difficult to find in cities and simply doesn't exist in most smaller towns. You may occasionally find it in pharmacies or hardware stores (it's called *petronafta liviana* or *bencina*), but don't count on it. Don't resort to burning automobile gas in white gas stoves since the potential for explosions is high. Bleuet Camping Gaz cartridges are available in major cities and in smaller towns that host lots of campers (e.g., Cuzco and Huaraz). Kerosene, though, is usually readily available, even in smaller towns. So if you have a choice, take a kerosene-burning stove. One of the multifuel stoves like the MSR would be ideal. You'll also need a fuel bottle and a pouring spout or small funnel. Remember, it is illegal to carry fuel on airplanes.

Pots. Bring at least two, depending on the size of your group. You'll also need utensils. Most people can get by with just a spoon, cup, and dish or bowl.

Freeze-Dried and/or Dehydrated Foods. If you plan on using this type of food, bring it with you. See the "Local Food" section in Chapter 2 for alternatives.

■ **Miscellaneous Equipment**

Knife. You'll need a medium-sized pocketknife for a myriad of camp chores—peeling fruit and vegetables, cutting cord, etc. Just remember, though, that your knife is a tool, not a weapon; therefore, carrying large, heavy sheath knives is usually unnecessary. Any normal task for which you need a knife can almost always be accomplished using a pocketknife. Some travelers to the Andes try to affect the look of explorers by carrying large hunting knives on their belts, even in larger towns. Aside from the pointlessness of this habit, we've talked to several local people who find it offensive.

Water Bottle. Water is generally readily available on most of the hikes described in this book, so you won't need vast water-carrying capacity. We usually carry a one-quart plastic bottle per person. Heavy drinkers, though, may want to carry a backup bottle for the occasional long, dry stretch.

Flashlight. Most experienced backpackers have learned to make do with the faint light of AA-sized flashlights, trading brightness for the substantial weight savings. And in practice, the light from AA flashlights is almost always adequate. Though both AA and D batteries are usually available in most towns and cities in the Andes, take at least one backup pair with you. Also take at least one spare bulb.

Medical Kit. See the section "Medical Preparation" above for suggestions on assembling a medical kit.

Iodine Tablets. Take plenty. If you run out, you can buy liquid iodine in pharmacies (ask for *yodo para llavar legumbres*), but it is much more difficult to use than tablets. Do *not* buy halazone tablets; they are not effective in killing amoebic cysts. See the section "Staying Healthy" in Chapter 2 for further comments on water treatment.

Toilet Articles. Take the smallest kit you think you can get by with. Remember, you'll be able to buy soap, razors, toothpaste, shampoo, etc., in most towns, so don't feel you need to carry large amounts of basic toiletries with you. Always carry plenty of toilet paper (available from market stalls and *bodegas*—small grocery stores). It is virtually never provided in public restrooms and often is not provided even in otherwise relatively decent hotels.

Towel. Indispensable. Not only will you need one while you're on the trail, but you'll also need one in many small-town hotels where they are not normally provided.

Lip Balm. Take a couple of tubes. You'll use it almost every day, and it is hard to find in the Andes.

Sunscreen. Take a bottle of strong screening lotion for the strong high-altitude burning rays, which will sometimes make you feel as if you have your head in a microwave oven.

Nylon Cord. You never know when you'll need a good, strong rope. Our coil has been used for everything from making clotheslines to constructing a rope slide to get our packs across a dangerous river.

Sunglasses. Take a pair. Not only will the bright high-altitude sun burn your skin, it can also burn your eyes, especially if you're walking on or near glaciers.

Spare Glasses. If you wear glasses, be sure to take a spare pair; you never know when you might lose or damage your only pair. If you wear contact lenses, consider switching to glasses for your trip. Cleaning and caring for contacts under Andean conditions can become quite a chore.

Insect Repellent. Take a small bottle unless you're planning to visit the jungle—in which case, take a large bottle.

Compass. You probably won't need it, but it's reassuring to know it's there if you do.

Plastic Bags. Take several small ones and a few large ones. They are virtually indispensable for carrying wet and/or dirty clothes, storing food, protecting a camera during a dusty truck ride, and a score of other uses.

■ Optional Equipment

Candles. A couple of long-burning candles can help brighten a campsite. They're also very welcome if you find yourself in small-town hotels where electricity is often either nonexistent or sporadic. If possible, buy what backpacking shops usually call "plumbers' candles"; they burn much longer than ordinary ones.

Binoculars. Obviously nonessential, but if you spot a condor at a distance, you'll wish you had a pair.

Earplugs. South American hotels, particularly those at the lower end of the price scale, can be amazingly noisy. You'll hear every sound from surrounding rooms as well as street noise that begins before dawn and continues until the middle of the night. Wax earplugs (at pharmacies in the United States) can help salvage at least part of a night's sleep even under the worst conditions.

Day Pack or Fanny Pack. If you are like most visitors to the Andes, you'll spend a considerable percentage of your trip *off* the trail —exploring ruins, sight-seeing in towns and cities, taking a side trip to the Amazon basin. For day trips, a small pack is convenient for carrying a sweater, camera, guide books, rain gear, snacks, etc.

Books. We'd feel lost without a couple of novels tucked away in our packs to help get us through long waits for planes and buses. Luckily, there are bookstores in Quito, Lima, and La Paz that carry a reasonably adequate selection of English-language books. Addresses of these shops are in the Resources sections for those cities.

■ Photographic Equipment

The Andes can be a photographer's dream, an overwhelming blend of awesome landscapes, timeless-looking villages, and colorfully dressed people. But unless you're a professional photographer on assignment, you don't need a heavy, bulky array of photographic equipment to return home with shots that will amaze you and your friends. Keep it simple.

Camera. A compact, lightweight single-lens-reflex camera is probably the most versatile instrument for the traveling photographer, though perfectly presentable photographs can be made with even simpler cameras. A strong case for the camera is vital.

Lenses. Don't get too ambitious here. Along with your normal lens, a wide-angle lens (preferably a 28 mm) for landscapes, and a telephoto (a 135 mm to 200 mm) for people and wildlife should be adequate. Be sure to take strong cases for the additional lenses to protect them from the shocks and dust to which they will unavoidably be subjected.

Film. 35 mm film is *very* expensive in South America, and finding particular brands and varieties can be quite difficult. Kodachrome 25, for example, is very rare. So be sure to take plenty of film with you. You may want to take a few rolls of "fast" film (ASA 400 or greater) along with your regular variety; jungle and cloud forest areas can be quite dim, even during the middle of the day, and you don't want to miss good shots of Machu Picchu just because the weather is gray and foggy the day you were there.

Batteries. Outside of major cities, it will often be impossible to replace camera batteries. Therefore, take at least one spare set.

Filters. An ultraviolet filter is helpful in screening these strong rays, which can cause color shots to be pale and washed out, especially at high altitudes.

Do not plan to mail your exposed film back to the United States from South America for processing. Mail is routinely opened for inspection, and your precious exposed film may be stolen, lost, or simply thrown away during this process. Remember to keep exposed film as cool and dry as possible. It is also a good idea to keep exposed film separate from other camera equipment; a thief looking for easily portable valuables might at least leave you with the shots you've taken.

Getting to the Andes

Though Eastern, Ecuadoriana, Faucett, AeroPeru, and Lloyd Aereo Boliviano all schedule flights between Miami and the Andean countries several times weekly, if you are a typical traveler, your first consideration in selecting an airline will probably be cost. If this is the case, it is usually much less expensive to fly with AeroPeru or Faucett, the Peruvian airlines. Fortunately, with these companies, air fares between Miami and the Andean countries have remained surprisingly inexpensive for quite some time. If Lima is your primary arrival city, you can take advantage of the excellent package fares these airlines frequently offer. In 1983, for example, both priced their round-trip Miami-Lima-Cuzco excursion flights at $399. In addition to these remarkable fares, both airlines frequently offer added incentives; for example, Faucett's Miami-to-Lima flight has the attraction of allowing a stopover in Iquitos on the Amazon River. AeroPeru's travel incentives regularly include a free overnight trip to Nazca, including a flight in small aircraft over the famous lines. Furthermore, AeroPeru will often allow foreign visitors to book unlimited domestic flights at the rate of $25 per ticket (1984 prices). However, these flights must be booked at the same time as your Miami-Lima ticket; once you're in Peru, you may be able to change the dates of these internal flights, but you cannot schedule additional flights at this bargain rate. AeroPeru's Miami-Lima flight stops in Guayaquil, Ecuador, allowing a visit to that country without additional charge. Don't underestimate the effect this sort of thing can have on your travel schedule and budget since it is often considerably less expensive to book a Miami-Cuzco ticket with

AeroPeru, staying a few days or weeks in Ecuador, than it is just to fly round-trip Miami-Quito on Ecuadoriana.

Since rates and special travel incentives change rapidly among the carriers servicing the Andean countries, we strongly recommend having a reliable travel agent collect all the current airline information you need to plan your trip.

When to Go

Because the Andes are south of the equator, the seasons are the reverse of those in the northern hemisphere; winter comes in June, July, and August. But because of proximity to the equator, season really makes little difference in temperature; average daily temperatures remain fairly constant year-round. Altitude plays a much more significant role in temperature variation than time of year. In fact, it has been said that in the Andes every day is a year—with spring in the morning, summer at midday, autumn in the afternoon, and winter at night. At altitudes above 12,000 feet, expect pleasantly warm days if the sun is out, but on cloudy days and at nightfall the temperature plunges, leaving you with little doubt as to why the Incas worshipped the sun, *inti,* as a god.

More important for trip planning than temperature is rainfall, which follows definite yearly cycles. The best time of year for outdoor travel in the Andes is during the dry period between May and October (June to October in the Ecuadorian highlands). Though rain is possible year-round, those months are most likely to offer fine, clear, dry days and crisp, cloudless nights. The worst of the rainy season usually lasts from January through March.

Table 1   Average Daily High-Low Temperatures (Fahrenheit)

	Ja	Fe	Mr	Ap	My	Je	Ju	Au	Se	Oc	No	De
Quito	72	71	71	70	70	71	72	73	73	72	72	72
	46	47	47	47	47	45	44	45	45	46	45	46
Lima	82	83	83	80	74	68	67	66	68	71	74	78
	66	67	66	63	60	58	57	56	57	58	60	62
Cuzco	68	69	70	71	70	69	70	70	71	72	73	71
	45	45	44	40	35	33	31	34	40	43	43	44
La Paz	63	63	64	65	64	62	62	63	64	66	67	65
	43	43	42	40	37	34	33	35	38	40	42	42

Table 2   Average Monthly Rainfall (in inches)

	Ja	Fe	Mr	Ap	My	Je	Ju	Ag	Se	Oc	No	De
Quito	3.9	4.4	5.6	6.9	5.4	1.7	0.8	1.2	2.7	4.4	3.8	3.1
Lima	0.1	0.04	0.04	0.04	0.2	0.2	0.3	0.3	0.3	0.1	0.1	0.04
Cuzco	6.4	5.9	4.3	2.0	4.3	0.2	0.2	0.4	1.0	2.6	3.0	5.4
La Paz	4.5	4.2	2.6	1.3	0.5	0.3	0.4	0.5	1.1	1.6	1.9	3.7

3
Getting Along in the Andes

Along with the mountains of the Andes and the exotic jungles of the Amazon, one of the primary reasons travelers go to the Andean countries is to experience a culture quite different from their own. On a fine day in a high Andean market town, where most everyone is speaking Quechua and wearing clothes that have changed little since Inca times, you may feel a little like a time traveler, and you'll probably be exhilarated by the differences in culture you see, hear, and smell all around you. On a bad day, perhaps after a brutal, dusty, all-day truck ride over rough roads or after an unexpectedly strange meal in a *restaurante típico,* you may want desperately to shut yourself up in your hotel room or to crawl into your tent and pretend you're at home in familiar surroundings.

Both the exhilaration and the despair are perfectly normal reactions that most travelers to unfamiliar cultures will experience. The exhilaration, of course, is no problem; you can handle that on your own. The despair, however, can become a genuine trip spoiler. But there are several things you can do to control it. Learning as much as possible about the culture before you arrive is helpful (see the Annotated Bibliography for suggested background reading). Having at least a rudimentary knowledge of Spanish and a few words of Quechua is essential to coping with culture shock since outside capital cities almost no one speaks English (see Appendices I and II).

The purpose of this chapter is to smooth your transition into Andean culture by letting you know how to get by with the day-to-day business of travel in a new cultural context. Above all, remember as you begin your trip to think of the normal sort of traveler's discomforts as cultural jet lag—relax, rest, give it some time, and it will disappear.

Cultural Impact

Much more important than the impact of the Andean culture *on you* is the problem of *your* impact on Andean culture. The number of travelers to the Andean countries has increased dramatically in the past decade. More significantly, the number of outdoor "adventure" travelers has increased even more dramatically. Visitors are no longer simply flying into Lima, dashing through Cuzco on the way to and from an afternoon at Machu Picchu, and flying out again. They're staying longer, using more local transportation, walking the trails, and interacting with the people.

Controlling our impact on the culture, particularly that of indigenous mountain people, is becoming a responsibility that all visitors to the Andes must share. Even a moderate number of relatively wealthy trekkers passing through a small mountain village can have a visible impact on the inhabitants. The impact is particularly strong on children. Kids from families largely outside the money economy quickly learn that a gruff demand for "Moneda, gringo" will often net them a few coins. Some trekkers, particularly, it seems, those led by agencies, distribute literally dozens of cheap plastic toys to children along the trails. Our extremely visible wealth becomes just one more pressure contributing to the growing exodus of *campesinos* out of the mountains and into the already overcrowded cities in search of modern objects, which the economies of the Andean countries simply cannot provide for everyone. A Peruvian social worker, whose job involves trying to help feed some of the thousands of indigent newcomers to Lima, once told us: "In the mountains these people have land, homes, and food. But they come to Lima to have TV and end up with nothing."

Of course, the pressures contributing to these changes are far more complex than simply the impact of outdoor travelers from industrial nations. However, we *should* try constantly to keep our impact as minimal and as positive as possible. One way to do that is to learn to interact with the *campesinos* on a level other than economic. Talk with them, even if only about the weather; exchange information about your respective countries; ask them to help you with difficult Spanish or Quechua pronunciations; share a little food that they may not be familiar with; play games with the children. But don't let your interaction with them be exclusively based on cash or cheap trinkets. That is a kind of cultural littering that concerned trekkers will avoid.

Sense of Time

Though the sometimes frenzied rush of downtown Quito, Lima, and La Paz belies the old and inaccurate cliche of the *mañana* Latin American lifestyle, one of the most difficult cultural differences for most travelers to get used to is the uncertainty of schedules in the Andean countries. We've seen more than one group of travelers at the edge of tears as they find their carefully planned trip suddenly self-destructing before their eyes because of unexpected schedule problems. Sometimes these problems can be quite large—for example, being stuck in a remote village for days, as one couple we met had been, because the only truck in the vicinity had broken down. But sometimes even the simplest things seem to conspire to slow you down, especially when you *really* have to be somewhere at a particular time. Just cashing a traveler's check or two can become a long and tedious process if you go to the bank and stand in a long line only to find that you're required to provide a photocopy of your passport. You then have to find a shop with a photocopy machine, get the copy made, return to the bank, work your way through the line again, and then confront the inevitable series of three or four bank officials who'll scrutinize your documents and demand signature after signature on form after form before you finally get your money. At worst, the process can eat a very large hole in a morning that you had planned for something much more pleasant.

Public transportation is a sure-fire schedule wrecker. In Lima we once left our hotel with plenty of time to spare to reach the bus station for our ride to Huarás in the Cordillera Blanca. We found a taxi, put our packs in the trunk, and a few blocks later coasted to a halt, out of gas in heavy traffic. Our driver, evidently a veteran of this situation, pulled a plastic gas jug from under his seat and started to walk away. "Momento," he said reassuringly, as though he knew of a gas station right around the corner. An hour and a half later when he returned, we were sitting on the hood of the car, our packs still locked inaccessibly in the trunk, and our Huarás bus already on the road. The driver seemed completely stunned by our anger. And the fact that we'd missed that morning's only bus and would have to wait twelve hours for the next departure seemed inconsequential to him. He, like most Latin Americans, took waiting as a matter of course, a fact of life that can't be changed.

Indeed, in very remote mountain regions and along the Amazon and its tributaries, delays are often measured in days rather than hours. On one trip we spent a *very* long week in a muddy town on the Ucayali waiting for the only down-river boat in port to complete its cargo load of machetes and beer before it could leave. Every day we'd make the muddy walk from town to the dock, and every day for a week the *capitan* would say, with a big confident smile on his face: "Tomorrow at ten we leave."

If you don't want to stay constantly upset by these sorts of delays, you'll adopt some of this looser Andean sense of scheduling yourself. Unless you're being led by a well-organized agency, don't plan on being able to follow an extremely rigid itinerary. You're bound to be disappointed if you do since it doesn't take too many long waits to destroy even the most carefully devised plans. The only real solution is simply to slow down and plan ahead for delays; build delay-days into your schedule. Be flexible. Don't spoil the trip by insisting on unrealistically rigid timetables. And during the inevitable long waits, tell yourself: "If I'd wanted efficiency, I'd have stayed at home."

Theft

One popular tourist spot in Cuzco displays prominently on its walls a warning about thievery. It reads: "Don't be careful, be paranoid." You'll encounter similar attitudes among other travelers everywhere you go, but particularly in Cuzco. And there *is* some basis for that attitude: theft, particularly on public transportation, is fairly common.

But if a constant state of paranoia is the only way to react to the possibility of theft, why travel in the Andes at all? By adopting that attitude, you'll enclose yourself in a cocoon of unrealistic paranoia, afraid that anyone who speaks to you is going to try to grab your wallet or steal your camera (and that kind of relatively minor grab-and-run thievery is by far the most common). Let's face it; there are many more serious things that could happen to you than to have a 35 mm SLR stolen. You could, for example, *rob yourself* of one of the important things you're spending money to come to the Andes for—to get to know the countries and the people.

Just remember, the *vast* majority of the people you'll meet are friendly, helpful, curious, and honest. By allowing fear of theft to control every encounter, you cut off any chance of communication, and you behave rudely to people who have done nothing to deserve such treatment.

A degree of common sense, wariness, and alertness is your best protection against theft. By all means, stay especially alert in train and bus stations and at airports. Since thieves often slit packs and steal whatever happens to be at hand, don't leave packs alone or unwatched for even a moment in public places, but to go to the extent of wrapping your pack in chicken wire, as we saw one group in Puno do, is probably well beyond the border of paranoia. Be wary of thieves working in teams; the usual approach is for one of the thieves to create a diversion (dropping something at your feet, for example) while the other grabs your camera or pack.

Watch out for crowded street and market situations when you can be easily distracted and robbed. Wear a money belt under your clothing for your main supply of cash, your traveler's checks, and, above all, your passport. Be particularly careful of what you display while on the streets. If possible, keep cameras out of sight when not in use. Otherwise, at least keep the strap around your neck and under an arm, rather than just dangling over your shoulder. Many travelers to Latin America replace their normal camera straps with chains to help prevent the camera from being yanked from their necks. This is largely a pointless precaution since in grab-and-run camera thefts it is almost always the little rings that attach the strap (or chain) to the camera that break rather than the strap itself. Wrist watches seem to be a frequent target of street thieves. If you feel lost without one, wear it underneath long sleeves. You'll inevitably hear horror stories of earrings allegedly being torn from pierced ears; this is very easy to prevent—simply don't wear earrings.

Almost anytime you get off an airplane, bus, or train in Peru, you'll be swamped by taxi drivers, hotel representatives, and enterprising kids (in the lexicon of travel, these people are officially called *touts*), all wanting to get your attention and your business. In these situations, in addition to the normal disorientation of suddenly arriving in an unfamiliar town or city, you'll have the confusion of a dozen hands thrusting pictures and price lists of hotels in your face and reaching for your bags. During those moments, keep an especially close watch on your things. Again, don't be paranoid; almost all of these people simply want to *earn* some money, not steal it. But in the confusion, a real thief could easily walk away with a bag while your attention is directed elsewhere.

On the trail, you'll need to take a few simple precautions to prevent camp theft. In inhabited areas pilfering is a frequent problem, so don't leave your camp unattended, and don't leave equipment, especially boots, outside the tent while you sleep (a barefoot walk on stony trails to the next town is no laughing matter). Remember, most *campesinos* earn less in a year than you'll spend in a few weeks on your trip to their country. To them you'll seem quite wealthy, perhaps so wealthy that you wouldn't really miss a pair of boots, a jacket, or a camera.

To help ease your mind about theft during the trip, take some precautions before you leave home. Check with your insurance agent and determine the exact amount of coverage your homeowner's or renter's policy will provide for travel-related loss. If this coverage is not adequate, purchase special short-term travel theft insurance. If for some reason your insurance agent cannot provide this service, any travel agent can supply you with a list of companies that will. Before you leave home, be sure to make a list of everything you take on the trip. If your entire pack should be stolen, such a list will be helpful in filing your insurance claim.

Finally, here are our two basic rules concerning theft:

1. If you can't replace it, don't take it.
2. Be wary, but don't be paranoid.

Trail Conditions and Trail Etiquette

Backpackers accustomed to U.S. trails must keep in mind the differences between the conditions they're used to and the conditions they'll encounter in the Andes. American backpackers are used to trails used primarily for recreational purposes. With the possible exception of the Inca Trail, you'll find none of these in the Andes. Andean trails are working trails. They are the primary means of transportation in roadless but inhabited areas. Over these trails farmers take their crops to market, herders move their animals to greener pastures, craftsmen carry their products into town for sale. The trails are, therefore, maintained largely through use; you won't find a National Forest Service trail crew clearing brush or repairing a washed-out footbridge. On these trails, you're on your own in a way that is hard to equal in the United States outside of Alaska. If you are injured or become sick or lost, no one will come looking for you. Unlike U.S. national parks, there are no rescue helicopters to airlift to safety hikers in poor condition and foolish enough to venture into the backcountry. When you begin a hike in the Andes, along with your pack, you shoulder the entire burden of responsibility for your own safety.

If you're a fit and experienced backpacker, you probably have all the backcountry skills you need to travel with safety and confidence through the South American mountains. But if you lack that fitness and experience, don't overestimate your abilities. At the very least you should plan to travel with someone who *is* experienced. Alternatively, guides and *arrieros* are available for most of the treks listed in this guide, or you could arrange a trip with one of the trekking agencies either in the United States or in the Andes.

Perhaps the one bit of advice we can pass along based on personal experience and that of other Andean hikers we've known is *always* take along a minimum of two days extra food per person. This will give you a margin of safety in case you run into a serious trail obstruction (e.g., a washed-out bridge over a deep ravine) or you become lost or ill. It will also give you the option of slowing down or taking a rest day if long climbs or inadequate acclimatization make your planned pace impossible to maintain.

Although you will be on vacation, you'll be sharing the trails and the countryside with working people carrying on the basic business of mountain life. You'll only be passing through for a few days, but these other trail users lead lives firmly rooted there. The following suggestions should help you to walk the trails with as little disruption as possible.

Above all, respect field boundaries. Subsistence farming is a life lived within close tolerances. A small corner of a barley field crushed by short-cutting trekkers may not *seem* important to us, but when every square yard of cultivation counts, it *is* important. Therefore, always skirt fields. On many hikes, you'll encounter narrow, shallow irrigation ditches. The banks of these can be quite fragile, so be careful when walking beside or crossing them. Trails will occasionally take you through stock gates. Be sure to leave these gates securely closed behind you.

Use stoves for cooking. Firewood is often scarce, especially along well-used routes. Leave what little there is for the people who live there. Avoid camping near houses and villages. If there isn't an alternative, always ask permission before making camp.

Litter is becoming an overwhelming problem on many of the most popular Andean trekking routes. Though it may seem incomprehensible, some people will travel halfway around the world to experience this landscape yet still toss a granola bar wrapper or empty sardine tin on the ground. With thousands of hikers a year, the Inca Trail is particularly hard hit. Because of the variety and magnificence of the scenery, the Inca ruins all along the way, and the goal of Machu Picchu at the end, the Inca Trail attracts large numbers of hikers with little mountain experience and evidently little sense of the impact that large numbers of hikers can have on the environment. Every Andean hiker, whether an Inca Trail first-timer or a seasoned veteran of the high *cordilleras,* should scrupulously attend to waste of all sorts. Take a garbage sack along and use it for everything—every wrapper, empty can, tea bag, and tissue. If you have a little extra room in your garbage bag, do pick up others' litter. Popular campsites benefit from a little trash pick-up.

Paper weighs next to nothing, and at the end of the trail you'll feel good about having done something to help improve trail conditions for everyone.

As when hiking anywhere, make your toilet *well* away from trails, campsites, and water supplies. If at all possible, bury feces or cover with a stone. Burn the paper. Be especially fastidious along the Inca Trail, particularly when camping in or near ruins. Do *not,* as many people have, use ruins as toilets.

People in remote areas are often initially quite shy, particularly in regard to cameras. Many will simply turn away from the camera or will cover their faces with their hands. Part of this reaction may be due to superstition, part to a feeling of violated privacy. In either case, respect their feelings. In most areas, few people will refuse to be photographed if you approach them first, talk a little, and then politely ask permission. A telephoto lens helps make photographing people less conspicuous, but always try to be sensitive to the wishes of the person being photographed. If you sense resentment, don't take photographs.

Gringo, Indio, Campesino

These epithets often cause trouble for travelers. You don't have to travel long in the Andes to become used to being called *gringo.* Everyone from shopkeepers to kids will use the word to get your attention when they want to talk to you, sell you something, etc. Don't be bothered by it. Though most *Norte Americanos* assume that the word *gringo* is always intended as an insult, most South Americans seem to use it merely as a general descriptive term, like foreigner or tourist, with no specific negative connotation at all. The word *Indio* (Indian), though, when used to refer to mountain people, *is* usually perceived to have negative connotations and may be taken as an insult. Much more preferable is to learn to call them *campesinos.*

Drugs

Coca leaves are both pharmacologically and legally different from the refined product cocaine. Though coca leaves are perfectly legal in Peru and Bolivia, cocaine laws are strictly enforced. In any town frequented by tourists, younger travelers will undoubtedly be approached by cocaine and marijuana dealers offering their goods at remarkably low prices. Don't be tempted. Drug laws are *very* harsh, and according to locals we've talked to, many of the dealers work as police informers. We've also met several younger, scruffier-looking travelers who've had their hotel rooms searched in middle-of-the-night raids by narcotics police. Anyone arrested for a drug offense can expect a very long wait in jail before trial and a stiff prison sentence if found guilty. And the American Embassy can offer virtually no help. Prison conditions in the Andean countries are medieval, and we're told that in Lima's central prison *gringo* prisoners often have to barricade themselves in their cells at night to prevent attacks from guards and other prisoners. Therefore, avoid any association with drugs while in the Andes.

Getting Around in the Andes

If you travel with an agency-led group, all of your ground transportation will be taken care of. If you travel on your own, though, you'll soon find that arranging transportation can become one of the most difficult parts of the trip. This is one more area in which you simply have to abandon many of your normal expectations of how public transportation works. Internal travel in these countries is almost always hard and tiring, especially if you are trying to cover great distances or if you are traveling to or from remote mountain areas. Your normal concept of the relationship between time and distance will have to change as well. To look at a map and find that the town you want to visit is sixty miles away by road means virtually nothing unless you also know the condition of the road and the kind of vehicle you'll be traveling in. We've been on truck rides of only sixty miles that have taken seven hours or more. And we've also been on hair-raising *colectivo* rides on straight, flat coastal highways when the driver roared along at unbelievable speeds, passing on blind curves, blowing the horn at every moving object within eyesight of the road, and getting us to our destination long before we had expected. There are, however, a few travel skills you can develop to help cope with the problems of getting around.

AIR TRAVEL

Because ground transportation is almost always slow, tiring, and difficult and because internal air fares are quite reasonable, we recommend that most of your long-haul trips within the Andean countries be by air, especially if your trip is a relatively brief one. Unless you're doing some fairly exotic jungle flying using private or military aircraft, virtually all of your internal air travel will depend on the services of the major airlines of the Andean countries: Ecuadoriana, AeroPeru, Fawcett, and Lloyd AeroBoliviana. Travelers constantly complain about the services of these airlines, often with just cause. Flights are frequently late and sometimes canceled altogether. Office staffs are notoriously inefficient, making even the simplest of transactions unnecessarily difficult. And if you have a complicated problem (such as changing your return flight date or checking to see if you have cleared a waiting list), plan on losing several hours to take care of it, even if you're at a main office. If you happen to be at a smaller office, you may never get a complicated problem resolved. And remember, the kinds of rights as a flyer that you expect in the United States are not in effect in South America. If you are bumped from a flight, don't expect the airline to provide you with accommodations and food. If your luggage is lost, you'll receive minimal compensation (another good reason to have adequate baggage insurance).

In dealing with these airlines, you'll be wise *never* to take anything for granted. Confirm and reconfirm every flight, both internal and external. Most flights fill up, and many people reserve tickets on several flights to ensure seats, so letting the airlines know that you fully intend to use your ticket is essential to avoid being bumped. You may encounter problems in reconfirming your return flight unless you are going to be in the city from which the flight leaves a couple of days before departure. The smaller offices are not connected to the computer communication system, and you may be told in those offices that you cannot change or confirm your flight there. If you're firm and persistent, though, these smaller offices will almost always telex the main office and take care of your problem in that manner. You should be especially careful to double check the confirmation of your return flight, especially during the peak travel period between late June and the end of August. During those weeks, most flights to the United States are fully booked, and the chance of problems increases.

For any flights in these countries, always get to the airport early, and get your baggage checked and pick up your boarding pass as soon as possible. Latecomers have a much greater chance of being bumped. If you do have trouble with the airlines, stay calm. They're quite used to hysterics; shouting, tears, and threats will get you nowhere. Be patient but firm in demanding that the problem be resolved. Don't let yourself be put off, and don't settle for vague answers. If you aren't satisfied that everything possible has been done to solve your problem, ask to speak to a manager.

One rather unexpected place you may have a little trouble with the airlines is with your pack. Evidently, luggage handlers sometimes don't feel like bothering with a heavy, unwieldy backpack. We've waited several times in small airports until all other passengers had claimed their suitcases to find our packs still not in sight. When the last luggage dolly was rolled away, the persistent fear of the traveler began to materialize—"What if all our gear is lost?" Each time, though, we've eventually found our packs. They've usually been left lying by themselves on the runway, just where they had been pulled from the cargo hold and thrown onto the ground because they wouldn't pack well on the luggage dolly. Once, though, we even had to climb into the hold of a jet revving its engines in preparation for takeoff in order to retrieve our packs.

Over the years, we've encountered almost every conceivable problem with South American airlines, and we've spent many long hours in more than a dozen different airline offices trying to solve those problems. We've also seen frustrated travelers stranded for days because of canceled flights, ticket foul-ups, etc. It is important to remember that though many of the problems are due to inefficiency, many others are not. Most late and canceled flights are the result of the very difficult flying conditions in the Andes. Weather is extreme and unpredictable. A few airstrips on which jets land are still unpaved (Juliaca near Lake Titicaca, for example), and therefore unusable in wet conditions. So be patient with unavoidable delays.

RAIL TRAVEL

Though South American trains hardly match up to European standards (see Paul Theroux's *The Old Patagonia Express*), they can be a very pleasant way to see the countryside and cover ground faster and more comfortably than by road. The railway systems in these countries are not extensive, but several of the lines that do exist are among the most spectacular in the world. Peru's Central Railway, for example, reaches the highest altitude of any standard-gauge railroad in the world, 15,981 feet, on its route from Lima to Huancayo. Almost as exciting in terms of scenery if not in sheer altitude are the trips from Quito to Guayaquil in Ecuador, from Puno on Lake Titicaca to Arequipa in southern Peru, and from Cuzco to Puno.

On most routes, you'll have a choice of tickets—second class, first class, and buffet or pullman. Though we've ridden second class several times, we could hardly recommend it. Unless you are on an extremely tight budget or unless you particularly enjoy the experience of being packed into a railroad car with twice as many people, animals, and bundles of produce as the car will comfortably hold, spend a little more money for first-class tickets. In those cars, you'll have softer seats, fewer animals, and a little more room to spread out. If you have a little more money to spend, we heartily recommend splurging on the buffet car. The cost is really very little higher than first class, and you'll have the luxury of adequate leg room and the option of having your meals served to you (as on trains everywhere, expect meals to be considerably more expensive than in local restaurants).

Trains are frequently full during peak travel periods, so buy your tickets as much in advance as possible. Even in first-class cars, luggage space is tight, so try to be at the station and ready to board early; if you wait too long, you may find no room in the overhead racks for your gear. On long rides, whether or not you plan on eating in the buffet car (only those with buffet car tickets can have meals there), take plenty of snacks since food at stations is unpredictable. Finally, be especially careful of thieves in dark, crowded train stations and on the trains themselves. The trains from Cuzco to Machu Picchu and from Arequipa to Puno have especially bad reputations for occurrences of theft.

ROAD TRAVEL

Most of your short-haul travel in Ecuador, Peru, and Bolivia will be by road. Because few people in these countries can afford to own their own cars, public ground transportation is well developed. Wherever a road goes, you can be nearly sure some bus, truck, or colectivo taxi will take you there, usually at a price that is unbelievably low. However, aside from the flat, straight coastal stretches of the Pan-American highway, most of the roads in these countries are convoluted, narrow, and sometimes poorly maintained, making travel slow and wearing. And the vehicles that travel these roads are often sixties-vintage American imports. They're well maintained, but hard-used, old and slow, and on their last legs. A full day of travel under these conditions can be exhausting, leaving you covered in a thick coat of road grit and feeling beaten-up by hours of pounding over potholes in a vehicle whose springs were worn out years ago.

To travel by road in the Andes, you have to learn to accept humanity in much closer proximity than North Americans are often comfortable with. Public road transportation will inevitably be crowded. You'll be packed into standing-room-only buses with people, almost all locals, jammed all about you. Andean public transportation is not for the squeamish. You'll be overwhelmed by odors of various sorts and sources, and opening a window for relief is often out of the question. Either the road is too dusty to open the windows or the window is jammed or the people on the bus object to the cold air. You'll also have to contend with the passengers' animals and produce. Chickens, goats, guinea pigs, sacks of potatoes, and (if you're lucky) bundles of fragrant herbs are all normal baggage on buses and trucks.

Your bus ride will be somewhat more comfortable if you take a few precautions. Board the bus as early as possible to ensure getting a seat. Check to make sure your window opens; if not, try to move to another seat. Since your pack will usually be loaded onto a luggage rack on the roof, keep your jacket with you inside. Even though it may be quite warm when you board, if your route takes you across a high pass, you may find yourself shivering uncomfortably in the cold, thin air. A jacket in your pack on the roof will do you no good. As always, keep your passport handy since you may have to show it to officials at police checkpoints along the way. For long rides, take along snacks—bread and fruit hold up well on bus rides—and a full water bottle. You'll usually be able to get food at stops along the way, but you never know what will be available or what you'll find in terms of cleanliness.

In Ecuador and Peru there are many buses and trucks traveling major routes. Minibuses ply the main roads with a frequency surprising to North Americans. We've never had to wait more than half an hour for a bus anywhere in Ecuador other than along remote dirt roads. In Bolivia, however, departures are much less frequent, and tickets are often scarce on short notice, so buy tickets as much in advance as possible or you may find yourself waiting days for an empty seat.

An alternative to buses for travel between most major cities and larger towns are *colectivos.* These are like regular taxis except they travel only when they have a full load of passengers sharing the cost of the trip. They cost a little more than buses, but they usually shave a considerable amount of time off the trip. But don't expect much more comfort in a *colectivo* than on a bus. In a full-sized car, drivers usually consider a complete load of passengers to be six, not counting the driver. So you'll be at least as crowded as on a bus, but for a shorter time. One of the problems with *colectivos* is that they will not leave without a full load. This is usually no problem on popular routes, but if you have to wait an hour or two for the car to fill, you'll have lost most of the advantage of traveling by *colectivo* instead of by bus. Another problem is unscrupulous drivers. We've had trouble over and over with *colectivo* drivers who quote one price at the beginning of the trip (the normal *colectivo* rate) and then when we reached our destination demand the full taxi rate for the trip. The only way to solve that problem is to ask the driver to write down the price of the trip before you begin. Though many travelers swear by *colectivo* travel, we use it only as a last resort because of the unpredictability of departure times and the extreme crowding of the passengers.

Often, especially in getting to trailheads, you'll have no choice but to travel by truck (*camión*). Trucks carrying goods, produce, animals, and people travel the back roads of the Andes on semiregular schedules. They're slow, rough, dirty, crowded, and an experience not to be missed. We've ridden on more trucks in the Andes than we'd like to remember, but every ride is in its own way unforgettable, an adventure the likes of which are unavailable in North America. On one special ride from Cuzco to Mollepata during a week-long fiesta, our truck turned into a rolling party with *chicha* (corn beer) flowing (and spilling) freely. But for every marvelous truck ride into the mountains, there is also one like a trip we took into the Cordillera Vilcanota. The only truck we could find had a load of oil drums and freshly slaughtered sheep carcasses. We rode among the drums and the sheep for eight hours over a torturously slow and brutally rough route that was so dusty we had to wrap our heads in our towels to breathe.

When traveling by truck, you should keep several things in mind. First, stake out your territory in the truck bed early. The ride will be much more bearable if you can sit on something approaching softness —a sack of potatoes, your pack, or, if you hit the jackpot, a bundle of blankets on the way to market. Keep your pack near you, and don't let it become covered by the other cargo; you may have to get to it to take out needed gear. For example, if you ride on a truck from Coroico to La Paz in Bolivia, you'll need to be able to get to your rain gear when the truck passes underneath a couple of waterfalls that drench everyone on the truck. Every time you get onto a truck, assume you'll need to have a bandanna handy to cover your mouth and nose for protection against dust. Also, as with trains and buses, take snacks and a full water bottle for long rides—you'll never know what will be available along the way. Be prepared for long and unexpected delays. Trucks stop and start at the whim of the driver; if he wants to visit with a friend along the way, you'll wait until he's through or until the other passengers threaten to mutiny. An unexpected delay on a truck ride, though, once netted us a free ride. The truck was uncharacteristically empty, and the driver, spotting the leafy branches left over from a grove of eucalyptus cut for firewood, stopped to load them onto the truck. To speed up the process, we worked for an hour with him, hauling the spicy-smelling boughs onto the truck. In town, he refused our payment, saying "No charge for *campesinos.*" Remember, since you'll usually pay for the ride at your destination, establish the price before you board.

In cities, of course, your choice of transportation is between taxis and city buses. Bus rides are always dirt cheap, but you may have trouble figuring out which buses go where you want to go. Lots of travelers avoid city buses because of this problem, but just stay loose and realize that if you do happen to get on the wrong bus, you can always get off and hail a taxi. City buses will invariably be packed, sometimes to the point of having "passengers" hanging on the outside or riding on the bumpers. Taxi fares are much cheaper than in the United States as well, and because of this, when we're in cities, we use them with abandon, especially if pressed for time or uncertain of how to get to our destination. You should, however, avoid taxis waiting outside higher-priced hotels, as well as the black "pirate" taxis in Lima; their rates will always be higher than ordinary cabs. For frequently used routes, such as from the center of a city to the airport, *colectivo* service is often available and can be a substantial savings over regular cab fare. Ask your hotel desk clerk if there are *colectivos* to the airport and where the pickup point is. Since South American cabs don't have meters, the fare will often depend on the whim of the driver. Therefore, always ask for the fare before you get into any taxi; if it sounds high, either bargain for a lower fare or wait for another taxi.

Mail, Telephone, and Telegraph

Even on relatively short trips to the Andes, you'll probably find yourself needing to use communications services. At the very least you'll probably be sending postcards to friends back home, and you may want to receive mail while on your trip. In cases of major and minor emergencies, you may need to get in touch with someone at home more quickly than the mails will allow, meaning you'll have to deal with telephone and/or telegraph services. In any of these cases, expect the going to be slow.

Postal service in South America is at best unreliable, but there are some precautions you can take that will improve your chances of successfully sending or receiving mail. To send mail, always go to the main post office (*correos*) of the town or city. Your chances of getting reliable service are much greater there. Of course, you should send everything by airmail, and be sure to write *via aereo* or *correo aereo* below the address. In our experience, airmail traveling between the Andean countries and the United States will usually take about two weeks for delivery—if it is delivered at all. Postal service for letters and cards is unreliable, and for packages, you might as well forget it. Most packages are opened for inspection, and whether or not your package reaches its destination largely depends on how appealing its contents are to whoever inspects it. On trips lasting several months, we've often wanted to receive packages of hard-to-find supplies—trail food, books, etc. This has not proved, however, to be very practical. If the package should happen to be delivered, the duty on imports often costs much more than the value of the package's contents.

If you want to receive mail in South America, you have a couple of options. You could have your mail sent in care of General Delivery in the town where you intend to pick it up; the South American equivalent of General Delivery is called *Lista de Correos.* Your other option—and a much preferable one if you are going to be passing regularly through major cities—is to have your mail sent to American Express offices. These are located in Quito, Guayaquil, Lima, Cuzco, Arequipa, and La Paz (for addresses, see the Resources sections in the chapters for the appropriate countries). It is always much easier to check for mail at these offices than at the *correos* since they keep a careful list of letters and will usually even let you look through the new arrivals for yourself. The only slight catch is that you must be an American Express customer to use this service; that is, you must show either an American Express card or American Express traveler's checks when you ask for mail.

Telephone service between the Andean countries and the United States has improved greatly in the past few years. International phone calls, however, are still quite expensive and usually frustrating to place. Normally you'll have two options on placing a long-distance call. If you're staying in a fairly good hotel, you'll often be able to place your call there. Normally, this is the simplest way to make a long-distance call since the hotel management will usually arrange the call for you. Then you can wait in your room for the call to be completed (this can take anywhere from a half-hour to a couple of hours). If your hotel can't make the call, you'll have to use the public telephone office. There you need to give the operator the information necessary to place the call—the country, state, person, and phone number you're trying to reach. If you're calling collect, ask for *cobro revertido.* Then you'll usually be asked to pay a deposit for the call, and you'll be given a receipt. Save this since you'll need it to get back your deposit after the call has been completed. Next, you'll settle in for what will often be a long wait, so long that we would never think of trying to make a long-distance call without taking a couple of good books along. When the connection is made, you'll be called to a booth (*cabina*) where the long-distance operator will probably make you repeat all the information you've already given to the local operator. When the call is completed, you'll need to check back with the local operator either to pay for the call or, if you called collect, to get your deposit back. Though you might get lucky and complete a call in short order, allow at least two hours to make a call to the United States from a public telephone office.

If your message is short and doesn't require an immediate response, you'll save yourself time and money by sending a telegram rather than making a phone call. Telegrams can usually be sent from post offices or from the public telephone office (ask for the *oficina de telégrafos*). Night rates are much less expensive than day rates. Your message will usually be delivered within a day. If you expect a reply, it is simplest to have the response delivered to your hotel. However, if you're not sure where you'll be when the response arrives, you can have it directed either to the *lista* at the *correos* or to American Express if you're a customer.

Our best general advice on communications between South America and the United States is to allow plenty of time for delivery, and if the message is important, send a backup. Don't assume that your letter or telegram will reach its destination.

Animal Hazards

Unless you're doing some fairly exotic jungle travel, you have little to worry about from wild animals. In the mountains, only one variety of mildly poisonous snake lives at altitudes over 12,000 feet. And there is virtually nothing to worry about from larger mammals. The Andean bear is extremely rare and offers little threat to trekkers. Rabies, though, is widespread among both wild and domestic animals, so be observant; don't go near any animal behaving oddly. Rabies innoculations are still a long and painful process, so you'll want to exercise every precaution in preventing being bitten by any animal.

Though not extremely common, vampire bats are a potential danger in jungle and cloud forest areas. Primarily for rabies prevention, you should take a few simple precautions against being bitten by vampire bats. These nasty creatures usually land on the ground away from their sleeping victims and walk to them. The bat then bites the victim, usually on an extremity, with its razor-sharp teeth. Since the vampire bat's saliva contains an anticoagulant, the wound bleeds freely, and the animal drinks its fill. The simplest precaution to take against providing a bat's liquid dinner is to sleep inside a tent when in vampire bat territory. Otherwise, make sure your feet and hands remain well covered throughout the night.

On a couple of occasions when passing through pasture land, we've encountered aggressive bulls. Though humorous in retrospect, there's nothing funny at the time in trying to escape from an angry bull when you're encumbered with a full pack. The best precaution is to keep your eyes open; make sure you spot a potential problem animal before he spots you. Give these animals a wide berth.

Far and away the most common problem animal in the Andes is the dog. Robert Louis Stevenson, in *Travels With A Donkey* [1879], wrote: "I respect dogs much in the domestic circle; but on the highway or sleeping afield, I both detest and fear them." After a few days of walking in the Andes, you may come to share Stevenson's feelings. Any time you're walking through inhabited countryside, you should be aware of the potential for dog trouble. Most country houses and many fields are aggressively guarded by one or more dogs. They'll rush at you with loud, vicious barking and give every indication that they mean to rip you to shreds. We've been the objects of literally scores of these attacks, and fortunately we've found Andean dogs to be living proof of the old cliché—"their bark is worse than their bite." Like dogs everywhere, Andean dogs understand the universal language of a well-aimed stone, so if you stand your ground, pick up a couple of stones, and throw them if necessary, these dogs will almost always keep their distance. After you've stalled their advance, walk away slowly; nothing incites a renewed attack like a hasty retreat on your part.

Beggars

One of the most difficult aspects of Latin American culture for many citizens of industrial Western nations to get used to is the extreme visibility of beggars. And it is especially difficult to decide what your personal policy toward beggars is going to be. Over and over we've met travelers who are made very uncomfortable by beggars and refuse to give money to them. These travelers usually rationalize their decision in one of two ways: either they say that the beggars probably make so much money from tourists that they live much better than the average person (a South American version of the old "Welfare Cadillac" routine), or they say that their small contributions will have no effect on the overall problem of poverty in Latin America and that their donations only perpetuate the system of begging.

We've come to somewhat different conclusions and think travelers to the Latin American countries should consider several cultural and political differences before deciding how to deal with beggars. First, remember that the Latin American countries have virtually no welfare assistance programs. Those who would be at least marginally taken care of in the United States, for example, are completely on their own in South America. Second, remember that despite what many travelers want to believe, begging is not strictly a tourist-oriented industry. Keep your eyes open, and you'll see that *many* South American citizens donate to beggars. In a small town in Ecuador, we once watched a brass band perform in the town square on a Sunday evening. A tiny, filthy beggar woman worked the crowd, pausing, palm extended, at group after group of tourists and locals alike. Over and over we saw the tourists wave her away with gestures clearly displaying their disgust and embarrassment. And over and over we saw the locals, even down to scruffy-looking shoeshine boys, give her a few small coins. To say that giving something to such a person does nothing to solve the problem of poverty in South America ignores the real issue: personal day-to-day survival. So the policy we've adopted is to follow the example of the Latin Americans and try to see begging—as they apparently do—as an informal system of social welfare. Therefore, we give to adult beggars obviously in need. We do not normally give to children because many children who beg from travelers are not particularly needy and because giving to children could lead to their exploitation.

Accommodations—What to Expect

One of the most consistent topics of conversations among travelers throughout the world is the exchange of information on hotel accommodations. This hotel rumor mill has more than once sent us on wild-goose chases for that wonderful little five-dollar-a-night place nestled under a waterfall with natural hot pools just outside the door and where maids change the roses in the rooms twice a day. Perhaps these sorts of oases of peace and tranquility exist somewhere, but unless you have plenty of money to spend on hotels, you'll be doing well simply to find a clean, quiet, reasonably priced room. In most major cities and towns in the Andes, you'll have the option of normal first- or second-class hotel accommodations—at normal first- or second-class prices. If you don't want to spend that much money or if you're in a small town, you're going to be limited to standard South American hotels. In our hotel recommendations later in the book, we've tried to include hotels in several price ranges—everything from North American-style hotels to very cheap and basic *alojamientos* (inns). In 1984 prices, double rooms in expensive hotels are above $20; moderately priced double rooms are usually at the low end of the $10 to $20 range, and inexpensive double rooms are often well below $10 a night. We've paid special attention in our hotel selections to indicate the hotels that act as *gringo* crossroads as a convenience both to those who seek them out and to those who avoid them with as much enthusiasm as we do.

In making your selection, never judge a hotel by its lobby—or lack of one. *Always,* even in upper-category hotels, ask to see your room before you check in since the rooms available can vary considerably in pleasantness. Many times we've been shown dank, chill, windowless rooms capable of throwing us into fits of minor depression, only to find that with a little prodding the desk clerk will eventually take us to a bright, airy room that he'd been holding back for later, more discriminating guests. So if you don't like what you see, push a bit for something more suitable.

While you're looking at the room, be sure to ask to see the bathroom (*baño*). In many lower-range Andean hotels, these facilities are quite informal. Broken toilets, inoperative faucets, clogged shower drains, etc., are all just part of the game, so before you commit yourself, make sure the bathroom is in reasonable working order. While we're talking about bathrooms, one of the things about South American plumbing, whether in hotels or elsewhere, that *gringos* find most difficult to get used to is the fact that toilets flush so weakly that they become clogged if toilet paper is thrown into them. The practice, then, is to throw paper into the waste basket. Though unsanitary, this is much preferable to the backed-up toilet that otherwise results.

Before you check in, you should also ask about hot water. You'll be surprised at the number of hotels, even relatively expensive ones, without regular hot water. So when checking in, ask not only *if* the hotel has *aqua caliente* but *when* it has *aqua caliente* because many hotels heat water for only a few hours a day. In Bolivia, most hotels do have twenty-four-hour hot water but only because they use water-heating shower heads. With these scary-looking devices, electrical wires run directly to heating coils inside the large shower head. The electricity is turned on with a lever just outside the shower stall. Remember always to turn on the water before throwing the switch to prevent burning out the coils and always to throw the switch while you still have your shoes on and are standing on a dry floor.

Even in better hotels, you'll have to get used to the absence of services you'd normally expect. For example, few hotels—even some higher-priced hotels—in the mountains have heated rooms. Of course, if you have a sleeping bag with you, a chilly night in a mountain hotel is no problem; if not, ask the desk clerk before you check in to make sure plenty of extra blankets are available.

Cheaper hotels, especially, can be unbearably noisy. If the hotel is located near a market, a train or bus station, or a busy downtown street, outside noise can make sleeping virtually impossible. If you think your hotel has a high potential for noise, be sure to ask for a room away from the street—either an interior room or a room at the rear of the building. Older hotels and those with very thin walls can generate quite a bit of interior noise; you'll hear every word and every move that other guests make. One partial solution is to ask for a room on the top floor; this cuts down on the noise from those above you and from people moving up and down the stairs. Finally, earplugs can offer a measure of relief from hotel noise.

One service that most South American hotels routinely provide that we've found very convenient is luggage storage. When we're getting ready for a short trek or a couple-of-day excursions to small villages and ruins and don't need all the gear we're carrying, we save weight by leaving the unnecessary items at our hotel. Usually this service is provided free of charge for hotel guests, especially if you intend to stay at the hotel when you return. Though most hotels have a locked room or closet for storage, some simply stack the baggage in a spare corner behind the check-in desk where it could easily be stolen. So before leaving your excess baggage with a hotel, *make sure* that it will be locked away. Also be sure to label your luggage clearly with your name as well as your passport number, and indicate the date on which you plan to return.

Restaurants

Many citizens of the United States suffer from the misconception that Latin American food is synonymous with Mexican food. That could hardly be further from the truth. In cities, of course, you'll find restaurants of all sorts—everything from French to Mexican (the only place you'll find those tacos you might have been expecting to be a staple). And in most tourist-oriented hotel restaurants, those desperate for at least somewhat familiar food will find the ubiquitous "international" menu. But if you confine your off-trail meals to these types of restaurants, you'll have no sense of what real Andean cooking is like.

After you've given your stomach a few days to acclimatize to the new strains of bacteria it will have to learn to cope with, be a little adventurous in your eating. Branch out from the tourist restaurants and try some of the local spots, usually called *típico* restaurants. Of course, if you're in a small town off the beaten path, you'll have no choice but to sample the local food. In these nontourist restaurants, it is virtually impossible to judge the quality or cleanliness of the food by looking at the facilities. Some of the best meals we've eaten in the Andes have been in quite unlikely looking places. One memorable meal of grilled trout, sauteed potatoes, and fresh vine-ripe tomatoes was served in a dark, windowless, dirt-floored, thatched-roofed hut where we had to wait to eat until the proprietor caught the fish from the glacier-fed lake outside. Conversely, there is seldom a direct correlation between clean tablecloths and either palatable food or clean cooking conditions.

One reason many travelers avoid local eating establishments is their unfamiliarity with the menu (called either *menu* or *lista*). But don't let that stop you. If you know that *lomo saltado* is a stir-fried dish of beef, tomatoes, and onions served over rice, you won't be totally lost in 95 percent of the restaurants in the Andes. If you know too that *bistek* is steak, that *corvina* is sea bass, and that *pollo* is chicken, then you'll begin to develop even more confidence. But don't stop there; far too many travelers confine their eating to *bistek con papas fritas.* Branch out and try local specialties usually not available in tourist restaurants, dishes like *cau-cau* (a spicy tripe, rice, and potato dish), *cebiche* (fish or shellfish marinated in lime juice), *anticuchos* (grilled beef hearts), *humitas* (cornmeal rolls stuffed with meat, eggs, and vegetables), *adobo* (pork stew), *rocoto relleno* (hot stuffed peppers), and *ocopa* (potatoes with a firey sauce). If you really want an eating adventure, try a traditional Andean favorite, *cuy* (roast guinea pig). To find these sorts of traditional Andean foods, look for restaurants with signs that include the words *picanteria* or *comidas criollas.* There you'll encounter a type of cuisine you probably didn't know existed—the cuisine of the Quechuas.

Two other categories of restaurants of which you should be aware are *chifas* and *parilladas. Chifas* are Chinese restaurants, and you'll find them almost everywhere throughout the Andes, a surprising discovery for many North Americans. The food in even the most out-of-the-way of these restaurants is usually surprisingly good, though somewhat different in preparation from most Chinese food served in the United States. Aside from typical items such as chow mein, look for the various *tallarine* (noodle) dishes. *Parilladas* are restaurants specializing in charcoal-grilled meats. Located primarily in larger towns, these restaurants are for devout carnivores only. A typical *parillada* meal may be served to you at a tableside individual hibachi and will usually include grilled pork, beef, chicken, sausages, and various and sundry internal organs.

Drinks are called *bebidas,* and though most restaurants serve beer and a wide selection of familiar soft drinks, many travelers have a difficult time getting used to the lack of refrigeration. Though it usually doesn't help, asking that your drink be *frío* or *helado* may get you a drink that is slightly below room temperature. Most brands of Andean beer are quite good, though we have an especial fondness for *Cuzqueña,* brewed in Cuzco. You should know, however, that the normal-sized bottle of Andean beer is nearly as large as a wine bottle; if you want a smaller bottle, you'll have to ask for a *cerveza chica* (because *chica* means young girl, just ordering a *cerveza chica* suggests something about your toughness). Other typical Andean alcoholic beverages include *pisco,* a grape brandy used in the quite good and easily overwhelming *pisco* sour, and *chicha,* a mildly alcoholic beverage brewed from corn. *Chicha*'s history is older than the Incas, and the still-popular drink can be found in local restaurants and street and market stalls throughout the Andes. Hot beverages include, of course, tea *(té)* and coffee *(café*—usually made by mixing liquid coffee concentrate with hot water to form a thoroughly unsatisfactory simulation of the real thing). More typically Andean is the widely available *mate de coca,* coca leaf tea. This very mildly narcotic drink is not only good for calming the symptoms of *soroche,* but it is also helps soothe frayed nerves after a hard day of travel. Finally, many restaurants serve excellent herb teas usually made by pouring boiling water over fresh herbs rather than dried herbs in tea bags.

In most upper-price-range restaurants, your bill will often include both a service charge (*servicio*) and a cover charge (*cubierto*). Cheaper restaurants add these charges less frequently. In either case you should leave a small additional tip for your waiter. Very low-end restaurants seldom have menus; you'll have to ask "Qué hay a comer?" (literally, "What is there to eat?"). The response to this question will sometimes simply be *almuerzo* or *cena* (lunch or dinner, respectively), in which case, you'll usually get the soup of the day and whatever main dish happens to be on the stove. Our least favorite response to the *Que hay* question so far has been "Cabrito, nada más" (goat, nothing more).

Food for the Trail

Whenever you're away from towns, you'll have to rely on nonrestaurant food sources. If you prefer commercially prepared dried foods for backpacking, you'll need to buy what you need in the United States and take it with you. But hauling enough food for the entire trip can be both bulky and heavy. Also, many hikers prefer not to eat freeze-dried foods exclusively. Fortunately, Andean markets and *bodegas* offer an extensive supply of foods adaptable to trail use. And outfitting yourself with foods from a colorful local market is much more exciting than simply stocking up on freeze-dried packets before you leave home.

Excellent, nutritious, and filling backpacking meals can, with a little imagination, be assembled from even the smallest of markets. The carbohydrate energy base needed for a strenuous activity such as backpacking is readily available in the form of rice (*arroz*), pasta (*tallarines*), corn (*maíz* or *choclo*), and potatoes (*papas*). Dried beans and lentils for nonmeat protein are also easy to find in markets and *bodegas.*

One authentically Andean food ideal for backpacking is the *chuño* potato. This small potato grown at high altitudes is quite bitter if eaten fresh, but since Incan times, and perhaps long before, the Indians have known about freeze-drying. The potatoes are left out during the cold mountain nights to freeze; then they are left out during the days to dry in the brilliant high-altitude sunshine. After several cycles of freezing and drying, the potatoes lose most of their moisture and can be kept almost indefinitely before eating. In the dried state they are quite light in weight and resemble mushroom caps. After cooking (boil them until tender, thirty minutes to an hour, depending on altitude), the *chuño* rehydrate and darken, and the finished product tastes something like a cross between a potato and a boiled chestnut. *Campesinos* tell us that the darker-colored ones are richer and better tasting (*más rico*) than the lighter ones, but they all taste pretty much the same to us.

Fresh vegetables also make excellent trail food if eaten during the first few days of the trip. Corn grown in the Andes is large-kerneled and tastes wonderful—excellent either on the cob or in soups and stews. Look also for large roasted corn kernels called *kamcha;* these make excellent trail and bus snacks. Other vegetables such as tomatoes (*tomate), carrots (zanahorias*), cabbage (*repollo*), and cauliflower (*coliflor*) are also widely available in markets and make excellent additions to soups and stews. Good, wholesome bread (*pan*) is easy to find in markets, bakeries, and from street vendors. Denser varieties will keep for several days on the trail if wrapped tightly in plastic.

In both markets and *bodegas* you'll see plenty of cheese, and though you may be tempted, remember that most of it is made from unpasteurized milk, so you'll be well-advised to avoid uncooked cheeses.

Remember that since the Andes range is fairly narrow, warm tropical regions are not far away, and excellent fruits and fruit juices are widely available. Whether you order them in restaurants or shop for them yourself in the market, take advantage of the wide selection and low price of tropical fruits such as papaya, mango, several varieties of banana, oranges and mandarines, pineapple, avocado, and guava. Sample as well some of the more exotic fruits such as the tamarind, a big, crude-looking pod inside of which is an edible pulp—a favorite food of ours for bus riding since it isn't messy and takes a long time to eat. Excellent and amazingly flavorful fresh fruit juices—everything from orange to papaya—are available in many restaurants and street stalls. These taste absolutely wonderful after a few days of iodine water on the trail, but make sure to buy your juice from the cleanest-looking vendor you can find.

In larger markets you will usually be able to find both excellent roast peanuts (*maní*) and plump, sweet raisins (*uvas secas*), from which you can make a simple trail mix.

In *bodegas* you'll find several kinds of trail-worthy foods. Even the smallest shops will have a few varieties of Knorr or Maggi dried soups —usually cream soups such as chicken (*pollo*), mushroom (*hongo*), and asparagus (*espárragos*). You'll also find canned tuna. In a pinch, we've put together marginally edible trail meals by combining noodles, mushroom soup, and a can of tuna. You'll also be able to get crackers, chicken bouillon cubes (*caldo de gallina*—we use them as a base for our vegetable stews), and chocolate (try the good but small *Sublime* bars rather than the gritty larger bars) in almost all *bodegas.* If you become inordinately nostalgic for familiar food, in larger shops you may be able to find imported U.S. brands of peanut butter, jelly, cookies, and canned goods—at very high prices.

So with all this wealth of good, cheaply priced food available to you in almost every town in the Andes, you really can get by with taking only a few packages of dried backpacking food to be reserved for emergencies and those occasions when speed of preparation is most important.

Fiestas

As you walk the trails of the Andes, passing villages and isolated farms, watching *campesinos* working in the fields, herding their animals, and weaving their fabrics, you soon develop a feel for the everyday lives of Andeans. And you may find them to be a fairly stoic group. Nothing provides the needed balance to this view better than visiting one of the many festivals of the region. Here you'll see a completely different side of the *campesinos,* the side that emerges when the hard work of living in the high mountains is put aside and forgotten for a day or two of sheer pleasure, a time when drinking, dancing, music, and laughter take over. There are so many festivals throughout the year that if you stay in the Andes for any length of time, you'll have a hard time *not* happening upon at least one or two. And aside from the usual procession to the cathedral and a general atmosphere of drunken revelry, you'll never know what to expect.

Some are raucous affairs with much throwing of water balloons. Others feature such things as the decoration of cars and trucks with flowers, after which the engines are sprinkled with holy water and blessed by the town priest. Others are simply occasions for drinking, dancing, and music, often throughout the night. One of our fondest festival memories is of a dark night near the winter solstice when we rode for hours in the bed of a truck to get from Ocongate to Cuzco. All around us for hours were the ritual fires on the mountainsides lit to brighten the longest nights of the year.

Most fiestas are religious in nature, of course. But *which* religious calendar—Catholic or Incan—is being celebrated is a matter of some ambiguity since the Spanish priests of the Colonial period very cannily substituted minor Catholic feast days for already existing Inca holidays. Thus, to this day much of the calendar of fiestas throughout Ecuador, Peru, and Bolivia are Incan with an overlay of Christianity. For example, Inti Raymi, the Inca Festival of the Sun on the winter solstice, became the feast day of Saint John the Baptist.

Many festivals are quite open to tourists. Cuzco's Inti Raymi, for example, has become a major tourist attraction, and finding a hotel room in the city the week of the celebration can be nearly impossible. Minor festivals in small, seldom-visited towns and villages, however, can be another matter. Remember that these festivals are not being staged for your benefit. Your presence, particularly if you are intent on taking photographs, may not be entirely welcome. In these situations, observe from a distance, keep your camera out of sight, and be sensitive to the feelings of the locals. If they want to include you in the festivities (often the case), you'll know it; otherwise, don't intrude.

The South America Explorers Club

The South American Explorers Club was founded by Linda Rosa and Don Montague in 1977 to act as a clearinghouse for those interested in scientific field exploration and research in South America, as well as those interested in outdoor adventure. Since then, the club has become an important source of information for Latin American travelers both before and during a trip to the Andes or Amazon. Aside from the interesting *South American Explorer* magazine, the club also has a good selection of maps and books on the region. The clubhouse in Lima (Avenida Portugal, 146, only a few blocks from the Sheraton Hotel) is always a friendly, pleasant place to pick up information, meet fellow travelers, and relax for a while in a spot of calmness in hectic downtown Lima. Clubhouse hours are 9 A.M. to 4 P.M., Monday through Friday. Nonmembers should limit their visits to thirty minutes, but they'll hardly be thrown out if they stay a bit longer. Though the club managers will willingly help anyone, if you are going to use club facilities and services, you really should join. The modest $25 annual membership fee includes a subscription to the magazine (published quarterly), full use of clubhouse facilities, discounts on books and maps (easily the best available for several trekking routes), and equipment storage. Further information on membership, maps, etc., can be obtained by writing to the club's U.S. office: South American Explorers Club, 2239 East Colfax Ave., #205, Denver, CO 80206.

Guides and *Arrieros* for Trekking

Hikers accustomed to U.S. trail conditions and practices sometimes feel that using porters is in some way cheating. We're used to carrying our own loads and traveling through the mountains at our own pace. To relegate those aspects of mountain travel to someone else *does* change the experience. But with only a few caveats, the change can be a thoroughly pleasant one. Especially at very high altitudes, being able to walk without a full pack can be the difference between fully experiencing the country around you and simply slogging out the day's mileage. Without the weight of your equipment to worry about, you'll probably travel faster and easier and be less tired at the end of the day than you can imagine if you've never traveled in this manner. Also, you won't have to worry about route finding, a decided advantage, especially when you find yourself confronted with an extremely confusing web of llama, cattle, or sheep paths obscuring the main trail. And in most cases you won't have to worry about being overly pampered; unless you specifically engage them to do so, most independent porters won't feel it is their responsibility to set up your tent or cook your meals. They (or more often their animals) will carry your gear and advise you on your route and suggest campsites; other services will usually have to be arranged beforehand.

As for those caveats mentioned earlier, just a bit of care in clarifying your arrangement with your guides before you hit the trail can head off most later unpleasantness. Many of the difficulties that arise between trekkers and their guides are generated by the vastly different reasons that draw the two parties into the mountains. You'll be there, of course, for recreation, adventure, personal enrichment, etc.—that whole complex of values that draws us out of our normal lives and into the wilderness. But you must never forget that your guides are there to earn a living. Your relationship with them is primarily a business one. However, you'll probably want to avoid haggling over money and hassling over who's responsible for what while you're on the trail; therefore, it is important to make these and other arrangements before beginning your trek.

First, you'll want to avoid hiring guides blindly if at all possible. Often you'll be able to get recommendations from other travelers, touring agencies, or, in the Cordillera Blanca, national park offices. If you can't get a recommendation, you'll have to go on instinct in trying to find the best guides available. Try to talk with them a bit before settling on anything definite. See if you're personally compatible. Get a feel for their experience in mountain travel. Then if you're ready to hire them, be prepared to haggle over the cost of the trip. Be sure both parties have a clear understanding of the *total* cost of the trip before you begin your trek. If your guide is literate, write up a simple contract indicating the per day charges as well as the total trip fees. Most experienced guides will insist on a contract. They'll also probably want an advance payment for part of the fee, usually no more than 25 percent of the total. If you are careful in arranging money matters before the trip begins, you'll save the irritation of having to deal with money discussions at a time when you won't want them—while you're enjoying your trek.

Aside from price, you'll also need to clarify responsibilities. Find out if your guides are bringing their own food and shelter or if they're expecting you to provide them. Even if they plan on bringing their own food, you should take a little extra to share with them; it is always greatly appreciated. You should also clarify your expectations on the trip's schedule. Most guides have a very definite idea of how many days are required for any given route. Getting them to vary from their normal schedule can be difficult, but if you want to go faster or slower than most people, let the guides know *before* you begin. In either case, expect to pay for your preference; of course, you'll have to pay for any extra days if you want to travel slowly, but you'll probably have to pay extra if you want to do a trip in fewer than the usual number of days.

Besides the practicalities of unloaded travel, guides can enrich your trip in other ways. One of the aspects of traveling with guides that we've enjoyed the most has been the opportunity to work on our Quechua. Guides are almost always eager to help you develop your vocabulary and improve your pronunciation by pointing out trailside objects and giving you the Quechua words for them. And they are usually just as eager to pick up a few words of English in exchange.

Staying Healthy

If you're serious about enjoying yourself in the Andes, you should also be serious about your health. It's foolish not to protect yourself when protection comes so easily. If you go through the series of innoculations and carry a medical kit as recommended in Chapter 2, you've already prepared yourself for the trip. But health should be one of the things on your mind during your trip to South America as well. The following sections should provide you with important information necessary to stay healthy while you travel.

SOROCHE

One of the drawbacks of modern travel is that it allows us to leave a city at sea level and in a very short time arrive in a city like Cuzco, which is nearly 12,000 feet above sea level. Without adequate time and a gradual ascent, most people, even the very fit, will have some difficulty with altitude sickness (*soroche*). But even as long ago as 1590, Father José de Acosta, without the benefit of air travel, had trouble adapting to the high-altitude conditions of the Andes. In *The Natural and Moral History of the Indies* [English translation, 1604] he wrote: "I therefore persuade myself that the elements of the air is there so subtle and delicate as it is not proportionable with the breathing of man, which requires a more gross and temperate air, and I believe it is the cause that doth so much alter the stomach and trouble all the disposition."

More than likely, Father de Acosta eventually adapted to the altitude, and so will you. But whether you make the ascent by burro or Boeing, expect to have a bout with *soroche* shortly after arriving. Plan to rest for a day or two and allow yourself another few days to get partially acclimatized before embarking on a strenuous trek into the mountains. At the very minimum, allow at least four days for acclimatization before beginning serious physical exertion. Take it easy and let your body adapt. Don't push.

We were never more sympathetic with fellow travelers than when we ran into a group that had had no opportunity to take this advice. They had contracted with an agency determined to get its customers to and from Machu Picchu in three days. These travelers were flown from Lima to Cuzco on a Friday morning. Supposedly Friday was to be their day for adapting to the altitude. Early Saturday morning, they were to ride the train from Cuzco to the ruins, walk through them for two or three hours, then ride back to Cuzco in the evening. Sunday morning, the group was to fly back to Lima. Now all of this sounds like very efficient planning, but what most of the group found out was that altitude sickness doesn't necessarily strike as soon as you get to high elevations. Though on arrival many people will feel a bit short of breath and weak, a full-fledged case of *soroche* often takes a day or two to develop. And that was the case with many of the travelers on that whirlwind tour of Machu Picchu. On the curvy train ride through the Urubamba River valley, many of them were nauseous and headachy, and at the ruins, they were in no mood to appreciate the architecture of the Incas when all they really wanted to do was crawl into bed and never think of eating again. By Sunday, the group had begun to recuperate. Some of them remembered their excursion with stoic good humor; others wanted to return to Miami on the next flight; and others, thinking they were fully adapted to altitude, were looking forward to seeing more mountains after a return trip to Lima. We didn't have the heart to tell this last part of the group that by returning to sea level, they'd soon lose what acclimatization they'd begun to develop.

Though not everyone reacts as strongly as this tour group, *every* traveler, no matter how fit, will experience some of the effects of altitude when he or she ascends above 10,000 feet at the start of a visit to the Andes. The body just can't escape certain critical changes, the first of which is hypoxia, a deficiency of oxygen reaching the tissues of the body. As soon as this deficiency is detected by the body's defense mechanisms, important compensations are made. In order to keep the vital organs supplied with adequate oxygen, blood is shunted from the extremities to more important areas. This means more blood will be forced through the lungs. And in some cases, this increased pulmonary blood flow can lead to lung congestion. While all of this is going on, medium-sized blood vessels, the arterials, are also reacting to the drop in oxygen pressure. These vessels contract and blood pressure rises. The heart beats more rapidly than normal under the least exertion.

Mild cases of altitude sickness may make you may feel breathless, dizzy, drowsy, irritable, and headachy. You may have trouble sleeping, and you may feel vaguely depressed. A full-blown case of *soroche* will feel like having a killer hangover on top of the twenty-four-hour flu. In either case, you should rest, avoid any strenuous activity, drink plenty of fluids (but not alcohol), eat lightly (mostly easy-to-digest carbohydrates rather than protein and fat), and realize that for the vast majority of people, most of the overt symptoms will dissipate in a day or two.

Other than that there is little else you can do. Breathing bottled oxygen (available at most first-class hotels) will provide some temporary relief from breathlessness, but it will have little effect on the other symptoms. Those who have a history of severe altitude sickness might ask their doctors about acetazolamide, a drug which many travelers we've met have found to be an effective prophylactic. As for ourselves, we stick by the old Andean remedy for *soroche*—coca leaf tea. This very soothing brew is available in most hotels and restaurants, and though it will not prevent altitude sickness, its calming properties may help reduce slightly some of the uncomfortable symptoms. Perhaps the most unusual remedy we've been exposed to was on a hike in southern Peru when we were both feeling weak and nauseous. Our guide, a Quechua, showed us a leafy plant called *muña,* which he claimed was a sure cure for *soroche.* The plant has a sweet sage odor, and we discovered that the treatment involved rubbing the leaves over our chests and backs. We actually *did* feel a bit better but have never been sure whether that was due to the unique properties of *muña* or to the fact that collecting the leaves and rubbing ourselves down with them took our minds off our illness. In any case, since then when we feel a mild attack of *soroche* coming on, we look for a few sprigs of *muña*.

Though a large portion of your body's adaptation to altitude occurs within a couple of weeks, full adaptation takes much longer. So remember that unless you stay in the Andes for several months, your body will remain only partially adapted to altitude. Don't expect to perform at your physical optimum. Realize too that if, for example, you descend from Quito to Lima and stay there for even three or four days before going on to Cuzco or La Paz or the Cordillera Blanca, you'll lose a significant amount of your hard-earned acclimatization.

An interesting sideline to the physical problems encountered at high altitudes is the effect on the human reproductive system. After arriving at high altitudes, men will undergo a drastically reduced sperm count. The few spermatazoa left tend to be less mobile than at sea level, and the number of abnormal and immature forms increases. Women arriving at altitude become more likely to experience dysmenorrhea— irregular menstrual cycles. Luckily, though, these symptoms for both men and women are mild and reversible.

HIGH ALTITUDE PULMONARY AND CEREBRAL EDEMA

Though a typical case of *soroche* can be miserable, it is hardly life-threatening. Reactions to altitude, however, can become much more serious. These reactions can take two possible forms—cerebral acute mountain sickness or pulmonary acute mountain sickness—both of them cause for extreme concern. Due to the potentially fatal nature of these forms, anyone traveling to high altitudes should be able to recognize the symptoms of these severe forms of acute mountain sickness because the *only* treatment is to get the victims to a lower altitude as soon as possible.

The most common symptoms for cerebral mountain sickness are drowsiness, uneven gait, hallucinations, abnormal limb tone, irrational behavior, inability to control urine flow, tremors, and coma. Symptoms for pulmonary mountain sickness include a dry cough, breathlessness, palpatations, vomiting, coughing up sputum and/or blood, clammy skin, chest pains, loss of coordination, and coma. Should these symptoms appear, be prepared to *descend* immediately. Delay will only aggravate the condition and increase the difficulty of reaching a lower elevation. It is much preferable to turn around and walk back to lower elevations if you detect early symptoms (e.g., persistent headaches) than to press on and have to be carried down by your companions later.

Don't make the mistake of thinking that if you happen to be young and fit, you'll be unlikely to develop serious mountain sickness. In fact, young adults between twenty and thirty years old are the most likely age group to develop pulmonary edema. An extremely fit young archaeologist we once met fit this profile exactly. He had to abandon a long-dreamed-of dig in the Urubamba valley due to pulmonary edema, and his case could have had much more serious consequences than it did because he refused to believe that he could have such problems until the symptoms were quite advanced.

So no matter what your age or level of fitness, when at high altitudes, get into the habit of monitoring your health carefully. To begin with, avoid dehydration, a common problem at high altitudes which can only complicate matters. Be conscious of your urine output, and be careful to drink enough fluids to maintain a minimum of a pint-a-day urine flow. Don't ignore or minimize early symptoms of acute mountain sickness. If you seem to be adapting more slowly than others in your group, be especially careful. Don't ignore persistent headaches, lung congestion, serious coughs, or frequent or continuing dizziness. Remember that once you're on the trail in the Andes, medical attention can be days away; there are no rescue squads, no helicopters to fly you out. You are responsible for knowing your body and being aware of what is happening to it.

DIARRHEA

When visiting southern climes, people who are normally modest and private when at home suddenly develop an inordinate interest in the operating condition of the digestive systems of everyone with whom they come into contact. Digestion becomes an almost mystical process for these people. However, in the cool light of clinical truth, diarrhea is simply the body's way of ridding itself of noxious agents to which it is not accustomed. And that last word "accustomed" is crucial. Don't simply assume that you'll become sick due to unsanitary conditions. Andean residents who travel to the United States will encounter bacteria to which *their* systems are not accustomed, and when traveling, they frequently have digestive difficulties too.

Typical traveler's diarrhea is caused by strains of *E. coli*, which give off a toxin that our bowels are not used to. This disorder is self-limiting; that is, the effects of diarrhea are also the way the body rids itself of the organism. The symptom is, in a sense, also the cure. Therefore, Lomotil or any other drugs that slow down bowel motility should be used with care since they often make matters worse or protract the course of the disorder. Though they may alleviate some of the immediate unpleasant symptoms, they won't solve the real problem.

The most important help you can give yourself if you come down with diarrhea is to keep your body fluids replenished. In letting your body get rid of those hostile organisms, you'll also be losing a great deal of salt and glucose, so as you work to keep from getting dehydrated, you will want to drink liquids containing salt and sugar. The U.S. government publication *Health Information for International Travel* provides a recipe designed specifically to help maintain adequate levels of fluid, salt, glucose, and other vital substances during bouts of diarrhea. You begin with two clean glasses. In one, pour eight ounces of fruit juice, a half-teaspoon of honey or corn syrup, and a pinch of salt. In the second glass, mix eight ounces of purified water with one-fourth teaspoon of baking soda. Drink alternately from each glass until your thirst is quenched.

Remember that traveler's diarrhea in itself is not a serious disorder. Keep replacing fluids and you probably won't be completely debilitated. You might not be happy or comfortable, but in two or three days, your body will have straightened itself out.

More serious forms of diarrhea, however, deserve real care. Blood or mucus in the stool, fever and shaking chills, persistence of diarrhea for more than a few days, and dehydration call for a doctor's attention.

Those who develop diarrhea after returning from a trip to South America should see a physician if the diarrhea is long term. Be sure to tell your doctor which countries you've been to in order to help identify possible parasites.

However, the prevention of intestinal disorders is more important than the cure. Clearly, your concern should be with making sure your food and water are clean. Though sanitation is important throughout your trip, be especially careful during the first week or so before your digestive system becomes accustomed to the new strains of bacteria that will invade it. We've seen too many travelers intent on saving money and savoring the "real" Andes hop off their plane from Miami and head immediately for a cheap *tipico* restaurant, shoveling down plates of at best marginally sanitary food. From our experience, though, North American travelers with less than cast-iron stomachs should exercise caution in restaurant selection early in a trip to the Andes. In fact, we always allow a somewhat higher food budget for the early days of a trip and eat in the cleanest places we can find. As the trip wears on and our internal flora and fauna become more decidedly South American, we branch out and take in those street-vended *humitas* (tamales) and *salteñas* (meat pies) we've been eyeing for days.

At all times, however, you should be particularly careful not to eat any raw foods that you cannot peel yourself. Be careful too of undercooked vegetables, especially in Chinese restaurants. Avoid as well all uncooked or unpasteurized dairy products to avoid both tuberculosis and undulant fever. Be careful, too, of the *cebiches* (a raw marinated shellfish dish) available along the Peruvian and Ecuadorian coasts. Inadequately cooked shellfish can harbor a nasty creature (a worm of sorts) called the trimatode or lung fluke.

WATER PURIFICATION

Though most common intestinal disorders originate from poorly prepared food rather than from unclean water, our study of the horrors of the microscopic world to which one opens oneself when drinking inadequately treated water has led us to the development of one hard and fast rule: when in doubt, drink beer. Of course, on the trail that rule is adapted to substitute iodine-treated water. Admittedly, treated water tastes rather bad and the process becomes tedious day after day during a long trip. But when you consider that some of the ugliest parasites ever to be enlarged by the microscope may inhabit that crystal clear stream, taste and tedium become small prices to pay for security. Follow the life cycle of a sheep liver fluke, for example, as it enters the liver and happily sets about forming a cyst, often necessitating the surgical removal of as much as half of the liver, and you'll probably never think of drinking untreated water again.

Though water can be purified by boiling, this process requires considerable fuel and becomes somewhat uncertain at very high altitudes due to the low boiling temperature. Water should be boiled five minutes at sea level, and the time should be increased considerably at high altitudes. By far the simplest way to treat water is with iodine tablets made especially for this purpose and available at most backpacking shops in the United States. The normal procedure is to allow one tablet per quart unless the water is cloudy or contains debris, in which case two tablets are required. If using tincture of iodine (available at pharmacies as *yodo,* but much messier to use than tablets), the dosage is five drops per quart. After the tablet dissolves (a couple of minutes), shake the water bottle, unscrew the cap, and slosh a bit of water into the cap, wetting the lip and threads of the bottle as well. Then allow the water to sit for at least twenty minutes before drinking. We've found that treated water tastes better (an admittedly relative term) if drunk soon after this waiting period. The longer it sits, the stronger the taste. Adding a pinch of salt and aerating the treated water by pouring it back and forth between two containers seems to help the taste a little.

In larger cities, the water is chlorinated and theoretically safe to drink. Nonetheless, since you can never be sure if chlorine levels are adequate for purification, you may want to be safe and drink bottled water, soft drinks, or beer.

HYPOTHERMIA

Hypothermia—clinically the lowering of the body core temperature below 95 degrees—is a serious, often life-threatening condition. Anyone who ventures into high mountains should be clearly aware of the dangers of hypothermia, the weather conditions conducive to it, the symptoms that indicate its presence, and the treatment of its victims.

The four factors that most directly lead to hypothermia are cold, wind, moisture, and fatigue—all of which you'll undoubtedly encounter on any Andean trek. Remember especially that hypothermia may occur even when air temperatures are well above freezing, so any time you're cold, wet, and tired, watch out for symptoms of hypothermia.

These symptoms include most of our normal reactions to cold: shivering, paleness, rapid heartbeat, slight feelings of numbness in the extremities. If the body continues to lose heat, symptoms become much more serious: disorientation, loss of coordination, slurred speech, amnesia, rigidity of muscles, irregular heartbeat, and, finally, unconsciousness.

Treatment should begin at the *first* appearance of even the most minor of these symptoms. Immediate care is important since hypothermia can kill its victims in as little as two hours. Once the core temperature begins to drop, it is often a slow and difficult process to raise it back to normal. The first order of business is to get dry clothes next to the skin as quickly as possible. Next, try to find shelter from the wind, and, if possible, drink hot liquids (not alcohol) and eat some high-calorie, easily digestible food. If undertaken at the first symptoms, these measures will usually correct the problem. In more severe cases, however, rewarming will take much longer. The victim should be dried and placed in a sleeping bag inside a tent. If the victim is fully conscious, have him or her drink warm liquids and eat. In severe cases, having someone lie in the sleeping bag with the hypothermia victim may speed the rewarming. Since hypothermia victims are highly susceptible to trauma, great care should be taken not to massage or abruptly move the victim.

Fortunately, with just a little planning it is possible to avoid hypothermia even under the worst conditions. First, you should know your physical limits; don't push yourself to the point of fatigue. Second, you should select your clothing and sleeping gear carefully to provide a wide margin of protection in cold, windy, and damp weather. In the Andes this means insulating yourself—especially the extremities—for the occasional night when temperatures fall well below freezing, and if you plan to camp near the 16,000-foot level, be prepared for near-zero temperatures. It also means preparing yourself for sharp winds by including a windproof shell garment in your trail wardrobe. For damp weather, you should *always* carry a spare set of dry clothes (socks, long underwear, and a sweater at the minimum) in a protective plastic bag. This little hoard of warm, dry clothes can mean the difference between being reasonably comfortable and barely surviving a windy night beside a glacier lake miles away from the nearest town. In the Andes, dampness can be a real problem even on a totally rainless trek under crystal clear skies because morning frosts, especially in high meadows, can be extremely heavy. After a couple of days of damp, frosty mornings, your tent, sleeping bag, and clothing can become almost sodden. Since most insulation—down in particular—can lose well over half of its heat-retention value when wet, be sure to take the time to dry your gear in the sunshine every day or two.

4
Ecuador

Ecuador is a country where the forces of mountain building are evident everywhere. Earthquakes regularly shake the countryside, sometimes disastrously as in 1949 when the large town of Ambato was destroyed. Violent landslides carve away the mountainsides and frequently block roads and railways and often take much heavier tolls than simply inconveniencing travelers. In 1983, for example, one slide killed 150 travelers on the central Guayaquil-to-Quito highway. Most characteristic of Ecuador's mountain building, though, is vulcanism. Part of the great "ring of fire" that surrounds the Pacific, Ecuador contains more than twenty active volcanoes and many more remnants of extinct volcanoes. The string of peaks that German naturalist Alexander von Humbolt called the "Avenue of Volcanoes" bisects the country from north to south, running over 400 miles in two parallel *cordilleras*. The western *cordillera* is dominated by the massive, 20,702-foot Chimborazo volcano while the eastern *cordillera* reaches its highest point at the 19,498-foot Cotopaxi, one of the world's tallest active volcanoes. Also notable are the beautiful Cayambe (18,980 feet) and the violent Sangay (17,464 feet), the most active volcano in the Andes.

This narrow band of mountains (only fifty miles wide) is separated by a broad central valley broken into several fertile intermontane basins situated at an altitude of approximately 7,500 feet. This *sierra* region is home to 45 percent of Ecuador's 7 million inhabitants. Here, despite the fact that Ecuador straddles the equator, the mean temperature is a pleasant 58 degrees Fahrenheit with only a three-degree differential between the year's warmest and coldest months. Yearly rainfall averages forty inches, the majority falling during the rainy season from January to May. In this benign climate, crops such as potatoes, maize, squash, beans, *quiñoa* (a grain), and barley flourish. Above the intermontane basins begins the cool, damp *paramos* region, the high-altitude grasslands used primarily as pasturage. Here, even during the dry season, fog and mist often shroud the higher peaks by early afternoon.

To the west of the *sierra* is the coastal lowland called *El Litoral*. It is rapidly becoming Ecuador's economic center, and its principal city, Guayaquil, has surpassed Quito to become the country's largest city. Over half of Ecuador's population now lives in El Litoral. Climatically a transition zone, this narrow band between the Pacific and the Andes is quite lush and junglelike to the north, becoming much more arid near the Peruvian frontier. The northern section of El Litoral is a hot and humid place, with daily high temperatures in Guayaquil averaging 90 degrees Fahrenheit, but it is also quite beautiful. To our mind, it is more quintessentially tropical than the Amazon—with lush foliage, slow rivers cutting through the jungle to the Pacific, banana plantations, parrots and toucans—the kind of place that makes us want to trade in our backpacks and hiking boots for panama hats and white suits.

To the east of the *sierra* is Ecuador's portion of the Amazon basin, much of it the subject of a long, bitter border dispute with Peru. Called *El Oriente* by Ecuadorians, this region makes up over a third of the country (much more if you allow Ecuador's claim to the disputed territory granted to Peru following the border war of 1941) but contains less than 5 percent of the population. Recent discovery of oil in *El Oriente* has given a much-needed boost to Ecuador's economy (Ecuador is a member of the Organization of Petroleum Exporting Countries—OPEC) and will probably lead to a dramatic increase in the area's population. Daytime high temperatures usually reach the 90-degree mark, and annual rainfall is very high—often exceeding 150 inches. The region is the site of one of the world's greatest journey's of discovery. In 1540 Gonzalo Pizarro sent one of his lieutenants, Francisco de Orellana, and a band of men eastward from Quito on a gold-searching expedition. Descending into the jungle by river, Orellana soon found himself trapped far from Quito—unable either to travel upstream along the river or to travel overland through the jungle. Exercising his only option, Orellana and his men continued downstream, following the Rio Napo to the Amazon. When he emerged from the jungle a year later at the Atlantic Ocean, Orellana had became the first white man to cross the continent.

Though Ecuador often enters the history books only with the conquest of the region by the invading Inca army under the command of Topa Inca in the fifteenth century, the real history of human habitation of the fertile coast and intermontane basins extends far back, thousands of years into the Stone Age past. At a site only twelve miles from present-day Quito, for example, archaeologists have uncovered the stone tools and projectile points of Paleo-Indians, who lived by hunting the now-extinct animals of the mountain valleys—the mastodon, bison, camel, and giant sloth.

Between Stone Age origins and the Inca conquest, the history of civilization in Ecuador is somewhat vague, still in the process of reconstruction by archaeologists, who must rely on the few artifacts that outlast the centuries in this damp climate. Outshown by the brilliance of the Peruvian cultures—especially the Incas who "rewrote" the history of the region to make its inhabitants appear to be savages elevated to civilization by the graces of the conquerors—the pre-Columbian civilizations of Ecuador are often ignored. We do know that while none of the Ecuadorian civilizations built great architectural monuments or controlled large geographical regions in the manner of the Peruvian cultures, the ancient coastal people of what was to become Ecuador did develop ceramics before any other known New World civilization—about 5,000 years ago. The probable reason for this puzzling early development is strange indeed. Archaeologists found that contrary to every normal expectation, the earliest forms of ceramics were technically superior to later forms. It was also discovered that the earliest Ecuadorian pottery almost exactly resembled Japanese pottery of the same period. So the archaeological record strongly suggests that a group of Japanese fishermen caught in the strong eastward currents of the Pacific made an unplanned transoceanic journey sometime before 3000 B.C., bringing with them the advanced technology of ceramics (and probably many other things less resistant to the passage of time, such as weaving, woodworking, etc.). In the 4,000 years between Japanese contact and the Inca conquest, the numerous cultures that inhabited the highlands and coast accomplished the kind of quiet, undramatic advances in agriculture, pottery, textiles, and animal domestication on which the development of civilization worldwide depended.

When the Incas arrived in about 1465, they found two dominant cultures, the Canari in the southern highlands and the Cara in the Quito-Otavalo region. The Cara resisted Inca invasion, and over a seventeen-year period fought a long series of losing battles for their independence. At the end of this war, the Incas protected themselves from future revolutions by executing large numbers of those who had resisted and by applying their system of *mitima* (forced relocation) with most of the remainder of the Cara people.

Finally in full control, Topa Inca and his son, the Ecuadorian-born Huayna Capac, constructed huge complexes of palaces, temples, and nunneries for the Chosen Women in Tomebamba in the Canari territory and Quito in the Cara territory. Unfortunately, nothing remains of either site. The Spanish, in building their colonial cities, destroyed all the Inca constructions in Ecuador except for the Ingapirca complex near Cuenca.

Though it does not offer the kind of remarkable trekking that you'll find further south in Peru, Ecuador is great for country-road rambles, native markets visits, volcano scrambles (as well as technical climbs, if you have the experience), and boat trips among the astounding Galapagos Islands. And there *are* a few very good backpacking trips in Ecuador as well. The terrain you'll travel through is, aside from the glaciated volcanoes, greener, gentler, more forgiving than the high, wild mountains of Peru and Bolivia. Ecuador also has the attraction of allowing the traveler to see a lot of the country—from the tropical coast to the volcanic highlands to the Amazon basin—in relatively little time since Ecuador is small enough and has a transportation system efficient enough to make land travel much simpler, quicker, and more comfortable than the kind of hard traveling you'll inevitably experience farther south in the Andes. Bus traffic—interspersed with Pepsi trucks, big U.S. cars from the sixties, bicycles, pedestrians, dogs, chickens, and pigs—is heavy on the Pan-American highway that runs down the center of the country through the Avenue of Volcanoes, so long waits for transportation are highly unlikely. For the outdoor traveler, Ecuador serves as a wonderful capsulized introduction to the landscape and culture of the Andes.

Quito

Quito is the gateway to the Ecuadorian Andes. Only fifteen miles south of the equator, but at an altitude of 9,500 feet, it has a wonderful climate, with days usually warm enough to make short-sleeved shirts comfortable and nights just cool enough for a light jacket. Quito is also the most physically attractive of the Andean capital cities. Its setting —a hilly green basin at the foot of an extinct volcano, 15,000-foot Mt. Pichincha—is lovely. And compared to a huge, sprawling city like Lima, Quito, with a population of only 800,000, seems comfortably small and well proportioned for foot travel. Even from a downtown hotel, it is possible to walk in an hour to the hills and grain fields above the city.

A large part of Quito's beauty is also due to the preservation of its colonial heritage. Among the narrow, hilly streets, the tree-shaded plazas, and the red-tile-roofed adobe buildings of the colonial district of the city, little seems to have changed architecturally in the past two centuries. In the cobbled streets of the old city, Indians dressed in their finely woven traditional clothing operate market stalls or sit resting in the parks.

But Quito also has its modern half. Separated from the colonial city by the large Alameda and Ejido parks, the modern district— Avenida Amazonas and the surrounding streets—is very much a part of the twentieth century. Here you'll find all the trappings of the modern world: high-rise hotels, fast-food restaurants, shops selling designer clothing, and the ubiquitous video arcades.

The best way to see Quito is by foot, and perhaps the best place to begin is to visit the Plaza Independencia, the center of the colonial city and one of the prettiest plazas in the Andean countries. Facing the plaza are the Presidential Palace and the Cathedral. If you walk south a block along Garcia Moreno, you'll reach the Jesuit church, La Compañia, the city's most ornate church with its gilded interior and gold altar. Turn right on Sucre and just two blocks away is the oldest of Quito's many churches, San Francisco. Construction of San Francisco began in 1536, and the dark, somewhat grimy, and quite faded structure shows every year of its age.

While you're wandering about the colonial district, don't neglect to climb the Panecillo, a round hill whose name means "little breadloaf," just south of the Plaza Independencia. Reach the top of Panecillo by walking along Avenida Garcia Moreno and following the steps that lead to the top. There you'll find the recently added statute of the

Virgin of Quito, but the main attraction is the panoramic view of the city and, if the day is clear, the surrounding countryside and nearby volcanoes.

As you return to the city from the Panecillo, take some time to wander about the vicinity of Avenida 24 de Mayo. On Wednesdays and Saturdays, 24 de Mayo becomes a colorful outdoor market filled with vendors and market stalls. While in this old section of town, be sure to walk down Calle Morales (downhill along 24 de Mayo); bordering this narrow, cobbled street are some of the finest of Quito's colonial houses.

Morales connects with Avenida Guayaquil, a crowded street of shops which leads toward Quito's large parks and the modern district. You'll first reach Alameda Park, and a few blocks downhill from it, Ejido Park; both are good places to sit and relax under the trees. Just past Ejido begins Avenida Amazonas, the center of modern Quito. Here you'll find a concentration of travel-related services—money exchange, travel agencies, bookstores, airline offices, sidewalk cafes, etc.

RESOURCES

■ **Hotels** Quito's finest and most expensive first-class hotels, the *Intercontinental* and the *Colon Internacional,* are both located in the modern district at Amazonas and Patria. Hotels in this area of Quito are rather expensive, but if you want a moderately priced hotel near the modern Amazonas district, try either the *Hotel Dan* (corner of 10 de Agusto and Colon) or the *Embajador* (corner of 9 de Octubre and Colon). Both offer clean, fairly modern rooms with private baths and hot water; rates at the Embajador include breakfast. A bit less expensive and conveniently located near Alameda Park, halfway between the colonial city and the modern district, is the *Hotel Coral* (90 Avenida Manuel Larrea), offering a small restaurant and clean, modern rooms with private baths and plenty of hot water. In the center of the colonial city, near the plaza, is an excellent medium-priced hotel, the old *Humbolt Capitol* (931 Espejo), which was once one of Quito's better hotels and still provides comfortable rooms and good service at reasonable prices. For budget old-town accommodations, try the *Hotel Guayaquil No. 1* (3248 Maldonado); rooms are basic but clean, and there is usually hot water. Perhaps the Guayaquil's best attraction other than price is its location near the Plaza Santo Domingo, the starting point for local buses out to the main *Terrestre del Sur* bus station outside the city. Quito's most popular *gringo* budget hotel, the *Gran Casino* (330 Calle G. Moreno), offers unusually good service and value for its kind. At the Casino, only a few dollars will get you a reasonably clean room and access to a frequently hot shower. The Casino will safely store luggage, and it also has a good, cheap restaurant with several vegetarian dishes.

■ **Restaurants** If you aren't on a tight budget and want a reasonably good, moderately expensive dinner, walk along Avenida Calama between Amazonas and 6 de Diciembre and try *Le Chalet Suisse* for steaks or the *El Delfin Dorado* for seafood. For very good Chinese food, try either the *Pekin* (197 Bello Horizonte) or the less expensive *Chifa Mayflower* (a few blocks down 6 de Diciembre from Patria). For a wide selection of inexpensive restaurants—everything from *pollos brasa* to regional specialties to pastries to ersatz McDonald's hamburgers, walk down Avenida 10 de Agosto near Alameda Park and take your pick. For a good, inexpensive lunch in the colonial part of town, try the *Balcon* (upstairs at 1170 Chile, right on the Plaza Independencia). Finally, for those suffering from terminal homesickness, Quito has a *Pizza Hut* (beside the Teatro Bolivar on Espejo).

■ **Transportation** Buses depart Quito for almost all parts of Ecuador at amazingly frequent intervals throughout the day, so you can usually go wherever you want at the spur of the moment. If, for example, you feel a sudden urge to get from Quito to Baños or Latacunga or even Guayaquil, you'll almost surely be able to find a bus going there within an hour or two. The only real problem is finding the bus station you need. Buses traveling to and from most southern, eastern, and western towns use the *Terrestre del Sur* station several miles from the city's center (some smaller companies don't use the station itself but pick up and drop passengers on the streets nearby). To get to the southern station take either a taxi or local bus #10 from the Plaza Santo Domingo. Inside the station, a dozen bus companies have offices and posted schedules; simply check destinations and departure times and take your pick.

For northern destinations, there is no central station. Several companies have small, hard-to-find stations scattered about the northern part of the city. *Flota Imbabura* (1211 Manuel Larrea) travels north on the Pan-American highway to Otavalo and the Colombian border. The following trip times are of necessity approximate: Quito to Ambato: two to three hours; Quito to Baños: three to four hours; Quito to Riobamba: four hours; Quito to Guayaquil: eight hours; Quito to Ceunca: ten hours; Quito to Huaquillas (across the border from Tumbes, Peru): fourteen to sixteen hours; Quito to Esmeraldas: eight hours; Quito to Otavalo: two hours.

The office for advance purchase of railway tickets to Guayaquil is at 441 Bolivar, only a few blocks from the Plaza Independencia; the train station is a half-mile down Calle Maldonado. There's more information on train travel in Ecuador later in this chapter.

If you fly into Quito, you'll arrive at Mariscal Sucre Airport where there is a tourist information desk to help you check on available hotel rooms before you get into the busy center of the city. To get into Quito, either take a taxi (surprisingly inexpensive) or catch one of the frequent and convenient airport-to-city buses. In Quito, all the major airlines have their offices in the Amazonas area: Eastern (376 Amazonas), Ecuadoriana (corner of Colon and Reina Victoria), TAME (1354 Amazonas). AeroPeru has recently opened an office at the corner of Amazonas and Washington, upstairs, convenient if you're going on to Peru and need to reconfirm a flight or to book internal flight tickets in advance.

Car rental rates are not particularly cheap in Ecuador, but considering how small the country is, you can see an awful lot of it in just a few days of driving around. Avis and Hertz have offices at the airport and on Avenida 10 de Agosto.

■ **Communications** The post office is at 688 Benalcazar, just off the Plaza Independencia. The simplest place to make international long-distance calls (aside from your hotel, if you have a phone) is the Ietel office in the gallery of shops at the Hotel Colon.

■ **Money Exchange** Money exchange is a much simpler process in Ecuador than in Peru. There are several exchange houses, which usually offer marginally better rates than the banks, on the Plaza Independencia and along Amazonas.

■ **Books** You'll find several bookstores along Amazonas selling a few English-language books, but for the best selection of English titles in the Andes, go to *Libri Mundi* (851 J. L. Mera, a narrow street between Amazonas and Victoria). Besides a good collection of fiction, Libri Mundi carries an excellent stock of books on South America.

■ **Volcano Climbing Information** Many of Ecuador's most spectacular volcanoes are climbable by acclimatized, physically conditioned trekkers. With the help of a guide, even those hikers without technical climbing experience and skills can experience the excitement of standing at the summit of a near-20,000-foot mountain like Cotopaxi. If climbing is your primary goal in Ecuador, you might consider the group trips organized by the American Alpine Institute (1212 24th St., Bellingham, Washington 98225). Open to inexperienced climbers, their trips (among the most reasonably priced Andean group tours) include climbing instructions and ascents of several major peaks, including Cotapaxi and Chimborazo. For those traveling in Ecuador on their own, information on climbing and arranging guides may be obtained in Quito from the *Nuevos Horizontes* climbing club (phone: 21–51–35) and the DITURIS office at Avenida Reina Victoria and Roca.

■ **Shopping** Lots of shops in the vicinity of the Plaza Independencia and Amazonas sell typical Ecuadorian craft items, but for high-quality, high-priced craft items, try the gallery of shops beneath the Hotel Colon, *La Bodega* (641 J. L. Mera near the Libri Mundi bookshop) or *Folklore Olga Fisch* (260 Avenida Colon). However, shopping for most craft items will be more entertaining and prices will be somewhat lower if you go to the markets at Otavalo or Saquisili.

■ **Movies** There are plenty of *cines* in downtown Quito, but the *Bolivar* and the *Atahualpa* usually have the newest movies in English. Check schedules in *El Comercio*.

■ **Maps** Ecuador's *Instituto Geografico Militar* (I.G.M.) is at Paz and Mino near the National Ministery of Defense (up the hill from the intersection of Patria and 12 de Octubre). To enter the grounds, you'll have to stop at the guard house and surrender your passport; in return you'll receive a visitor's badge. Inside the building, the map room is to your left. The series of 1:50,000 and 1:25,000 scale topographic maps will be of most interest to hikers; unfortunately, coverage of the country is still somewhat sketchy, so don't count on the availability of the maps you need. Check the books of maps scattered about the counters. The I.G.M. has good road maps of the country along with a huge four-sheet colored map for only a few dollars. It also has aerial photos of most of the volcanoes of Ecuador, which they will print up fresh for you at very reasonable prices—if you can wait three days.

■ **Fiestas** The Quito Festival, celebrating the founding of the city, is held during the first week of December. Beginning on December 28 and ending January 6 (Epiphany), Quito's streets are filled with costumed celebrants welcoming the New Year. Quito's observation of Good Friday includes processions and self-flagellation by penitents.

■ **U.S. Embassy** At the corner of Patria and 12 de Octubre.

■ **Tourist Information** There are two very helpful offices of the National Tourist Board, DITURIS: a main office at 514 Reina Victoria in the Amazonas district, and a smaller one in the Palacio Municipal on the Plaza Independencia. Try the main office for current information on transportation, climbing, the Galapagos, etc.

There are dozens of tourist agencies along Amazonas, but the following offer special services. American Express business and mail pickup is handled by *Ecuadorian Tours* (339 Amazonas). The *EthnoTouring* agency (1238 J. L. Mera) specializes in jungle trips, Galapagos cruises, and mountain trekking/climbing. *Transturi* (1810 Orellana) books passage on the "floating hotel," the Flotel Orellana, an expensive, plush way to see something of the Amazon. *Economic Galapagos Tours* (Amazonas and Pinto), as their name implies, arranges very good and relatively inexpensive small-boat tours of the islands.

■ **Museums** Quito's most interesting museum is in the *Banco Central* (Avenida 10 de Agosto across from Alameda Park). The collection of colonial paintings, furniture, coins, etc., is worth a look, but of considerably more interest is the well-displayed pre-Columbian collection, which includes examples of Valdivian pottery—the pottery that led to the theory of ancient Japanese-South American contact. Closed Mondays.

Also worth visiting are the following museums: the *Casa de la Cultura* (on Patria across from the American Embassy) with collections of Ecuadorian art and musical instruments; the *San Francisco* convent museum of religious art (Plaza San Francisco, closed Sundays); the *Jijon y Caamaño* museum (in the library of the Catholic University, Avenida 12 de Octubre) with a good collection of pre-Columbian Ecuadorian artifacts.

Climbing Mt. Pichincha— an Acclimatizing Hike from Quito

Pichincha, a 15,729-foot volcano, which last erupted 300 years ago, looms directly above Quito to the west. On its slopes Ecuadorian national hero Antonio Sucre and his men won the country's independence in the Battle of Pichincha on May 24, 1822. The day hike/climb to the volcano's summit is an exciting excursion that you can make right from your hotel. The climb will take eight to ten hours, so start early. Remember, too, that even during the dry season the summit of Pichincha is often cloud-covered by early afternoon. Under these conditions, cold, soaking mists can make the higher parts of this hike extremely unpleasant unless you take along rain gear and a warm jacket. These dense mists can also make finding routes difficult, so keep your bearings as you climb, and take along a compass just in case you become completely fogged in.

You begin the climb by ascending Cruz Loma, the lower mountain just to the south of Pichincha. The mountain is covered with trails, but the simplest route from the colonial city is just to walk up either Avenida 24 de Mayo or Calle La Gasca to their ends and continue on paths heading west straight up the mountain (if you want to shorten the hike a bit, take a taxi to the end of 24 de Mayo). You should reach the top of Cruz Loma (look for the antennas) in three to four hours.

There the trail to Pichincha turns right to follow the ridge between the two mountains. You'll walk across this high, grassy *paramo* country for an hour or so to reach the base of Pichincha's rocky summit cone. The final ascent to the summit will take about an hour, and though it requires no technical climbing, it can be a tough scramble if you've had only a day or two in Quito to acclimatize. Arrows painted on rocks along the way mark the route. If you're lucky enough to climb Pichincha on a day with clear afternoon skies, the view of the Quito valley and most of the mountains of the Avenue of Volcanoes will be well worth the climb.

Otavalo

Located just two hours north of Quito (you cross the equator along the way), Otavalo (population 15,000) is one of the most pleasant of the Ecuadorian highland towns in which to spend time relaxing and hiking in the lovely country nearby. Surrounded by extinct volcanoes, beautiful rolling hills, and the villages of Indian weavers, Otavalo offers enough excellent walking to justify a week-long visit if you're in the mood for settling down and getting to know the area's land and people a little better than a quick pass through allows.

For most travelers, though, Otavalo's big attraction is its large Saturday market, the most famous in Ecuador. The market is something that no visitor should miss, and from the large numbers of *gringos* in town on Saturdays, apparently none does. Most of them come in from Quito on slick tour buses and leave a couple of hours later with armloads of sweaters and weavings. But despite the hoards of tourists, the Otavalo market is still well worth a visit; it is a colorful, exciting view into the lives of the highlanders, who pour into town early on Saturday morning, crowding the streets to sell their high-quality weavings.

The quiet, dignified Indians of the Otavalo region are among the most beautiful and most distinctively dressed people of the Andes.

Weavings in the Otavalo market, Ecuador

Their clothing displays a purity of style that is quite dramatic. The men wear felt hats with broad flat brims, heavy, closely woven ponchos—usually navy blue—and clean white trousers; traditionally, the men do not cut their hair, so most of them have waist-length braids. The women wear turbanlike headcloths, great piles of golden-colored beads around their necks, navy shawls, white blouses, and layered navy skirts. On market days, these expert weavers transform the otherwise plain town by covering the bushes, trees, and plazas of Otavalo with displays of their bright tapestries and ponchos. Though the weavings are the focus of travelers' attention, in other areas of the market locals do a lively business in produce, livestock, household goods, and clothing; these areas are in their own way as interesting as the craft market.

If experiencing the market is one of the primary objectives of your stay in Otavalo, be sure to arrive a day or two in advance (remember, though, hotels fill up early on Fridays). This will allow you to wake early on Saturday (the market begins at dawn) and have a few hours in the market before the crowds of tourists arrive by bus at around 9:30 A.M. Considering the market's popularity with tourists, prices are still incredibly low, but examine the weavings carefully since synthetic fibers have begun to creep into use. When shopping in Otavalo, as in virtually all Latin American markets, you are, of course, expected to bargain. However, tourists sometimes misunderstand the purpose of bargaining. Contrary to what some people think, bargaining is not a way to keep from being cheated; neither is it an opportunity to exercise aggression and beat the other person into total submission. For most market

Market scene, Otavalo, Ecuador

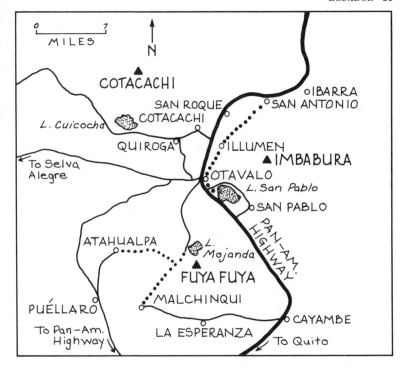

vendors, bargaining is an enjoyable, entertaining form of social contact, not a contest of wills. In the meeting of minds that successful bargaining represents, both sides gain a little and lose a little and walk away from the encounter with a feeling of accomplishment and pleasure.

RESOURCES

Otavalo's hotels are all rather basic. The town's best hotel, the moderately priced *Yamor* (north of town on the Pan-American highway), has pretty grounds, but the rooms are dark and damp, and the private baths have no hot water. A marginally better choice is the inexpensive *Hotel Otavalo* (on Calle Roca near the center of town). Though the rooms here are dark too, the Otavalo is quite clean, and the private baths frequently have hot water. Less expensive still is the clean and fairly pleasant *Residencia Santa Ana* (Calle Colon).

Our favorite restaurant in Otavalo is the *Chifa Tien An Men* where the servings of Chinese food are very generous and the prices low. For sandwiches, ice cream, and excellent coffee (the real, brewed item, not the instant you find most everywhere else), stop at the *Camba Huasi Fuente del Soda* (on the main plaza). For vegetarian food try the *Ali Micui* (on the Poncho Plaza).

Otavalo's principal festival is El Yamor, a harvest festival with a reenactment of the arrival of the Inca in Ecuador. It is held annually, usually during the first week in September.

San Pablo

Some of the best country rambles in the Otavalo area are in the direction of San Pablo, a large lake and village of the same name situated at the foot of the green slopes of volcano Imbabura. The beautiful countryside is quite inhabited, so it is marked by a maze of trails, allowing you to put together walks—everything from a simple two-hour hike to the lake and back to an all-day climb of Imbabura— that suit your physical and mental mood. A dozen or more trails link the two towns by crossing the ridge to the east of Otavalo; simply walk east from anywhere in town, and you'll almost certainly hit a trail or cobbled lane crossing the ridge. Most of these strike the *laguna* (lake) near the Hotel Chicapan (turn left on the paved road between the ridge and the lake). The paved road swings around the north shore of the lake to reach the village of San Pablo, a couple of hours walk from Otavalo.

From San Pablo, those who left Otavalo very early (or who take an Otavalo-San Pablo bus) and who are in the mood for a hard uphill slog with a bit of scrambling along the way can climb Mt. Imbabura. There is no real trail up this 14,502-foot volcano, but the way is apparent—straight up the open, grassy slopes toward the summit. Begin the climb in San Pablo, and simply work your way up the north flank of the mountain. From the top there are, of course, excellent views in the directions of Cotacachi and Cayambe.

The Weaving Villages

Many of the weavers who sell their goods at the Otavalo market live in the typically Andean villages of Peguche and Iluman, a few miles north of town. The easy walk (also a good running route) to the villages follows aloe-lined country lanes (virtually no vehicle traffic) that wander through the rolling hills and farmland. If you're interested in weaving and want to buy tapestries or ponchos directly from the Otavalo Indians' workshops, ask around in either Peguche or Iluman. Though the rather reserved Indians won't clamber about trying to sell their crafts, you should be able to find someone who will direct you to a weaver's home. Don't expect prices drastically below Otavalo market rates.

The easiest way to begin this hike is to walk north out of Otavalo on Calle Bolivar. Just past the Hotel Yamor on the Pan-American highway, turn right on a lane bordered with big eucalyptus trees and follow it to the railway. Walk north along the tracks until you reach the first lane to the right; walk uphill a short distance and then turn left at a house. You're now on the main lane traveling north. Though there are numerous side paths, stay on the fairly obvious main route and you'll soon reach Peguche (three miles from Otavalo) and not long after that, Iluman (five miles from Otavalo). In Iluman, you can turn west (left) on any of several lanes that reach the Pan-American highway in less than a mile. There, catching a ride back to Otavalo should be no problem. More ambitious hikers can continue north from Iluman on

Otavalo weaver

the main dirt lane, following it another seven miles to the village of San Antonio de Ibarra, of interest because it is home to some of Ecuador's best wood carvers; several shops in town sell their work. San Antonio is beside the Pan-American highway where, again, catching a ride south to Otavalo should be easy.

Laguna de Cuicocha

This easy, pleasant day trip takes you through the countryside northwest of Otavalo to the beautiful Laguna Cuicocha. Situated beneath 16,204-foot Mt. Cotacachi, the lake partially fills the collapsed crater of an ancient volcano. From its center rises a double-peaked island. Something of a tourist attraction, Cuicocha has a good hotel and restaurant at lakeside (a good place to sample *tipico* Ecuadorian food); there is also a cheaper restaurant at the top of the trail to the crater's rim. Boats can be rented to get out to the island. With just a bit of bushwhacking, it is also possible to walk around the lake on an occasionally rough trail.

The route to Cuicocha from Otavalo passes through some of the prettiest countryside in Ecuador—eucalyptus groves, grain fields, and frequent views of Cotacachi and Imbabura. It begins along a cobblestone and dirt road with light vehicle traffic, so you have the choice of either walking or catching rides (or of doing a bit of both). Begin the walk just north of Otavalo past the Hotel Yamor. Here, near a gas station, a paved road turns left; not far along it, the dirt road to the town of Quiroga (six miles) turns right. In Quiroga, a paved road climbs west to Cuicocha (six miles). If you don't feel like walking, a truck or two per hour leaves for the lake from Quiroga's plaza. To return to Otavalo, either take a truck from the lake to Quiroga and then another truck from Quiroga to Otavalo, or, alternatively, continue northeast a couple of miles from Quiroga along the paved road to the town of Cotacachi with its numerous shops selling good-quality leather goods. From Cotacachi, buses leave fairly frequently for Otavalo.

Laguna Mojanda

Laguna Mojanda is a lovely, isolated spot nine miles above Otavalo, and it makes a wonderful overnight backpacking trip. This walk will take you into the high, grassy world of the *paramos,* away from the farms down below. The lake itself is fairly large and set deep among ragged mountains, primary of which is 13,987-foot Mt. Fuya Fuya. Some of the mountains around the lake are good for scrambling, and Mojanda is also reputed to be a good spot for fishing, though the day we were there the lone *campesino* angler we met seemed to be having no luck.

To reach Mojanda from Otavalo, walk south out of town along Calle Sucre. Cross the Pan-American highway and take the immediate left-hand dirt road. This very lightly used road climbs for miles into the *paramo.* Early into the hike, look to the southeast for good views of volcano Cayambe, and as you gain altitude, look to the north for views of Cotacachi and Laguna Cuicocha. The road (very lightly traveled, so don't count on catching a ride) climbs continuously for 5.5 miles to the first left-hand fork. Turn onto this rough, rutted road and continue climbing four miles through the *paramo* to the lake.

There is a *refugio* at Mojanda, but it is rather bleak and offers no sleeping facilities other than a concrete floor, so most hikers would probably rather take advantage of the many good campsites near the lakeshore. Expect cold nights on the high open plateau, and be sure to take a stove since there is no wood.

After a night at the lake, you have several options, the first of which is simply to return to Otavalo. Alternatively, two trails that begin across the hillside just above the *refugio* allow you to finish the trip without backtracking. Just above little Laguna Chiquita, the trail forks. The left-hand trail runs south, descending to the village of Malchingui; the right-hand trail travels west to the village of Atahualpa. Either village is nearly a day's walk from Mojanda, and since both are fairly remote, transportation back to Otavalo may be a little hard to find, so try to arrive as early in the afternoon as possible.

The Zumbagua Market
and Quilotoa Crater

This long loop trip—partly by foot and partly by bus or truck—through the mountains and *paramo* is one of our favorite trips in Ecuador. It offers wonderful scenery, fine walking, exciting campsites either in the caldera or along the rim of the Quilotoa crater, and, with a little care in scheduling, a chance to visit one of the most authentic highland markets in the Andes. Quilotoa is a huge collapsed volcano crater, the bottom of which is filled with a lake. The Zumbagua market is held on Saturday mornings and draws hundreds of *campesinos* in from the little mountain villages to do their weekly trading. Though the market offers little in the way of crafts and therefore draws few tourists, it is one of the best markets in Ecuador for people watching.

The beginning point for the trip is Latacunga, a large town on the Pan-American highway between Quito and Ambato. Though it has little else to recommend it, Latacunga does offer excellent views of nearby Cotopaxi, especially from the tower on the hill to the east of town. The best hotel value in Latacunga is the clean, moderately priced *Cotopaxi* on the plaza; for meals, try the *Careta* or *Ejecutivo*. Buses for Zumbagua leave frequently throughout the morning from the row of shops and restaurants just across the Pan-American highway from town. But if you're going to the Saturday market, try to make the 6 A.M. bus. The trip to Zumbagua takes about two hours (along the way are occasional good views of Cotopaxi as well).

The bus stops along the Latacunga-Quevedo road a half-mile above Zumbagua. Simply take one of the trails running downhill into town. On market days Zumbagua, normally a quiet little village, is filled to overflowing with highlanders dressed in dark ponchos and narrow-brimmed hats. They spend the morning cooking and eating food in numerous market stalls or buying and selling produce and livestock (the

Laguna de Quilotoa, Ecuador

slaughterhouse area of the market is only for those with strong stomachs).

The route to Quilotoa is a dirt road that begins below the town. Even on market days there is little traffic, so don't count on catching a ride. Walk downhill from the main plaza and cross the concrete bridge over the stream. This road meanders north through open, heavily farmed hills and is paralleled for much of the way by a strange, labyrinthine canyon to the right of the road. There are several branching roads, but if you continue to bear to the right on the most traveled route, you'll have no trouble. And since there are many adobe houses and foot travelers along the road, finding someone to ask for directions is a simple matter.

As the road climbs to its high point (seven miles from Zumbagua near two thatch huts), a wide but vague roadway that soon becomes a path enters from the right. The crater is less than a half-mile along this path, though from the main road you'd hardly think anything was there. Only at the very last moment does the vast bowl of the crater open up before your feet, a startling sight. The rim makes a wonderful camping spot, with Quilotoa and the surrounding mountains to occupy your vision throughout the evening. Alternately, a trail leads down to the caldera floor where there are more campsites beside the lake (its water is not drinkable, so carry what you'll need).

From Quilotoa, continue north along the main road, which soon descends into a valley but quickly climbs again to contour along the mountainsides. There are frequent good views of the mountains to the east. The road continues eight miles past Quilotoa to the village of Chugchillan. Arranging transportation from Chugchillan back to Latacunga can be a little difficult, but arriving as early as possible in the day will improve your chances of finding a truck making the half-day trip.

Illiniza

Illiniza is a twin-peaked mountain in the western chain, easily accessible from Quito. The southern peak (17,268 feet) requires technical climbing skills, but the northern peak (16,790 feet) is a fairly easy scramble. The short backpack across the *paramo* to the mountain and the climb to Illiniza Norte makes a good three-day trip. The Nuevos Horizontes climbing club in Quito has a bare *refugio* below the saddle between the two peaks (call the club for information on hut availability).

To get to Iliniza, travel south from Quito on the Pan-American highway to the El Chaupi road, about three miles south of Machachi. The side road branches west and reaches the village of El Chaupi in about five miles. Though a rough but driveable road runs from the village to within two miles of the Nuevos Horizontes hut, unless you hire a taxi in Quito or get very lucky in catching a ride (as usual, weekends are your best bet), plan on walking in from El Chaupi (eight miles). Walk out of town to the west; this road quickly turns to the south to reach the Hacienda Refugio and immediately begins to climb.

In an hour or so you will reach a junction; the main road continues to the left, but the route to Iliniza turns uphill to the right. If you hire a taxi in Quito, your driver should take you to this point. In another two hours of following the jeep road and trail that take you through the open highlands, you should reach the hut, just below the gap between the two peaks.

Cotopaxi

At 19,342 feet, Cotopaxi is one of the world's highest active volcanoes. The extremely popular climb up this perfect, massive cone to the summit, though not technically difficult, is long and exhausting, and it does require negotiating glaciers and crevasse fields. Therefore, those not experienced in above-snowline climbing should hire guides. From the José Ribas hut at snowline, the round trip to the summit will take approximately ten hours and requires a *very* early departure to avoid the soft snow and dense cloud cover that afternoon brings. Due to the large numbers of climbers, the route to the summit is usually quite apparent.

For those less interested in climbing than in mountain scenery, Cotopaxi still makes an excellent destination. Lots of people with no aspirations for a summit attempt spend a night or two at José Ribas where, at an altitude of 15,750 feet, you can get a good feel for the heights. There is a small charge for use of the large hut, and the attendant will safely lock away your gear while you're out. Nonclimbers can easily fill a couple of days scrambling about the lava fields, exploring the fairly gentle lower portions of Cotapaxi's snowfields, and taking in the excellent views of Ecuador's mountains.

The simplest—and of course most expensive—way to reach the José Ribas hut from Quito is to hire a taxi for the seventy-two-mile trip (the final sixteen miles are over a dirt road that ends just below the hut). A much cheaper but more uncertain alternative is to travel south by bus along the Pan-American highway to the entrance to Cotopaxi National Park (look for the sign). There the road to the hut turns back to the northeast, and to reach the hut, you'll either have to walk or rely upon the kindness of strangers for a ride. Traffic is fairly frequent on weekends when lots of climbers travel to the hut, but on weekdays, hitching a ride may be difficult.

Chimborazo

For a while during the nineteenth century, Chimborazo (20,571 feet) was thought to be the tallest mountain on earth. In a sense it still is. Because of the earth's equatorial bulge, the peak of this extinct volcano is the farthest point from the planet's center. The climb to the glaciated summit is not for novices, but as with Cotopaxi, conditioned hikers with a little experience with crampons, ice axe self-arrest, and ropes can make the climb with guides. Nonclimbers can get the flavor of the mountain by spending a day or two at the Edward Whymper hut, just below the Thielman glacier at the 16,400-foot level. As at the Ribas hut on Cotopaxi, the Whymper hut is large and has an attendant who'll safeguard your gear while you're out.

The hut is easily reached from Riobamba (three to four hours south of Quito). Though there is no regular public transport to the hut, taxis can be hired in Riobamba for the hour-and-a-half trip. For information on hiring guides for the climb, try the DITURIS office in Riobamba (2306 5 de Junio).

Baños

East of the Avenue of Volcanoes the land drops away precipitously, plunging thousands of feet to the Amazon basin in only seventy-five horizontal miles. Partway down from the intermontaine basins, in the sheltered valley of the Río Pastaza, is Baños, one of the prettiest towns in Ecuador. Baños is such a perfect spot for both hiking and relaxing that many travelers settle here for a long visit. With an elevation just below the 6,000-foot level, Baños enjoys a wonderful climate, with days warm enough for an enjoyable swim in the pools that give the town its name. And the physical setting of the town could hardly be more attractive. Wherever you go in the area, you're accompanied by the sound of rushing water from the Pastaza River and its side streams, and the valleys these waters have carved into the eastern slope of the Andes are lush and green compared to the grassy brown *paramos.* Among these steep slopes towering to the north and south of town, you'll find a maze of trails for day hikes. Above all, looming over the town—like the goddess that an ancient tribe of the region took it to be—is the snow-capped cone of volcano Tungurahua, an easy climb for those with just a bit of experience.

With all this physical beauty, Baños is hardly unvisited. It has long been a popular resort town for residents of the nearby highlands, and on weekends, Ecuadorians from Riobamba, Ambato, and Quito crowd the town, filling the pools, restaurants, and hotels. Foreigners too have discovered the attractions of Baños, so expect to see more fellow travelers here than any other town in Ecuador with the possible exception of Otavalo. If at all possible, try to schedule your arrival in town during the week since finding a decent hotel room on weekends may be impossible.

RESOURCES

By far the best hotel in Baños and one of the best hotel values in the Andes is the extremely pleasant and very moderately priced *Sangay* (101 Plazoleta Isidro Ayora, beneath the waterfall visible throughout town). Here you'll find good service, modern accommodations (especially in the newer back annex), private baths, a clean swimming pool, tennis and squash courts, and a sauna. The Sangay's restaurant, the best in Baños, serves four-course dinners nightly. Every other hotel in Baños is a long step down from the Sangay in both price and comfort; expect very low prices and very minimal comfort. For the best budget accommodations in town (tiny rooms, noisy, and not very clean) try

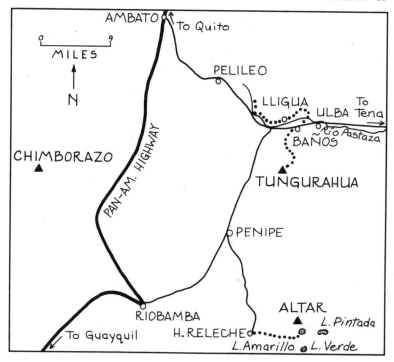

either the *Residencia Teresita* (on the plaza) or the *Residencial Patty* (554 Eloy Alfaro, behind the market).

Most of Baños's virtually identical restaurants are on the plaza and along the main street (Calle 5) in the direction of the bus station. Few of them have menus, so if you speak no Spanish, you may have trouble. Just ask for *almuerzo* or *cena,* and you'll get whatever the special of the day happens to be—usually soup, a main course of meat, vegetables, and rice or potatoes, and fruit or dessert. For Chinese food, try the *Chifa Oriental* on the main street. For vegetarian food and surprisingly cold drinks, try the *Mercedes* (on Martinez near the cemetery). If you'd like to acquire a taste for roast guinea pig, you'll find a restaurant outside the market building that always has a few *cuy* (guinea pig) turning on spits. If you enjoy taking fresh-baked bread on day hikes, stop at one of the bakeries along the main street on your way out of town.

Transportation to and from Baños is a simple matter since it is only an hour from the major highland city of Ambato (three hours south of Quito). Buses travel between the central Ambato station and the Baños station (just off the main Ambato-Puyo highway) every half-hour or so throughout the day. There are also direct buses between Baños and Quito (three to four hours; several departures daily from the main station in Baños and the *Terrestre del Sur* station in Quito).

Neither of Baños's two thermal baths and swimming pools (one in town across from the Sangay, the other, called Salado, outside town past the school on a cobbled street that turns left off the Ambato road) is a model of cleanliness. But after a long walk—especially on a weekday when crowds are light and the water is cleaner—a soak in the hot water can be soothing.

An interesting excursion from Baños is to the Sunday market at Salasaca. This village, partway between Ambato and Baños, is home to weavers of colorfully patterned strips of cloth called *tapices.* Their market is well worth the half-hour trip from Baños both for shopping and for observing the Salasaca Indians in their distinctive dress—black ponchos and white pants and shirts.

Hikes Outside Baños

Baños is the hub of a set of trails that radiate from the town like spokes, linking the farms and pastures of the surrounding countryside. You can easily find lovely walks into the *campo* (countryside). Take care to keep yourself oriented. We've included below a few of our favorite walks outside Baños.

One of the best hikes in the Baños area takes you along the Río Pastaza west of town. Walk along the main highway toward Ambato; at the edge of Baños, just before the police control station, turn right onto a dirt road that drops sharply into the canyon of the Pastaza, a deep and narrow cut in the rock through which the river rushes muddy and fast during the wet season. On a rock outcrop above the bridge that crosses the river is a shrine to Saint Martin. Beyond the bridge is the old Ambato road, and on it you can walk as far as you like—even the forty miles to Ambato. Only a couple of miles beyond the bridge, the road has been swept with landslides and is, therefore, untraveled by vehicles. Following the road, whether for a long or short distance, makes a nice ramble through green country with the Pastaza on the left and vegetated hillsides on the right. A mile or so beyond the bridge, be sure to walk through Lligua, a little village of rustic tile-roofed houses that fills a small valley north of the road.

Another good day hike (allow five to six hours) takes you across the Pastaza into the open farmland north of Baños where the hillsides are a patchwork of pale green fields cut into squares by the darker green rows of low trees and tropical plants that grow along fence lines and paths. From the bus station walk across the Ambato-Puyo highway, and look for the wide trail that plunges into the gorge. One minute you're in town and the next you're deep in a canyon on a donkey trail. Cross the river over the suspension bridge, the Puente San Francisco, and start climbing into the hills. Be sure to stay on the main trail, avoiding shortcuts through the many cultivated fields. When near houses, watch out for the inhabitants' guard dogs; their small size in no way prepares you for their ferocity. Beyond the bridge, trails proliferate confusingly, splitting again and again as you go along. But try to follow the most traveled path, which bears somewhat to the right (east) as it heads fairly directly up the mountain. Early in the hike, avoid trails that branch to the left, but as you climb high above the Pastaza, leaving the houses and cultivated land and entering high pastures, begin to look for trails ascending to the left. As you work your way up the mountain, remember that your objective is the ridge line to the north (trails get fainter as you climb beyond the heavily farmed lower slopes). There a trail swings west, first following the ridge and later, near the radio antenna, dropping through switchbacks to culminate at the San Martin shrine. In good weather, there are excellent views of Tungurahua from the ridge line.

Other trails out of Baños climb the wet green ridges to the south of town. These damp north-facing slopes are beautiful areas of high jungle, and the trails take you through lush, heavy foliage. Trails beginning near the cemetery climb the mountain to the little collection of houses called Runtung. Other trails begin near the Salado pools (look for the broad path to the right just before the baths); these ascend the broad valley first on the right-hand side of the stream, then on the left bank. Eventually this trail intersects with a newly cut dirt road, but only 100 yards or so up the road, a wide trail branches off and climbs into beautiful high pastures and dense forest. To return to Baños, walk back to the new road, and follow it back to the outskirts of town.

The area east of Baños is also good territory for country rambles. Along the Ambato-Puyo road are dozens of waterfalls, most notably the Agoyán falls six miles down the road. Buses leave from town regularly for Agoyán. More trails into the countryside begin a couple of miles east of Baños near the little town of Ulba. Look for a *bodega* near the highway bridge. If you follow paths to the north, you'll find a newly constructed footbridge crossing the Pastaza. Across the bridge you can ramble for hours on trails that climb into the farming country to the north.

Tungurahua

By far the most spectacular hike from Baños is the climb to the summit of 16,457-foot Tungurahua. While neither as tall nor massive as Cotopaxi and Chimborazo, Tungurahua has a graceful, symmetrical beauty of its own. Though the climb is not very difficult or technically demanding, it will take you into the snow, so the inexperienced are advised to seek the services of a guide (the British owner of the Hotel Sangay will help guests arrange equipment and guides for the climb). There is a *refugio* and campsites below snowline, so for nonclimbers, this route also makes a good overnight backpacking trip.

The path to the volcano begins on the western edge of Baños. Near the police control station, turn left (south) onto a dirt road. Less than 100 yards from the main highway, a heavily used trail turns to the right and immediately begins to climb, passing a cross on a hill overlooking Baños. In about two miles the trail reaches the village of Pandua where it is usually possible to hire *arrieros* to transport your gear up to the *refugio.* From Pandua the clear trail climbs south, first through heavy foliage and then breaking out onto open slopes. The steep climb from

Pandua to the *refugio* should take about four hours. Past the hut, the route to the summit is usually fairly clear due to large numbers of climbers. The final ascent will take four to five hours, so begin early.

Altar

This hike was one of our first in Ecuador, and it served as a perfect introduction to the unpredictability of the country's weather patterns. Many hikers we've met claim this is the most beautiful hike in Ecuador. We can't verify the claim because when we made this walk (during the "dry" season), a slow rain fell incessantly, and the highlands were blanketed in thick fog that kept visibility to only a few hundred feet for days on end. We began the walk wet, stayed damp for the duration of the trip, and saw nothing but blank, gray mist for our trouble. If you're lucky enough to have clear weather for the trek, however, what you'll see is, by all reports, stunning—the remnant of a great glaciated volcano crater more than a mile across. At some point in the past, however, a powerful explosion virtually gutted the mountain, blowing away the western wall and part of the mountain's center to form a magnificent cirque. The approach to Altar is directly toward the blown-out west wall, providing excellent views of the sheer rock walls, hanging glaciers, and ragged peaks of the cirque.

The walk to Altar from the trailhead will take only a day, but allow at least three days for this trip since you'll need at least one day for exploring the area. You'll certainly want to climb up to the cirque and perhaps do a little scrambling around on the ridges nearby. And the best camping area—the valley just below the cirque—is in itself a wonderful place to spend time. So if you're the type who likes camping better than walking, Altar makes a wonderful spot for a several-days visit. Expect cold nights, and be prepared for rain at any time of the year.

The most difficult aspect of this walk is reaching the trailhead at Hacienda Reliche, just above the village of Candelaria (the farthest point to which you're at all likely to catch a ride). The closest you can get to Candelaria by public transportation is the town of Penipe on the Baños-Riobamba road (buses leave in either direction at hourly intervals). The problem is that Candelaria is fourteen miles above Penipe on a very infrequently traveled dirt road. We sat so long in the fog by the side of this road waiting for a ride that Penipe's police force, apparently out of boredom, finally came over and ran a long and involved document check and desultory backpack search on us. After failing to turn up anything interesting enough to liven up the day, their best advice on transportation was to be in town by 6 A.M. since a couple of vehicles apparently do go up to Candelaria early most weekdays; they claimed that on weekends, especially Sunday, traffic was considerably heavier. With the help of a couple of rides in small trucks, we did, finally, manage to get to Candelaria that day, but it took hours. If you're pressed for time and want a degree of certainty in transportation, we'd suggest hiring a taxi either in Baños or Riobamba for the trip to Hacienda Reliche and trying to plan your return for a Sunday.

If you begin this hike in Candelaria, cross the bridge and walk along the road for somewhat more than a mile to Hacienda Releche. Here the trail begins, turning to the left and climbing past thatched houses, fields, and pastures. Within a mile you'll reach a potentially troublesome area of pastures. The trail becomes obscured by many livestock paths in this area, but follow it as best you can up the side of the valley (aim for the ridge to the left of the waterfall). You'll soon reach the main trail, which remains quite clear as it travels east to Altar up the valley of the Río Colanes. The final five miles of the walk to the foot of the crater are quite easy, with no serious climbing and frequent good views of Altar ahead.

The climb into the crater is a steep one, and though it is possible to camp near the Laguna Amarillo in the crater's grassy floor, you'll find more pleasant campsites in the valley of the Río Colanes (only a stream at this point) just below the crater. These campsites are more protected and allow you to climb up to the crater (an hour away) to explore without having to haul all your equipment. Several rough trails will take you up to Laguna Amarillo, but the easiest one begins its ascent along the left bank of the stream.

By *Autoferro* to the Coast

The most interesting way to travel between Quito and Guayaquil, Ecuador's largest city, is by *autoferro* on what is one of the world's most interesting railroad journeys. Done early in a visit to Ecuador, this trip provides a panoramic one-day introduction to the landscape and people of the country. The *autoferro* is simply a bus on rails, and it travels along a 288-mile railroad south from Quito through the Avenue of Volcanoes, providing good views of both Cotapaxi and Chimborazo, especially if you ride on top of the car with the luggage. As it passes through the heavily populated intermontane basins, the *autoferro* also offers a quick look at the people and towns of the highlands. Along the way, the line reaches a maximum altitude of 12,000 feet, and it plunges to the wet west coast through an amazing series of switchbacks and loops.

Because the *autoferro* is small—holding only about three dozen passengers—tickets are often in short supply, so be sure to purchase tickets as far in advance as possible (the ticket office is in Quito at 441 Calle Bolivar). Departure for the ten-to-eleven-hour trip is at 6 A.M. daily except Sunday (especially during the wet season; however, service is often off schedule or canceled altogether because of landslides). There is a brief lunch stop at Riobamba, but you may want to take snacks along as well. The end of the line is in the town of Duran, across the broad Río Guayas from Guayaquil. To get to the city, take one of the ferries crossing the river several times an hour; they're much less expensive than taxis, which must take a roundabout route over the new bridge.

Ingapirca

Ecuador's only significant architectural remnant of the Inca occupation is Ingapirca, a large *tambo-pucara* (inn-fortress) built by Huayna Capac in the fifteenth century. Situated along the Inca road between Quito and Cuzco, Ingapirca—with its polished stonework, semicircular walls, baths, and fine chambers—served primarily as a resting place for traveling royalty.

To get to Ingapirca from Cuenca in the southern highlands, early risers could try to get tickets for the *autoferro* (departure time: 4 A.M.), which stops at the Ingapirca station. More sensible travelers will take a bus (departures at least every hour throughout the day) north to Cañar (about two hours), but get out just before town at a road junction (look for the "Ingapirca" signpost). The ruins are eight miles up this dirt road, and traffic is frequent enough to make catching a ride fairly easy.

El Litoral

Between Guayaquil to the south and Esmeraldas to the north, Ecuador's Pacific coast is hot, green, and wet—tropical in the extreme. Though El Litoral offers no overwhelmingly major tourist destinations, it is a wonderful region for a relaxed style of travel—a few days of swimming and sunning at a beach and a few days of bus travel through the banana groves, the coastal jungle, and the faded little towns of the lowlands.

Guayaquil is normally just a quick stopover for travelers on the overland route between Quito and Peru or for those waiting for an open seat on a TAME flight to the Galapagos Islands. But the city does have a certain tropical attractiveness. With nearly a million inhabitants, Guayaquil is Ecuador's largest city, and though Quito remains the country's governmental center, Guayaquil is very definitely the commercial center. Much of the town's center (near the Parque Centenario, the Parque Simon Bolivar, and along Avenida 9 de Octubre) is quite modern—with a multilevel enclosed shopping mall and franchises of several U.S. fast-food chains. But the riverfront district with its old buildings and Malecon Park is much more picturesque. The park is a relatively cool, shaded spot in a hot, humid city, and it stretches for blocks along the Río Guayas, sometimes full of floating hibiscuslike flowers. At dusk the Malecon is full of strolling lovers, bats wheeling around the old clock tower, and prostitutes in flowered dresses beginning the evening's business in the arched portals of the grand but decaying waterfront buildings.

For clean, moderately priced, air-conditioned hotel accommodations, try the *Italia* (only a block from the Malecon at the corner of 10 de Agosto and Pichincha) or the *Cervera* (1036 Cordoba). For a good value in inexpensive, un-air-conditioned rooms, try the *Boston* (711 Chimborazo). Food in Guayaquil's restaurants is surprisingly good. For a wide selection of restaurants, walk along Avenida 9 de Octubre. For very good Chinese food try the *Gran Chifa* (on Pedro Garbo). Guayaquil's very helpful tourist office (DITURIS) is at Malecon and Olmedo.

The nearest beach to Guayaquil is Playas, about sixty miles away. Once a fishing village, Playas is rapidly being transformed into a resort area. Its primary attractions are sea, sun, and fresh seafood. For accommodations, try the moderately expensive beachfront *Humbolt* or the moderately priced *Cattan.* Another beach resort primarily of interest for its relatively clean beaches and deep-sea fishing (especially for marlin) is the expensive resort town of Salinas (two to three hours by bus from Guayaquil). To arrange boats for fishing, contact *Pesca Tours.* For moderately expensive accommodations, try the *Mirimar;* for moderately inexpensive rooms, check the *Yulee.*

The normal route north through El Litoral to the major north coast town of Esmeraldas travels inland through Babahoyas and Quevedo. However, committed beachcombers can continue up the coast on short-haul buses and trucks to the port of Manta, stopping at quiet fishing villages like Palmar and Manglaralto along the way. From Manta, the route to Esmeraldas turns inland, running northeast to Santo Domingo de los Colorados, a town noted for its Sunday market, which attracts a few members of the Colorado Indian tribe and many tourists from Quito. From Santo Domingo, frequent buses make the four-hour trip to Esmeraldas.

A little cooler than Guayaquil but situated on an even lusher coastline, Esmeraldas (population 65,000) is a raw seaport town in the process of being transformed into a resort area. Though banana, tobacco, and cocoa crops still make their way through town to the port, Esmeraldas depends increasingly on tourists from Quito for its livelihood. Many of the inhabitants of the coast in the Esmeraldas area are the descendants of shipwrecked slaves.

Esmeraldas itself is not particularly interesting; most visitors are attracted by the outlying beaches. The closest of these is the new resort area of Las Palmas (try the moderately priced, air-conditioned *Hotel Cayapas*). But more relaxing and typical is Atacames, about fifteen miles south of town. Atacames is a quiet little beach town where the main activities are swimming, sunning, and eating seafood. There are several adequate inexpensive hotels and collections of *cabañas* along the beachfront.

The Galapagos Islands

At first glance, it is difficult to see why the Galapagos Islands have become one of the world's premier adventure travel destinations. Until very recently, few people came to the remote Galapagos (600 miles off Ecuador's coast) other than sailors blown off course, pirates looking for a hideout, and whalers looking for water and turtle meat—and just possibly the Inca Tupac Yupanqui on a voyage of discovery in the fifteenth century. The 400 scraps of volcanic rock that make up the Galapagos (only fifteen could be called major islands of the group and only five are inhabited) are about 3 million years old. They are for the most part bleak and barren, a raw young corner of the planet not yet smoothed by time. Novelist Herman Melville, who visited the islands in 1841, described them in this way in *The Encantadas:* "Take five-and-twenty heaps of cinders dumped here and there in an outside city lot;

imagine some of them magnified into mountains, and the vacant lot the sea; and you have a fit idea of the general aspect of the Encantadas, or Enchanted Isles. A group rather of extinct volcanoes than of isles; looking much as the world might after a penal conflagration."

Despite the hoards of travelers who descend upon the islands every year, little has changed on the Galapagos since Melville's visit. It is still a forbidding place of black rock and spined cactus, a place of sharp edges where just a short jaunt over a lava field can reduce a new pair of sneakers to shreds. But if the bleak, uninviting landscape has changed little since Melville's visit, neither have the amazing animals of the islands changed since Charles Darwin made his landmark observations of them in 1835. And above all else it is the chance to view the unique wildlife—about half of which is found nowhere else—that brings most visitors to the islands today. In 1835 Darwin, aboard the *H.M.S. Beagle,* spent several weeks in the Galapagos, and what he found was a natural laboratory for the study of adaptation of plant and animal life to environmental conditions. Observing the ways related species (especially finches) had adapted to the various environments the islands provide, Darwin was able to develop his theory of natural selection, which shook the world when *The Origin of Species* was published twenty-five years later.

Today, thousands of visitors each year are attracted by this wealth of amazingly tame-acting wildlife. Traveling from island to island in simple boats or luxurious ships, visitors can swim with fur seals in the cool waters of the Humbolt current, sit on a rocky escarpment above pounding surf with primitive-looking marine iguanas, and walk through lava fields to volcanic craters.

The best time to visit the Galapagos is December through May, when you're most likely to have warm sunny days. From June through November, the *garua* (mists and clouds) sets in, keeping the sky gray much of the time.

Galapagos National Park

In 1959 the Ecuadorian government, in an admirable move, declared the Galapagos Islands a national park. Since then the park service has worked to protect the islands and their animal life from disruption by humans and by nonnative plants and animals. One of the first stops any visitor to the Galapagos needs to make is at the National Park headquarters in Puerto Ayora. There, along with getting your passport stamped, paying the park entry fee, and obtaining the permit necessary for travel among the islands, you should familiarize yourself with park rules and restrictions.

Because the Galapagos ecosystem is unique, irreplacable, and quite fragile, virtually all land travel in the National Park is restricted. Though it is possible to camp in a very few designated areas on the islands, you'll need to get permission from park officials first; for the most part, visits to the uninhabited islands are restricted to daylight hours. Also, to ensure the protection of the plants and animals, you'll have to have a certified guide (usually the captain and/or the cook of your boat if you go on your own) accompany you any time you go ashore outside the few inhabited areas of the islands. That means virtually all hikes on the islands are of necessity guided hikes. During all hikes and shore visits from boats, observe the cross-shaped markers installed by the park service to indicate where to walk.

Guidebooks often call the animals of the Galapagos islands "tame." They are not. Rather, they simply have little instinctive fear. Therefore, park regulations prohibit touching, feeding, or harassing animals. Be particularly careful to give nesting birds a wide berth in order not to scare them from their nests, possibly harming eggs or chicks in the process. Because each of the islands is unique in flora as well as fauna, be careful not to carry seeds between islands; check clothing before shore visits to ensure that you do not introduce any nonnative plants.

GALAPAGOS FAUNA

The animals most often associated with the Galapagos are the giant tortoises that gave the islands their name. Growing to as much as six feet in length and 600 pounds in weight, Galapagos tortoises feed primarily on various grasses and prickly pear and spend most of the rest of their time resting partially submerged in pools. Giant tortoises once inhabited many of the Galapagos islands, but today they are found only on Isabela, San Cristobal, Duncan, Española, Santa Cruz, and Santiago. There is noticeable variation from island to island in size, shape, and coloration of the tortoises' shells.

Though they may live 150 years or more if allowed to, in the nineteenth century the tortoise was hunted almost to extinction for its meat. Whaling ships, for example, made the islands a regular stop in their long voyages; live tortoises were stored on their backs in the ships' holds until time for slaughter and were reported to live for as long as a year without food or water. Though now protected from human hunters, the tortoises are still threatened by nonnative animals imported by man. Rats and feral pigs, dogs, and cats disrupt tortoise nests, eating the eggs and hatchlings. Part of the work of scientists at the Charles Darwin Station at Academy Bay on Santa Cruz is to protect the species from these depredations by collecting newly laid eggs, hatching them, and releasing the tortoises back into their natural environments once they're mature enough to be safe from attacks by nonnative mammals.

Another reptile unique to the Galapagos is the marine iguana, the only sea-feeding lizard in the world. These dark, three-foot-long lizards inhabit most of the islands and are often seen in thick groups clinging tenaciously to wave-swept lava flows. Able to stay submerged for as much as an hour, the marine iguana survives by eating mainly seaweed. It also drinks sea water, ridding itself of the salt through ducts near its eyes. If disturbed, it can shoot jets of water from these ducts.

Less common is the larger land iguana whose numbers were drastically reduced due to pointless killing by man and by lack of food as a result of competition from nonnative mammals such as goats and donkeys. Growing to as much as four feet in length, the land iguana is lighter in color than the marine iguana and usually has a yellowish head. They are most populous on Fernandina. Another notable and extremely common reptile is the small and fearless lava lizard, whose coloration and size vary from island to island. Lava lizards are one of the primary food sources for the Galapagos snake, a nonpoisonous constrictor. Growing to between two and three feet in length, the snake is brown, often with yellow stripes down its back.

Naturally occurring mammal life in the Galapagos is quite limited. On land, only bats and rice rats (much less common than the imported black rat) are native to the islands. More interesting are the sea mammals—fur seals and sea lions. Both species flourish in these equatorial waters only because of the cold Humbolt current. Sea lions are quite common on most of the islands. They prefer sandy beaches and are relatively fearless of man, so it is easy to walk among them as they lie sunning in groups. Bulls are sometimes aggressive, though, so don't get too close. Fur seals are often harder to find because they avoid the open beaches in favor of rocky shoreline where they can find shade against the hot sun.

Entire volumes could (and have) been written just on the bird life of the Galapagos. Over two-thirds of the varieties are unique to the islands, and most Galapagos birds are startlingly fearless of man. Among the most common seabirds of the islands are the various types of boobie—the blue-footed, the white or masked, and the red-footed. Also common is the frigate bird; one variety is aptly named the magnificent frigate bird because of its seven-foot wingspan. Another large seabird is the Galapagos albatross, whose eight-foot wingspan allows it to soar all the way to the coastline of the South American continent before returning to Española Island for breeding. The flightless cormorant and the Galapagos penguin both inhabit only Fernandina and Isabela islands because of the colder waters there. Both birds are quite awkward on land but have adapted into marvelous swimmers, catching fish as their primary food source. Also inhabiting the islands are gulls, petrels, pelicans, and flamingos. Land birds of the islands include the Galapagos hawk, owls, herons, egrets, and the thirteen species of finches that were instrumental in the development of Darwin's theory of evolution. For more information on the birds of the islands, see M. P. Harris's *A Field Guide to the Birds of the Galapagos* (New York: Taplinger, 1974).

THE ISLANDS

One source of potential confusion in traveling among the Galapagos Islands is their names. The major islands of the group have both English and official Ecuadorian names, and some of them have local names as well. Though the English names are most often used in scientific studies of the islands, they are less often used by the locals. Sometimes even the official Ecuadorian names are ignored; Santa Cruz, for example, has at least a half-dozen local names. Below is a list of the major islands; the most commonly used name is given in italics.

English	Ecuadorian	Local name
Abingdon	*Pinta*	
Albemarle	*Isabela*	
Barrington	Santa Fe	
Bindloe	*Marchena*	
Charles	Santa Maria	*Floreana*
Chatham	*San Cristobal*	
Culpepper	Darwin	
Daphne	Mosquera	
Duncan	Pinzon	
Hood	*Española*	
Indefatigable	*Santa Cruz*	
James	San Salvador	*Santiago*
Jervis	Rabida	
Narborough	*Fernandina*	
North Seymour	*Seymour*	
South Seymour	*Baltra*	
Tower	*Genovesa*	
Wenman	Wolf	

Unless your tour of the Galapagos is quite extended, you'll have to be selective in deciding which islands to visit. The following list of major islands and their most notable sights and activities should help in planning your itinerary.

■ **Santa Cruz** Virtually all visitors begin their visits to the islands on Santa Cruz, the tourist and transportation center of the Galapagos. There are several interesting excursions on the island to keep you busy while waiting for your boat. A short walk outside the principal town of Puerto Ayora is the Charles Darwin Research Station. Here scientists are working to increase the populations of Galapagos tortoises through a program of controlled breeding and protection of eggs and hatchlings. Visitors to the station can observe the tortoises Monday through Friday.

There are also a couple of good day hikes on Santa Cruz. The first of these is to the Tortuga Reserve on the southwest corner of the island. The hike begins at the village of Santa Rosa in the center of the island (take an early morning bus or hire a car or jeep for the fourteen-mile trip). There a trail turns south to reach the reserve, home to hundreds of tortoises. Allow a full day to reach the reserve, explore about, and return to Santa Rosa. Another excellent all-day hike is to Santa Cruz's central highlands, an area of much lusher vegetation than the coastal regions that you'll spend most of your time exploring from the boats. Trails to the highlands begin in the village of Bellavista (five miles from Puerto Ayora) and climb into the mountainous area of Media Luna,

Cerro Crocker, and Cerro Mesa. To hike either to the Tortoise Reserve or into the highlands, you are required to have permission from the park service and be accompanied by a certified guide. Check with park headquarters in Puerto Ayora for information on permits and guide services.

■   **South Plaza**   This island, just east of Santa Cruz, is an excellent spot for observing sea lions, the bright red Sally Lightfoot crab, and land iguanas.

■   **Seymour**   Just north of Baltra and Santa Cruz, Seymour is home to frigate birds, land iguanas, sea lions, boobies, and seals.

■   **Daphne**   Little Daphne Island, located between Santa Cruz and Santiago, is mostly just a volcanic cone, but the floor of its crater is the island's chief attraction. In the pale rocks of the crater floor, hundreds of blue-footed boobies sometimes nest. The severe El Niño of 1982–83, however, drastically reduced the numbers of boobies on Daphne to only a few dozen pairs, and it may take years for the population to return to normal. Visitors have been prohibited from descending to the crater's floor.

■   **Santa Fe**   Only a half-day's boat ride from Puerto Ayora, Santa Fe makes a logical first stop on many circuits of the islands. It is notable primarily for the beautiful little bay along its north shore. Arguably the best beach in the islands, it is an excellent spot for a long swim or snorkel in the clear and relatively warm water. About twenty-five feet deep, the bay's floor is covered with sand dollars. You may swim with sea turtles, manta rays, and harmless varieties of shark (though the waters around the Galapagos are home to large numbers of shark, almost all of them are varieties like the hammerhead, which pose no threat to man—only a very few shark attacks on humans have been recorded).

■   **Isabela**   This is the largest island of the Galapagos group, and it is inhabited, especially near the towns of Santo Tomas and Puerto Villamil. Perhaps the most interesting excursion on Isabela (or in the whole group of islands for that matter) is the hike up Volcano Alcedo. Aside from offering some of the most beautiful scenery anywhere in the Galapagos, climbing the volcano will give you an excellent lesson in the adaptation of plant life to climate and altitude, for as you ascend, you soon leave the rocky coast behind and enter the higher altitudes where the *garua* (heavy fogs and mists) settles, promoting relatively lush plant life as well as open grassy slopes a little reminiscent of the *paramo* in mainland Ecuador. Several thousand Galapagos tortoises live on the green slopes of Alcedo, though you may not see them due to the remote areas they prefer to inhabit. The view from the crater's rim—about four hours from the landing—is awesome. Fumaroles steam and the far wall is almost four miles away. In the distance you can see Santiago on the horizon to the east. The climb to the rim of Alcedo can be done in a long day, and you will, of course, need a guide. In the past it has been possible to obtain permission to camp at Alcedo, allowing time to explore the area in more detail than a day hike permits. Check with the National Park office in Puerto Ayora to arrange permission to camp.

- **Fernandina** West of Isabela is Fernandina Island, a single volcanic cone that has been quite active since man has frequented the Galapagos. The climb to the lake-filled crater's rim makes a hard but rewarding day's hike. The water off Fernandina's shoreline is the coldest in the islands, so penguins, cormorants, seals, and sea lions flourish there.
- **Santiago** This island is notable primarily for its black lava formations and its seal colony. Most of Santiago's coastline is made up of dark forbidding cliffs, but if you're lucky, you may be able to swim with the seals at Espumilla beach. Just north of Espumilla is Buccaneer Cove, a spot used as a refuge by pirates because there is a nearby spring —an unusual feature on these water-poor islands. Santiago's shoreline is a good spot for observing sea lions, the bright Sally Lightfoot crab, and marine iguanas. While visiting the island, make sure to talk your guide into taking you on a walk across the lunar landscape toward the volcanic cones of the interior (wear sturdy shoes or boots for this one).
- **Bartolome** If you visit Santiago, don't neglect stopping at nearby Bartolome (just off the eastern shore). The island has extraordinarily beautiful beaches, and it is possible to hike up the island's main mountain where there is much evidence of volcanic activity.
- **Española** This is an interesting and pretty island with high cliffs along much of its southern shoreline. The normal landing spot is Point Suarez to the west. There you'll see sea lions, crabs, blue-footed boobies, and marine iguanas. Española is also the nesting ground of the Galapagos albatross. You might ask your captain to try one of the less frequented landings along the north shore if Suarez is crowded with other visitors. Gardner Bay is one of the island's best beaches.
- **San Cristobal** This is one of the five inhabited islands, and you can pick up additional supplies at Moreno on the island's southwest point. It is also possible to walk inland from Moreno to the village of Progreso and on to the San Joaquin crater and El Junco Lake.
- **Floreana** Most boats stop at Post Office Bay. There a barrel has served as an unofficial mail drop since the days of the whalers in the late eighteenth century.
- **Genovesa** Remote and desolate, Genovesa Island, far to the northeast, is seldom visited. But during April and May—breeding season—the sky is full of frigate birds. And so is the ground where they perform their extraordinary mating dance, the most interesting feature of which is the puffing of the brilliant scarlet neck sac by the males.

GETTING TO THE GALAPAGOS

Visiting the Galapagos is expensive. Round-trip air fares for the 600-mile flight from Guayaquil to Baltra cost nearly as much as a Miami-Cuzco round-trip ticket. And travel among the islands, whether you go with an agency or hire a boat for a week or so on your own, is vastly more expensive than traveling in the Andes. The Ecuadorian airline, TAME, is the sole commercial air carrier serving the Galapagos Islands. Daily flights from Quito with connections in Guayaquil arrive at the Baltra landing field (an old U.S. air base). However, tour agencies frequently book large groups of seats for their customers, so last-minute ticket purchases are sometimes impossible to arrange. If visiting the islands is a high priority for your trip to South America, be sure to book Galapagos air tickets with your travel agent well in advance. If you should find yourself in Ecuador with a spur-of-the-moment desire to go to the Galapagos but are unable to book a ticket through TAME, check with Ecuadorian Tours (399 Amazonas, Quito; 1500 9 de Octubre, Guayaquil) or Economic Galapagos Tours (Pinto and Amazonas, Quito; 424 Avenida 9 de Octubre, Guayaquil); if they haven't filled their group tours, they'll sometimes sell excess TAME tickets.

To get from the Baltra landing field to Santa Cruz, the tourist center of the islands, you first have to take a bus, then a ferry across to Santa Cruz, and then either a taxi or truck to the town of Puerto Ayora. Upon arrival, have your passport stamped at the National Park Office.

TRAVELING AMONG THE ISLANDS

You have two basic choices for travel among the Galapagos islands: either book a tour in advance with an agency that will arrange everything from ship to food to itinerary, or go to Puerto Ayora and hire an independent boat captain to take you where you want to go; you'll have to hire a cook, buy food, decide on an itinerary, etc. There are, of course, trade-offs either way.

Perhaps the greatest advantage an agency tour offers is certainty, something virtually impossible to ensure on independent trips. A prearranged group tour will also free you from the details, negotiations, and inevitable frustrations of trying to set up a tour on your own. And on the larger ships that agencies usually book, you'll surely be more physically comfortable than in the rough, cramped boats that work independently. A reputable agency will also make sure your guides are knowledgeable and informative, prepared to enrich your visit educationally. On the other hand, agency tours will be much more expensive (rates for some of the more luxurious ships average well over $100 a day—three times the cost of an independently arranged tour) and will lock you into a schedule not of your own making. Perhaps the most serious drawback to most (not all) of the agency tours is the size of the group. Shuttling as many as 200 passengers between the ship and the islands is quite a logistical problem, and it means that your time on shore will almost inevitably be much briefer with an agency tour than on your own. You'll also have to share the experience with larger numbers of fellow travelers. Unless luxury of food and accommodations is a more important consideration for you than actually seeing the Galapagos, we'd highly recommend booking a tour with an agency that uses small ships (fifteen to thirty passengers). One agency we'd like to single out for recommendation is Economic Galapagos Tours, which offers island tours in eight-passenger boats very similar to and only slightly more expensive than the independently arranged excursions described below.

If you decide to travel on an independent boat, the responsibility for all arrangements falls upon your shoulders, not the agency's. But with a little work, you can put together a trip that will have a feel of adventure impossible to attain on an agency-led tour. The boats on which you'll travel are mostly thirty-to-forty-footers and carry six to eight passengers. Accommodations are basic: a toilet, all the bunks in one cabin, a rudimentary galley, maybe a shower, and a skiff for shuttling to and from the islands.

Since you can't really prearrange these trips, you are taking a chance that boats will be available in Puerto Ayora when you get there since the number of boats is somewhat limited. Many people arrive in the Galapagos thinking they'll hop right off the plane and into a boat. You might get lucky and be able to do just that, but for your own protection, schedule at least two or three days just for hiring a boat, buying food, etc.

Also, unless you're already traveling with six to eight people, you'll have to arrange a group. Many groups form spontaneously on the way in from Baltra or on the waterfront in Puerto Aroya. But if at all possible try to get your group together in Quito or Guayaquil. That will give you a little more time to decide on which islands you'd like to visit and how many days you want to stay out (most captains prefer trips of about a week), both of which you'll need to know before you get to the waterfront. You'll be traveling in *extremely* close proximity to these people for at least a week, so take a little time to make sure you can bear one another's company under those conditions (according to one captain, it is not at all uncommon for major disagreements to break out among these casually formed groups after only a few days at sea).

At the waterfront, don't take the first boat that comes along; shop around. There is considerable variation not only in prices but in the boats themselves and the knowledgeability of the captains. Check out cabins, toilets, and equipment; make sure, for example, that the boat has adequate numbers of dishes and eating utensils. Remember that once you're on the water, what's there is all there is—you'll have to live with any inadequacies. Another important consideration in selecting a boat is speed; some boats are much faster than others, allowing you to see more of the islands during the time you're out. The cheapest boats are not always the best value for your money. Haggle a bit with the captain, but don't expect huge reductions of the original price. During these negotiations, you'll have the option of hiring a cook for the trip as well. We'd strongly recommend including a cook in your crew; he will be well worth the small additional charge, especially if he is also a certified guide as most cooks are.

After you've arranged the boat, your next job is buying food for the passengers and crew. There is no real grocery store in Puerto Aroya, just several *bodegas* and markets (shop early in the morning for best selections). On your trip, you'll catch fish and perhaps dive for lobster for many dinners, but you'll need much more for a week or more at sea. From the simple fare available to you, you'll probably want to buy bananas in mass quantities (both cooking and eating bananas), oranges, rice, flour, sugar, cases of soft drinks, beer, mineral water, eggs, beans, lentils, bread (there's a bakery in town), tomatoes, and peppers. Most of the cooks can work wonders with these basic ingredients.

On-your-own travelers in the Galapagos should be sure to bring a sleeping bag since not all boats provide blankets. All visitors will also need a wide-brimmed hat, sunglasses, *lots* of strong sunscreen, insect repellent, sturdy boots (sneakers won't hold up against the sharp lava), a swimsuit, seasickness pills, and plenty of film. If you want to dive, bring a snorkel and mask and fins. Most boats have a few sets onboard, but there are seldom enough to go around, and the quality leaves something to be desired. If you're going on from the Galapagos to travel on the mainland and don't want to carry them along, you'll have no trouble selling them in Puerto Ayora. If you plan to camp, bring a tent; mosquitoes make camping impossible otherwise.

Finally, because of the numbers of people visiting the Galapagos, there is talk of limiting or even banning independent travelers, giving the agencies a monopoly on travel in the islands. Before planning an on-your-own tour, check with a travel agent for possible current restrictions.

For those forced to wait in Puerto Ayora for several days for an available boat, hotel accommodations and restaurants are quite limited. For moderate to expensive accommodations, try either the *Hotel Delfín* or the *Hotel Galapagos,* both of which have pleasant surroundings, hot water, and adequate restaurants. For inexpensive rooms, most people try the very basic *Cabiñas Angermayer* first, though budget rooms are also available at the *Colon* or the *Gloria.* If your hotel doesn't have a restaurant, try *Don Pico's.* Puerto Ayora is most crowded in June, July, August, December, and January, so accommodations can be full. If you're going to the Galapagos during these months, hotel reservations are recommended. There is also a campground with shower facilities outside town.

5
Peru

There are a few countries of the world where landscape, history, and culture come together in completely unique ways—ways that make otherwise fairly normal kinds of experiences into adventures, countries where the new, the picturesque, the significant vision waits around every turn for the perceptive traveler. Nepal and Greece are countries of this sort. And so is Peru.

For the first-time visitor, Peru's geographic diversity may seem astonishing. Its landscape falls into three major regions, three vast curved longitudinal strips, each running over 1,500 miles down the South American continent. And so unlike are these strips of land in almost every way—culture, economy, landscape, rainfall, vegetation—that they are virtually separate nations.

Peru's Pacific coast, the *chala,* is a long thin desert, 1,500 miles long but only about forty miles wide (sometimes much narrower). Though some sections of this coastline receive less rainfall than the Sahara, fifty rivers flowing through the desert from the mountains have made it an important population center for thousands of years. Today this region is the home of over half of Peru's 18,000,000 inhabitants, and it is the center of both the economy and government. In this region, summer temperatures (October to May) may reach the eighties, and days are often clear of the pervasive coastal fog. Winter temperatures (June to September) are noticeably cooler, with daytime highs often reaching the low sixties. The coastal area receives on average less than two inches of rainfall yearly, but the humidity is frequently above 90 percent.

Peru's center strip, the *sierra,* is of course the Andes range, the country's backbone and the home of most of the nation's Indian population. Here, rising from the high *puna* literally scores of peaks exceed 18,000 feet, with 22,205-foot Huascarán the highest. The range is broken into several relatively separate and compact aggregations of densely packed peaks, and in these *cordilleras* the backpacker and trekker will find high alpine scenery that is unsurpassed anywhere. In the *sierra,* temperature varies little throughout the year; in fact, daily fluctuation is much greater than annual fluctuation. In mountain towns at the 11,000-to-12,000-foot level, evenings are almost always cool, with temperatures routinely dropping below the freezing mark. Daytime temperatures are usually very pleasant, usually reaching into the sixties (and often feeling much warmer due to the strong sunlight). Though this region averages only fifteen inches of yearly rainfall, during the wet season (November to April) be prepared for short periods of rain almost daily.

East of these lofty mountains, the land falls away dramatically to the *selva,* the Amazon basin, only about seventy-five feet above sea level. This resource-rich area contains less than a tenth of Peru's population, but it is very much the nation's hope for its economic future. Already roads are beginning to be cut through the jungle, and vast expanses of forest have been cleared for ranches, farms, and energy production. In the *selva* there is little annual temperature fluctuation; expect 85-to-100-degree days year-round. Rain falls almost daily, giving the region a yearly average of well over 100 inches of precipitation. The period of heaviest precipitation is from November to April.

Peru has been called a huge outdoor museum. The description is an accurate one, for its history manifests itself to the traveler at every turn. Remarkably, considering the difficulty of the desert, the mountains, and the jungle, Peru has been occupied by humans for thousands of years. And though the Incas were certainly the most spectacular of Peruvian cultures, they were also just the last in a long line of amazing and diverse peoples who adapted themselves to the hard conditions of this land. The remains of these civilizations are densely scattered throughout the country, and more examples of the complexity of Peru's past are discovered every year. Not only will you experience Peru's history at such magnificent spots as the vast desert ruin of Chan-Chan or the lost mountain city of Machu Picchu, but you'll also find wonderful, out-of-the-way sites that you can explore undisturbed by other travelers. You'll even discover bits and pieces of the past—burial towers, old agricultural terraces, sections of stone wall—as you walk the ancient trails of the Andes and realize that most of the treks described in this chapter are along routes centuries old, often predating the Incas.

Culturally, Peru is an exciting mix of the ancient and modern. Though a handful of Spanish conquistadores quickly toppled the Inca government with amazing ease, centuries of effort on the part of Spanish administrators and Catholic priests failed to wipe out the strong culture of the Peruvian highlanders. The resiliant Quechuas simply adapted their folk art, dance, festival, and religious beliefs to incorporate the Spanish and Catholic influence while retaining the essence of their indigenous culture.

For example, the official language of the Inca empire, Quechua, has survived the efforts of colonial administrators to wipe it out, and it is now recognized by the government of Peru as the nation's second official language; nearly 40 percent of the country's population speaks Quechua as their first language. And for today's highlanders, the cycle of the year and the pattern of work and celebration is also very much the same as it was for their Incan forebears. The Catholic calendar of feasts was adapted to fit the Incan solar holidays and the ancient celebrations of *anta-situa* (one of the Inca months), which fell naturally after harvest time in July. Wherever you go in Peru, but particularly in the mountains, you'll find one of the most pervasive reminders of Peru's ancient culture, the wonderful traditional music of the Andes. Characterized by the *kena* (wood flute) and the *charango* (armadillo-shell mandolin), this music will become the soundtrack to your trip. Particularly in the mountains, you'll hear it in every circumstance from the mundane (blaring from tinny speakers in a bus) to the ethereal (hearing, as we once did, a lone *campesino* playing his *kena* as he crossed a high pass).

Lima—Entry City to the Peruvian Andes

If you've never traveled in Latin America before, visiting Lima at the beginning of your trip is rather a crash course in the subject. It is a grim-looking city, shrouded for months of the year by the *garua,* the thick gray fog created by the cold Humbolt current off the Pacific shore. On days when the *garua* is particularly heavy, the city seems strangely isolated, an urban landscape cut off from the rest of the world, a place devoid of any color other than shades of gray.

Lima lacks the colonial charm of Quito with its rustic old-town streets and tree-shaded plazas. Neither does it have the distinctive vista of La Paz, with glaciated Mt. Illumani looming over the city. Lima is big, crowded, noisy, chaotic, and expensive. But it is also fascinating. In our travels through the Andes, we've been in and out of Lima over and over again and have gradually overcome our initial aversion to the city. We've come to like it for its museums, its history, its busy life, its representation of the vitality of Latin American culture.

Lima is a desert city, receiving less than two inches of rainfall annually. And totally rainless years are not an unknown phenomenon here. But the course of the Rimac River as it cuts its way from the nearby mountains through the desert to the coast is a relative oasis. Because of the guaranteed availability of year-round water, the area was a population center long before the Spaniards arrived. The large ceremonial center of Pachacámac outside present-day Lima is only one of the more recent expressions of a very long habitation.

But it was Francisco Pizarro who is credited with founding Peru's capital city in 1535, and his desiccated body in a sense still presides over the city from the glass case in which it remains on view inside the Cathedral. Today's Presidential Palace sits at the site of Pizarro's home, and the 117-block portion of the city that he mapped out is still the capital's heart, the vital business and governmental center of the city and the nation. Though Pizarro's choice of arid locale for the capital may seem unlikely at first glance, it is clear with the benefit of hindsight that his decision was a wise one. The area has the benefits of being only ten miles from the port of Callao on the Pacific coast, making Peru the only Andean nation with a coastal capital. The city also has the benefit of being located on the broad flat alluvial plain of the Rimac River, so in addition to the water supply necessary to support a large population, Pizarro's city is also situated in an area without natural obstructions to growth.

And grow it did, quickly becoming the largest city in the Americas and remaining so through the eighteenth century. In the twentieth century, Lima's growth has been at a breakneck pace, with its population increasing from a half-million residents in 1940 to nearly 6 million today. And this figure is projected to rise to over 10 million by the end of the century. You'll feel the press of these abstract numbers in very concrete terms wherever you go in Lima, whether you're walking the crowded sidewalks of the Colmena, or sitting stuck in a traffic jam with a hundred other cars all blasting their horns, or trying to work your way through a busy side street filled with vendors and market stalls.

Lima's explosive recent growth has spread the city over a nearly thirty-square-mile area, incorporating the old central city with its remnants of colonial glory, the sprawling new suburbs for the growing middle class, the grim *barrios* where indigent newcomers build roofless cardboard huts, and the well-to-do oceanfront community of Miraflores with its shops and restaurants and nightclubs. Lima is thus a capsulized version of Latin America, exhibiting at every turn the problems and the promises that the continent carries into the future.

Your stopover in Lima will probably begin at the newly expanded and very modern Jorge Chavez airport, ten miles from the center of the city. And if you're doing very much air travel in Peru, you can be sure you'll pass through Chavez again and again. As you leave customs, you'll be swamped by taxi drivers reaching for your bags and hotel representatives thrusting price lists and brochures for their hotels into your hands. If you don't already have reservations, you'll be much better off, however, if you go directly to the airport tourist office (near the exit from customs) and have them help you select a hotel and then call to check on room availability before you make your way into the city. The major decision involving hotel selection is whether to stay in the noisy but convenient center of the city or in the much more pleasant but out-of-the-way Miraflores district.

To get into Lima from the airport, you can take a taxi directly to your hotel (fairly expensive, and since Lima taxis have no meters, drivers almost always inflate the fares for incoming passengers not familiar with the usual prices) or if you plan to stay near the center of the city, you can take a *colectivo* (very inexpensive) from just outside the airport's front door to the Colmena (near the Plaza San Martin). There, for a very small fare, you can catch a taxi to your hotel. AeroPeru runs a shuttle between the airport and downtown, but prices are rather high, so if two or more people are traveling together, it costs about the same to take a taxi right to your hotel. To get to Miraflores, either take a taxi or try the Morales Moralitos shuttle bus.

AROUND TOWN

Lima's Plaza de Armas, only a block from the Río Rimac, is as good a place as any to start your tour of the city. Though no longer the center of activity that it once was, the plaza is bordered by the Cathedral, the archbishop's palace and the Presidential Palace, where each noon the changing of the presidential guards is accomplished with considerable ceremony. Lima's Cathedral sits on the spot designated for it by Pizarro when he laid out his plans for the city. The construction of the current structure began in 1746 after the original building (1555) was destroyed in an earthquake. Pizarro's remains (some question their authenticity) are in the first chapel to the right as you enter the Cathedral; at the back of the building is a religious museum.

The Church and Monastery of San Francisco, a block beyond the rear of the Presidential Palace, is also worth a visit. Completed in 1674, the massive construction displays both baroque and Arabic influences. Be sure to visit the catacombs beneath the church.

Near the Plaza de Armas on Ucayali (walk down Carabaya a block and turn left on Ucayali for a block and a half) is the Torre Tagle Palace, one of the finest examples of Colonial Spanish architecture in Latin America. Built in 1735 for the Marqué Torre Tagle, the building is now the home of Peru's Ministry of Foreign Affairs but is open to the public daily.

Across the broad Avenida Abancay from the Plaza de Armas (four blocks along Jiron Junin) is the Plaza Bolivar, location of the Museum of the Inquisition (closed Sundays). Here, from 1569 until 1813, the Court of the Inquisition reigned, passing judgment in the ornately carved courtrooms and inflicting torture in the underground chambers below.

After you've visited Lima's principal historical sights, you'll probably want to take in some of modern Lima. The best way to do this is to walk the five blocks from the Plaza de Armas to the Plaza San Martin along Jiron de la Unión. These five blocks of Unión have been closed off to vehicular traffic, and the area has become a pedestrians-only shopping district. The big, open Plaza San Martin, circled by shops, restaurants, and theaters, is very much the center of modern Lima. As you stand facing it from Jiron de la Unión, the Parque Universitario, the center of long-distance bus transportation, is to your left, only a couple of blocks away on Avenida Nicolas de Pierola. To your right begins the Colmena (also Avenida Nicolas de Pierola, but seldom called that), a busy, modern street lined with some of Lima's best hotels and restaurants.

When the noise and crowds of downtown Lima begin to wear on your nerves, it's time for a visit to the oceanfront district of Miraflores. Though the beach at Miraflores is not particularly appealing, the town itself makes a welcome break from the *centro de Lima.* This fashionable city-in-itself has increasingly over the past few years become the home of some of Lima's most fashionable hotels, restaurants, and shops. While in Miraflores, be sure to walk through the central shopping district, the Avenida Larco, and relax for a while in the Parque de Salizar, which overlooks the Pacific. Miraflores is a rather long taxi ride from central Lima, but those on a tight budget can get there for pennies by taking bus #2 from the Plaza San Martin.

RESOURCES

■ **Hotels** If you want first-class accommodations at first-class prices, the *Sheraton, Bolivar,* and *Crillón* have what you want. Otherwise, the hotel selections listed below begin at a moderate price range and work their way down to the cheapest decent rooms we could find in Lima.

Hotel Maury (Ucayali 201). Located only a block from the Plaza de Armas, the Maury is a nice old hotel, once one of Lima's best. Private baths and hot water, of course. A good restaurant. Good service.

Hotel Wilson (Chancay 639). Though the rooms are small, they have private baths and plenty of hot water. The interior rooms are particularly quiet for a downtown Lima hotel at the price. The Wilson has a very good one-day laundry service and will store luggage. Friendly service, good value.

Hostal Miraflores (Avenida Petit Thouars 5444). If you don't want to stay in downtown Lima, the Hostal Miraflores offers reasonably priced, clean rooms with private baths and hot water. Conveniently located near the center of Miraflores.

Hotel Oriental (Jiron Cuzco 696). This large hotel offers clean rooms with private baths and hot water for a surprisingly low price. The trade-off, though, is that it is a bit inconveniently located in a somewhat rough market district on the far side of Abancay, still only a six-block walk to Jiron de la Unión. Rooms on the front are very noisy.

Hotel Gran (Avenida Abancay 546). Entering this once-fine old place is a bit like stepping back into history; it has a certain shabby, eccentric charm at a very low price. Private baths, some hot water, friendly service, good location, and not too noisy, but a bit on the rough side.

Hotel Europa (Jiron Ancash 376, near San Francisco and the train station). The Europa is Lima's low budget *gringo* hotel, the kind of crossroads for long-term travelers that you'll find in every major town in the Andes. Very inexpensive, reasonably clean. Hot water, perhaps.

■ **Restaurants** If your food budget is fairly high, try some of Lima's better restaurants serving international food along the Colmena, places like *The Chalet Suisse* (Avenida Nicolás Piérola 560) and the *Casa Vasca* (Avenida Nicolás Piérola 734). For a very special and expensive meal, try the *Tambo de Oro* (Belén 1066, not far from San Martin) where you can sample Andean specialties in an elaborately decorated colonial dining room. For steaks, try the *Parrilladas San Martin* on the Plaza San Martin.

For quick meals, lots of snack bars on the Colmena, around San Martin, and along Jiron de la Unión serve sandwiches, hamburgers, etc. Our favorite is *Googeys* on San Martin for huge sandwiches, good ice cream, cakes, and cold drinks. Whether in these snack bars or in one of the many street stalls throughout Lima, try *salchipapas,* a Peruvian fast-food mixture of french fries, sliced sausages, and a variety of sauces ranging from mild to firey.

For good inexpensive meals, branch out from Union and the Colmena to nearby but less fashionable side streets. There you'll find numerous *chifas* serving big plates of Chinese food at surprisingly low prices. By walking just a couple of blocks up Carabaya from San Martin, for example, you'll not only find two good *chifas,* but also a very inexpensive vegetarian restaurant. For an authentic *criollo* meal try *Rosita Rios* at 100 Cajatambo in the Rimac district.

- **Transportation** Offices for the major airlines are located near the Plaza San Martin. The central station for service to La Oroya and Huancayo is behind the Presidential Palace. Most bus transportation centers around the Parque Universitario and surrounding streets.

- **Money Exchange** All the money exchange offices along the Colmena change dollar bills, and most of them cash traveler's checks—with far less difficulty than the Banco de la Nación (across from the Hotel Crillón).

- **Communications** Most of the hotels listed in this section are quite good about helping guests place long-distance international calls either from their room, if it has a phone, or from the lobby. Otherwise, you can make long-distance international calls from the ENTEL office at 347 Bolivia (between San Martin and Plaza Bolognesi).

The most convenient *correo* is a few blocks up the Colmena across the street from the Hotel Crillón. The main post office is near the Plaza de Armas on Jiron Junin.

- **U.S. Embassy and Consulate** Both at 1400 Garcilaso de la Vega.

- **News** An English-language weekly newspaper, the *Lima Times,* is available at most San Martin area newsstands, as are the international editions of *Time* and *Newsweek.*

- **Maps** The *Instituto Geografico Nacional* (1190 Avenida Aramburu in Lima's San Isidro district) is Peru's only outlet for topographic maps. A few years ago, before the *Instituto* changed its name from *Militar* to *Nacional,* entering the grounds was a little unsettling—a fenced compound, machine-gun-armed guards, a general atmosphere of suspicion. But now, buying maps is a much more pleasant business. Though you may still have to show your passport to enter, the guards no longer carry their automatic weapons, and no one acts as if you're there to acquire vital classified information. You merely locate and identify specific quadrangles on a large guide map of Peru hanging on the wall. You can examine these quads in sample books, and if you want to purchase them, give the names and numbers of the maps you want to one of the uniformed attendants. Along with topos, the *Instituto* also sells maps of the departments of Peru and a very good, detailed road map of the country.

■ **Fiestas** Principal fiestas in Lima are the Festival of Kings (January 6), Carnival (February), and Festival of Señor de los Milagros (October 18–28).

■ **Books** The *ABC Bookstore* at 689 Avenida N. Piérola sells a limited number of English-language books and magazines. But for a much better selection, try the *Book Exchange* at 211a Ocoña, just a block off San Martin, where you'll find a whole room full of used paperbacks.

■ **Movies** There are nearly a dozen *cines* in the vicinity of San Martin, most of them showing recent American movies in the original English with Spanish subtitles. Tickets are very cheap.

■ **Crafts** Though you'll be much better off buying crafts when you visit the regions in which they are produced, inveterate shoppers may want to have a look at some of the several downtown and suburban Lima shops that sell handcrafts at fairly reasonable prices. There are numerous craft shops along the Colmena, but for better-quality articles, walk down Calle Belén toward the Sheraton; several shops along the way carry excellent examples of carvings, textiles, silverwork, etc. The government-run EPPA shops (610 Avenida Orrantia, San Isidro; 305 Avenida Benavides, Miraflores; 1065 Calle Belén, downtown) also offer a wide selection of quality native handcrafts.

■ **Tourist Information** American Express business (lost or stolen traveler's checks, mail pickup, etc.) is handled by *Lima Tours,* 160 Ocoña. *Enturperu,* which handles reservations for Peru's State Tourist Hotels (including the wonderful Hotel Machu Picchu), is on the Plaza San Martin. The *Dirección General de Turismo,* which has brochures, maps, posters, etc., is near the Tambo de Oro restaurant at 1066 Belén.

■ **Museums** Perhaps the best museum in the Andean countries is the *National Museum of Anthropology and Archaeology.* Located on the Plaza Bolivar in the Pueblo Libre section of Lima (not the same Plaza Bolivar as the Museum of the Inquisition), this museum is devoted to the study of Peru's many pre-Columbian cultures. It serves as a wonderful corrective to those who think of the Inca empire as the *only* native Peruvian civilization. Here you'll find the relics (especially fine textiles) of the ancient and little-known coastal desert peoples— the Paracas, Chimu, Nazca, and Mochica cultures. And you'll find as well the work of the highland Chavin and Tiahuanaco cultures. Though located a long taxi ride from Lima's center, the museum is not to be missed for those interested in understanding the long history of human life in Peru. Closed Mondays.

Also well worth a visit is the *Gold Museum,* which, as its name implies, houses a fine collection of gold relics from the Inca empire as well as from most of the other pre-Columbian cultures of Peru. The extensive collection consists of mostly smaller pieces that somehow escaped the pillaging of the Spanish conquistadores, but from them you do get a clear idea of both the material and artistic wealth looted from Peru. The museum also houses a collection of weapons. The main museum (privately owned) is located in Monterrico, a long taxi ride from central Lima, but a good portion of the museum's holdings have been moved recently to the Gran Hotel Bolivar, just off the Plaza San Martin on the Colmena.

The *Larco Herrera Archeological Museum* houses a fine private collection of pottery and weaving, particularly of the Chavin, Chimu, Mochica, and Nazca cultures. Perhaps the most unusual feature of the Herrera Museum is its extensive collection of erotic pottery. It is near the National Museum at Avenida Bolivar 1115 in Pueblo Libre. Closed Sundays.

For those without the time to visit the National Museum, the *Museum of Art* provides a convenient survey of Peru's long cultural history. Exhibitions include everything from ancient Chavin pottery and fine Paracas weavings to colonial furnishings and the paintings of the Cuzco school. The museum's holdings also include Inca mummies. The Museum of Art is located an easy walk from the Plaza San Martin at Paseo Colon 125, down from the Sheraton Hotel. Closed Mondays.

Pachacámac

The extensive ruins of the ceremonial center of Pachacámac (the name of the ancient god to which the site was devoted) make an excellent and quite inexpensive half-day trip from Lima. Located in the Lurin valley, twenty miles south of the city, Pachacámac is most famous for its great temple pyramid, constructed in the fourteenth century. However, the site was in use long before the Incas by the Cuismancu people, the culture native to the area. Archaeological studies indicate that Pachacámac may have attracted worshippers for as much as 2,000 years. The ancient religious tradition of the ceremonial center was so strong that when the Incas conquered the coastal region, they wisely recognized the powerful hold the god Pachacámac held over the Cuismancu and allowed them to continue worshipping him, simply adding worship of the sun to the preexisting ceremonies. So Pachacámac remained throughout the Inca period an important religious center, attracting pilgrims from all over Peru.

What remains of this sacred city, once inhabited by 30,000 people, is an extensive sun-blasted ruin. The main temple, a massive adobe pyramid, covers almost twelve acres. Other temples include the Inca Temple of the Sun and the recently restored Temple of the Virgins of the Sun near the entrance to the ruins. Just as interesting, though, are the remains of the city where crumbling adobe walls mark the locations of ancient houses, streets, and plazas.

Getting to Pachacámac is a simple matter, and if you take the bus rather than a taxi, the whole trip, including admission to the ruins, can be done for just a few dollars. Microbuses, which pass by Pachacámac at km 31 of the Pan-American highway, leave Lima from the corner of Jiron Puno and Andahuaylas (near the Parque Universitario). Let the driver know your destination so he'll be sure to stop at km 31. The ruins are closed on Mondays.

Marcawasi

If you tire of Lima's traffic, noise, and *garua,* a wonderful overnight excursion that really qualifies as a short trek is the trip to the strange prehistoric site of Marcawasi. Located fifty miles east of Lima in the foothills of the Andes on a plateau above the little town of San Pedro de Casta, Marcawasi is not really a ruin; it is rather a ceremonial ground distinguished by its mysterious collection of carved stones and lines. Much of the mystery of Marcawasi involves the question of exactly who made use of it and when. The site is apparently quite ancient, and its age may perhaps be more accurately measured in thousands rather than hundreds of years. To compound the puzzle, the style of some of the artwork is quite unlike typical New World patterns.

Aside from these historical and archaeological questions, much of the site's mystery resides in the stones themselves. Some students of the site claim that the carvings were quite carefully designed to change appearance depending on the angle of sunlight striking them; as the shadows cast on the stones shift, the image undergoes a metamorphosis. Some carvings, these people say, make several transformations in the course of a day, and some perhaps transmogrify much more slowly, depending on the changing angle of the sun in the course of a year. For example, the massive *Cabeza de Humanidad* (head of mankind) allegedly begins the day as a child and ends it as an old man; as it ages, it also changes racial characteristics (if true, this is a mystery in itself since it is difficult to imagine how these ancient people could have been familiar with the physical characteristics of people from other continents).

Though we found some of these claims a little far-fetched, Marcawasi is, nevertheless, a place of considerable enigma, a little-known, isolated spot where you can speculate to your heart's content on the complex workings of the so-called "primitive" mind. And on a clear day Marcawasi is also a place of considerable beauty, sitting as it does on a plateau within sight of both the Andes and the Pacific. The site makes a wonderful campsite, and you'll almost assuredly have the place to yourself.

To get to Marcawasi, you must go to Chosica by either a *colectivo* or one of the regular Lima-Chosica microbuses (both leave from near Parque Universitario; a few buses go on to Santa Eualaia, and these are more convenient if you can find one). Chosica, a pleasant old resort town just far enough above sea level to avoid the coastal fog, was once a favorite spot for Lima's elite, and it still retains a certain measure of time-worn charm. Here you can catch frequent microbuses to nearby Santa Eulalia, situated in the lovely valley of the same name. At Santa Eulalia, wait for a truck going either to San Pedro de Casta or Cruce (only a mile or so below San Pedro).

In San Pedro de Casta, the trail to Marcawasi begins near the cemetery; allow a couple of hours for the climb. If you plan to camp at Marcawasi (it's difficult to make this trip in one day), you'll need to make arrangements to carry adequate water to the site; there is none in the vicinity. We had no trouble finding gallon plastic bottles for this purpose in Lima. In San Pedro de Casta, you may want to hire an *arriero* to help haul your pack and heavy water bottles up to the site. Be sure not to leave your empty water bottles at the site.

INTO THE INTERIOR
ON THE TREN DE LA SIERRA

The 260-mile train trip on Peru's central railway line from Lima to Huancayo is an adventure in itself. And it is also something of an international engineering marvel. Built throughout the latter decades of the nineteenth century, primarily by Chinese labor, the route was planned by an American, Henry Miggs, and a Peruvian, Ernesto Malinowski. It passes through some of the most difficult topography imaginable, and its construction necessitated the building of sixty-one bridges and sixty-five tunnels. More significant, though, is the fact that the Lima-Huancayo line is the highest railway in the world. When it crosses the Andes at Ticlio Pass through the Galera Tunnel, the line's altitude is only a little short of the 16,000-foot mark, and white-jacketed stewards with bottled oxygen circulate about the cars for those suffering from the effects of the thin air (read Paul Theroux's account of this trip in *The Old Patagonia Express* for a vivid description of how unpleasant sudden elevation gain can be for the unacclimatized). As the train works its way into the mountains, the scenery that unfolds outside the windows is unsurpassed. You cross deep canyons and pass through quiet valleys, and as you switchback into the Andes, the mountains tower around you. For rail buffs as well as anyone who values grand scenery, the central railway is definitely one of the great train journeys of the world.

The eight-to-ten-hour trip to Huancayo begins at Lima's Desamparados Station (a rather ominous beginning since in Spanish *desamparados* means "the abandoned"), on the banks of the Rio Rimac. The train departs Monday through Saturday at 7:40 A.M. First-class and buffet car tickets can be bought one day in advance (we've found the small extra charge for buffet tickets to be money well spent on this and all other Andean trains providing the service). Though it may be warm in Lima, you'll want to be sure to keep a jacket out of your luggage for the crossing of the cold pass.

If the day is clear, as the train moves east across the narrow coastal plain, you'll see the mountains ahead of you looking high and impenetrable. But the train begins its climb into them through a narrow canyon beyond the town of Chosica. Overshadowed by high cliffs, the train climbs steadily into the Andes, often through switchbacks. Finally, at about a hundred slow miles into the trip, the line reaches its highest point at Ticlio and the Galera Tunnel. Beyond Galera, the

Andes open up, spreading across the horizon and into the far distance. The train stops at Oroya and Jauja (for a brief time Pizarro's capital city, 178 miles into the trip) and works its way through the heavily populated Mantaro valley before reaching Huancayo.

Most travelers schedule their trip to Huancayo (10,700 feet) for Saturday in order to be able to take in the large Sunday market. *Campesinos* from throughout the Mantaro valley flood Huancayo on market day, bringing with them their handcrafts. Huancayo's market is Peru's largest and arguably its best, offering almost any Andean handcraft item you can think of. It is an especially good place to buy blankets, ponchos, and other woven articles. Lots of tourists come to the Huancayo market, so don't expect astounding bargains.

Huancayo's best hotel is the moderately priced, state-operated *Turista* (Plaza Huananmarca) with private baths and hot water (if you plan to stay at the Turista on Saturday night before the market, you should make reservations ahead of time at the Enturperu office in Lima). A step down in price is the *Kiya* (Plaza de Armas) with private baths and hot water. For those on a tight budget, the *Hotel Prince* (578 Calixto) offers clean rooms and some hot water.

The restaurant in the Turista serves good meals, as is typical of the restaurants in almost all of the Enturperu hotels we've tried. The *Olimpico* at the Plaza de Armas is also worth a stop. For Chinese food, try *La Gran Chifa* (Plaza de Armas) or the *Chifa Porvenir* (Jiron Real).

After attending the Sunday market, most visitors to Huancayo return to Lima on the Tren de la Sierra, departing at 7 A.M. Monday through Saturday. However, some travelers may want to try to go to Cuzco from Huancayo without returning to Lima. Though the trip is certainly possible, it is very difficult. The road south through the mountains is a rough one, frequently disrupted by slides and washouts. And commercial transportation on this route is often filled well ahead of departure time. Several bus lines in Huancayo do make the two-day trip all the way to Cuzco (even longer if road conditions are bad). Alternatively, it is also possible to go overland south to Ayacucho by bus or *colectivo* (twelve to fifteen hours) and then take AeroPeru's daily Ayacucho-Cuzco flight (usually full, so book ahead in Lima and reconfirm as soon as you get to Ayacucho). For a grueling but evidently spectacular trip, you can go to Cuzco by truck (about three days; for hardcore road-trippers only).

THE NORTH-COAST ROUTE

The dry land of Peru's north coast looks bone hard and virtually changeless, but it is in reality a fragile place, easily disrupted by fluctuations in climate. Life there is a delicate business. Because the people of the north coast live primarily by farming the fertile river valleys and fishing the cold waters of the Humbolt current offshore, they are thus dependent on a very narrow range of climactic conditions. But the north coast is a place of sometimes severe climactic variation, susceptible to both prolonged drought and abnormally heavy rain. In the early years of this century, for example, the Trujillo area experienced nearly a decade of drought, receiving less than two inches of rain over an eight-year period. Conversely, every few years the patterns of the ocean currents shift, forcing warmer water over the surface of the Pacific to cover the Humbolt current. Because this usually happens near Christmas time, the conditions associated with the shifts in ocean currents is called *El Niño,* the child. The warmer offshore water that El Niño brings both kills and drives away the normally dense fish populations, and the reduction in catch can virtually shut down the economically important fishing industry. At the same time, the unusually warm air offshore changes precipitation patterns, bringing extraordinarily heavy rains to the coastline and the nearby highlands. The resulting flooding often severely affects crop growth and disrupts transportation due to landslides and washed-out bridges. For thousands of years, though, people have somehow managed not only to survive but actually to flourish in this harsh and unpredictable environment.

Here the conquistadores made their first explorations of Peru in search of gold, and everywhere they turned they found evidence of long habitation. They scoured the desert for a civilization they had heard called Viru (one possibility for the origin of the name "Peru"), but they found instead the Incas. And in the process of capturing and ransoming Atahualpa, the Spanish explored vast regions of the north coast and the nearby mountains, even traveling into the Cordillera Blanca as early as 1533. The chronicles these original travelers wrote about their explorations are filled with passages suggesting their genuine amazement at both the overwhelming beauty and difficulty of this region.

Unlikely as it may seem at first glance, this barren north coast with its adjacent mountains is also a fascinating destination for the modern traveler, and it is still relatively uncrowded by tourists. Most first-time visitors to Peru still set their travel sights farther south—to the Cuzco and Machu Picchu region. Considerably smaller numbers of travelers work their way up the north coast and into the mountains just to the east, but for those willing to savor less familiar and celebrated travel experiences, the northern route has much to offer. There is first the desert coast, a barren land dotted with the strange, crumbling ruins of massive temples and powerful ancient cities predating the Incas. As for mountains, the Cordillera Blanca, less than fifty miles inland from the coast as the condor flies, is a trekker's dream, with peak after peak rising above 20,000 feet and hundreds of miles of trails. Further north is Cajamarca, the attractive highland town where Pizarro captured and executed Atahualpa, the beginning of the end of the Inca empire.

The Cordillera Blanca

With some of the most magnificent high alpine landscape anywhere in the world, Peru's Cordillera Blanca (White Mountains) offers what many hikers consider to be South America's finest trekking area. To talk about the Blanca is, of necessity, to indulge in superlatives. Only fifty air miles from the Pacific Ocean, the peaks of the *cordillera* soar far into the sky, forming the highest tropical mountain range in the world. In an amazingly compact area (a little over 100 miles long but only about fifteen miles wide), more than two dozen peaks exceed 19,500 feet, and another two dozen or so exceed 18,500 feet. The range also includes Peru's highest mountain. Huascarán, at 22,205 feet, rises almost a mile and a half higher than California's Mt. Whitney. The many dazzling glaciers that continue to carve the mountains and give the Blanca its name constitute the highest concentration of glaciers in the world's tropics. Too, these mountains offer one of the last places of refuge for such distinctive Andean wildlife as the spectacled bear and the giant condor.

Yet the Cordillera Blanca is relatively accessible to trekkers. Located only 215 miles north of Lima on an all-paved road, the range can be reached in eight hours by bus. It is crisscrossed by several hundred miles of trails, most of them climbing the long, lovely *quebradas* between mountains to cross high passes. But with a permanent snowline above 17,000 feet, nearly all of these passes remain unglaciated. For the trekker on a relatively short trip to the Andes, the

Laguna Paron and Piramide de Garcilaso, Cordillera Blanca, Peru

Blanca is also accessible in terms of time. There are several interesting trekking routes (e.g., the Olleros-Chavín walk) that take conditioned hikers only a few days to complete. The Blanca does, however, have plenty to offer those with more time; the Grand Tour of the Cordillera Blanca route described later in this section is a spectacular two-week circuit through a large portion of the range.

Primary access to the Cordillera Blanca is through the Callejón de Huaylas, a beautiful twenty-five-mile-wide valley bounded on the east by the Blanca and on the west by the Cordillera Negra, an unglaciated, black volcanic rock range with a 15,000-foot ridge line. The Río Santa, largest of Peru's coastal rivers, flows north through the valley. The Callejón is a wonderful, light-filled valley of rich farm and grazing land, and the two-hour ride through it is not to be missed (if on a bus, sit on the east side for the best views of the mountains). As you move through the Callejón de Huaylas, the entire Cordillera Blanca spreads itself out for you in one grand panorama after another. In fact, many of the views from the valley of the range's major peaks, particularly Huascarán, rival those seen from the trails.

The inhabitants of the Callejón and the Blanca are primarily *mestizo* (mixed blood), so the existing culture is not as heavily influenced by the Inca past as it is further south in the Cordilleras Vilcabamba and Vilcanota. Though you'll see fewer *campesinos* wearing traditional dress, the people are friendly, and the trails, all of them used by locals, will take you past their homes and villages, giving you close-up views of day-to-day life in the high mountains.

The principal towns of the Callejón de Huaylas are (from south to north) Catac, Recuay, Huarás, Carhuáz, Yungay, and Carás. Except for Carás, these towns are all rather stark, consisting primarily of hastily constructed concrete buildings. You'll find little colonial charm here. This is understandable considering that the towns of the Callejón have been hit hard by devastating natural disasters twice in the past half-century. In 1941 *Laguna Palcacoche* broke through its moraine and swept away a third of Huarás, killing more than 5,000 of its inhabitants. The town was reconstructed, but the disaster was only a grim dress rehearsal for a much more widespread tragedy.

Peru is part of the great earthquake belt that follows the border between land masses and the Pacific Ocean from Tierra del Fuego to Alaska. In 1970 a powerful earthquake with its epicenter just off the coast of Peru devastated most of the towns and villages throughout the Callejón de Huaylas. Little of Huarás was left standing; its adobe buildings were shaken to rubble. Throughout the valley, more than 80,000 people were killed, and many more thousands were left injured and homeless. Though none of the valley towns was without substantial damage, the most awesome forces were loosed on Yungay, a little village just beneath Huascarán that many people considered to be one of the most beautiful in Peru. During the quake, a massive slab of rock and ice a half-mile wide was shaken from the face of Huascarán's north peak. The original mass broken from the mountain was estimated at 35 million cubic feet of rock and ice, and it moved down the 70-degree slope, accumulating more material as it fell, at speeds of as much as 200 miles per hour. At that velocity, the mass simply jumped a hill that had been thought to protect Yungay from slides from Huascarán. The entire town and almost all of its inhabitants were completely buried.

The town of Carás to the north, though hard-hit too, sustained the least damage, and today it is the only town in the valley retaining much of its pre-1970 appearance. Though the extent of the quake's damage is probably unimaginable to those who did not directly experience it, it is possible to get something of an idea of what was lost. In Huarás's hotels and restaurants today, you'll see faded photographs of the lovely old town with its cathedral, red-tile-roofed houses, and palm-shaded plaza. Sadly, when you look about you, the only similarity between the town in those photographs and the new Huarás is the background view of the great glaciated peaks of the Cordillera Blanca.

Huascarán National Park

Peru is one of Latin America's leaders in the area of conservation of natural resources and wildlife. Under the general administrative blanket of the *Sistema Nacional de Unidades de Conservacion* (SNUC), established in 1972, several national parks, wildlife reserves, and historical sanctuaries (e.g., the Inca Trail) have been established. The *Parque Nacional Huascarán* is part of this system, and its existence is the result of years of work by Peruvians and others concerned with the protection of this remarkable mountain range. The park was established in 1975, and its boundaries include not only the area immediately around Huascarán but also all of the Cordillera Blanca above 13,000 feet.

The stated efforts of the park staff are directed primarily at protecting the plants, animals, geology, and archaeology of the Cordillera Blanca; promoting and controlling tourism in the park; encouraging scientific study of natural resources; and improving the living conditions of the mountain people of the park's high *cordillera*. Though the staff is small, their work is having measurable positive effects in limiting the impact of the growing numbers of hikers who visit the park. One of the most visible recent changes is the establishment of group campsites on some of the more popular routes. These help concentrate and control the inevitable damage of campfire scars, improper waste disposal, etc., that comes with increased visitation. When establishment of these campsites throughout the park is completed, camping outside designated areas may be prohibited. So check with park headquarters in Huarás for current camping regulations.

Regulations governing visitors to Huascarán National Park are similar to those at national parks in the United States. Visitors are prohibited from removing plants or animals from the park, cutting trees or making fires with branches from live trees, hunting or carrying firearms, fishing during the trout spawning season (May to October), feeding wildlife, and destroying animal habitat, natural resources, or park signs.

Visitors to the park are required to register before entering. This can be done at park headquarters in Huarás. The office is on the outskirts of town; walk east on Avenida Raymondi beyond where the paving ends and look for the office on the right. If you are entering the park at Lagunas Llanganuco, Laguna Querococha, or Carpa, you may register at separate control stations near those locations. Along with registering, you will have to pay a small daily fee for using the park. Though some visitors grumble loudly and try to avoid paying this minimal fee, remember that since visitors are the chief users of the park, it seems fair that they help pay for its protection. Be sure to retain your entry pass; you may have to show it at control stations.

MAPS OF THE CORDILLERA BLANCA

Especially if you plan to travel off the more popular routes, you may wish to carry more detailed maps of the Cordillera Blanca than those provided in this chapter. Maps of the Blanca can be obtained from the following sources.

The *Instituto Geografico Nacional* (I.G.N.) (Avenida Aramburu 1190, in the San Isidro section of Lima) has 1:100,000 scale topos covering the entire Cordillera Blanca. Quads covering the range are 18–h (Corongo), 19–h (Carhuáz), 19–i (Huari), 20–i (Recuay), and 18–i (Pomabamba). A word of caution: trail locations on these maps are not 100 percent accurate.

INGEMMET (*Instituto Geologico Minero y Metalurgico*, Avenida Guzman Barron 528, Huarás) sells 1:100,000 scale dyeline maps of the Cordillera Blanca. Trail locations are more accurate than on the I.G.N. topos, but the dyeline maps are harder to read than colored topos.

The South American Explorers Club (Avenida Portugal 146, Lima) offers maps covering specific treks in the Cordillera Blanca, and they sometimes have some I.G.N. maps. Try calling first to see what's in stock (31–44–80); you might save yourself a hectic cross-Lima taxi ride if they don't have what you need in stock.

GETTING TO THE CORDILLERA BLANCA

Though an airport has been built at Anta, a few miles north of Huarás, flights are, to say the least, unpredictable. For a few years, AeroPeru scheduled three flights per week between Lima and Anta, though these were often canceled. In 1982, Lima-Anta commercial flights ceased altogether for an indefinite period of time. AeroPeru tells us, however, that the route may be reopened in the future, so check with a travel agent or with AeroPeru's office in Lima *(Plaza San Martin).*

Most likely, you'll travel to the Cordillera Blanca by bus, following the Pan-American highway along the coast before turning inland at Pativilca and beginning the long climb into the mountains. Several companies cover the eight-hour Lima-Huarás route, most of them leaving from stations near Lima's *Parque Universitario* (a few blocks southeast of the *Plaza San Martin* on the *Colmena*). Prices are nearly identical from company to company, but *Transportes Rodriquez* (Roosevelt 354, Lima; Tarapaca 422, Huarás) and *Expreso Ancash* (Avenida Carlos Zavala 145, Lima; Fitzcarrald 125, Huarás) maintain reasonably modern buses and provide fairly reliable service. Most companies have two daily departures between Lima and Huarás and vice versa, usually leaving in each direction at approximately 9:30 A.M. and 9:30 P.M. Afternoon departures are also possible; check with bus companies.

Another way to get to Huarás from Lima is by *colectivo* taxi. These normally cost about double the price of a bus ticket, but they shave a couple of hours off the trip. *Colectivos* also depart from near the *Parque Universitario*. *Comités* 11 (Leticia 587) and 14 (Leticia 630) make the trip daily. *Colectivos* traveling from Huarás to Lima may be found in Huarás near the intersection of Fitzcarrald and Raymondi.

If you're traveling to the Cordillera Blanca from northern Peru, *Transportes Chinchay-Suyo* (720 Jiron Bolivar, Trujillo) operates nightly buses from Trujillo to Huarás, taking about ten hours for the trip down the coast and up into the mountains on the Pativilca route.

Finally, an unusual way to get to the Cordillera Blanca that turns a bus ride into something of an adventure is to make the trip from Chimbote on the coast to Carás at the northern end of the Callejón de Huaylas. This all-day trip climbs on a very rough dirt road that winds its way through the deep Cañon del Pato of the Río Santa, and it is, to our minds, the quintessential hair-raising, gut-wrenching Andean bus ride. The buses that travel this route are hardly confidence-inspiring. They are cramped, crowded, and ancient, and their suspensions have been beaten to uselessness by years of pounding over the rutted roads. In these vehicles, you'll cross rickety wooden bridges and ford the river where these bridges have collapsed; you'll pick your way across recent landslides and pass through several tunnels, skirting several others that have fallen in. And to cap off the day, you'll climb into the Callejón de Huaylas through a series of switchbacks on a road narrow enough to leave you looking straight down through a few thousand feet of empty space when you're unlucky enough to be on the outside of a turn. *Transportes Morenos* buses (Avenida Pardo 758, Chimbote) allegedly leave Chimbote daily at 6:30 A.M. and 8 P.M., though in our experience this schedule is, let's say, rather hopeful. If you're going to do this trip, be sure and take the morning bus so you won't miss the spectacular scenery. Take along some snacks, a full water bottle, and your bandanna to cover your mouth when dust blows through the windows. And you might want to consider covering your pack with a plastic garbage bag; luggage rides on the top of the bus and becomes absolutely saturated with fine, powdery dust.

HUARÁS—RESOURCES

Despite its violent past and its grim modern appearance, Huarás is very much alive. It is the capital of the Department of Ancash (*ancash* is the Quechua word for "blue") and the focus of activity for the Callejón de Huaylas. It is also the trekking and climbing center of

Peru. Between May and September, Huarás usually has a healthy complement of foreigners in transit either to or from the mountains. And with at least twenty-five hotels and about as many restaurants, Huarás is equipped to take care of them all.

■ **Hotels**   The most pleasant hotel in Huarás is not really *in* Huarás; the *Monterey* with its beautiful surroundings and thermal pools is located a little more than four miles north of town but is easily reached by local bus. The Monterey is a great spot for a peaceful rest after a long trek. In town, the *Turista* (Avenida Centenario) and the *Andino* (Pedro Cochachin 357) provide relatively expensive lodgings. Hotels a step down in price include the *Tumi* (private baths, some hot water, clean, friendly, some rooms with mountain-view balconies, good value; on San Martin) and the *Pacifico* (private baths but scant hot water, can be noisy; on Luzuriaga). For budget-minded travelers the *Barcelona* (Avenida Raymondi 612), the *Raymondi* (Avenida Raymondi 820), and the *Edwards* (basic but clean and very friendly, hot shower available; on Avenida Bolognesi) are all worth a look.

■ **Restaurants**   Several restaurants are located near the intersection of Fitzcarrald and Raymondi. The *Tabariz* and *Ebony 76* offer good, clean, reasonably priced food, particularly the various *saltados* they both make. Also near this intersection is the *Chifa Familiar,* which offers quite good Chinese food. Across the bridge past the market is the *Pio Pio* (Centenario 329) recommended for its fish dishes and reasonable prices. Numerous smaller restaurants along Luzuriaga offer good, filling, cheap meals—with more authentic creole cooking than the larger restaurants.

■ **Transportation Through the Callejón de Huaylas**   Crowded half-sized buses travel north on the Huarás-Carhuáz-Yungay-Carás route (they'll have these names painted on their sides) from 6 A.M. to 6 P.M. daily. In theory, departures are scheduled every half-hour, but in practice there is seldom a time during the day when there isn't a bus ready to leave on this route because before leaving the buses shuttle back and forth through town until they have a full load. Catch these north-bound buses either at the corner of Raymondi and Fitzcarrald or on Fitzcarrald near the bridge at the market. Huarás to Carás is a two-to-three-hour trip on these buses.

The larger bus companies such as *Transportes Ancash* also travel this route with regular-sized buses as part of their Carás-Lima service. These buses are much faster (ninety minutes from Huarás to Carás) and much more comfortable, though they travel much less frequently than the smaller Callejón de Huaylas buses.

Similar buses travel south on the Huarás-Recuay-Catac route (again, names on the sides) frequently throughout the day from the market area.

Passenger-carrying trucks also travel the Callejón de Huaylas road. These too leave from the market, usually early in the morning and at midday, but check beforehand on departures since their schedules are, to say the least, not particularly rigid.

■ **Mountain Transportation**   One very welcome addition to travel services in Huarás is Paraih Tours (on Luzuriaga). Besides organizing sightseeing tours, treks, climbing expeditions, renting some equipment, and arranging for guides, the most useful service they provide is transportation into the mountains. Getting to trailheads in the Cordillera Blanca can be time-consuming, frustrating, and uncertain if you depend on local transport, but Paraih Tours will arrange truck transportation from your hotel to virtually any trailhead in the *cordillera* for reasonable fees. They have fixed rates for the more popular destinations —charged by the vehicle, not by the person—so you'll save money if you can get a group together to make the trip. Though this service is considerably more expensive than taking public transport, it will get you from Huarás to the trailhead and ready to hike *much* more quickly, an important consideration if your time is limited.

More detailed information on transportation to specific trailheads is included in applicable trail description sections.

■ **Communications** The post office is across from the Plaza de Armas on Luzuriaga. Huarás's unusually efficient ENTEL office for international communications is located at 1001 San Martin.

■ **Money Exchange** *Banco de los Andes* (on Fitzcarrald) and *Banco de la Nación* (behind the new cathedral) cash traveler's checks with a minimum of difficulty. Hotels in Huarás are also becoming more accustomed to dealing with traveler's checks.

■ **Trekking Equipment and Supplies** Huarás is probably the only small town in the Andes where you can find almost anything you need in the way of camping equipment. Several shops and touring agencies, mostly along Luzuriaga, sell or rent equipment. *Pepe's* at the Hotel Raymondi (look for his signboard on the sidewalk) serves as a clearing house for hikers and climbers (as well as a cheap, mattresses-only sleeping place) and is a good spot to try if you need to replace or add to your camping gear. As usual, Bleuet camping gas cartridges are easy to find, as is kerosene. White gas is another story. Though the hardware stores and pharmacies in Huarás sometimes carry *bencina* (white gas), we've had little luck in catching them when they have it in stock.

Pepe's often sells dried backpacking foods. Otherwise, there are several *bodegas* in Huarás, all with similar selections of food—Knorr dried soups, rice, dried beans, pasta, tuna, chocolate, crackers, and expensive canned goods. The two stores on Raymondi near Fitzcarrald are the most convenient. Fresh-baked bread is readily available from vendors who spread their goods on plastic sheets on the sidewalk along Fitzcarrald and in the market.

■ **Arrieros** If you'd rather see the mountains without the burden of a heavy pack, horse or mule drivers are available for most routes in the Cordillera Blanca, and if you ask around, they can be found in most of the towns of the Callejón de Huaylas near trailheads. The simplest place to find *arrieros* is in Huarás where they congregate outside the National Park headquarters. You'll need to make arrangements with them a couple of days in advance of your trek in order for them to be able to get the animals to the trailhead to meet you. Before you hire an *arriero,* be sure to check with park headquarters to find the current daily rate for their services; this standard rate is usually not negotiable, but the speed with which the trek is carried out is. In the Cordillera Blanca, the practice is that trekkers are responsible for providing meals for their *arrieros.*

■ **Museum** The *Museo Regional de Ancash* (near the Plaza de Armas) contains some interesting pre-Inca stone carvings. Open Tuesday through Friday.

■ **Tourist Information** There are two offices, one at Luzuriaga 459, and another at the corner of Fitzcarrald and Raymondi. Basic maps of the area and tourist information are available, but don't count on English being spoken.

Puya Raimondi Park

If you are in the Cordillera Blanca in April or May, make every effort to see the flowering of the amazing *puya raimondi* plants. These are a type of large bromeliad that grows only in the Andes. Each plant flowers only once at the end of its one-hundred-year life, and when it does, the results are both unique and spectacular. The *puya raimondi* has the world's tallest flower stalk, up to thirty feet high. And on each stalk bloom literally thousands of blossoms. These rare plants are now protected in the Puya Raimondi Park in the Carpa sector of Huascarán National Park. Before making the trip, though, check with park headquarters in Huarás to make sure the *puya* are in bloom.

The simplest way to reach Puya Raimondi Park is to take one of the day trips offered by commercial tourist agencies in Huarás. Paraih Tours offers such a trip, as do all of the tourist agencies along Luzuriaga, so making arrangements for this trip is quite easy. Alternatively, you can arrange your own trip and have a larger voice in planning the excursion by hiring a taxi (not too expensive if you have four or five people sharing the cost). The trip takes two to three hours each way.

For a much cheaper, more exciting, but more uncertain and difficult trip to the *puya,* take a bus south from Huarás to a point about six miles south of Catac (look for the National Park's *Carpa* sign). Wait there for a truck going up the dirt road along the *Río Pachacoto.* Puya Raimondi is about ten miles up this road.

Chavín de Huantar

Whether you walk there on the Olleros-Chavín trek or go by bus, the visit to the remote pre-Inca Chavín de Huantar site is worth the long, hard trip. The ceremonial complex there was built around 500 B.C. and was evidently a religious and artistic center for the Chavín culture, earliest of the higher cultures in Peru. The Chavíns (probably a widespread religious and artistic influence rather than a political force) developed an art style centered around renderings of the puma or jaguar, and though many of the relics and carvings are now in museums in Huarás and Lima, the remaining stone carving around the main temple, the Castillo, is in fine condition, and the work is of excellent quality.

Since the area around the site appears not to be well suited to supporting a large population, some archaeologists speculate that Chavín may have been a pilgrimage destination for inhabitants of the more densely populated coastal oases. Two and a half millennia ago, these people would have made the long walk across the Cordillera Blanca after harvests and may have spent their time at Chavín both worshipping and working to build the grand buildings. Despite the natural forces of time and earthquakes, their work is remarkably well preserved —and remarkably sophisticated.

The Castillo, for example, is a considerable architectural achievement. The building is immense, nearly 250 feet square, and its three-story height was never matched, even by the Incas. Inside, the Castillo is full of windowless rooms, most of them filled now with rubble and unenterable, but still connected by an elaborate, carefully planned ventilation system. The elaborate system of underground passageways associated with the Castillo has been extensively damaged by earthquakes, but nonclaustraphobic visitors may still squeeze through some of the upper levels, accessible through a tunnel near the front of the Castillo. Take a flashlight if you want to go into the passageways. (It's always a good idea to carry one in any case; friends of ours once made this trip and had to use their little AA-battery flashlights to lead their

Campesinos threshing grain near Chavín, Cordillera Blanca, Peru

bus without headlights through a long, dark tunnel on the way back from the ruins.) To the side of the main temple are broader passageways (ask the site attendant to turn on the lights if you're not with a tour group). Here, at the intersection of crossing passageways, was discovered the large monolithic dagger stone, the *Lanzón*. The original stone is now in Lima; however, a full-sized replica effectively occupies its place.

Chavín encompasses a fairly extensive group of plazas, terraces, and mounds. And since Chavín is seldom crowded, you'll be able to examine them without the distraction of too many fellow travelers.

If you aren't doing the Olleros-Chavín trek, you can get to the ruins on regularly scheduled *Cóndor de Chavín* buses. But to make the ten-to-twelve-hour round-trip in one day, arrange a tour with one of the agencies in Huarás. They'll pick you up at your hotel early in the morning and have you back in time for dinner. However you go, expect cold temperatures along the way and take a warm jacket.

The road to Chavín leaves the main Callejón de Huaylas road at Catac and travels east, providing excellent views of the mountains of the southern sections of the *cordillera,* Yanamarey and Huantsan especially. Before crossing a high pass through *Tunel Cahuish,* the road passes Laguna Querococha, a high, cold glacier-fed lake in which there are wonderful trout. If you tell the friendly owners of the rough, dirt-floored, thatch-roofed restaurant just above the lake approximately when you'll be returning from the ruins, they'll catch some trout and have them ready for you when you get back. On a particularly cold evening, amid blowing snow, we had an excellent lamp-lit meal there.

Willcawain

If you arrive in Huarás (9,845 feet) from lower altitudes, your body will need a day or two to adapt itself to the change before you are ready to go into the high mountains. A good conditioning walk from Huarás is the 9.5 mile round-trip to the Willcawain ruins, a well-preserved Tiahuanaco temple dated at about A.D. 1000. This temple is a much smaller version of the Castillo at Chavín. Like the Chavín culture, the Tiahuanaco was probably an influential art style rather than a political or social order. The Willcawain temple is a windowless, earth-roofed structure. The rooms and winding passages inside are pitch dark, so take a flashlight.

To get to Willcawain, follow Avenida Centenario north out of town. About three-quarters of a mile out of Huarás, look for a small sign indicating a right turn onto the dirt road leading to the ruin. This road climbs gently through beautiful grazing and farming land, and along it are frequent views of the brilliant peaks to the east. Since the way to Willcawain is through inhabited areas, this is a particularly good walk for observing the *campesinos* as they go about their everyday work of tending their animals and crops, often using techniques and tools that have changed little over the centuries. The people along the way are friendly, especially if you speak first. A question you'll probably hear several times along the way is "De qué pais?" ("What country are you from?"). Enough hikers walk this road that some of the children have learned to ask for money ("Plata, gringo" or "Moneda, gringo"). Instead of giving money, try sharing some snacks or talking with them; it's a great way to practice your Spanish, and it helps humanize the whole situation, teaching kids that *gringos* are people too, not just sources of easy money.

As it winds its way toward Willcawain, the road passes eucalyptus groves, clusters of rustic houses, and rushing water. If the switchbacks of the main road become tedious, watch for well-used shortcut paths, many along lovely stone-walled lanes. At the ruins, you'll be charged a very small admission fee. The hillside on which the ruin sits makes an arresting lunch spot. It overlooks a broad valley cut into a patchwork of green pastures, beige grain fields, and chocolate-brown plowed earth. Several clusters of round, yurtlike houses with conical thatched roofs are scattered throughout the valley. All in all, the view across this valley from Willcawain appears to have changed little since the temple was constructed a thousand years ago.

From the ruins, the dirt road continues thirteen miles up the Quebrada Llaca to Laguna Llaca, a rather unattractive body of water from which, nonetheless, outstanding views of the *cordillera* can be had. Taxis to the lake can be arranged in Huarás.

The Llanganuco-Cashapampa Trek

Though this walk is often called the Llanganuco-Santa Cruz trek, most people stop walking at Cashapampa because connecting with transportation into Carás is easier there. With the exception of the Inca Trail, this loop is probably the most popular trek in Peru. Its popularity is justified. The trek begins at one of the most beautiful spots in the Cordillera Blanca, the Lagunas Llanganuco, two high lakes situated between two of the most beautiful mountains in South America, Huascarán and the 21,103-foot Huandoy. Within its forty-one-mile course, this trek exposes the hiker to a typical Andean village, the heady crossing of Punta Unión pass with its unparalleled view of Taulliraju (arguably the most beautiful mountain in the *cordillera*), and the green and peaceful Quebrada Santa Cruz. And all along the way the hiker is treated to the dazzle of the high white peaks in the sun, the roar of avalanches rushing down glaciers in the afternoons, the rose light of alpenglow on snow-corniced ridges in the evenings.

Though this hike is only forty-one miles long, due to the altitudes and the climbs involved, most hikers take five days for the circuit. This is a much-frequented route and is suitable for all but very poorly conditioned or very inexperienced backpackers.

To get to the trail from Huarás, take the Huarás-Carhuáz Yungay-Carás bus. From Yungay, you'll have to arrange truck transport for the two-to-three-hour ride up to the Lagunas Llanganuco. A truck leaves every morning at around seven (depending on how long it takes to get a full load of passengers) from the tourist office on the square across

To Cañón del Pato

SANTA CRUZ ▲
CASHAPAMPA
SANTA
CRUZ
L. Jatuncocha
TAULLIRAJU ▲
CARÁZ
▲CARÁZ
L. Perón
PIRÁMIDE ▲
Quebrada Huaripampa
HUANDOY ▲
CALLEJÓN DE HUAYLAS HIGHWAY
YUNGAY
L. Lianganuco
PORTACHELO
COLCABAMBA
HUASCARÁN ▲
▲CHOPICALQUI
YANÁMA
Pasaje Yanayacu
CONTRAHIERBAS ▲
Pasajé de Ulta
LLIPTA
SHILLA
L. Auquiscocha
ULTA ▲
CARHUÁZ
HUALCAN ▲
To Chavin
POMPEY
CHACAS
MARCARA
CHANCOS
COPA ▲
JUITUSH
VICOS
Portachuelo

0   7
MILES

N

from the new market. The problem is that unless you're very lucky and catch the first bus out of Huarás *and* unless it makes the trip to Yungay more quickly than usual, you may not be able to get there in time to catch the morning truck.

It is often possible to catch other trucks going to the lakes later in the day, but don't absolutely count on it. After the scheduled truck leaves at 7 A.M., the price of a ride often rises drastically, so if you simply *have* to get to the lakes in the middle of the day or in the afternoon, expect to pay a premium, but bargain as hard as you can. If you want to cut at least a day's walk off this hike, you might be able to catch a ride on one of the trucks that travel two or three times a week across the Portachuelo to the construction camp near Colcabamba. For information about all trucks to the lakes and beyond, ask at the tourist office.

If you arrive in Yungay in the afternoon and can't find a ride to the lakes, you'll have spend the night in Yungay where the choice of accommodations is severely limited—only a couple of very basic hotels. Though its tiny rooms with concrete floors and saggy-mattressed cots feel a little like jail cells, the *Hostal Gledel* (a couple of hundred yards north on Avenida Arias Graziani from the market) is quite clean, and the owners, the Gamboa family, are very friendly. If you wish, Señora Gamboa will cook for you, or you might try the *Turista* restaurant just down the hill from the Gledel on the main Callejón de Huaylas highway.

Once you've completed the bumpy, dusty but spectacular ride to the lakes, simply walk along the road by the side of Laguna Orcancocha (the second lake in the chain). Just past the lake, you'll pass the Yurac Corral campsite on your right, a good place to camp if you manage to get to the lakes in the afternoon. After the road begins to climb, watch for the beginning of the wide, rocky trail on the right. If you should somehow miss the trail, don't worry; between the Yurac Corral and the Portachuelo, the trail crosses the road over and over again. Though road construction has disrupted some of the earlier sections of the trail, the road itself is narrow and unpaved, and traffic is almost nonexistent. So the Llanganuco-Cashapampa trek, though somewhat damaged, has not been destroyed by the construction.

The walk from the Llagunas (12,599 feet) to the Portachuelo (15,639 feet) is an often steep five-mile climb that takes most reasonably conditioned hikers about four hours. Be sure to look behind you occasionally as you climb; the views of Huascarán and Huandoy are excellent. Look also along the boulders alongside the trail for *viscachas*. These relatives of the chinchilla look like a combination rabbit-squirrel and, like North American marmots, often live among the rocks in boulder fields.

From the Portachuelo, you'll see the tiny Lagunas Morococha a couple of miles below the pass. Camping is possible near some of the lakes, but most ground flat enough for tents is quite marshy. The new road switchbacks from the pass toward the chain of lakes while the trail takes a steeper, more direct route. Views of the 20,846-foot Chopical-qui dominate the descent from the pass. Below the lakes, the trail becomes more severely disrupted by recent road construction. The trail is often covered in rock slides and is sometimes difficult to follow. Sometimes, too, grading for the road has left the trail dead-ended at the top of twenty-foot dirt banks. Until the road construction is completed and the trail is reestablished, hikers might consider walking along the road between the Llagunas and Vaqueria.

Approximately three miles below the Lagunas Morococha, the descent becomes much less steep, and after crossing the stream several times (no bridges, so be prepared to wade), you'll descend the Quebrada Morococha on the left side of the stream. There are several good campsites along this stretch of trail. Just before Vaqueria, a small village of a half-dozen houses, you'll cross to the right bank of the stream on a log bridge. From Vaqueria to Colcabamba (two miles), the trail is a wide, well-used path through inhabited land, so you'll be sharing the trail with *campesinos* and their animals.

Just beyond Vaqueria, watch for an unmarked fork in the trail. The ascending right-hand trail goes to Yanama where it connects with the Pasaje de Yanayacu trail to the Quebrada Ulta, so be sure to stay on the descending left-hand trail. If you want to bypass Colcabamba and save 1.5 miles of walking, watch for a trail branching to the left (near a couple of houses) just below the Yanama trail junction. This trail crosses the stream and shortcuts past Colcabamba toward the Quebrada Huaripampa. Most hikers, though, want to go through Col-cabamba. This small, typical mountain village makes a good rest stop. The friendly Calogne family operates an inn near the plaza in Col-cabamba where you can drink cool beer under a thatch-roofed shelter and even order a meal if you wish.

Leaving Colcabamba, you'll begin to climb gradually toward the Quebrada Huaripampa. Walk through the town's plaza and pick up the trail that follows the left side of the main stream through the valley. At about 0.7 miles up the stream, you'll cross to the right bank over a footbridge near a house. The trail on the left bank continues up the Quebrada Ranincuray to the Lagunas Tintacocha below Chacraraju and Piramide (three miles on a steep, narrow trail). Unless you plan to climb to the Lagunas, keep a close watch for the crossing to the stream's right bank.

About 2.5 miles out of Colcabamba, you'll approach the clearly visible conjunction of the Quebradas Ranincuray and Huaripampa (the right-hand canyon). Be prepared for a brief, steep climb on a wet, rocky section of trail into the Quebrada Huaripampa. Once fully into the *quebrada,* you'll find yourself in a wide, swampy meadow that serves as an immense pasture for numerous cows. The trail is often indistin-guishable from cow paths as you ascend this long meadow, but stay near the trees on the right side. Venturing out into the flat, grassy meadow is a sure way to end up knee-deep in black mud.

The Huascarán National Park staff has established two sign-posted camping areas in this meadow. The first is about 1.5 miles into the *quebrada,* the second another mile on up the meadow. Since the meadow is so heavily used as pasturage for cattle and sheep, try to collect water from one of the numerous side streams descending from the canyon walls.

Above the long, marshy meadow, the trail continues somewhat indistinctly its mostly gentle ascent of the *quebrada,* keeping to the right bank of the stream. Watch for a large stone column on the right wall of the canyon and a grove of trees in the center of the valley; the trail crosses to the left side of the stream *before* the grove. Here the real ascent of Punta Unión begins. The trail, switchbacking up the left side of the canyon, is often very muddy. After passing the Pomabamba junction (a faint trail to the right, eight miles from Colcabamba), the trail climbs on open, boulder-strewn hillsides past a series of small lakes. Views of Nevado Taulliraju become increasingly impressive as the trail climbs toward the pass. After switchbacking up open granite slopes, you'll reach Upper Laguna Morococha (almost three miles from Poma-bamba junction; yes, the name is the same as the lakes below the Portachuelo). This beautiful, deep lake makes a good place to rest before tackling the final steep 0.7 mile ascent of Punta Unión, visible above as a faint notch in the dark wall of granite below and to the left of Taulliraju. The trail winds over bare granite and is often indistinct. Watch carefully for the rock cairns and rock rows that mark the route. Don't underestimate the difficulty of this ascent; we've crossed higher passes in the Andes, but we've never crossed a harder one.

Punta Unión itself is a spot you'll never forget. The route across the pass is an ancient one, surely in use by the mountain people for hundreds of years. As you approach from below, the deep notch that is the pass becomes more and more distinct, and you'll begin to see the marvelous stonework switchbacks leading to it. From the pass, you'll have wonderful views back down the Quebrada Huaripampa, and in the other direction, Taulliraju looms directly over you. Just below Taul-liraju lies the small, brilliantly blue-green Laguna Taullicocha (*cocha,* by the way, is the Quechua word for lake; *raju,* is the word for snow mountain). Farther down the long Quebrada Santa Cruz ahead of you, you'll see Laguna Grande, seven miles away by trail.

Descending from the pass, the trail is quite distinct until it reaches meadowland below. There, cow trails again multiply confusingly. How-ever, be sure to cross to the right bank of the stream soon after you reach the meadow since the stream soon drops into a small gorge, making crossing later very difficult. Below this small gorge are several adequate campsites. Again, try to collect water from side streams.

Past these campsites, the trail soon reaches a very large and very swampy meadow. Be sure to cross to the left side of the stream *before* entering this meadow. The trail runs along the extreme left side of the meadow, and it is sometimes quite faint. Should you lose it, however, simply walk along the boundary between the meadow and the boulders and you'll soon pick up the trail again. The trail along this long meadow

Nevado Taulliraju from Punta Unión, Cordillera Blanca, Peru

above Laguna Grande is a frustrating one, alternating between being very muddy and very rocky. At the lake, an extensive rockslide has covered the trail. The current route across this slide area is easy to follow and climbs high above the lake.

Between Laguna Grande and Cashapampa (ten miles) the trail is quite clear as it follows the left bank of the main stream down the beautiful Quebrada Santa Cruz. The descent is gentle, and the trail winds through meadow after meadow and crosses numerous small side streams. About halfway between Laguna Grande and Cashapampa is another established, sign-posted camping area, the Llama Corral.

When the stream begins to flow much more rapidly and to drop into a deep gorge, you are approaching the final stage of the hike. Soon the trail drops *sharply* in its three-mile descent out of the *quebrada*. At the end of this steep descent, you'll pass a National Park sign and a small building where permits may be checked. When you reach a cross on a hillside, turn left and follow the trail along irrigation ditches into Cashapampa.

Though there is no restaurant in the village, two stores sell snacks, soft drinks, and beer. A truck leaves town every morning at 6 A.M. for the two-to-three-hour ride into Carás; transportation from Santa Cruz (2.5 uphill miles from Cashapampa) is much less regular. Though it may be possible to arrange a ride from Cashapampa to Carás later in the day, be prepared to pay extra for off-schedule transportation. If you have to wait overnight for the morning truck, camping is possible in Cashapampa in the stone-wall-enclosed area just to the left of the trail where it enters the town. Finally, if you're really stuck or if you find yourself with loads of excess energy, an eight-mile trail runs from Santa Cruz to Carás.

Carás

Travelers often arrive in Carás after hiking the Llanganuco loop, take a quick look around, and then hop the first bus back to Huarás. But there are several good reasons for spending a day or two here rather than rushing through, not least of which is that Carás is a quiet little town, a good place to rest after a long trek. And Carás is certainly the most physically charming town in the Callejón because it suffered considerably less damage during the 1970 earthquake than the towns farther south. Here you'll still find old adobe buildings with red-tile roofs, and a pretty little central plaza with trees and a band shell. And if you have a bit of energy left, you'll also find Carás to be a center for a couple of excellent excursions.

The first of these excursions is to Laguna Parón, one of the most remarkable alpine lakes in the Andes. Opaque turquoise from the accumulation of glacier flour, the waters of Parón fill the upper end of a deep *quebrada* (which provides excellent scenery in itself) surrounded by some of the most awesome peaks of the Cordillera Blanca. The great glaciated massifs of Nevados Caráz (19,768 feet), Artesonraju (19,768 feet), Chacraraju (20,086 feet), and Huandoy (20,981 feet) flank the lake on the north and south. But dominating the landscape is Pirámide Garcilaso (19,308 feet), looming to the east directly behind the lake. This mountain, as its Spanish name indicates, is a near-perfect pyramid of rock and ice, surely one of the most beautiful mountains anywhere. Parón is an excellent spot for photography, but remember that clouds tend to pile up around the peaks most afternoons, so go early.

Laguna Parón lies at the end of a sixteen-mile dirt road from Carás. The road itself is quite spectacular, climbing sharply through switchbacks into a very deep, sheer-cliffed canyon with an impressive tower of rock above one of the walls. But the road is so rough that the one-way time for getting to the lake is nearly two hours under the best of circumstances. Near the lake, you may be asked to identify yourself and sign in at the control station, so be sure to take your passport. *Colectivo* taxis and small vans travel this road, usually leaving from the plaza in the morning. Their rates are quite reasonable; however, they go only if they can collect a full load of passengers, not always a sure thing in a sleepy little town like Carás. If *colectivos* are not available, you can always hire a taxi or perhaps a truck from the plaza to take you to the lake (expensive), or you could take your chances and walk up the road to Parón a bit (from the plaza, walk past the market, and take the main road out of town going first north and then east) and hope for a truck going all the way to the lake (very cheap, but pretty uncertain). In Huarás, most of the touring agencies schedule regular day trips north through the Callejón de Huaylas with a stop at Parón.

For inveterate country road ramblers like ourselves, Carás offers an interesting opportunity to travel into the Cordillera Negra. Located across the Río Santa from Carás at the base of the Negra is the pleasant little mountain town of Huata, with its big ficus-shaded plaza accented by shrubs displaying someone's rough attempts at topiary. It is a seldom visited spot, and the infrequently used dirt road leading to it winds along the Río Santa for several miles before turning west toward Huata, offering good views of the peaks of the northern Cordillera Blanca. A truck leaves from the plaza in Carás for Huata daily, usually at mid-morning, returning at mid-afternoon; this schedule is very rough though. Just taking the truck to Huata and walking back to Carás makes an enjoyable conditioning day hike of about eight miles (don't leave Huata on the switchbacking road; take the steeper and much shorter broad trail that descends directly and intersects with the road near a bridge).

But Huata is also the beginning point of either a long day hike or a short overnighter into the Cordillera Negra to Cantu, a small Inca ruin. To reach Cantu from Huata's plaza, walk uphill out of town on the main path. Look ahead of you and you'll see a wide *quebrada* leading to the left. The trail to the ruins follows that canyon, and the walk takes two to three hours of steady climbing. Actually, several trails work their way up the canyon, but the area is inhabited, so assistance in route finding shouldn't be hard to come by. The ruins themselves are not particularly impressive, but the main attraction here is in taking a hike that few visitors to the Callejón de Huaylas make and meeting *campesinos* relatively unaccustomed to *gringos.* Hikes from Huata are covered on the I.G.N. topo, Carhuáz (19–h).

For those wanting to make Carás a base for excursions, accommodations are simple but adequate. The *Hostal Chavín* on the plaza is clean and has plenty of hot water in the private baths, a rarity in very inexpensive hotels. The *Hotel Suiza Peruana,* just a couple of doors up from the *Chavín,* is a reasonable second choice. The *Restaurant Yanet* on the plaza serves decent *lomo saltado* and *bistek,* as does the *Comedor* at the Suiza. But for a taste of *tipico* food, walk up Sucre to the *Lareno* where you'll find a good selection of Andean food, especially *tamales* and *humitas,* along with cold drinks. If you're leaving from Carás for a trek, several *bodegas* and the main market (up Sucre from the plaza) offer the usual supplies.

The Huarás-Carhuáz-Yungay-Carás minibuses leave Carás traveling south through the Callejón de Huaylas regularly, picking up passengers at the plaza. More comfortable and faster buses also travel to Huarás and on to Lima, leaving less frequently but throughout the day. Offices for Morenos, Ancash, and Huarás bus companies are all located near the main plaza. Money may be changed at the Banco de la Nación, but it is rather out of the way; walk up Sucre past the market, and turn right on Minerva. The *correo* is located a block up San Martin and a half-block right on Olaya from the plaza.

The Quebrada Ulta-Honda Loop

This sixty-mile loop is recommended for experienced backpackers. It crosses two high passes, takes you through a typical Andean village, and offers scenery equal to that on the much more crowded Llanganuco-Cashapampa loop. Good campsites and water are readily available except in the immediate vicinities of the passes. Most well-acclimatized hikers should allow at least six days for this trek and should be prepared for the usual cold nights of the high Andes. Though some limited supplies are available in Pompey, take all the food and fuel you'll need for the trip; do not plan on any significant resupplying in Pompey.

For those not ready for a week's walk through the mountains but who want instead an easy, short hike into the backcountry of the Cordillera Blanca, we know of no better destination than the beautiful, accessible, and uncrowded Quebrada Ulta. Without having to cross a pass, you can sample some of the best views the *cordillera* has to offer. During the approach to the *quebrada*'s mouth, magnificent close-up views of Huascarán and Hualcan (20,086 feet) dominate the landscape, and near its head Nevados Ulta (19,276 feet), Contrahierbas (19,804 feet), and Chopicalqui (20,847 feet) fill the sky with glaciers. And this abbreviated hike has the added attraction of being very flexible; you can make it an overnighter by hiking up to the area of the Quebrada Matara one day and walking out the next day, or you could extend the walk to two or three days by exploring trails that climb into several interesting side *quebradas* to the high alpine lakes of Auquiscocha and Huallcacocha.

Magnificent as the Ulta-Honda trek is, though, perhaps some of our enthusiasm for this trip is due to the special circumstances of our visit there. As we approached the Quebrada Ulta from Carhuáz, riding in the bed of a small pickup truck, we found ourselves in the middle of a wonderfully rustic fiesta that seemed to be very slowly ambulating its way along the road between the villages of Shilla and Llipta. A couple of hundred *campesinos*, accompanied by a little band—a trumpet, a tuba, a fiddle, and a drum—blocked the road, dancing to the very rough but festive Andean music. They were in no mood to entertain the pressing needs of two *gringos* to get through, and we were so entranced by the fiesta that we were in no mood to insist on passing, as our driver wanted to do.

Instead of letting us through, the *campesinos* simply incorporated us into their party, pulling us from the truck with a chorus of *holas* and handshakes and offered mugs of beer and *chicha*. After they all satisfied their curiosity and exercised some welcome hospitality, they finally let us pass. We made our camp that night near the head of the *quebrada*, feeling as if the day had been magic, the kind of day that makes the hardships of Andean travel worthwhile. And the next morning as we climbed from our tents at first light, almost as a good omen for the rest of the trip, we saw our first condor. Impossibly massive, it came gliding along the lower slopes of Chopicalqui with its huge wings extended, the foot-long wimple feathers at the wing tips spread like fingers.

Unfortunately, as with the Llanganuco trek, a new road is currently being built through the Quebrada Ulta, over the Pasaje de Ulta, and down the Quebrada Potaca to Pompey and on to Chacas on the east side of the Cordillera Blanca. But the very narrow dirt road that is slowly inching its way across the mountains hardly appears to destroy the quality of the backcountry experience in the Quebrada Ulta. And even when the road is completed, traffic should be very light, probably limited to only a vehicle or two a day if traffic on similar roads in the *cordillera* can be used as a comparison. The head of the *quebrada*, of course, will remain undisturbed. For those crossing the Pasaje de Ulta to Pompey and the Quebrada Honda, though, road construction does currently complicate route finding a bit in the area of the pass. But since the route the new road takes begins its climb west of the old trail, the traditional route, at least as far as the Pasaje, stands a good chance of remaining relatively undisturbed.

To reach the Quebrada Ulta from Huarás, take one of the regular Huarás-Carhuáz-Yungay-Carás buses to Carhuáz. Trucks leave on irregular schedules (but most frequently in the morning and fairly often throughout the day on Sundays) from the plaza in Carhuáz going at least as far as Shilla (6.5 miles) and sometimes on to Llipta (7.5 miles). If nothing seems to be going into the mountains from Carhuáz, you can, in a pinch, also hire trucks (much more expensive than the regular trucks to Shilla) in the plaza to take you on the rough road beyond

Llipta, at least as far as the broad stream that marks the junction for the trail to Laguna Auquiscocha (9.5 miles). On the truck ride to Shilla, be sure to look ahead for some of the best views of Huascarán anywhere in the *cordillera*. And as you ride toward Shilla, use the opportunity to orient yourself—the deep canyon between Huascarán Sur and Hualcan is the mouth of the Quebrada Ulta.

Assuming that you'll be starting from Shilla, walk uphill toward Llipta on the main dirt road. Above Llipta, turn right onto the trail just past the bridge. This rock-wall-bordered path crosses the road over and over. It climbs steadily, taking you past fields, pastures, and houses (watch for dogs) and offering excellent opportunities to observe typical daily life in the high Andes. After almost three miles, the route reaches the Auquiscocha trail junction at a broad stream, which crosses the road (to avoid having to wade this stream, look for the trail that descends steeply from the road to a rough bridge before climbing back to the road). The Auquiscocha trail branches to the right just before the stream crossing and winds four steep, rough miles to Laguna Auquiscocha (campsites scarce) just below Nevados Ulta and Hualcan.

Past this stream, the road into the Quebrada Ulta begins a series of switchbacks (look for obvious shortcutting trails) before passing through a wooden gate that marks the true entrance into the *quebrada*. The road climbs gradually into a huge meadow cut by meandering streams and used by *campesinos* as pasturage for their cattle. The new road skirts to the left of the meadow, eventually climbing high above it on the north wall of the canyon. The old trail continues through the meadow, crossing to the right bank of the stream early on. Both routes up the *quebrada* are equally direct.

At 8.5 miles from Shilla, you'll reach the Laguna Huallcacocha trail junction. This 2.5-mile trail (to the south) climbs steeply to the beautiful lake where good campsites make this an excellent side trip (but if you want to go to Huallcacocha, be sure to stay on the trail rather than the road because at the point of the junction, the road is high above the valley floor).

Past the Huallcacocha junction, you'll begin to see the seemingly endless series of switchbacks the new road makes in its ascent toward the tunnel in the process of being cut underneath the Pasaje de Ulta. As the road begins to turn toward these switchbacks, the route becomes somewhat obscured by the construction and by the many cow paths near the stream. Stop and take your bearings. Whether you're walking the trail or the road, at this point you should be on the right bank of the stream (if you're walking on the road, look for a crude log and stone bridge that crosses to the right bank before the road fords the stream).

Past this stream crossing, the trail climbs a small hill. Watch for the rather faint trail continuing up the valley as the road begins its switchbacks toward the pass. Soon after Nevado Chopicalqui appears up a side canyon to the north, the trail forks. The left branch is the three-mile-long trail into the Quebrada Matara; the main right branch continues up valley for less than a mile before reaching another junction. Here, the right branch climbs to the Pasaje de Ulta while the left climbs to the Pasaje de Yanayacu and descends to Yanama (fifteen miles from the head of Quebrada Ulta). Good campsites in dry meadows filled with blue-blossomed lupin with easily accessible water and excellent views of the surrounding mountains are abundant in this junction area, both near the head of the Quebrada Ulta and into the Quebrada Matara. Because of the use of the area as pasturage, however, exercise particular care in water treatment. Also, because the Quebrada Ulta is much frequented by herders, to prevent minor pilferage it is not recommended that you leave your camp unattended.

From the head of the canyon across the Pasaje de Ulta to Pompey is eighteen miles. The ascent to the pass is a very steep and hard 5.5-mile climb through switchbacks. It is best to begin the climb first thing in the morning since campsites and water are unavailable until well after the crossing of the pass. The upper sections of the trail to the pass are both rough and often fairly indistinct, but the Pasaje de Ulta (16,080 feet) is clearly visible above (look ahead of you for the notch between Contrahierbas and Ulta).

When we made this hike, the potential effects of the road and tunnel construction on the pass itself and on the trail descending to Pompey were somewhat unclear. But it appears that crossing the pass over the trail rather than having to walk through the tunnel may remain possible after construction is completed. Below the Pasaje de Ulta, it appears likely that the trail may be considerably disrupted. Route finding, though, should be no problem whatsoever. Should the trail become difficult to follow, you can always walk along the road, which will probably follow the stream that flows from the small lakes below the pass (passable but cold campsites near the lakes), entering the Quebrada Potaca (eight miles from the pass to the point where the stream from the Quebrada Coyo enters on the right), and descending to Pompey (12.5 miles below the pass).

Pompey is a typical small highland village, a pleasant enough place to sit for an hour, drinking a warm beer and resting. If you've had nearly enough walking and don't feel like crossing another high pass, you can take the road from Pompey down to Chacas where trucks and infrequent buses will take you to San Luis on the main road; there more frequent transportation can be found south to Huari, Chavín, and on to Catac and Huarás. Considering the difficulty of road travel on the eastern side of the Cordillera Blanca, however, it's probably simpler to continue with the loop.

From Pompey the route back to the Callejón de Huaylas is easy to follow and, for the time being, at least, mercifully free of road construction. The trail begins only a short way below Pompey, branching right (south) from the road. This trail soon begins to parallel the right-hand bank of the stream flowing down the Quebrada Juitush, one of the loveliest valleys in the Cordillera Blanca. This clear trail climbs gradually to the little village of Juitush (six miles above Pompey) before beginning the real ascent to the pass, the Portachuelo de Honda. The upper sections of the *quebrada* are particularly beautiful as the trail passes numerous waterfalls (a couple of miles above the village), and there are plenty of good campsites with easily accessible water supplies along the way. The trail crosses and recrosses the stream and its tributaries in this area but generally stays on the left-hand bank.

The final mile or so of the ascent to the Portachuelo (15,595 feet, twelve miles from Pompey) is quite steep, but the view from the pass should make the efforts of the climb disappear immediately. The Portachuelo offers one of the truly great vistas of the entire *cordillera,* with excellent views of the big mountains to the south—Palcaraju (20,585 feet), Pucaranra (20,198 feet), Chinchey (20,415 feet), Tocllaraju (19,798 feet), and a host of lesser peaks.

Two trails descend from the pass, uniting a short distance down below. The left-hand trail descends more gently than the steep right-hand trail for the benefit of pack animals. In a meadow about 4.5 miles below the pass, you'll reach a trail junction. The main Quebrada Honda trail continues to the right, heading down valley on the right bank of the stream. The trail to the left dead-ends at Laguna Pucaranracocha, six miles away. From this junction, your route gradually descends on a clear trail for twelve miles through the lovely Quebrada Honda to the town of Vicos. There are plenty of good campsites throughout the *quebrada,* but, again, don't leave your camp unattended because there is considerable foot traffic through the canyon. After beginning its descent on the right bank of the stream, the trail crosses to the left bank, and the much-frequented foot path soon becomes a rough road (virtually no vehicular traffic above Vicos, however). As this road begins to switchback out of the *quebrada,* watch for obvious time-saving shortcutting trails that descend more directly.

Unless you arrive in Vicos late in the day, you should have no trouble catching a truck going the 4.5 miles down to Marcará on the Callejón de Huaylas highway. About halfway to Marcará you'll pass through Chancos, where there are hot springs if you have the time and inclination for a soak. In Marcará, frequent buses travel the short distance south to Huarás.

The Grand Tour of the Cordillera Blanca

The Grand Tour links together the Llanganuco-Cashapampa loop and the Ulta-Honda loop to make a very long, spectacular trek through a large portion of the *cordillera.* The route covers ninety miles, crosses four high passes at the 16,000-foot level, and requires approximately two weeks to complete. Because of the length of the trip and the lack of opportunities to resupply food stocks along the way, all but those hikers able to carry very heavy loads will need *arrieros* for this circuit.

Since all but the Quebrada Ulta-Colcabamba legs of the trek are described in detail elsewhere in this chapter and since your *arrieros* will know the trails well, our description of the route will be brief. Starting in Vicos (reached by truck from Marcará on the Callejón de Huaylas highway), the trail climbs gradually to the east through the Quebrada

Honda toward the Portachuelo (seventeen miles). From this pass, the route descends, swinging north through the Quebrada Juitush to the small town of Pompey (27.5 miles).

Turning to the northwest at Pompey, the route climbs the Quebrada Potaca along the new road to the Pasaje de Ulta (thirty-nine miles). From the pass the trail descends sharply to the head of the Quebrada Ulta (45.5 miles) where, rather than following the main trail down valley to exit the *quebrada*, it begins immediately to climb to the pass at Punta Yanayacu (50.5 miles). From Yanayacu the main trail descends toward the town of Yanama, but six miles or so below the pass, the Grand Tour route turns left, crossing the stream at a bridge and soon reaching another junction. Here the trail divides, the right-hand branch going north to Colcabamba (sixty miles). From Colcabamba, the trail follows the usual Llanganuco loop route up the Quebrada Huaripampa to the pass at Punta Unión (seventy-two miles) and then descends through the length of the Quebrada Santa Cruz to the conclusion of the trek at Cashapampa (ninety miles). There, trucks leave each morning for Carás.

Quechua child, Cordillera Blanca near Colcabamba, Peru

The Quebrada Cojup

This two-day trip takes you to the head of the beautiful Quebrada Cojup where the Laguna Perolcocha and the Laguna Palcacocha lie directly beneath Nevados Ranrapalca (20,218 feet), Palcaraju (20,585 feet), and Pucaranra (20,198 feet).

The simplest way to make this hike is to hire a taxi to take you up the Laguna Llaca road to km 15 where a clear trail descends to the right to intersect in less than a mile with the main Huarás-Palcacocha trail before reaching the livestock gate that marks the entrance to the *quebrada.* Here the trail begins its climb through the canyon, at first on the stream's right bank but crossing after five miles or so to the left bank for the final two to three miles to Laguna Palcacocha. The walk from the Llaca road to Palcacocha is a pleasant morning's work. Good campsites are available in the *quebrada,* but not so good at the lake. If you're in the mood for a scramble, Laguna Perolcocha is a mile or so above the canyon floor (reached by clambering up the northwest canyon wall below Palcacocha).

To return to Huarás, walk back down the Quebrada Cojup. But instead of crossing below the livestock gate to the Llaca road, continue on the main trail, a very wide, often stone-wall-bordered foot and animal thoroughfare, that descends to the village of Unchus (12.5 miles) where the Pitec road continues on to Huarás (16.5 miles from Palcacocha).

The Olleros to Chavín Trek

Though not one of our favorite walks, this rather short and very popular trek has something to offer hikers of all experience levels. For beginners, the hike is the easiest in both physical and route-finding demands of any cross-*cordillera* hike in the Cordillera Blanca. Though views of the big, glaciated mountains are rather more scarce on this trek than on the others described in this section, the walk, nevertheless, offers lovely, if not spectacular, scenery throughout the inhabited valley of the Río Negro, working its way through crop and pasture land and passing numerous little *estancias* (collections of houses too small to be considered villages). And with a 15,355-foot pass and excellent views of Nevado Huantsan (20,982 feet), it would be unfair to say that this walk is entirely lacking in high alpine scenery. Also, the trail has the historical appeal of following an ancient route; much older than the Inca period, the trail closely duplicates the route coastal pilgrims would have taken to get to the great ceremonial center at Chavín de Huantar, and some sections even display pre-Inca paving. Finally, the trail offers an exciting conclusion—the Chavín de Huantar ruins—which will most certainly be more impressive to you after tracing the ancient Chavíns' path than had you ridden a bus over the road from Catac.

Most people take three days for this trek, though conditioned and acclimatized hikers can do it in two days. As with all Andean treks involving higher altitudes, trekkers should be prepared for frosty

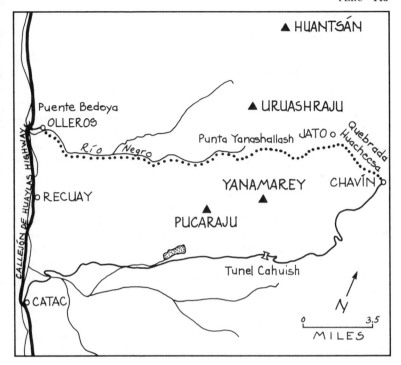

nights. Except for the area near the pass and the lower sections of the trail on the descent to Chavín, adequate if not memorable campsites are frequent.

Transportation from Huarás to Olleros, the trailhead, is either by bus or truck (unless you hire a taxi or arrange transport with Paraih Tours). Trucks leave fairly frequently from the Huarás market for Olleros on schedules too loose to mention. Ask around in the market. Otherwise, take one of the Recuay-Catac buses south to Puente Bedoya (let the bus driver know you're going to Olleros, and he'll let you out at the right spot), and then walk the mile and a quarter east to Olleros.

Walk through town, cross the Río Negro over a stone bridge, and continue walking east along the south bank of the river (with the Negro on your left). The trail parallels the river all the way up the valley, making route finding extremely simple. As you begin the walk up-valley, you'll pass cultivated fields, eucalyptus groves, and several of those *estancias* we mentioned. Of course, you'll be sharing the trail with *campesinos* and their animals. But before long, cultivated land gives way to pasture and boulder-strewn meadow. The clear trail continues to climb alongside the Río Negro through the valley.

The only difficulties in following the trail come about 10.5 miles into the walk. Here, at the entrance of the Quebrada Otuto, in a marshy area near where the Ríos Quilloc and Araranca enter the Negro, the trail becomes indistinct. Remember, though, that the route follows the southern bank of the Río Negro (though not too close to the river due to the marshy ground), so work your way across the Río Quilloc (the first of the crossing streams), climb a slight ridge toward the Río Araranca, and the main Chavín trail will reappear soon beyond the collection of herders' huts called Pampacancha.

Though camping is possible near Pampacancha, better sites lie a couple of miles farther ahead. Unfortunately, a fairly steep climb separates Pampacancha and these campsites. Following this climb, the clear trail crosses a *pampa* (flat place) and begins in earnest its ascent toward Punta Llanashallash, the 15,355-foot pass (14.5 miles from Olleros) where you may want to add a stone to one of the sacred *apachetas* (rock cairns) that weary travelers have erected there.

Beyond the pass, the trail descends sharply into the valley of the Río Shongo. And, again, the easy-to-follow trail follows (except for a very brief crossing) the river's southern (right-hand) bank. For nearly five miles, the Shongo is a calm meandering stream; eventually, though, the river tumbles into a canyon, leaving the trail high above it. Watch for, but don't cross, the bridge to the Quebrada Jato (eighteen miles from Olleros). Instead, continue on the main trail that descends to Chavín, only five miles away now.

Below where the Ríos Jato and Chico enter the Shongo, the main stream becomes the Río Huachecsa, and the trail parallels it through the Quebrada Huachecsa to Chavín. As you make the final steep descent of the trek on a broad, clear trail, you'll see below you the complex of temples and plazas dominated by the Castillo, which was the ceremonial center of the Chavín culture.

If you arrive in Chavín after noon, you'll certainly want to spend the night to give yourself time to explore the ruins (open 8 A.M. to 12 noon, and 2 P.M. to 4 P.M.). Accommodations in this small town are pretty basic, but the *Alberque de Turistas,* a couple of miles north of town on the road to Huari, is quite nice. If you want to stay in town or are on a tight budget, try the *Hotel Montecarlo.* In our experience, restaurants in Chavín are pretty uniform (and pretty bad), offering the usual *saltados* and *bistek,* so take your choice.

The return to Huarás is over the Cahuish pass and through Catac on the Callejón de Huaylas highway. Both *Cóndor de Chavín* and *Ancash* travel this route twice a day (seven hours, Chavín to Huarás). Or you might want to catch a truck over the pass to Catac and then catch one of the regular Huarás-Recuay-Catac buses there. Alternatively, if you're ready to leave the Cordillera Blanca, Cóndor de Chavín offers a direct Chavín-Lima bus daily (thirteen hours). However you return though, don't forget to keep a jacket out of your pack for the cold crossing of Cahuish.

Trujillo

If you like ruins, Trujillo (350 miles north of Lima) with its deep and varied layers of human history, is the town for you. The valley of the Río Moche near Trujillo is a fertile strip through the desert, one of the several linear oases up and down the coast that have been centers for human population for thousands of years. Because of the proximity to the coast and the reliable fresh water supply of the Moche, inhabitants of the valley eventually developed a strong economy based on both fishing and agriculture, so strong, in fact, that two of the great (and little-known) cultures of the New World developed here. The Moche and Chimu cultures that inhabited the area around Trujillo left behind them some of the largest structures and one of the largest cities of the New World, and these ruins are Trujillo's primary attraction to the traveler.

When the Spaniards came to the Moche valley in 1534 and founded Trujillo, 350 miles north of Lima, the area was almost uninhabited, but they found the coastal desert area filled with the ruins of the Moche and Chimu peoples. Conquered by the Incas and perhaps decimated by disease, most of the descendants of the builders of these temples and cities had either died out or moved on. The Spaniards, then, were free to move into the area with a minimum of effort. After the requisite looting of the desert ruins, they, like the native peoples before them, recognized the agricultural potential of the area and soon began growing sugar cane on large *haciendas* in the Moche and Chicama valleys. With this strong agricultural base, Trujillo prospered throughout the colonial period, and it has continued to do so, recently supplanting Arequipa as Peru's second largest city. It is a growing, vital, industrial city, but reminders of its pre-Columbian and colonial roots are always a forceful presence.

Though your primary interest in Trujillo will probably be in its ruins, you may also want to have a look at some of its Spanish past, for despite its rapid growth, downtown Trujillo remains very much a city of colonial churches and houses. Begin at the spacious and pleasant Plaza de Armas. There, of course, you'll find the Cathedral, a large but relatively undistinguished building, many times reconstructed after earthquake damage. Also on the plaza and much more interesting are the Casa Urquiana and the Casa Bracamonte, occupied, respectively, by the Banco Central de Reserva and the Banco Central Hipotecario. Both banks are happy to allow visitors to walk through during business hours to examine fine examples of colonial architecture. Three of Trujillo's most interesting colonial churches, San Francisco (a block from the plaza on Independencia), the Convento del Carmen (four blocks up Pizarro at Estete), and La Merced (just off the plaza on Pizarro) are currently being restored, so you may not be able to enter them.

Chan-Chan

When we think of important, highly developed pre-Columbian civilizations, we think almost exclusively of the Aztecs, the Mayans, and the Incas. But the Chimu civilization that inhabited the Moche valley and was one of the most developed, organized cultures of the Americas, has never entered the popular imagination. It remains largely unknown except to the specialist. At the height of its power, the Chimu empire stretched up and down Peru's north coast for hundreds of miles, but its center was Chan-Chan, only three miles north of Trujillo. The remains of the empire's grand capital city are a strange and mysterious desert ruin, probably unlike anything you've ever seen before. At first approach, Chan-Chan seems almost a natural feature of the bleak desert landscape surrounding it. The rounded, eroding adobe walls of the city are gradually melting into the desert, worn away by time, wind, and the occasional rainstorm. They rise like hills from the sand. As you walk among the walls of the empty city, recognizing it as the product of human effort, it begins to feel a little like one of the mysterious labyrinthine ruins from a story by the Argentine writer Jorge Luis Borges—remote in both time and our ability to understand the lives of the people who worked to build this empire in the desert.

As you stand in this somewhat alien-feeling ruin, it is hard to imagine that in the fourteenth century when the Chimu empire was at its peak, the dead city around you was one of the great cities not only of the Americas but of the world, for at that time it was larger than either London or Paris. With a population estimated to have been as high as 100,000, the city, surrounded by a thirty-foot-high wall, occupied a huge site of over six square miles. It would have been alive with the activities of a large capital city—the busy center of the empire's government, religion, and military. In its prime, the brown city around you would have been alive with color in the form of bright wall paintings and gold decorations on the principal temples. And due to irrigation water diverted from the Río Moche, the city would have been much greener than today.

The Chimu were a highly organized society, and their capital is the product of a considerable knowledge of urban and social planning (so much so, in fact, that the conquering Incas adopted many of the Chimu practices of social control to help in establishing and governing their new and largely unconsolidated empire). This careful planning is clearly apparent in the efficient design of the capital city. Inside the enclosed area, Chan-Chan's houses, courtyards, temples, and plazas are connected by a very modern-feeling grid of streets. The city is divided into ten districts, which are very much cities within themselves. Each district is set off by its own walls and was presumably governed by its own chief. Each district also has a well, a central plaza, a temple, a burial ground, and of course numerous houses. And, in addition, each district has artisan workshops, storerooms, military posts, and assembly halls. Separating the districts are open spaces, perhaps used for agriculture.

While at Chan-Chan first spend some time in the reconstructed section called Ciudadela Tschudi in order to get a feel for how the city may have looked when it was occupied. But don't neglect to walk about the extensive unrestored sections as well. Here you'll most likely have the ruins to yourself. Take time as you walk through both the Ciudadela Tschudi and the unrestored sections of Chan-Chan to look on the adobe walls for expressions of the artistry of the Chimu people in the form of the bas-reliefs and murals—mostly geometric patterns and animal motifs—which once decorated much of the city. Another interesting feature of Chimu art is their pottery, specifically the whistling *huaco,* a double-chambered, double-spouted vessel with one spout fashioned into a whistle. When water is poured from one of the *huaco*'s chambers to the other, air rushes out the spigot, producing a whistle. You can see *huacos* at the Cassinelli Museum (see "Resources").

To reach Chan-Chan, either hire a taxi or take one of the Huanchaco buses from the corner of Orbegozo and España, letting the driver know you want out at Chan-Chan.

THE MOCHICAN HUACAS

The predecessors of the Chimus in the Trujillo area were the Moche people, who began their rise to prominence about 2,300 years ago. Despite the great age of their culture, the Moche are much more accessible to our imaginations than other ancient Peruvian cultures because their fine pottery depicts their daily lives in great detail. In modeled and painted pottery, Moche artisans show us their houses, dress, ceremonies, food production methods, medical practices, and even their sex lives (see the collection of erotic Moche pottery at the Larco Herrera Museum in Lima).

On a larger scale, the Moche culture also left behind some of the most imposing temples of the ancient world. You can see the remains of these temples just south of Trujillo where the massive ruins of the Huaca del Sol and the Huaca de la Luna rise out of the desert. Both ruins are gigantic terraced platforms, which once supported smaller temple structures. The larger of the two, the Huaca del Sol, is topped with a flattened pyramid, and its construction required something on the order of 200 million adobe bricks. Its base dimensions are an amazing 750 by 450 feet. To reach the site, either hire a cab or take any of the local buses marked "Salaverry," which travel south of town to Trujillo's port, passing near the Huacas on the way. Let the driver know that you wish to get out at the Huaca del Sol.

Not far from the Chan-Chan ruins is another Moche Huaca, the Huaca Arco Iris (also sometimes called Huaco del Dragon). The distinguishing feature of this large temple is the elaborate frieze work covering the structure. Admission to Arco Iris is included in the nominal charge for entrance to Chan-Chan.

BEACHES

If you come to Trujillo weary from a trek in the cold mountains and tired of being constantly bundled in sweaters and jackets, one of the things you'll enjoy most about the area is its warm weather and nearby coastline. Relatively clean by South American standards, the beaches near Trujillo will give you a chance to let the warm sun bake out some of the cumulative cold you've absorbed in the Andes. As is typical of the Peruvian coast, however, in all but the warmest weather, the water is often a bit more bracing than is comfortable. Though the beaches at Buenos Aires (three miles north) and La Delicias (four miles south) are closer to downtown, Trujillo's most pleasant beach is the little port and fishing village of Huanchaco, about eight miles north of the city past the ruins of Chan-Chan. Interestingly, some of Huanchaco's fishermen still use a type of reed *balsa* in use for at least a thousand years (as evidenced by Mochican pottery picturing similar boats). Called *caballitos del mar* (literally "sea ponies"), the boats are reminiscant of the *totora* reed craft used by the Uros Indians of Lake Titicaca; however, the Mochican boats are really more like reed surfboards in that they are simply a flat platform from which to fish.

To reach Huanchaco from Trujillo, either take a taxi or one of the buses that leave frequently, passing Chan-Chan along the way. If you want to stay at the beach, try either the *Hosteria Sol y Mar* or the *Hotel Caballitos de Cotora,* both of which are very inexpensive and pleasant. For very good fresh seafood, don't miss the *Lucho del Mar.*

TRUJILLO RESOURCES

■ **Hotels** If you want to stay outside the central city, try the moderately priced and very quiet *Hotel Los Jardines* (1245 Avenida America Norte) with bungalow-style accommodations, a large, clean swimming pool, and a good restaurant. Closer in and a bit less expensive is the *Hotel Opt Gar* (595 Avenida Grau) with private baths, hot water, pleasant rooms, and a good restaurant. An excellent value in a lower-priced hotel is the *Chan-Chan* (Avenida Sinchi Roca), with large, clean rooms, private baths, hot water, and a restaurant. Also good for the price is the *Hotel Turismo* (747 Gamarra). Trujillo's *gringo* crossroads is the cheap and basic *Hotel Americano* (758 Pizarro).

■ **Restaurants** If you choose not to take meals in your hotel's restaurant, you might try one of the many places along Avenida Gamarra, such as the *Restaurant Gamarra,* the *Peña Vegetariana,* and the *Chifa Oriental.*

■ **Transportation** Both Faucett (532 Avenida Pizarro, just off the plaza) and AeroPeru (421 Jiron Bolivar) schedule daily flights between Lima and Trujillo. Air time between the two cities is about an hour. From Trujillo, AeroPeru has Monday, Wednesday, and Friday flights to Cajamarca, and Faucett flies on Saturday and Monday to Iquitos.

Buses making the eight-hour trip between Lima and Trujillo leave from both cities fairly frequently throughout the day. Try Tepsa or Roggero. For those traveling south to the Cordillera Blanca, Chinchay-Suyo (720 Jiron Bolivar, Trujillo) operates a nightly bus between Trujillo and Huarás (ten hours) on the paved Pativilca route. Empresa Diaz travels to Cajamarca daily. For those going overland to Ecuador, both Tepsa and Roggero schedule daily buses to Tumbes on the Ecuadorian border. A word of caution: though southbound buses are seldom full, those traveling north to Tumbes are often booked well in advance; also, most of Trujillo's bus companies very confusingly maintain separate ticket offices and bus departure stations, so it is best to check with the Tourist Office (509 Independencia) for detailed directions.

■ **Museums** To get a feel for the Moche and Chimu cultures, be sure to visit the Archaeological Museum (446 Jiron Bolivar) or the privately owned Cassinelli Museum (601 Jiron Nicolas de Pierola), both of which have good collections of pottery and other artifacts from the north coast civilizations. Both museums are usually open Mondays through Saturdays from 8 A.M. to 12 noon and from 2 to 6 P.M., but since these schedules sometimes change, check with the tourist information office first.

■ **Money Exchange** The Banco de la Nación is near the corner of Gamarra and Independencia, a block off the plaza. There is also a money exchange office on the plaza.

■ **Tourist Information** The main tourist office is at 509 Independencia. In addition, Trujillo has a very active, friendly, and helpful Tourist Police force, so if you're approached by an armed, uniformed policeman at the airport or near the plaza, don't immediately assume trouble; more than likely they're Tourist Police trying to be of help and practice their English. We found them to be full of the kind of very current information on which no travel book can keep up to date (how far you can expect to bargain down a taxi driver for the Trujillo-Chan-Chan fare, for example).

If your time in Trujillo is limited but you still wish to see the primary Moche and Chimu ruins, Guia Tours (519 Independencia) operates convenient tours to all of the sites in the area.

Cajamarca

The high, dry, light-filled valley where Cajamarca lies is strikingly similar to the setting of Cuzco far to the south. It was here that the Spanish under Pizarro captured and ransomed Atahualpa, the ruling Inca. The conquistadores could hardly have come to Peru at a more propitious time. Disorganized by a just-completed civil war between Atahualpa (the victor), who had controlled the northern provinces, and his half-brother, Huascar, who had controlled the south, the Inca empire proved to be incredibly weak—so weak that it could be taken by a mere 180 men. Using the civil war and the old legends of the return of the god Viracocha and his followers to his advantage, Pizarro advanced from the coast to Cajamarca, where Atahualpa was soaking a battle wound in the nearby hotsprings and preparing to travel to Cuzco to assume the throne.

In Cajamarca, Pizarro took Atahualpa captive, killing hundreds (some contemporary accounts say thousands) of Inca soldiers and civilians in the process. To ransom Atahualpa, gold was brought from all over the empire, filling, according to the Spanish chroniclers, a room of 25 by 17 feet to the height of Atahualpa's raised hand. Based on records of the Spanish court, it is estimated that the gold collected in this ransom alone amounted to at least 15,000 pounds, virtually all of it worked by Inca craftsmen into jewelry, statutes, and decorative wall plates. This great cultural and artistic wealth was immediately melted down into bullion by Pizarro's men. Though the full ransom was apparently collected, much of it by removing vast amounts of gold from the

Temple of the Sun in Cuzco, Pizarro refused to release Atahualpa, and finally, in August of 1533, had him baptized and then strangled to death.

Today, little evidence remains of Cajamarca's Inca heritage. The Temple of the Sun and other Inca buildings were dismantled, the stones recycled for use in colonial constructions. Virtually all that remains are the Cuarto del Rescate (just up Calle Junin from the plaza), supposedly the room where Atahualpa's ransom was collected, and the foundations of Inca structures on Cerro Santa Apolonia, the steep little hill just above town from which Atahualpa viewed his city and his troops. Though the Inca remains are not extensive, the views of Cajamarca and the surrounding countryside and mountains from Cerro Santa Apolonia make the climb worthwhile (walk up Jiron Dos de Mayo from the plaza).

Because of Cajamarca's slow growth, the colonial character of the town has been little affected by modern construction. The Plaza de Armas is dominated by the rather raw-looking Cathedral, begun in the seventeenth century but only recently completed, and the Convent of San Francisco, also begun in the seventeenth century. Of interest as well is Belén, an elaborate eighteenth-century church.

In addition to the appeal of Cajamarca's Inca history and its strong colonial feel, it is also a wonderful base for long rambles on little-used roads into the countryside, and it is the start of an excellent trek in the mountains. Though the landscape of the region is not as overwhelmingly spectacular as the Cordillera Blanca or Cordillera Vilcanota, it is pleasant country to travel through on foot. It is a gentle landscape where the little villages of the valley are linked by agave- and eucalyptus-lined lanes. And at an altitude of 9,050 feet, the valley is high enough to provide a wonderfully crisp climate with warm days and cool nights. But it is also high enough to make you feel the elevation gain if you've come directly from the coast, so take a day or two to acclimate before beginning strenuous activity.

RESOURCES

■ **Hotels**   Cajamarca's best hotel is the moderately priced *Turista* (on the Plaza de Armas) where you'll find pleasant, clean accommodations, private baths, hot water, and the best restaurant in town. Also good is the inexpensive *Hostal Cajamarca* (311 Jiron Dos de Mayo, just off the plaza), an attractive colonial building with clean rooms, private baths, and hot water. In the very inexpensive category is the *Hostal Jusovi* (a block below the plaza at 637 Amazonas) where the small but relatively clean rooms have private baths but little hot water.

■ **Restaurants**   Aside from the restaurant at the Turista, the best places to eat in town are the *Salas* and the *Taverna* (both on the plaza) with the usual *saltados* and *bisteks.* For filling, inexpensive meals, try the *cena* at the restaurant below the Hotel Jusovi on Amazonas.

■ **Transportation**   The overland route from Trujillo to Cajamarca runs north along the coast to Pacasmayo, at which point a good paved road branches east from the Pan-American highway toward the high-lands. The road climbs through the Jequetepeque valley, reaching its highest point at Gavilan Pass (10,500 feet) before descending into the valley of Cajamarca. The 175-mile trip takes about eight hours, and several bus companies travel the route. Try *Tepsa* (on Cajamarca's Plaza de Armas) or *Expreso Cajamarca* (926 Avenida Puga). Expreso Cajamarca's daily departure continues from Trujillo to Lima, taking about fifteen hours for the entire trip. Inexpensive AeroPeru flights of only twenty-five minutes duration operate between Cajamarca and Trujillo (with easy Lima connections) on Mondays, Wednesdays, and Fridays, saving two days' travel if you fly round-trip. The AeroPeru office is on Jiron Lima near the Hotel Turista. Be sure to get to the airport early and check in as soon as possible since even ticket-holding passengers are frequently bumped from this flight.

■ **Money Exchange**   Cajamarca's very inefficient branch of the Banco de la Nación is a couple of blocks along Avenida Lima from the plaza.

■ **Communications**   The ENTEL office is on Avenida Cajamarca just above the plaza. The *correos* is at 406 Jiron Lima.

■ **Supplies**   Along with the usual *bodegas* scattered throughout the town, Cajamarca also has a remarkable shop (a couple of blocks along Avenida Lima from the plaza) with an unusual stock of international food supplies—everything from U.S. peanut butter to French wines. Several shops on the plaza and along Avenida Amazonas sell chocolate and cheese. The market area is along Avenida Amazonas (and connect-ing side streets) beyond Avenida Arequipa. However, it has little to offer in the way of handcrafts.

■ **Movies**   Because Cajamarca is a university town, the several *cines* all within a few blocks of the plaza schedule a distinctly better class of movies than is normal in Andean mountain towns.

Ventanillas de Otuzco-Baños del Inca

This all-day walk is one of the best country rambles outside Caja-marca. It links two Inca sites and takes you through the beautiful pasture and farmland of the Cajamarca valley. You'll walk first to the Ventanillas (literally "windows"), which are Inca burial niches cut into a cliff, and then on to the Baños del Inca, the natural sulphuric hot pools where Atahualpa bathed.

Begin the walk by leaving Cajamarca on Avenida Arequipa, turn-ing right on the outskirts of town onto the main airport road (Avenida Aviación). Just before the airport (2.5 miles) turn right on the dirt road crossing a stream. Several roads converge shortly after the stream, but the route to the Ventanillas (turning first left, then right) is clearly the main road. However, be sure to remember the first right-hand turning after you cross the stream; you'll return to this seldom-used, aloe-lined lane to get to the Baños del Inca.

The road to the Ventanillas (three miles beyond the airport) is wonderfully pastoral, taking you past the fields and houses of the valley's *campesinos.* The Ventanillas are just above the road by a short trail, the beginning of which is marked by a signpost. The form of burial practiced here was typical of the Incas. The bodies of the dead, usually eviscerated, were wrapped into compact bundles, sometimes by forcing the knees into the empty chest cavity, and placed in small niches, which were then walled up with mud.

From the Ventanillas, return to the aloe-lined lane near the stream, and follow it for a mile or so through a beautiful eucalyptus grove to a river. Don't cross the river; instead, turn right and follow the sometimes sketchy trail along the river bank. Don't get discouraged if you feel you've lost the trail; simply stay near the river on its right bank, and within a couple of miles you'll reach the Cajamarca-Calendin road. The Baños del Inca are just across the river to the left. The waters of the hot springs have been diverted into rows of bathhouses, so though there is little here that is identifiably Incan, you can, if you wish, soak in the hot water in private pools. To return to Cajamarca, you can take one of the crowded minibuses that leave from in front of the baths every few minutes, but as long as you've come this far, why not walk the 3.5 miles back into town?

The Cajamarca-Cumbe Mayo-Kuntur Wasi Trek

Though neither very difficult nor very long, this three-to-four-day trek into the mountains outside Cajamarca is a wonderfully pleasant one. While it lacks spectacular, glaciated mountains, it takes you instead through green, isolated agricultural areas—some of the most beautiful countryside in the Andes and a nice contrast to the dry, barren *altiplano* of southern Peru. In addition, the trail both begins and ends at fascinating pre-Inca Chavín sites—Cumbe Mayo outside Cajamarca, and Kuntur Wasi near the town of San Pablo. (*Note:* when asking directions along this route, ask for the way to San Pablo rather than Kuntur Wasi.) One other enjoyable feature of this walk is that the ascents to the two passes you'll cross are gentle enough in comparison to the passes of the Cordillera Blanca or the Cordillera Vilcanota that they hardly even merit being called passes. In addition, the walk is extremely flexible in that there are several options for shortening or lengthening the trip—either make it a simple overnight hike to Cumbe Mayo and back to Cajamarca or walk a little farther but shorten the hike by turning off the main route either near the first pass or near the village of Chetilla on trails that descend to the main Cajamarca-Pacasmayo highway. It is also an extremely rare Andean trek in that it involves no bone-crunching truck ride to reach the trailhead. You can begin the trek from the plaza in Cajamarca if you wish.

Simply walk out Jiron Cajamarca. Just past Cerro Santa Apollonia, the road, which switchbacks wildly up the mountain, bears to the left, but the much shorter trail begins climbing directly into the hills. Cumbe Mayo, a Chavín ceremonial center, lies about nine miles above Cajamarca by way of this trail. The trail is quite wide and often

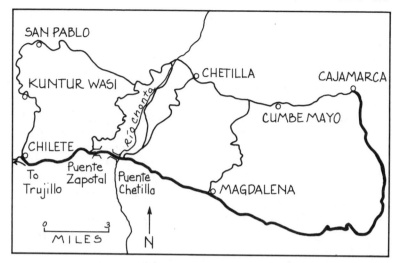

rock-lined, and it stays in fairly close proximity to the road, working its way up open hillsides and past thatch-roofed houses. Route finding is not difficult. After a long but not terribly steep climb up this trail, you'll walk the last mile or so to Cumbe Mayo on the road. From the main dirt road, look for a secondary road, which branches to the left, descending a short way into a valley and dead-ending at a turn around. Walk down this short road to reach Cumbe Mayo.

As you stand at the end of this road, the area all around you is the site of the ancient ceremonial center, and though the site has no structural ruins, it is still fascinating. In the distance you'll see groups of large naturally standing stones, which the *campesinos* call *frailones* (friars), seemingly guarding the area. Near the end of the road is the site's most distinctive feature, a huge boulder roughly resembling a human head with a man-made cave as the mouth. Inside the cave are Chavín petroglyphs. Don't neglect, too, to walk into the small canyon beyond the cave. It is a beautiful, lonely spot that surely has changed little in the 2,500 years since the Chavíns occupied it. Scattered through the canyon are several flat altar stones. There are also narrow aqueducts cut into the bedrock of the canyon that still carry water in the wet season. These too may have had a ceremonial purpose since they apparently were not designed to irrigate crops.

There are plenty of good campsites with available water in the area of Cumbe Mayo. If you wish to reach the site by vehicle, you'll probably have to hire a taxi in Cajamarca because few trucks travel the road.

From Cumbe Mayo, it is an easy twelve-mile walk to Chetilla. Simply walk back up to the main dirt road. Turn left and follow the road (very seldom used beyond Cumbe Mayo) for a mile or so until you see a group of braided trails branching to the left and climbing toward a rocky ridge. The road swings widely around at this point, so the trail across the ridge saves at least a mile of walking. Follow the trail across the ridge and across open grassy hillsides until it rejoins the road. Soon you'll reach the pass, and just below that, near a small double-barred cross and a couple of thatch-roofed huts, a trail branches to the left, descending six miles to the town of Magdalena on the main highway; there you can easily find transportation back to Cajamarca. The main route, however, begins to drop into a valley that very rapidly becomes green and cultivated. The town of Chetilla lies below you, and if the day is clear, you'll be able to see its rooftops during much of the descent. But if you find the valley obscured in dense fog, as we did, route finding can be a bit difficult. After descending from the pass, the dirt road, apparently almost never used by vehicles these days, gradually becomes grassy and dwindles to little more than a wide trail. And since Chetilla and the surrounding valley support a fairly large population, numerous wide trails cut through the valley, not all of them actually passing through Chetilla. If in this welter of paths you become uncertain as to the main route, just continue to descend, keeping generally to the right hand (northern) side of the valley. Make sure not to take trails leading too far toward the left side of the valley since some of them do not continue to descend but contour along high above the village, eventually bearing south and descending approximately ten miles to the main highway.

Chetilla is a simple little village without a hotel, restaurant, or reliable supplies. It is connected to the outside world only by trail. Chetilla apparently sees very few travelers, and as we passed through, we quickly became the day's main attraction. Soaking wet from the heavy fog and light rain, we became a source of excitement for the children who poured from the schoolyard and followed us through town in an impromptu parade. And we were a source of comedy for the adults who could not believe that anyone could get disoriented enough, even in the thick fog, to miss what they call *el camino real* (the royal highway) to San Pablo.

Several trails radiate from Chetilla, one going north to strike a road from Cajamarca, another going south to follow the Río Chonta to the main highway. The Kuntur Wasi route, however, continues generally west, descending sharply to the Río Chonta, crossing the river over a bridge, and then ascending through more cultivated land. Eventually (about six miles from Chetilla), you'll come to an obvious trail junction. The left branch is another of the trails descending to the Río Magdalena and the main highway (while most of the trails turning south in the Chetilla area unite a mile or so above the main highway, ending at Puente Chetilla, this wider trail descends to Puente Zapotal; at either spot, catching bus or truck transport back to Cajamarca should not be too difficult unless you reach the road very late in the day). The right-hand branch is the main route to the pass (about four miles ahead) and on to San Pablo and Kuntur Wasi.

The trail initially climbs fairly steeply but levels out for a stretch as it follows a stream later on. After crossing the stream over a bridge, the trail continues to climb, working its way westward to the pass. At the pass, a broad level area, several trails come together. Don't take the northerly, ascending trail that branches to the right; instead, look for the descending left-hand branch. This clear trail will take you through pleasant, inhabited, agricultural land for the last leg of the trek. From the pass it is six fast miles to San Pablo, all downhill except for the final, mile-long climb to the town.

The Chavín ruins of Kuntur Wasi are another couple of miles beyond San Pablo, just off the main San Pablo to Chilete road near a collection of houses called Pueblo Nuevo. You'll almost certainly have the overgrown ruins of the Chavín's large, truncated temple-pyramid to yourself. Though the guard probably won't let you camp at the site itself, it is possible to camp in the vicinity.

If you prefer not to camp, you'll find basic hotel accommodations back in San Pablo. Buses leave San Pablo early every morning for Chilete on the main highway. We managed, however, to catch a truck out at midday, and you might be able to do the same should you not want to spend the night either at San Pablo's hotel or camping near Kuntur Wasi. In Chilete, you should be able to catch buses either back to Cajamarca or on to Trujillo.

THE SOUTH-COAST ROUTE

Peru's south coast is profound desert. This barren strip of land between the mountains and the ocean is robbed of moisture by the cold offshore currents and the prevailing winds of the nearby *sierra.* It is as dry as any spot on earth. And as bleak. There is no vegetation, and in good weather there are only three colors in the *desierto,* the gray-brown of the sand, the pale blue of the sky, and the much deeper blue of the Pacific. In bad weather, when winds whip the loose sand into the air —first in thin plumes, then in thick clouds—the world becomes entirely beige, and thin grit works its way through even the most tightly closed window. For long stretches along the Pan-American highway that runs through this bleak landscape, the only features along the side of the road other than ocean and desert are the dozens of crosses and tiny shrines, some with candles burning through the night, that mark the spots of fatal accidents.

For life of any sort, the south coast is a precarious land indeed. Only where the rivers flow through the desert to the sea can life exist with any degree of security and comfort. But along these linear oases man has made a permanent home, occupying this hard land for perhaps as long as 10,000 years. It seems entirely fitting, given the landscape they chose to inhabit, that the ancient civilizations that occupied this harsh, arid coast are among the most mysterious cultures found anywhere in the New World. Of the people of Paracas and Nazca we know little. We have some of their textiles—excellent, tightly woven tapestries still flexible after hundreds of years—that experts have called the finest examples of weaving in the world. And we have the strange lines and figures cut into the desert floor at Nazca and Paracas, the puzzling

work of complex ancient minds we are still trying to understand. And
in Paracas and Nazca, we have the bones of the people themselves
scattered in the sand, covered and uncovered again and again by the
winds and blowing sand.

All too often, the relatively few travelers who venture down the
south coast either roar through on Lima-Arequipa express buses, or
they rush down to Nazca, overfly the lines, and rush back to Lima. The
desert, though, deserves better travelers; it repays the ones willing to
slow down and explore.

Travel along the south coast is a fairly simple matter. Fast buses
from several companies run the long, straight Pan-American highway
south of Lima, taking around fifteen hours for the 640-mile trip to
Arequipa, stopping, among many other towns, at Pisco, Ica, and Nazca.
Transportes Ormeño is the best of these, offering frequent departures
throughout the day and operating reasonably new buses (177 Avenida
Carlos Zavala, not far from the Sheraton). *Tepsa* (on Paseo de la
República) and *Roggero* (1324 Parque Universitario) also travel the
Lima-Arequipa route. For those going only as far as Pisco or Paracas,
Transportes General José de San Martin (581 Montevideo near Parque
Universitario in Lima; 136 Callao just off the Plaza de Armas in Pisco)
make frequent and cheap Lima-Pisco runs. *Colectivos* (fast and
crowded) for either Arequipa or any of the oasis towns along the way
leave from near the Parque Universitario. Comité 3 (581 Montevideo)
travels to Ica and Nazca, and Comité 2 (148 Avenida Carlos Zavala
Loayza) goes to Paracas.

The Paracas Peninsula

The first stopover on a trip down the south coast is the Paracas
peninsula, a fascinating if barren spit of gray sand sticking out into the
Pacific like an extended thumb hitching a ride to nowhere. Admittedly,
our first glimpse of Paracas was not one designed to instill great affec-
tion for the place—we arrived in a blinding sandstorm. Visibility
through the brown whirling air was limited to perhaps twenty feet. Our
colectivo driver let us out on a deserted stretch of highway, vaguely
indicating a side road as the way to Paracas. After a walk through the
stinging sand, we sat out the afternoon in the bamboo-walled bar of the
Hotel Paracas, where a stuffed condor and a whale jawbone hang above
the fireplace. "Mucho aire" (lots of wind), the bartender said, in what
had to be one of the most extreme understatements imaginable. The
wind shook the building, and drove fine sand around the closed windows, gradually dusting our tables and our beer. Why, we wondered,
had travelers whose judgment we valued insisted that we shouldn't miss
Paracas?

The next day, after the winds had died down and the skies cleared,
we found the answer to that question. Strapping on water bottles, we
set out on a long run across the peninsula, and within a few miles we
were converted. The beauty of the stark, pure desert landscape and the
rugged cliffs of the coastline began to erase the sandstorm from our

memories. And we soon found that the barren peninsula was not as void of life as we had expected. In fact, Paracas is one of Peru's National Wildlife Preserves, home to a healthy population of birds and mammals. The rocky Pacific shoreline is habitat for colonies of both sea lions and seals. In the winter, flamingos frequent the marshy areas skirting the Bay of Paracas. Various shore birds such as gulls, terns, and even penguins inhabit the coast and offshore islands. In the summer, especially during birthing periods for the seal and sea lion colonies, large numbers of condors cruise down from the mountains to sweep the beaches looking for carrion.

The area is also the possessor of a deep history, a fact that became strikingly obvious to us when we occasionally noticed beneath our feet shards of human bone lying half-buried in the sand. Two thousand years ago the people of the Paracas civilization used the peninsula as their sacred burial ground. In 1927, Peruvian archaeologist Julio Tello excavated the site, discovering over 400 mummy bundles at Paracas. The bodies, along with articles of clothing, pottery, textiles, and jewelry, were wrapped in fabric and buried in a seated position in baskets. Though most of the findings from the site are in Lima, a representative sample of mummies, textiles, and pottery is on display at the Julio C. Tello Museum at Paracas. One further and rather mysterious mark of an ancient civilization on the peninsula is the so-called "Candelabra," a huge Nazca-style earth drawing on a hillside along the peninsula's northern end. The Candelabra is best viewed from the sea and is visible to those making the trip out to the Islas Ballestras.

Your visit to Paracas should begin with a trip across the peninsula. The dirt road that crosses the peninsula ends at a beautiful spot called the Lagunillas. Here a small, protected bay is set in an otherwise wild coastline of sheer cliffs and pounding surf. On a warm day, Lagunillas is a perfect place to sunbathe and swim in the calm little bay. And you can sample the day's catch at the two very simple bayside restaurants that serve wonderful fresh seafood. It is possible to camp at Lagunillas, and there are usually several tents along the beach there, but water availability can be a problem. If you plan to camp there, bring water and check with park headquarters at the museum for current regulations or restrictions. An easy walk north along the coast from Lagunillas (a sign points the way) will take you to the Mirador Lobos. Here from the top of a high cliff over the ocean you can usually observe seals sunning on warm rocks and swimming in the surf.

Another dirt road (turning left off the main road about a mile before the park headquarters) crosses south of the peninsula's neck, running parallel to the coastline down to Laguna Grande with its large bird population and nearby sea mammal colonies. The seldom-visited area is wonderful for wildlife observation and general wandering around, but the long trip over rough roads requires a vehicle.

An interesting excursion in the Paracas area is the boat trip out to the Islas Ballestras. These rocky, guano-covered islands off the northern point of the peninsula are a good place to observe birds (especially the colony of Humbolt penguins) and sea mammals. Boats leave from the Hotel Paracas every morning for the four-hour round trip to the Islas.

To get to Paracas from Lima, you'll first need to take one of the regular coastal buses south to Pisco. The Bay of Paracas is ten miles down the coast from Pisco, and *colectivo* taxis and vans make the trip throughout the day. The Hotel Paracas also operates a van for its customers, which picks up passengers in Pisco late in the afternoon, usually around 5 to 6 P.M., and shuttles them to the hotel.

At the bay, there are really only two choices of accommodations. The moderately high-priced *Hotel Paracas* with many sea-view rooms, a clean swimming pool, and an excellent restaurant is one of the most pleasant Peruvian hotels we know of, an excellent spot to relax and enjoy wonderful seafood. The *Hotel Bahia,* nearby, is a step down in price and several steps down in quality. Neither hotel, however, is blessed with a reliable hot water supply (surprising at their prices).

The best restaurant in the area is at the Hotel Paracas, with relatively expensive but excellently prepared meals. Try any of their several superb *corvina* (sea bass) dishes. The *conchita* (sea scallops) are wonderful as well. For much cheaper meals, try the seafood stalls at the dock near the Hotel Paracas (just below the intersection of the main road and the Paracas road). There you'll eat seafood fresh off the boats, and you'll be eating with the crews of these boats, usually with their sacks of fresh, shell-clacking scallops thrown beneath the table.

Transportation through the peninsula is somewhat difficult to arrange. The Hotel Paracas operates short bus tours, which stop briefly at the museum, Lagunillas, and Mirador Lobos. You'll get a much better feel for Paracas, however, if you take more time and get out on your own. For conditioned walkers, the trip across the peninsula and back is well within comfortable day-hike range, especially if you catch a ride as far as the park headquarters. We found the peninsula to be an excellent location for long-distance running. We came to Paracas with a degree of high-altitude acclimatization, and the rich sea-level oxygen supply combined with the gently rolling terrain and firm off-road footing made us feel as if we could run all day. If you do head off into the peninsula afoot, though, be sure to take a full water bottle with you. If you venture off the dirt road (very little traffic beyond the pavement), pay attention and keep your bearings; it is easy to become disoriented in the featureless desert.

Ica

From Paracas, the Pan-American highway turns inland and within fifty miles reaches the oasis city of Ica, in the fertile valley of the Río Ica. One of the prettiest towns of the south coast, Ica's older sections are full of mature trees and shaded plazas, a welcome relief from the surrounding desert. The Ica valley is Peru's most famous wine-producing region, home of the Tacama, Ocucaje, and Vista Alegre vinyards, which offer winery tours and wine-tasting visits. But Ica's most famous product is the grape brandy called *pisco*, main ingredient in the *pisco* sour. The city's annual harvest festival in March is a lively combination of fiesta and agricultural fair.

The primary reason for a stopover in Ica, however, is the *Museo Regional*. Better than the Paracas or Nazca museums, the *Museo Regional*'s collection includes artifacts and mummies from all the coastal civilizations. It makes an excellent introduction to the region for those going on to overfly the Nazca lines. Though the huge lines and figures may always remain a mystery, seeing the artistic and domestic products of the Nazcans helps a visitor put the lines into human cultural context and makes the "flying saucer" theory look as silly as it is.

Nazca

Pampa San Jose, the arid plain on which the Nazcans hundreds of years ago (some say thousands of years ago) scratched out their gigantic complex lines and figures, is one of the most mysterious places on earth. The site is vast, indeed, stretching for miles over the *pampa*, and the sheer numbers of lines and figures drawn into the desert floor by the Nazcans (and perhaps by their predecessors as well) are staggering. Undetected for centuries, the site was rediscovered only as recently as the 1930s when Peruvian pilots spotted the strange desert markings from the air. The markings are virtually unnoticeable from ground level, but from above, it is clearly apparent that over a huge area the *pampa* is crisscrossed by hundreds of intersecting lines and the amazingly large and accurately drawn figures of birds, spiders, monkeys, fish, and even a strange human figure drawn on a hillside. The largest of the drawings exceeds 300 feet in length, and each one is drawn in a continuous line (leading to the speculation that they may have been ceremonial paths).

As interesting as the drawings are in themselves, the real puzzle of Nazca is what motivated the ancient desert peoples to fill the *pampa* with them. Determining the origin and purpose of these lines and figures has occupied researchers since their discovery. The fact that the lines are visible only from the air has led to some rather outlandish theories. One popular theory calls the lines spacecraft landing strips, and pilots of the small aircraft that fly visitors over the site usually drop down for a mock landing on one of the wider lines as "proof" of the theory. Another theory involves the speculation that the Nazcans constructed hot air balloons from their finely woven fabrics and floated over the *pampa* in religious ceremonies.

Calmer heads have looked for an answer to the puzzle of Nazca in the stars, seeing the site as a huge calendar, which, like Stonehenge, could be used by ancient astronomers to determine among other things the seasons, agricultural planting and harvest periods, and the dates of religious ceremonies. According to this theory, the lines might mark the rising or setting points of significant stars or star groups (like the Pleiades, an important constellation for several South American civilizations). Dr. Paul Kosok, one of the first scientists to study Nazca, called it "the largest astronomy book in the world." Recently, though, computer studies, which reconstructed the star patterns of the ancient skies, found little correlation between the lines and the rising or setting points of significant stars, deepening the mystery.

The most comprehensive study of the Pampa San Jose has been made by mathematician Dr. Maria Reiche, who came to Nazca in 1946 and stayed to spend her life studying the significance of the lines and protecting them from destruction. It is due largely to her efforts that the lines continue to exist because she fought proposals to irrigate the *pampa* and helped protect the lines from damage by vehicles. Despite the negative results of the computer studies, Reiche's long work at Nazca has convinced her that the lines and figures *are* of astronomical significance. She has also done much work to determine the methods of construction of the lines and figures and the levels of mathematical sophistication needed for planning them. Dr. Reiche lives at the *Turista* hotel in Nazca, where she continues her work and lectures in the evenings to hotel guests.

One of the most interesting explanations for the lines and figures is also the simplest. Author, filmmaker, and South American explorer Tony Morrison traveled throughout the Andes looking for other line patterns and found that they are a common feature of primal Andean religion. In the highlands of Bolivia he found lines still in use by the natives. There the lines are ceremonial pathways forming straight connections between points of religious significance, called *huacas.* On special days the paths are walked as a kind of simple worship. The lines and figures at Nazca, he speculates, served a similar function.

The final answer to the mystery of Nazca may never be found, but the Pampa San Jose remains a place of magnetic fascination, a place where the puzzle of the past is an overwhelming presence. The best way to see the vast work of the Nazcas is, of course, to fly over the *pampa.* Two companies, *AeroCóndor* (Sheraton Hotel Shopping Gallery, Lima) and *Aeroica* (677 Nicholas de Pierola #702, Lima), operate daily flights in single-engine aircraft. The flights last about an hour and circle all of the major figures. The flights are not cheap, but it's hard to imagine anyone taking the trouble to go to Nazca and not flying over the lines. If you plan to visit Nazca, you might check with a travel agent before you book your U.S.-Peru air tickets; AeroPeru sometimes offers a free promotional package with their Miami-Lima flights, which includes Lima-Nazca bus tickets, a night's accommodations, and an AeroCóndor flight over the lines.

For those not interested in the flights, Maria Reiche has built an observation tower near the Pan-American highway a few miles north of the town of Nazca, from which a couple of the smaller figures can be seen.

While you're in Nazca, you should visit the municipal museum with its collection of artifacts from the Nazca period. You may also want to visit the Nazca necropolis and a place called Cahuachi or the Estaqueria where ancient peoples erected tree trunks, perhaps as support for a pavilion. For reasonable fees, taxis in Nazca will take you on a tour of the area, usually including the necropolis, Cahuachi, and the observation tower.

The best hotel in Nazca is the moderately priced and very pleasant *Turista* (Avenida Bolognesi) with a clean swimming pool, a nice courtyard, and a good restaurant. A bit lower in price is the *Montecarlo,* also with a pool and their own flights over Pampa San Jose. The cheapest recommendable hotel is the *Hotel Nazca* (438 Calle Lima), which is clean and better than basic.

From Nazca you can either continue down the coast to Arequipa or you can turn east into the mountains to Abancay and on to Cuzco. Transportes Ormeño and Moralitos (not recommended) travel this route, taking around fourteen hours for the long, slow trip to Cuzco.

The Pan-American highway continues south, returning to the coast at Puerto de Lomas and continuing on to the tiny fishing village of Chala, a little over 100 miles from Nazca and about 250 miles from Arequipa. During Inca times, this was Cuzco's port, and from here Inca runners rushed fresh seafood back to Cuzco's royal court. There are still traces of Inca highways and buildings in the area. If you're taking your time getting to Arequipa, Chala, with its seafood restaurants and clean, inexpensive little *Turista* hotel, makes a good stopover along the way. Below Chala, the Pan-American highway skirts the bleak coast until it reaches Camana, at which point it turns inland for the climb to Arequipa.

Arequipa

Arequipa makes an excellent gateway to the Andes. Situated in the valley of the Río Chili and overlooked by El Misti, a nearly 20,000-foot unglaciated but often snow-capped volcano, Arequipa is often called Peru's most beautiful city. At its altitude of 7,608 feet, it offers travelers into the higher mountains a chance to acclimate to the heights in stages often gradual enough to avoid *soroche.* Arequipa also has an excellent climate. Average yearly rainfall is only a little over four inches, and daytime temperatures seldom drop below the fifties or rise above the seventies.

Since Inca times, Arequipa has been an important crossroads, the spot where the highway descending from Cuzco branched north toward the coast and south to the lower regions of the empire. The Spaniards took over the city in 1540, establishing a central Plaza de Armas and a surrounding grid of streets, as was their practice. Arequipa flourished during the Spanish colonial period, and the beautiful city still reflects as much colonial charm as any in Peru. Even some of the cheap, *tipico* restaurants of the center city have wonderfully arched, heavily beamed colonial ceilings. Many of the city's buildings, both colonial and modern, are built of a volcanic substance called *sillar,* a lightweight, cream-colored stone, which gives Arequipa its distinctive bright appearance and earns it its nickname, "The White City." Arequipa's central plaza, with its palm trees, massive cathedral, and excellent view of the great cone of El Misti, is one of the prettiest in the Andes.

While you're in Arequipa, by all means walk through the huge Cathedral (reconstructed in the nineteenth century after the original building was largely destroyed in an earthquake), and visit La Compañia (a Jesuit church constructed in the seventeenth century). Be sure as well to walk up the hill to Selva Alegre, a large park above the Río Chili. But the most remarkable feature of Arequipa is the Convent of Santa Catalina (on Calle Santa Catalina, three blocks above the Plaza de Armas). Built in the sixteenth century, the convent was opened to the public in 1970. Inside its high walls, Santa Catalina is a little colonial city in itself, with plazas, courtyards, and narrow cobblestone streets that wind their way among the surprisingly comfortable homes of the nuns, most of whom were from wealthy Peruvian families. There is a large, domed *sillar* church, an interesting laundry courtyard, a gallery of religious art, and even a bakery where you can stop for tea and cakes. You'll notice as you work your way through the convent that the various sectors of the complex are marked by the symbolic colors of the walls—progressing from earthy orange nearest the entrance, through sky blue, pure white, and finally blood red at the center. Finding your way through the labyrinth of streets is not easy, so you may benefit from the very reasonably priced services of the helpful guides who'll lead the way and explain the day-to-day routine of the convent during its 400 years of seclusion.

You'll also want to visit Arequipa's suburbs, once small villages but now swallowed up by the city's expansion. To the northeast, an easy walk across the Río Chili from central Arequipa, are Yanahuara and Cayma, both with fine old churches (climb to the tower of the Iglesia de Cayma for good views of the mountains and the city) and narrow streets. Also good for general wandering around are the areas of Tingo and Tiabaya below Arequipa. These make good lunchtime destinations since they are the home of several *picanterias.* Tingo is something of a recreation area with swimming pools and a small lake (good local food there). To get to these areas, either take a taxi or one of the frequent Tingo-Tiabaya buses that run down La Merced.

A simple, relaxing acclimatizing walk from downtown Arequipa is to ramble through the green valley alongside the Río Chili for a couple of hours. From the plaza walk uphill along Santa Catalina or San Francisco. At Calle Ayacucho, turn left; immediately after crossing the Chili at Puente Grau, look for paths leading down to the river. At the bottom, take the upriver path in the direction of Misti.

RESOURCES

■ **Hotels** For very good moderately priced accommodations, it's hard to beat the *Hotel Crismar* (in the same block of Calle Moral San Jose as the post office); it is clean, well run, and centrally located. A step down in price and service is the *Arequipa Inn* (a little out of the way on Calle Riviero) with clean rooms and private baths. At the lower end of the scale but a good value is the *Los Portales* (a half-dozen blocks from the Plaza de Armas at 306 Calle Puente Grau) with clean rooms, hot water, and a very pleasant sun deck.

■ **Restaurants** Arequipa is probably the best place in Peru to sample a wide variety of Andean cuisine. The city is full of *picanterias,* restaurants specializing in the highly seasoned food of the region. But so popular is the local food that even the pizza restaurants on the plaza include such items as *rocoto relleno* (stuffed hot peppers), *adobo* (a spicy pork stew), and *ocopa* (boiled potatoes with a creamy hot sauce). For the best in authentic *picanteria Arequipeña* food, don't miss the *Sol de Mayo* (107 Calle Jerusalem in the Yanahuara district; there is also a Calle Jerusalem in the central city, so don't be confused). For more ordinary meals and sandwiches, simply walk up Calle San Francisco from the plaza and take your choice of several restaurants along the way. For adequate pizza, spaghetti, and lasagna, try *Pizza Nostra* on the plaza.

■ **Transportation** The AeroPeru office is on the Plaza de Armas. There are daily AeroPeru and Faucett flights to Lima and Cuzco. AeroPeru also schedules daily flights to Juliaca near Puno (if you're on a tight schedule, this half-hour flight is really not much more expensive than the train, and it is infinitely easier and quicker; the flight doesn't go in bad weather because the Juliaca landing strip is dirt).

The very heavily booked train from Arequipa to Puno on Lake Titicaca allegedly leaves daily at 9:30 P.M., on Mondays, Wednesdays, and Fridays at 8:30 A.M. (a good choice since the scenery along the way is wonderful and deserves to be seen in the daytime), taking around nine hours to reach Puno. This schedule is very much subject to change, especially the daytime departures. Buffet car service for the day train and pullman service for the night train are usually available and well worth the reasonable extra charge. Tickets may be bought a day in advance at the station (down La Merced from the plaza; tickets are only sold from 11 A.M. to 1 P.M. and from 3 P.M. to 5 P.M.).

■ **Money Exchange** Banco de la Nación, 204 Palacio Viejo, is extremely tedious in changing money and may not honor traveler's checks. The Casa de Cambio at 115–B Rivero will change dollars. Interbanc, a block up Mercaderes from the plaza, will cash traveler's checks with reasonable dispatch.

■ **Communications** The post office is at 118 Moral San Jose. The ENTEL office for international calls is on Calle Palacio Viejo, a block south of the Plaza de Armas. Another office is on Calle La Salle near San Agustin University.

■ **Tourist Information** The Ministry of Tourism is at 117 La Merced. There is also a tourist office on the plaza (friendly and helpful staff).

■ **Museum** The small *Museo Arquelogico* is near the intersection of La Salle and Independencia, upstairs in a San Agustin University building. You may have to ask the museum's director, Professor

Linares, whose office is a few doors down the hall from the museum entrance, to unlock it for you. He is appreciative of small donations for the museum's upkeep. The museum has a representative sample of pottery and other artifacts from the major periods of Peruvian civilization.

Excursions from Arequipa

After you've explored this beautiful colonial city, you'll want to get out into the countryside around Arequipa, which offers the outdoor traveler several outstanding excursions—everything from climbing El Misti to visiting the strange petroglyphs at Toro Muerto to touring the Colca valley where at one point the canyon is reportedly the deepest in the Western hemisphere.

The problem in planning an outdoor trip in the Arequipa region is that transportation can be very difficult. The points of interest are widely separated, and public transportation over the rough roads is slow. On top of that, public transportation is often extremely inconvenient. For example, if you want to visit the Toro Muerto site and have a look at the nearby Majes canyon as well, putting together bus and truck transport that will take you where you want to go and return you to Arequipa by nightfall will be nearly impossible. Of course if you don't mind extreme uncertainty, you could simply set off and hope for the best, but based on our experience in getting around the area, we'd recommend more definite transportation.

An agency called *Turandes* (130 Mercaderes, #14 upstairs) offers a variety of services ranging from simple excursions to Majes or Colca all the way to guided climbs of El Misti and Chachani. By far the most extensive range of trips in the Arequipa region is offered by Anthony Holley, an enterprising and lively British gentleman who knows the countryside like few others (contact him in the evenings by phone, 22–44–52, or look for his Land Rover parked near Santa Catalina Convent when he is not on tour). Mr. Holley drives his Rover on excursions ranging from simple trips to the Majes Canyon and Toro Muerto to an excellent tour of the Colca Valley to an ambitious journey to Cailloma, headwaters of the Amazon. In addition, Mr. Holley provides the valuable service of transporting climbers. For a very reasonable fee, he'll drop you off at Aguada Blanca Dam, the starting point for the ascent of El Misti, and pick you up at a prearranged time a day or two later. Of course, another way to get around the Arequipa area is to rent a car for a couple of days. If you have several people sharing the cost, car rental is probably less expensive than traveling with one of the touring agencies (contact Arequipa Rent-a-Car, Calle Pierola).

The Colca Valley

This lovely, isolated region in the Caylloma Province of the Department of Arequipa is a wonderful place to visit for anyone wishing to get a real feel for life in the Andean highlands. Scattered all along the terraced valley are little villages and settlements where rural life goes on much as it has for centuries.

Just getting to Colca is an interesting excursion in itself. The unpaved road leaves Arequipa, climbs between Misti and Chachani, and then crosses the Pampa Cañahuas. In this area is the Aguada Blanca National Reserve where the rare vicuña and *taruka* are protected from hunters. Then before descending into the Colca valley, the road reaches its high point of over 15,000 feet, offering along the way excellent views of Nevado Ampato (20,900 feet).

Chivay, the principal town of the province, is a typical Andean village, relatively unspoiled. While there, you might enjoy a soak in the hot springs at Calera, just a mile outside of Chivay. Not to be missed is the road that runs between Chivay and Cabanaconde (thirty miles), often following the rim of the Colca canyon. Along this road, near the village of Pinchoillo, is an overlook from which it is a 4,000-foot drop to the river below. The Colca region is also evidently one of the best spots in Peru for observing condors; though we didn't spot any while we were there, practically everyone we ran into along the way had seen at least one.

Empresa Silva buses (219 Pampita de Zeballos, just off Avenida Ejercito across the Río Chile) leave Arequipa daily at 6 A.M. for the five-hour trip to Chivay. Occasional buses and frequent trucks (better views) travel the canyon rim road between Chivay and Cabanaconde. If you plan to spend the night in Chivay, however, don't expect much in the way of accommodations. The town's one hotel is very basic and not particularly clean. Alternatively, several touring agencies in Arequipa (see below) operate one-day round-trips to the Colca valley, usually with stops at Aguada Blanca, Chivay, and the canyon rim (but make sure to find out just how far down the canyon road the agency goes; you'll want a tour that goes at least as far as Pinchoillo).

Toro Muerto

Located about ninety miles from Arequipa not far from the Río Majes is the strange Toro Muerto site. Here, scattered across the high desert plane, literally thousands of petroglyphs estimated to be 1,200 years old depict animals, birds, reptiles, and dancers.

Though it is possible to reach Toro Muerto from Arequipa by taking a bus to the town of Corire (four to five hours) and then walking to the site (one to two hours), making the trip and returning to Arequipa by nightfall is difficult. The trip is much more enjoyable if done by car or with a touring agency.

El Misti

Though a long, steep haul, the climb up El Misti is not technically demanding. Few mountains in the 20,000-foot range are as accessible as this one. Recently, we're told, a foot race up the mountain was staged. Still, those with no mountaineering experience whatsoever should probably hire a guide from Turandes before attempting the ascent. The route up the mountain is quite clear; a path (actually numerous parallel paths) beaten down by previous climbers makes the ascent. If you arrange transport to and from the dam at Aguada Blanca with either Turandes or Anthony Holley (*much* simpler than trying to take buses), you may be able to make the ascent and return in two days if you begin climbing very early on the second day and arrange for a late afternoon pickup. For most climbers, though, three days is a much more comfortable pace. Most people camp at the stone enclosure about a half-day's walk from the dam, ascend the mountain to its cratered summit the next day, and walk out the third day.

Puno

Puno is a high, cold city. If you arrive here on a gray day when bitter winds whip across Titicaca, the lake is the color of lead, and everyone walks the streets huddled and wrapped in dark ponchos, you may think it is the bleakest place imaginable. But when the weather is fine and clear and the brilliant sun of the *altiplano* warms the air a bit and the sky and water are dazzling shades of blue, Puno is invigorating.

The city itself has little to attract the visitor—a fairly undistinguished Cathedral on the Plaza de Armas and a fairly good Museo Municipal with an interesting collection of Tiahuanaco artifacts. Puno is, however, one of the best cities in Peru for handcrafts. If you're interested in shopping, you should begin at the market, in the covered section of which you'll find a good selection of regional crafts including sweaters, ponchos, alpaca items, and stone carvings. You might also try some of the craft shops near the plaza; for example, the Artesanal de Puno (corner of Lima and Deustua near the plaza) or the Fraternal de Artesanos (106 Jiron Arequipa).

Puno's real attraction, of course, is its proximity to Lake Titicaca, the world's highest navigable lake, and the mythical birthplace of Manco Capac and Mama Occlo, the original ancestors of the Incas. To fully appreciate the Puno region, you must get out onto the lake and into the harsh *altiplano* that surrounds it.

Excursions from Puno

An interesting trip into the *altiplano* is to the pre-Inca *chullpas* of Sillustani, twenty miles outside Puno. The *chullpas* are stone or sometimes adobe burial towers that contained the bodies of the dead along with the food, pottery, clothing, and other articles they would need in the afterlife. *Chullpas* are a fairly common feature of the Andes, but these at Sillustani are particularly interesting because of their size (up to forty feet tall) and their setting overlooking the bleak *altiplano* and the lagoon of Umayo. To reach Sillustani, either hire a taxi or arrange a trip with any of Puno's touring agencies.

The most popular excursion from Puno is the half-day trip out to the floating islands of the Uros Indians. As you cross the lake to the islands, you'll surely see men and women in boats gathering reeds in the shallows. These are the Uros, people whose lives are remarkably linked to the *totora* reeds they gather. From these reeds they make their distinctive boats, little canoelike craft constructed by lashing together

four long bundles of reeds and sometimes propelled by a reed sail. The
Uros even built a boat for one of Thor Heyerdahl's expeditions. The
homes of the Uros, too, are entirely constructed of reeds. Most remarkably of all, though, even the islands they inhabit are made of reeds. The
so-called floating islands were built and are continuously maintained by
simply piling dried reeds into the shallow lake. Walking across one of
these islands is like walking on a damp sponge; with each step you feel
the reeds beneath you give and rebound. Each small island holds a reed
hut or two and perhaps a miniscule plot for growing potatoes. Even the
small degree to which the Uros have entered the money economy is also
based on the reeds because they now sell small replicas of their boats
to tourists who visit the islands. Boats traveling to the floating islands
leave from Puno's waterfront. Rates are fixed, depending on the number of islands you wish to visit.

An excellent all-day trip across Lake Titicaca is the voyage to the
large island of Taquile. Make sure to leave early for this trip because

Uros child, Lake Titicaca

it involves six hours of round-trip boat travel from Puno, and you'll want to have plenty of time to walk about the village and explore the island a bit. There are old agricultural terraces and several small ruins on the island, the remains of both Inca and pre-Inca cultures. The people of Taquile live mostly by fishing and selling handcrafts (several shops with excellent weavings, ponchos, carvings, etc.). Though Taquile has no hotels, it is possible to spend the night on the island since the local handcraft cooperative regularly arranges lodging and meals in the homes of its members. If you plan to spend the night, take a sleeping bag.

To reach Taquile for a day trip, it is best to make your arrangements the day before with one of the boatmen on the Puno waterfront, establishing in advance the cost of the trip and the amount of time you wish to spend on the island (otherwise you may feel unpleasantly rushed by a pilot impatient to return to Puno). If you plan to spend the night on the island, a more convenient and much cheaper way to get to Taquile is on one of the local *colectivo* boats that leave from the dock very early, usually about 7 A.M., but ask around the dock the afternoon before you want to leave. Other good lake excursions include trips out to either Amantani or Soto islands. Similar to Taquile, but even less frequently visited, these large islands (four to five hours, round-trip from Puno) are the homes of Aymara fishermen. Again, arrange transportation a day in advance with the boatmen at the dock.

Finally, for those going on to La Paz, a much more interesting way to make the trip than going by bus is to take the steamer *Ollanta* across the lake to Guaqui in Bolivia where it connects with a train to La Paz. Scheduling this trip, though, can be difficult because the *Ollanta* sails only once a week, leaving for Guaqui on Wednesday evenings and returning to Puno on Friday evenings (bunks for sleeping included in ticket price). Buy tickets ahead of time at the dock.

RESOURCES

■   **Hotels**   If you have a few *soles* to spare, the expensive new *Turista* hotel built on a small island just offshore from Puno is a spectacular place to spend a day or two overlooking Lake Titicaca. It has wonderful lake-view rooms and a good restaurant, but the heating system is poor (guests spend the evenings huddled around the fireplace in the lobby, not out of camaraderie but because their rooms are freezing). Very convenient for those arriving or departing by train is the moderately priced *Hotel Ferrocarril* (185 Avenida de Torre, just across from the train station). The hotel is clean and quiet and has private baths and some hot water; surprisingly, the rooms are heated. The Ferrocarril has a good restaurant with Andean music in the evenings. Also good is the *Hostal Italia* (122 Avenida Valcarcel, near the train station) with private baths, hot water, and a restaurant. Puno's inexpensive *gringo* hotel is the *Europa* (corner of Ugarte and La Torre, near the railroad station).

■ **Restaurants** In Puno it is generally preferable to eat in your hotel's restaurant rather than wander the cold, empty streets looking for an independent restaurant, especially since Puno restaurants are undistinguished. A couple of places, *Las Rocas* and the *Paititi* (vegetarian), both on Jiron Valcarsel near the Hostal Italia, are recommendable. The *La Isla* (on Alfonso Ugarte between La Torre and Valcarsel) serves good, inexpensive meals.

■ **Transportation** Puno-Cuzco trains depart at 6:45 A.M. Monday through Friday and at 9:30 A.M. on Saturday for the eleven-hour trip. The train is often full, so tickets should be purchased in advance at the station (on Avenida La Torre). The long but exciting railway crosses the bleak *altiplano,* pausing for a sometimes frustratingly long stopover to change cars at Juliaca. Later in the day, the line reaches its high point of over 14,000 feet at La Raya before passing first through the beautiful Vilcanota valley, rimmed with glaciated peaks, and then winding through the Huatanay valley on the last leg to Cuzco. The train makes more than two dozen stops along the way, at most of which vendors sell sweaters, ponchos, bread, sandwiches, cakes, soft drinks, etc., through the train's windows. Those who want a meal served to them on the train should buy tickets for the buffet car.

The Puno-Arequipa train departs nightly at 8:30 P.M. for the ten-hour trip (pullman cars available). Day trains may be scheduled as well, but this service is frequently canceled, so check with the train station for current information.

Bus travel to either Cuzco (ten hours) or Arequipa (twelve hours) is available through both the *Morales Moralitos* and the *San Cristobal* companies. The train, however, is much more comfortable.

For Bolivia-bound travelers, there are two overland routes to La Paz. The more direct route skirts the lake, passing Juli, crossing the Bolivian border at Desaguadero, and pounding over rough dirt roads across the very desolate *altiplano* before finally reaching La Paz. Morales Moralitos travels this route in worn out buses, which leave from Puno daily at 9 A.M. for the all-day trip. A word of caution: Bolivian immigration officials at Desaguadero are the worst we've ever seen; we had discounted the tales we'd heard about them in Puno, but as we passed through customs these officials very flagrantly stole an expensive ballpoint pen from one man and fabricated a problem with documents to elicit a bribe from another. Have your documents in order and watch the officials *very* carefully.

The alternate route to La Paz crosses the Bolivian border between Yunguyo and Copacabana (much less mercenary officials) and requires a ferry ride across the Straits of Tiquinia before the final leg of the trip into La Paz. The scenery along this route is much more interesting than along the Desaguadero route, but you'll have to change buses several times along the way, making for a cumbersome trip. Take either a Moralitos or La Perla bus from Puno to Yunguyo, then catch a local bus from Yunguyo to Copacabana, then find a Copacabana-to-La Paz bus. Buses travel frequently between these towns, so unless you're extremely unlucky, you should be able to make connections quickly enough to complete the Puno-La Paz trip in one day. For an overnight stop along the way, though, Copacabana is a pleasant town with several good hotels (see Chapter 6 for details).

If you wish to fly to Arequipa or on to Lima, buy tickets from the AeroPeru office in Puno's old Hotel Turista (255 Alfonso Ugarte) as far in advance as possible. Flights depart from the Juliaca airport, a half-hour taxi ride (cheap *colectivos* sometimes available) from Puno.

■   **Money Exchange**   The Banco de la Nación (156 Tacna) will exchange dollars and traveler's checks but may require a photocopy of your passport. The Money Exchange Gladys (280 Jiron Puno near the plaza) changes cash and checks with much less difficulty. For those coming from Bolivia, Puno money changers offer very poor rates for Bolivian pesos.

■   **Touring Agencies**   Both Amantani Travel (464 Avenida Titicaca, toward the waterfront) and Kinjyo Travel (410 Calle Arequipa) offer several land and water tours of the area around Puno.

HEARTLAND OF THE INCA EMPIRE

Cuzco

If you fly to Cuzco, you'll arrive early in the morning, and if the weather is good, as you step out of the plane, the brilliant, high-Andes light and the thin, crisp air become immediately palpable forces. As you look around the valley where Cuzco sits, you'll know immediately how the Incas arrived at its name, which is derived from the Quechua word for *navel*. Not only does the hill-ringed valley physically resemble a navel, it was also, as the capital of the empire, the center of the Inca's world. Here, according to Inca legend, the empire's founders, Manco Capac and his sister and wife Mama Ocllo, came after their emergence from Lake Titicaca, establishing the city and bringing civilization to the world.

Whatever the actual origins of the city were, it was probably originally inhabited by the people who became the Incas sometime in the eleventh century, and it remained little more than a small mountain village until the reign of the greatest of Inca emperors, Pachacuti, in the fifteenth century. Under Pachacuti—whose son, Topa, could be considered the New World's Alexander the Great—the domain of the Incas expanded dramatically as the result of a brilliantly planned series of conquests that eventually, during Topa's rule, brought virtually all the territory between northern Chile and Ecuador under Inca control. While Topa was conquering the scattered civilizations of the Andes, Pachacuti was planning the expansion of his capital city. He is supposedly responsible for laying out the plan for the city and for much of the construction of the Temple of the Sun, as well as many of the other public buildings of Incan Cuzco. By the time Pachacuti abdicated in favor of Topa Inca in 1471, Cuzco was near the height of its power. For only a very brief period of little more than a half-century before the Spanish arrived, Cuzco was indeed the navel of the Inca's world, a great governmental and religious center filled with massive palaces and temples. The city was laid out in the form of a puma, an animal considered sacred in Andean civilizations for thousands of years. The fortress of Sacsayhuaman was the puma's head, the Río Tullumayo (now underground) its backbone, and the city proper its body, with its center at the Huacaypata plaza. This great plaza was circled by the palaces of previous Inca rulers and the House of the Chosen Women.

Cuzco was also the busy hub of the *capac nan,* the radiating system of roads that connected the widely separated quarters of the Inca world, called the four *suyos.* On these roads Inca runners, the *chasquis,* would have stayed busy carrying imperial messages in relays from Cuzco to the far-away provincial capitals. They could, for example, make the trip to Lima in three days, a time you'd be hard pressed to match by bus today. Also over these roads came pilgrims from all over the empire to worship at their religion's source, the huge and lavish Temple of the Sun. Others undoubtedly came to conduct governmental business—representatives of the governing *apus* and *quipucamayocs,* the Inca equivalent of a Certified Public Accountant. All in all, Cuzco, during its few decades of grandeur, would have been one of the great cities of the world.

This grandeur was hardly lost on the conquistadores. When the first members of Pizarro's group entered the city in 1533, they found the closest thing to El Dorado, the city of gold, that ever existed in the New World. The Temple of the Sun (the Coricancha) is representative of the grandeur of the Incas. This huge religious complex housed hundreds of priests, and the walls of many of the rooms were covered with panels of solid gold. According to some chroniclers, the Sun Temple's focal point, a great gold representation of the sun, was hidden by the priests and never found by the looters. In the temple's gardens, an entire life-size farm of solid gold—with corn, animals, and even a farmer —reportedly existed until the Spanish melted it down into bullion. So golden was the city than even after Cuzco donated its large share to Atahualpa's incredible ransom, the Spanish still were able to relieve the city of another 15,000 pounds of gold.

We hardly expect conquerors to be particularly sensitive to the values of the cultures they invade, but Pizarro and his men surely rank among the most callous and ethnocentric men in history. The last of the Inca gold had hardly been melted down and sent back to Spain when they began dismantling what Pachacuti and Topac Inca had built. Following the battles of 1536 when the successor to the Inca throne, Manco Capac, led a concerted and very nearly successful uprising, the Spanish began a sustained effort to rebuild Cuzco in the image of their homeland, building first the Triunfo church (1536, but since reconstructed) to celebrate the victory over Manco Capac, and then moving quickly to other churches, municipal buildings, and *casas.*

Street musician and Inca stoneware, Cuzco, Peru

In the interests of expediency, however, they often used the lower walls of principal Inca palaces and temples as foundations for their construction. Nowhere is the deep division in the city's character more apparent than in its architectural schizophrenia. As you walk through the narrow, cobbled side streets, the buildings themselves with their massive Inca walls and colonial superstructures are clear representations of Cuzco's dualism. The Cathedral, for example, is also the site of the Temple of Viracocha; the Convent of Santo Domingo incorporates much of the stone work of the great Temple of the Sun; the Plaza de Armas where Tupac Amaru, the last descendant of the Inca emperors to fight for the throne, was executed by the Spanish is also the site of the Huacaypata, the town square where once a year the Incas held the Festival of the Dead, displaying there the corpses of their ancestors. It is in this contrast and the very visible historical schism it represents that Cuzco's uniqueness lies, a uniqueness that draws travelers of all sorts from throughout the world.

Because Cuzco is a small city and while there you'll undoubtedly want to begin getting in shape for the mountains, the best way to get to know the Inca half of Cuzco is by walking its streets. Begin at the Plaza de Armas. Imagine the spot in Inca times when it was much larger, extending to the southwest all the way to the area of the Plaza Regocijo. On the hills to the west you would have seen jutting into the sky the stone towers that marked the solstices, indicating planting and harvesting periods. Standing on the northwest side of the plaza was the palace of Pachacuti (Pizarro appropriated the palace as his residence during his time in Cuzco), a corner of which is still visible as part of a restaurant. Across the plaza on the southeast end is some of the best of Cuzco's remaining Inca stonework. There stood the Acllahuasi, the House of the Chosen Women, where women selected for their beauty and weaving skills served as the equivalents of both nuns and concubines to the royalty. Perhaps appropriately, part of the structure now houses the Convent of Santa Catalina. Beside Acllahuasi, separated by the narrow, cobbled Calle Loreto is Amarucancha, the palace of Huayna Capac, now the foundation of La Compañia church (founded in 1571 but rebuilt in 1668). As you walk down Calle Loreto with the walls of Acllahuasi on your left and those of Amarucancha on your right, notice how tightly the stones fit together without benefit of mortar. These buildings have repeatedly withstood earthquakes that have crumbled colonial buildings.

If you continue walking down Loreto and its extension, Pampa del Castillo, you'll eventually come to the Convent of Santo Domingo, which incorporates perhaps the finest example of Inca stonework in Cuzco, the rounded tower of the Coricancha. This once-huge structure, most of which stood below the present street level, was the center of Incan religion, and inside it were also smaller temples dedicated to lesser dieties, such as the moon, Venus, thunder, and the rainbow.

At Santo Domingo, turn left and walk a block along Zeta to an area known as Limacpampa Chica, turning left there onto Romeritos. Follow Romeritos to Marui, turn left there, and then right on Arequipa, which leads you back to the Plaza de Armas. All along this route, you'll again walk beside the foundations of Inca structures. If you turn right on Triunfo just as you reach the plaza, in two blocks you'll reach one of the most massive Inca walls in Cuzco. This is the palace of Inca Roca, and halfway down its wall you'll find the famous twelve-angled stone, a good example of the skill of Inca stonemasons.

To help put Inca history into context, be sure to visit Cuzco's Archaeological Museum, only a couple of blocks from the plaza at 165 Tigre. The museum's fairly small but interesting collection includes fine examples of Inca artifacts, including ceramics, tools, metal implements and ornaments, weavings, and even a few gold and silver items that somehow escaped the attention of the Spanish. One of the museum's rooms contains a collection of mummies and other exhibits related to Inca burial practices.

Cuzco's colonial heritage, the second half of the city's split personality, is almost as fascinating as its Inca origins, and you should not miss visiting some of the town's excellent examples of Spanish architecture. Begin at Plaza de Armas, site of the executions of the last of the Inca successors to the throne. The first colonial building project was the Triunfo, a chapel built on the site of an Inca storehouse, which the conquistadores used as a fortress during the battles of 1536. Construction of the Triunfo, which stands just to the right of the Cathedral, began immediately after Manco Inca's defeat, but the present building dates from 1733. The Cathedral itself is one of the most remarkable in the Americas. Notice in particular the many examples of Quechua craftsmanship in both the stonework of the structure and the fine metal work (especially the silver pulpit) and woodwork (the elaborately carved cedar choir) of the interior. Note too the hundreds of religious paintings, particularly those of the Cuzqueña school. These Quechua artists sometimes had a rather vague sense of traditional European religious imagery, leading to interesting anachronisms in some of the paintings: for example, a depiction of the Last Supper with Jesus and the apostles sitting down to a hearty meal of roast *cuy* (guinea pig). Also of interest is La Compañia, the huge Jesuit church also on the plaza.

Three of Cuzco's best examples of colonial nonpublic architecture have the added attraction of now housing museums. For one of the best illustrations of colonial domestic architecture make the short walk to the Admiral's Palace (a block up Tucuman from the plaza). The restored mansion, built in the early seventeenth century, is now the Regional Historical Museum, so in addition to viewing the structure's interesting interior, you can see a collection of both Inca and colonial artifacts. For another example of colonial architecture, visit the archbishop's palace (the corner of Hatunrumioc and San Agustin). Constructed on the walls of the palace of Inca Roca, this structure now houses the Museum of Religious Art with its large collection of Cuzqueña paintings and religious paraphernalia. Also worth visiting is the house of Garcilaso de la Vega (on Heladeros opposite the Hotel Turista Cuzco). Garcilaso, of both Incan and Spanish descent, was the most famous though not the most reliable of the early chroniclers. The building is now the archives of the Department of Cuzco, housing exhibits of colonial furniture, paintings, etc.

Entrance to almost all of Cuzco's Inca and colonial historic sites and museums requires a combined admission ticket (fairly expensive; individual admission tickets are not available).

RESOURCES

■ **Hotels** Since it is the unrivaled tourist mecca of the Andes, Cuzco is filled with hotels, ranging in price from the quite elegant and very expensive *Hotel Libertador* to filthy, $2-a-night, hole-in-the-wall pensions. For good, moderately priced lodgings, we've found nothing nicer than the friendly, centrally located *Hotel Garcilaso* (233 Calle Garcilaso). The hotel occupies a fine old colonial mansion, but the rooms are modern and carpeted, with private baths and plenty of hot water. Offering similar accommodations is the *Conquistador* (149 Santa Catalina, just off the plaza), another good moderately priced hotel, though its rather dark rooms make it a second choice to the Garcilaso. A step down in price but still quite pleasant is the *Hostal Mantas* (115 Calle Mantas, second floor), with clean, carpeted rooms, private baths, and hot water. Another step down in price is the *El Sol* (338 San Andres, about four blocks from the plaza). The plain, clean rooms have private baths and frequently hot water. We've stayed at the El Sol a couple of times and have been pleased with their service; they've very happily stored our luggage while we're out on the trail, done our laundry, and even uncomplainingly opened up in the middle of the night to find rooms for us. The *Hostal Corihuasi* (561 Suecia), with clean rooms and good service, is among the best of Cuzco's inexpensive hotels. For very inexpensive lodgings, try the numerous pensions on Plateros and its extension, Sapphi. A final word of advice on hotels: if you visit Cuzco outside the peak travel months, June through August, or if the hotel seems fairly empty, bargaining for lower rates is usually successful.

■ **Restaurants** Having been in and out of Cuzco over and over, using it as a place to rest and eat something besides trail food after trips into the mountains, we've had meals in most of the restaurants in town. We've gradually developed a theory, which we have yet to be able to prove, that all of the restaurants facing the Plaza de Armas operate out of a single, huge, underground kitchen beneath the plaza. Their food is not particularly bad, but both the menus and the food are virtually identical from place to place, so take your choice. The *Tumi* and the *Paititi,* both with good, moderately priced steaks and chicken, are perhaps worth singling out as a cut above the rest of the plaza restaurants. For a special and relatively expensive dinner, try *El Truco* (on Calle Santa Teresa at the little Plaza Regocijo). Here you'll find some of Cuzco's best food (excellent trout from the Urubamba) and a nightly *folklorico* show with Andean music and dancing. El Truco is a popular spot for trekkers on their last evening in Peru. One place we find ourselves returning to fairly often for its adequate Italian food and pleasant dining room is the moderately priced *Trattoria Adriano* (corner of Mantas and Sol). Should you find yourself desperate for pizza, try *La Mamma* (on Plaza Regocijo, a block from the Plaza de Armas) or *Chez Maggie* (up Procuradores, the narrow pedestrian street that begins at the plaza). One of our favorite Cuzco restaurants and probably the best value in town is the very inexpensive *Govinda,* a vegetarian restaurant run by the Hare Krishnas. But don't let that put you off; they won't try to sell you anything but good three-course meals, yogurt, and excellent bread and cakes at prices you won't believe. For years the Govinda was in a tiny bare room on Procuradores, but they've recently moved to very calm and pleasant surroundings at 128 Calle Espaderos, a half-block from the plaza. If your stomach is ready for local specialties, you might try *chicarrones* or *adobo* at one of the dark little restaurants up Plateros from the plaza, and if your stomach is really acclimated, walk over to the Plaza San Francisco or to the market and try *anticuchos.* These strips of beef heart cooked on skewers over charcoal by street vendors taste better than you'd think.

■ **Transportation** Both AeroPeru (corner of Quera and Matara) and Faucett (567 Avenida Sol) have two flights daily (sometimes three during peak travel periods) between Cuzco and Lima. These airlines also have flights several times a week to Puerto Maldonado, Arequipa, and Iquitos. Twice-weekly Lloyd-AeroBoliviana flights between Cuzco and La Paz have only recently been instituted, but most people would probably prefer to make the trip overland by rail to Puno and then on to La Paz either by the steamer across Lake Titicaca or by bus through Copacabana in order not to miss the scenery along the way. Remember to reconfirm any flights out of Cuzco well in advance because all of the flights are heavily booked.

Cuzco has two train stations. The station for trains to Juliaca, Puno, and Arequipa is down Avenida Sol beyond the post office; the San Pedro station for trains to Machu Picchu is by the market on Ccascaparo. The Puno train departs Monday through Saturday at 8:10 A.M. for the nine-hour trip; the buffet car is available for an additional charge. The tourist train to Machu Picchu departs daily at 7 A.M. for the three-and-a-half-hour trip; this train does not stop at km 88 for Inca Trail hikers. The local train, which does stop at km 88 (and dozens of other places along the way), leaves daily at 6 A.M. Try to buy tickets for all rail travel a day in advance.

Though several bus companies travel to Lima, Arequipa, and Puno, any long-distance road travel from Cuzco is extremely time-consuming and difficult. Durations for most trips are measured in days rather than hours. So we recommend air or rail travel if at all possible. One possible exception is the so-called "luxury" bus *Transturin* (191 Portal Harinas, on the plaza), which operates between Cuzco and La Paz. Buses leave Cuzco on Tuesday, Thursday, and Sunday at 6 P.M., and the trip takes a full twenty-four hours, including stops for breakfast at Puno and lunch at Copacabana.

Transportes Caparo (700 Calle Sapphi) operates buses through the Urubamba valley, with departures scattered throughout the day. Some buses go all the way to Ollantaytambo; others turn around at Urubamba.

■ **Money Exchange**   The Banco de la Nación (corner of Avenida Sol and Almagro) cashes traveler's checks, but they are agonizingly slow and tedious, usually requiring a photocopy of your passport in order to complete the transaction. Much more efficient is the Banco de los Andes (only a couple of blocks further down Sol).

■ **Communications**   The main post office is down Avenida Sol at the corner of Garcilaso. The new and reasonably efficient ENTEL office for international calls is just above the *correos* on Avenida Sol.

■ **Car Rental**   The Avis office (900 Avenida Sol) rents small imports at high prices.

■ **Tourist Information**   The tourist office beside La Compañia church on the plaza provides city maps and up to date information on bus and train schedules.

■ **Touring Agencies**   Cuzco has a number of travel agencies that offer a broad spectrum of services. Virtually every agency in town operates tours of the city, the principal outlying ruins, the Urubamba valley, and Machu Picchu. However, these tours are rushed and touristy, so you'll probably want to avoid the agencies unless you're very

pressed for time. *Lima Tours* (567 Avenida Sol) are American Express
representatives in Cuzco, though they do little more than hold mail.
Exprinter, a reservation agency for EnturPeru hotels, including the
Hotel Machu Picchu, is in the Hotel Turista Cuzco (Plaza Regocijo).
Río Bravo (236 Portal de Carnes, Plaza de Armas) operates whitewater
raft trips on the Urubamba and Apurimac rivers. Several agencies
around the Plaza de Armas and up Procuradores offer a number of
valuable services for trekkers, including equipment rental, guide and
porter services, transportation to trailheads, and river-rafting trips. It
is best to shop around town for these services as the prices seem to be
influenced by how busy the individual agency is at the time. *Ex-
plorAndes* (372 Procuradores) offers a particularly comprehensive
range of outdoor excursions.

■   **Fiestas**   Cuzco's principal festivals are Inti Raymi (June 24–30)
and the Festival de la Virgen de la Puerta (December 8–15).

■   **Shopping**   Most visitors to Cuzco spend quite a bit of their time
there shopping for the handcrafts of the region, and despite the easy
market such hordes of free-spending tourists make, Cuzco is still among
the better towns of the Andes in which to buy crafts. Prices are not
terribly inflated compared with more remote areas, and the selection
and quality of most craft items are very good. Though the Plaza de
Armas area is full of craft shops, you'll find better bargains and more
interesting items by branching out a bit. Don't miss the main *mercado*
near the San Pedro (Machu Picchu) train station. This daily market

Llamas near Cuzco, Peru

offers a little of everything—from wool and alpaca items to kerosene stoves to coca leaves to freshly slaughtered meat.

Even if you may want to make major craft purchases elsewhere, the market is an interesting way to have a look into the lives of the *campesinos.* Simply walk about the crowded, open-air lanes and stalls and watch the often traditionally dressed highlanders bargaining and buying. Those with weak stomachs should avoid the meat market area. Since the market is a fairly high-risk area for thievery, you'll probably be able to relax and enjoy your visit there more if you leave your camera, daypack, purses, or any other valuable items at your hotel.

For quality craft items, try the Artesania collective on Calle Maruri. Here you'll find a couple of dozen shops, mostly specializing in alpaca sweaters, ponchos, rugs, and wall hangings. For a wide selection of some of the best handmade items in Cuzco, walk to the San Blas section of town. Here, numerous shops and a couple of collective areas sell well-made weavings, rugs, sweaters, leather items, carvings, pottery, and jewelry.

■   **Supplies**   Cuzco is one of the simplest towns in the Andes to supply yourself for a trek. For fresh vegetables, bread, kerosene and the like, simply walk to the *mercado* and shop around. Several *bodegas* in town carry a pretty good selection of trail-worthy foods, but the best we've found is the *El Chinito* (Avenida Sol 210) where, along with the usual supplies, they carry harder-to-find foods like oatmeal, dried fruit, and a variety of U.S. canned goods.

Day Hikes and Excursions Outside Cuzco

We are including here two of our favorite day hikes in the Cuzco area, but all of the countryside in the area is excellent for rambling. The land is open and visibility is good; getting lost should not be a problem if you make minimal efforts to keep yourself oriented. So don't hesitate to get out of town and wander about on your own. On days when we've just gotten off long treks and our trail-sore legs need stretching, we usually start at Sacsayhuaman or Q'enko and tramp about the hills for a few hours, using the Pisac highway, the Viva Peru earth-art markings, and Ausangate as landmarks. Dogs can occasionally be a problem, but on one of our excursions we learned a little trick from a *campesino* named Hernan that has stood us in good stead. He was walking with us back toward town one day and laughed at us when, every time a vicious barking dog approached, we stooped to pick up rocks. He just made a loud clicking sound with his mouth, and the dogs almost always calmed down. Since then, we've done the same with considerable success—but we still scan the ground for likely stones.

THE RUINS WALK

This is an exciting day hike of about ten miles that you can make right from your hotel room. It takes you into the countryside near Cuzco and allows you to visit all of the major Inca constructions nearby

The fortress of Sacsayhuaman

—Sacsayhuaman, Tambo Machay, and Puka Pukara. The combined entrance ticket is required to enter these sites, so purchase it either before you leave town or at Sacsayhuaman. Should the lingering effects of a bout with *soroche* make you hesitant to set off on an all-day walk, you could cut the walking distance almost in half without missing any of the Inca sites by taking either a taxi or a bus (the Cuzco-Pisac bus from Calle Sapphi) to Tambo Machay and walking back to Puka Pukara and Sacsayhuaman.

If you begin at the Plaza de Armas, walk up Procuradores, turning right when it dead-ends. Climb a set of steps, cross Sueca, and turn left on Resbalosa, another pedestrian street. Resbalosa ends at the Pisac road. Across the road, steps lead up to the San Cristobal church and the imposing nearby walls of Colcampata, supposedly the palace of Manco Capac, the first Inca. After visiting Colcampata, continue walking up the main road until you reach a broad path turning uphill to the right. After a short climb that will, nevertheless, make the unacclimated feel the altitude, this trail quickly brings you to the great Inca fortress of Sacsayhuaman.

In Quechua, a *sacsayhuaman* is a particular kind of hawk, a name that seems absolutely appropriate for the fortress when you consider the aerial view from this strategically important hilltop overlooking the Cuzco valley. Here, probably under the reign of Pachacuti, the Incas constructed their massive, hulking fortress, and the ruins of Sacsayhuaman, even after the Spanish dismantled much of it to quarry stones for their colonial city below, remain as one of the most impressive constructions of the pre-European Americas. The dominant impression as you stand in the flat parade grounds in front of the fortress is of great muscular bulk. The rounded stones from which it was constructed are extraordinarily massive, the largest being nearly twenty feet tall and weighing an estimated 200 tons, and all of the stones are fitted into place without mortar but so perfectly that you can seldom find even a paper-thin crack between them. The obvious difficulty of building a huge and complex structure like Sacsayhuaman provokes, of course, the question tourists the world over always ask when confronted with the unbelievable constructions of the ancient world—how did these "primitive" people, without machinery or even the wheel, move such massive stones? The answer to such a question lies neither in the occult nor the extraterrestrial but in the vast manpower the Incas were able to command under their system of *mita,* a requirement for a yearly period of public labor from every able-bodied citizen. It has been estimated that as many as 25,000 laborers, most of them fulfilling their *mita* service, were needed to build Sacsayhuaman.

Above the walls, at the summit of the hill, commanding a wide view of the valley below, stood a complex of storage houses, water reservoirs, and three towers, all destroyed by the Spanish but for their foundations. According to the chronicler Garcilaso de Vega, tunnels running through the hill connected the towers and the battlements below. As you climb through the massive lower walls, notice the careful and brilliant work of the Inca planners in their design of the fortress. In order to reach the summit, attackers following the zigzag passages between the walls were forced to expose their backs and flanks as they made the 180-degree turns. In 1536, however, during Manco Inca's revolt, the Spanish successfully attacked the fortress. Approaching from the parade grounds, they reached the summit by climbing the walls with ladders rather than by following the passages. The conquistadores massacred all the Incas who held the fortress, breaking the back of the revolt. The chroniclers claim that the skies above Sacsayhuaman were dark for days after the battle with the broad wings of condors circling the carrion.

When you're ready to move on, walk across the parade ground and climb the large rock outcrop opposite the fortress. Carved into this outcrop is a seat overlooking the parade ground, from which it is supposed that the Inca surveyed his troops. Continue walking across the top of the outcrop and begin to descend. Here you'll find the Rodadero, a smooth, grooved rock slope, which you'll probably find being used as a slide by local kids. Look carefully as you descend beyond the Rodadero, and you may find some of the caves and passages between the rocks. Several of these were carved and enlarged by the Incas and probably were considered *huacas* (sacred spots).

Look ahead of you (to the northeast) as you descend the rock outcrop, and you'll see a line of eucalyptus trees running alongside a lane straight ahead and a main road turning to the right. Walk to that junction. There you'll need to decide whether you want to walk several miles along the road, which links up with the Pisac road, to the next site, Tambo Machay, or whether you want to do a bit of cross-country walking. The road is not so terribly busy that walking along it is unpleasant, but the cross-country walk is quite pretty, though the final sections to Tambo Machay are trailless.

If you decide to go cross-country, walk up the eucalyptus lane; soon, you'll reach a group of houses; a well-used trail turns uphill, bearing to the right. The trail is somewhat sporadic through this inhabited, agricultural area, but if you keep your bearings (easy to do in this wide-open countryside), you should have no trouble. Within a mile or so you should find yourself climbing steadily up a seldom-used dirt road; when you reach two abandoned adobe structures, turn right and climb to a gap between round grain-covered hills. From the gap, you'll simply have to find your own route among the potato and barley fields that cover the hillsides, but if you continue to the northeast, you should find yourself descending steeply into the valley of Tambo Machay within a mile. Remember that you're traveling in a generally northeast direction, paralleling the paved road to Pisac. This road is often visible off to the right as you walk through the hills and fields on the way to Tambo Machay, as is Nevado Ausangate, just visible on the horizon far to the southeast. If you keep these landmarks to your right rather than to your back, you should have no trouble navigating your way. Be very careful to skirt cultivated fields as you pass through this area. If you haven't walked too far to the north or northwest, you should enter the valley either at Tambo Machay or just below it on the dirt road that connects the site to the Pisac road.

Tambo Machay is a series of walled terraces through which the Incas diverted water, which still flows from the stone spouts today. There is apparently some disagreement among authorities as to whether Tambo Machay was simply a rather elaborate bathing spa for the Inca royalty or whether it was a temple dedicated to water and where, perhaps, ritual bathing ceremonies took place. If you begin this walk first thing in the morning, you should reach Tambo Machay around noon; the pretty little valley makes a good spot for a picnic lunch.

To finish the hike, walk downhill along the road. As you reach the ticket hut just above the Pisac road, the ticket taker may be a bit confused by your exiting without having passed through the entrance, so be prepared to soothe him with your already-purchased combined entrance ticket. At the Pisac highway, turn right and walk only a short distance until you see the ruins of Puca Pucara to the left of the road. Puca Pucara was probably a fortress, and as you walk through it, enjoying its commanding view of the surrounding countryside, you can easily see that situated as it is, directly on the ancient Inca road from Cuzco to Pisac and perfectly positioned for observation of approaching attackers, this outpost was quite crucial to the defense of Cuzco.

From Puca Pucara, walk along the Pisac road in the direction of Cuzco for only about a quarter of a mile until you see a trail descending to the left. This is part of an Inca road, and though it is occasionally somewhat indistinct, it descends in a southerly direction to Cuzco. This is one of the most attractive sections of the hike, passing beside irrigated fields (be careful not to damage the fragile irrigation ditches) and perhaps an occasional grazing llama. You'll descend through a small, rocky valley, with the fairly clear trail following the right side. Eventually you'll come to a tempting-looking dirt road, but the Inca road crosses over it and continues its gradual descent through the fields. Keep your bearings by looking for the large "Viva Peru" earth inscriptions on the hills near the airport; these should frequently be visible ahead of you.

About three miles beyond Puka Pukara, you'll see before you, across open fields, a large eucalyptus grove. There you'll find a dirt road that branches just beyond the trees. To return to Cuzco, you can either walk down the left branch, crossing a paved road and descending into town, or you can take the right branch that passes by the Q'enko site (see below) and leads you to the main Pisac road. Along this road, you can make the short walk back to Sacsayhuaman and return to town from there.

The Huaca Walk

The concept of the *huaca* was central to the spiritual life of Andeans for centuries, and even today in remote areas of the mountains *huacas* are still respected. The *huaca* is a sacred spot, the home of a spirit. Every high mountain peak is a special kind of *huaca,* and Quechuas often call the big, glaciated peaks *apus* (master). At high mountain passes throughout the Andes, you'll still find *apachetas,* rock cairns that serve functions similar to *huacas.* But many *huacas* are much less spectacular than high peaks and remote passes. In fact, virtually any natural object can be a *huaca*—a spring, a strangely shaped rock, a cave, or even a man-made pile of stones to mark the otherwise undesignated home of a local spirit. According to chroniclers, there were literally hundreds of *huacas* in the Cuzco vicinity alone. Most of these were strewn along a system of forty-two lines that radiated like the sun's rays from the center of the Coricancha.

Visiting several of these *huacas* makes a good half-day hike from downtown Cuzco. Begin at the Plaza de Armas, and walk up Triunfo. As it climbs out of the city, this street changes names several times— from Triunfo to San Blas to Suitu Qhatu—before eventually becoming a pedestrian lane climbing through a poor suburb. When you reach the main paved road, continue across it and walk up a dirt road to the right of a steep, eucalyptus-covered hillside. Q'enko, the first of the *huacas* along the route, lies above the eucalyptus slope. To reach it, either turn left on the steep, switchbacking path through the trees, or continue on the dirt road, climbing until you reach another dirt road entering from the left; Q'enko is about 200 yards down that road.

Q'enko was one of the most important *huacas* of the Cuzco area. This sacred spot was perhaps used for sacrifices, though the zigzagging channels cut into stone at the site are more likely for ritual libations of *chicha* than for carrying away the blood of the sacrificial victims as some would have it. The Incas did, by the way, occasionally practice human sacrifice, but unlike the Aztecs of Mexico, they resorted to human victims only under fairly unusual circumstances, such as prolonged drought or other serious threat to the welfare of the state. More normal sacrificial victims were llamas and guinea pigs. At any rate, ritual sacrification was probably not Q'enko's primary function, though what that primary function might have been remains largely speculative. The focal point of the site is the huge upright stone that was carved by the Incas, and its shape has led some to argue that the site may have been dedicated to phallus worship. Be sure to walk into the underground passage beneath the great central stone. Here, surely, religious ceremonies were held, and you'll find carvings, platforms, and niches in which were kept gold and silver statues and perhaps mummies. At the site you'll also see a small amphitheater, the purpose of which remains uncertain.

To continue the walk, turn right on the dirt road above Q'enko, and walk through the eucalyptus grove. As you leave the trees, you'll find yourself in the *campo,* the open, grassy fields and pastures that make up the countryside near the city. If you look to the right across this wide open area, you'll see a rocky knoll. This is the next *huaca,* Salapunco. A path along an irrigation ditch leads toward it. At the site, you'll find several fissures and caves, and in one of these are mummy niches and an altar, dramatically lighted by an overhead opening in the rock. You might want to take a flashlight along with you.

From Salapunco, there are several alternative routes. Just behind the *huaca,* you'll see a wide path crossing a stream. This is part of the old Inca highway system. If you follow it for a half-mile or so, you'll see a conical rock knoll. This *huaca,* like the stone towers that stood on the hills to the west of Cuzco, was part of the Inca astronomical, calendrical system. These spots marked points at which the sun rose or set on summer and winter solstices, crucial periods of the year for an agrarian society.

From this *huaca* you can continue up the Inca road to the Pisac highway three miles or so away. The Inca road climbs through the valley, ascending above the stream on its left bank and then crossing the stream before reaching Yuncaypata and finally the highway; there you can catch a bus or truck back to Cuzco. Alternatively, you could do a little cross-country walking, descending along the creek through the little gorge below the *huaca.* Shortly after you pass the ruins of Spanish kilns on the hillside to the left, look for a trail turning to the right and climbing that side of the gorge. High above the valley floor, you'll find a broad path contouring around the hills. This wonderful stretch of trail will eventually lead you back to Cuzco, providing good views along the way of the patchwork green, brown, and gold fields of the countryside and of Nevado Ausangate in the distance. Don't get impatient and turn downhill too soon, however, or you'll end up in "Cuzco moderno," a long way from the Plaza de Armas. Instead, keep contouring and the broad path will become a dirt road leading back to the direct Suitu Qhatu-San Blas-Triunfo route to the plaza on which you began the walk.

The Urubamba Valley

The valley of the Vilcanota and Urubamba rivers is one of the most beautiful regions of the Andes. Fifteen hundred feet lower in elevation than the Cuzco valley, the Urubamba enjoys a warmer climate and has, therefore, for centuries been well populated and a major producer of agricultural products. The waters of the Río Vilcanota and later the Río Urubamba flow through the glacial valley between the mountains of the Cordillera Vilcabamba and the Cordillera de Urubamba. Along this valley you'll find more than a little of everything that comes to mind when you think of the Andes—Inca ruins, *campesinos* in traditional dress, colorful Indian markets, beautiful landscapes, charming little towns and villages, highlanders leading llamas. Yet too many tourists rush through the valley on one-day group tours, usually on Sunday in order to catch the Pisac market. Of course, if one day is all you have to spare, the Urubamba still makes an enjoyable excursion, but the so-called "sacred valley of the Incas" really merits a slower visit in order to enjoy fully its many attractions.

If you have a few days to spend in the Urubamba, transportation is no problem; simply go by bus (hourly departures with Transportes Caparo, 700 Sapphi), making either Urubamba or Ollantaytambo your base of operations since both have adequate hotels and restaurants. Even if you only have a day to spare, there are still several ways to travel through the valley more enjoyably than signing up for one of the crowded group tours. If you have several people traveling together and sharing expenses, hiring a taxi for a full day—with long stops in Pisac, Urubamba, Ollantaytambo, and perhaps Chinchero—will cost no more than the combination of four or five tour fares, and *you* will be able to control the itinerary and the length of your stops. If you have less money to spend, you could make a day trip through the valley by bus. We suggest that you take one of Transportes Caparo's buses all the way to Ollantaytambo first (two to three hours) and then work your way back up the valley by bus and/or truck. With an early start, you should be able to see much of the valley and still make it back to Cuzco by dark. Remember that Sunday is market day in several of the towns of the valley, so expect buses and trucks to be full throughout the day.

Pisac

Pisac, twenty-five miles from Cuzco by paved road, is a sleepy little town of old brown adobe buildings with faded red roof tiles, but two days a week it fills up with large numbers of tourists for its markets— a principal one on Sundays and a smaller one on Thursdays. Held in the Plaza de Armas, the tourist market is still a good place to find a wide selection of crafts, but don't expect bargain prices. However, it is still an excellent place to observe the *campesinos,* many of them in

Quechua highlander, Pisac, Peru

traditional dress. Notice the women's hats, for example. Those in the fringed pancake hats are pure blood Quechuas, most of whom speak little or no Spanish; those in white straw hats are of mixed ancestry and will usually speak fluent Spanish. Following mass, the mayors of nearby villages still parade through the market dressed in their Sunday best carrying the silver canes that designate their positions in the community.

Of considerable interest too are the Inca ruins in the Pisac area. As you enter town from the main highway, notice the Inca canal the Río Vilcanota flows through. Notice too the extensive agricultural terracing along the valley walls. But most impressive are the extensive ruins of a large Inca fortress and city high above Pisac. The site of this mountain fortress, with panoramic views of the valley below, is nearly as dramatic as Machu Picchu itself. To reach the ruins, you can hire a taxi to take you on the newly built road up the mountain; at the entrance, either ask the driver to wait or walk back to Pisac, only about an hour away by trail. Alternatively, you can walk both ways, but plan at least four hours for the trip to allow time for the steep climb (one to two hours) and adequate time to explore the very large site. Well-used trails leave directly from town (from the plaza, walk up the street to the left of the church), climbing through the agricultural terraces toward the ruins.

More than likely, the fortress was designed as a place of retreat for the people of the valley in times of attack. It had a safe water supply, and the terraces were both a means of food production and protecting walls impeding attackers from below. As you explore the site, remember that the extensive ruins are not concentrated but are scattered about the ridges and mountain spurs of the area. These are connected by paths and Inca steps. The central area of the site is the Intihuatana, the ceremonial area of the city and perhaps the location of a Temple of the Sun similar to the Coricancha in Cuzco. If you follow the trails that climb above the Intihuatana, you'll find more ruins and a typical Inca burial site, a cliff with niches cut into it where the bundled bodies of the Inca dead were placed. The combined admission ticket from Cuzco also allows entrance to the Pisac ruins, so don't forget to bring it along.

If you wish to spend the night in Pisac (not a bad idea if you want to get to the market early, before the tourist buses arrive), there are a couple of adequate hotels—the moderately priced *Hotel Chongo Chico* (a half-mile south of town on the river road) with pleasant surroundings and a good restaurant, and the inexpensive *Hotel Turista* in town, also with a restaurant.

Ollantaytambo

As you make your way through the valley below Pisac, you'll pass through several small towns. Among these, Yucay and Urubamba are very pleasant. Urubamba is an especially nice town in which to spend a restful day or two. Either the *Hotel Turista* or the *Hostal Naranja-chayoc* (both with clean rooms, restaurants, and swimming pools) makes a comfortable, inexpensive base of operations for exploration of the valley. The countryside around Urubamba is among the loveliest in the Andes, so be sure to get out for rambles on the roads and lanes either across the river in the direction of Maras or to the northeast in the direction of the Río Chicon. Not far from Urubamba is the strange little village of Pichinjoto, just across the river from Tarabamba, four miles down the main highway from Urubamba. The village is built underneath an overhanging cliff and looks very much like a slightly more contemporary version of the Anasazi cliff dwellings of the southwestern United States; the countryside around Pichinjoto also makes for enjoyable rambling.

Of all the valley towns, though, our favorite is Ollantaytambo, a quiet little village disturbed only by a flurry of tourist activity every afternoon for a couple of hours when the tour buses make their quick stop. One of the things that makes Ollantaytambo so appealing is that most of its buildings sit upon Inca walls, and its street plan is still virtually identical to that laid out by its Inca builders. The town is also surrounded by a variety of Inca ruins, principal of which is the great *pucara* or fortress.

This impressive stepped fortification (use your combination ticket for entrance) looks very much like a massive amphitheater, but its curving walls and terraces were purely defensive. Here, after the defeat at Sacsayhuaman, Manco Inca and his troops made a determined stand against the conquistadores, turning them back and forcing them to wait for reinforcements before they could take the fortress. At the top of the fortress, you'll find a group of buildings—among them a temple and, of course, the practical structures (storehouses, barracks, and the like) needed for an outpost such as this one. Not far from the entrance to the fortress is the Baños de la Nusta, an Inca bath, and on the walls of the valley of the Patacancha River (just below the fortress) are the ruins of several buildings traditionally said to be either the dwellings of the Chosen Women or a kind of college for the children of Inca royalty, though both explanations seem a little unlikely.

Aside from being an exceedingly pleasant town to wander about, Ollantaytambo is also a good base for rambles in the surrounding countryside. You can walk for several miles up the Patacancha, or cross the Urubamba at the bridge and explore the many trails that run along the river and back into the hills.

Accommodations in Ollantaytambo are inexpensive and very basic. The *Alberque* (near the railroad station) is clean and pleasant enough, and it attracts lots of *gringos*. Should it be full, the *El Tambo* is also clean enough to recommend. For meals try the *Parador,* near the plaza.

Chinchero

Chinchero is a pleasant little highland town with good views of the mountains and plenty of evidence of the Inca past. The hills around the town are ringed with ancient agricultural terraces, and much of the town is built upon Inca foundations. In the plaza you'll particularly notice that the church is built upon massive Inca walls, purportedly the remains of the palace of Inca Tupaq Yupanqui. And if you enjoy Indian markets, you'll probably find the Sunday market at Chinchero of considerably more interest than the one in Pisac, though even here you'll find plenty of tourists. The *campesinos* of the Chinchero region still use their market primarily for trading food and essential goods, so don't expect a wide variety of crafts. The market's primary attraction is the opportunity it provides to observe the mountain people.

A little off the beaten path, Chinchero is located high above the Urubamba valley floor about two hours away from Cuzco by truck, the only way to get there unless you hire a taxi. Trucks leave Cuzco for Chinchero from Avenida Arcopato at around 6 A.M., but you might want to check a day in advance with the tourist office near La Compañia church for current times.

To make your visit to Chinchero an exciting all-day trip, instead of taking a truck back to Cuzco, walk one of the several trails that descend from Chinchero and culminate in or near the town of Urubamba down in the valley. Since most trails leaving town in a generally northern direction will take you down to the main Urubamba highway, you're safe in doing some exploring on your own. The main trail, however, begins among the old terraces north of town. On this clear, direct trail you should reach the Río Urubamba in about three hours. At the river, turn downstream and follow the trail to the village of Huayallabamba where a bridge crosses the river to the main highway. There, unless you arrive late in the afternoon, you should have no trouble catching a bus or truck to Calca and on to Cuzco. Allow four hours for this walk.

The Cordillera Vilcabamba

The Cordillera Vilcabamba is a region of deep mystery. Into this complex landscape, cut into a maze of canyons and valleys by the tributaries of the Urubamba and Apurimac rivers, the last of the Incas retreated after the defeats at Sacsayhuaman and Ollantaytambo. They held out for four decades, making their last stand in this country of towering snow mountains and convoluted, heavily forested hills, until 1572 when the Spanish executed Tupac Amaru, the last direct descendant of the Incas to fight for the throne. Vilcabamba became the stuff of legend. Tales of hidden cities and unfound treasure drifted for centuries to the outer world, attracting men like Hiram Bingham, who, during several trips to the region in the second decade of this century, discovered not only Machu Picchu, but ruin after vine-covered ruin scattered through the mountains. But despite years of exploration by archaeologists and adventurers, the Vilcabamba still has a few secrets hidden away. As recently as 1982, in fact, some Inca ruins, hidden for centuries by dense vegetation, were discovered high above the Urubamba River only a short distance from Machu Picchu. And no doubt other ruins still lie waiting in the cloud forest for their own Hiram Bingham.

The Vilcabamba is no less fascinating for the outdoor traveler than it is for the historian or archaeologist. Here you'll find miles and miles of wonderful trails into the mountains, more picturesque scenery and mountain people than you'll have film to capture, and Machu Picchu, one of the world's premier historical sites.

The Inca Trail

The are many Andean roads and paths built and used by the Incas, but there is only one Inca Trail, and it attracts hikers from the world over who want to walk the ancient, ruin-studded path to Machu Picchu. This is certainly not a walk for those who want to experience the mountains in solitude—not when several thousand people walk the trail annually. But despite the crowds, the Inca Trail is still one of the most justifiably famous and exciting hikes in the world. Ignoring the ruins for a moment, the scenery itself is lovely; the trail takes you over high passes with views of glaciated mountains and down into the folded hills of a green, junglelike cloud forest. Along the way you walk over long sections of trail paved with Inca stonework, and you pass at convenient intervals the ruins of Inca outposts and towns. And above all else, you have the satisfaction of entering the astounding ruins of Machu Picchu not by train and shuttle bus with the hoards of tourists, but afoot through Intipunku, the Sun Gate, as did the Incas centuries ago.

Most people begin walking at km 88 (also occasionally called Qoriwayrachina) on the Cuzco to Machu Picchu rail line. Since the 7 A.M. tourist train does not stop there, hikers must take the very crowded 6 A.M. local train, which requires a very early departure from your hotel, especially if you are unable to buy your tickets a day in advance. The dark, cold San Pedro station is always crowded and apparently so full of thieves that even the locals, not just paranoid tourists, guard their baggage vigilantly. When the gates open, there is a wild dash for seats because the cars are routinely overbooked. By the time the train reaches Ollantaytambo, the aisles are filled with seatless passengers, and those passengers lucky enough to have seats will probably find themselves holding a lapful of fresh produce one of the standers found too bulky to fit anywhere else. By the time the train reaches km 88, you'll breathe a sigh of relief to be away from the press of humanity, but even there you'll have to stand in line with all the other trekkers to pay your entry fee (it covers use of the trail and entrance to Machu Picchu). Everyone begins walking at roughly the same time, so during the first few miles of the trail—until people begin to spread out a bit —it will feel a little more like the start of a 10-km footrace than the beginning of a relaxing backpacking trip.

There is, however, an alternative to this hectic beginning to a fine walk that few people know about. A very pleasant trail begins in Ollantaytambo, just across the bridge from town, and runs downstream along the south bank of the Río Urubamba to Chillca and on to Llactapata, a mile up the Inca Trail from km 88. This alternative will add about thirteen miles of easy, mostly flat walking to the trip, and it has

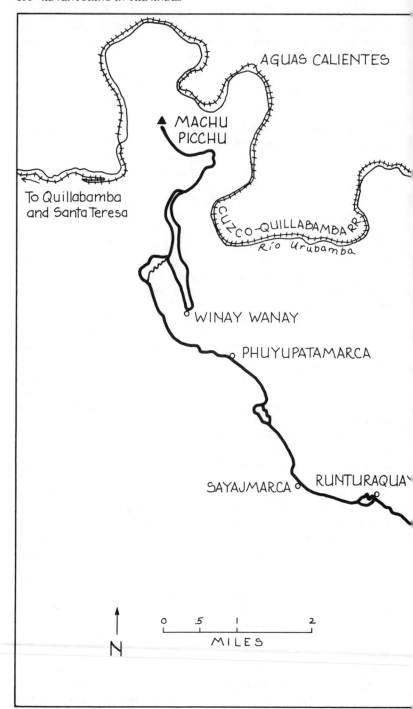

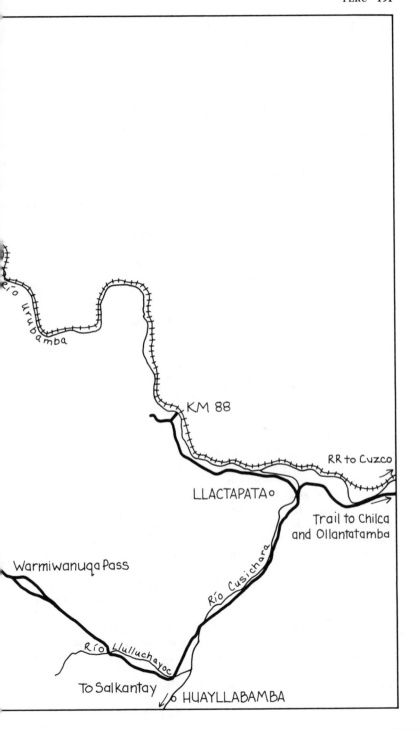

a couple of distinct advantages: if you spend the night in Ollan-taytambo, you can start walking when you want, and you can plan your arrival at the main trail so as to avoid the crowds (e.g., you could camp the first night near Llactapata and get an early start the next morning to put yourself a couple of hours ahead of hikers taking the train).

If you decide to begin this hike with the train ride, you may be able to eliminate having to get to the station when the ticket window opens at 5 A.M. in order to buy tickets for the frequently full train by trying to buy tickets a day in advance. When we did this walk, the ticket officer told us that only tourist train tickets were sold in advance, but on another visit to Cuzco we were told that tickets for the local train could be purchased between 4 P.M. and 5 P.M. the day before departure. At any rate, it's worth a try.

Quite a few hikers fret over the possibility of missing their stop, but you need not worry about figuring out which of the train's score of stops is km 88; locals in your car will let you know when to get out if you ask. If you want to keep up with the train's slow progress through the valley, try to sit on the right side of the car and watch for the frequent kilometer posts along the way.

Because of its fame and its obvious attractions, the Inca Trail is walked by much larger numbers of inexperienced hikers than any other in the Andes. Perhaps this lack of backcountry experience accounts for the often flagrant breeches of trail etiquette committed by many Inca Trail hikers. Because the trail is so heavily used, everyone—experienced hikers and novices alike—must strictly observe matters of common courtesy, especially in garbage disposal and defecation. Though it should be unnecessary to have to request that hikers make their toilets *well* away from trails and especially ruins and that they carry out *all* garbage, the condition of the trail suggests such requests are necessary.

Both experienced and inexperienced hikers frequently underestimate the physical demands of this walk. Though the Inca Trail is only a little less than thirty miles long, it does, nevertheless, involve considerable climbing, especially during the first half of the walk. And during all this climbing, it crosses three passes, the first near 14,000 feet, so the unacclimated are advised not to rush. Since you'll surely want to take some time to explore the major ruins of Sayajmarca, Phuyupata-marca, and Winay Wayna, we'd recommend planning four days for the hike.

The Instituto Geografico Nacional has only a very poor dyeline map of this area, and since it doesn't indicate trails, it is virtually useless for hikers. If you want a larger map, the South America Explorers Club in Lima and several of the bookstores around the plaza in Cuzco sell maps of the trail. If you want to use a guide and porters for the trip, any of the trekking agencies in Cuzco can arrange them for you. Since these eastern mountains catch the moisture rising from the Amazon basin, be prepared for wet weather, even during the dry season. By all means, take a camp stove and do not plan to cook over fires; if you must have campfires, build them away from Inca walls in order to prevent smoke blackening the stonework.

At km 88, you'll begin the walk by buying your entrance ticket and crossing the Urubamba River. For years this was accomplished with a little two-passenger, hand-powered cable car, but we understand that a footbridge is nearing completion. Across the bridge, the trail swings to the left and passes through a pretty eucalyptus grove as it leaves the river. Within a mile, you'll pass the minor ruins and terraces of Llactapata on your right. Just beyond Llactapata, the clear trail crosses the Río Cusichaca over a log bridge and climbs steeply up a rocky ridge to enter the very lovely valley of the Cusichaca. The walk up the open valley to the village of Huayllabamba is a wonderful morning's work, climbing gradually along first the left and then the right bank of the stream. Views of the surrounding glaciated peaks are frequent, especially if you remember to look behind occasionally. The walls of the valley are dotted with bromeliads, and the floor with cactus. As you work your way up the valley, you'll pass fields, pastures, and several collections of thatch houses.

The village of Huayllabamba is six miles from km 88. At the outskirts of the village, you'll reach the point of convergence between the Cusichaca and the Río Llulluchayoc. Here, just across the footbridge over the Llulluchayoc, is an important trail junction. The trail to the left continues through the village and becomes the trail that swings around Nevado Salkantay and descends to Mollepata, several days away. The Inca Trail, however, turns right (northwest) and begins the long, steep climb toward the Warmiwanunqa (dead woman) Pass.

If the day is getting late, camp near the village; if not, follow the trail as it begins its climb along the left-hand bank of the stream. If you aren't completely acclimated to Andean heights, you're guaranteed to feel it on the slow, steep one-mile climb between Huayllabamba and the forks of the Llulluchayoc. Watch for the convergence of the two streams and their obvious canyons ahead of you as you climb, and get your bearings since the trail becomes a bit indistinct at the forks. The trail follows the left branch for only a very short distance, then crosses the stream over a log bridge. Past the bridge, the trail swings to the right, climbing over the round hill separating the two streams and entering the small canyon of the right branch of the Llulluchayoc. There the trail ascends into forest, following the left bank of the stream. Though there are several potentially confusing side trails near the area of the forks, you should have no trouble finding the main route because it is marked by arrows on trailside boulders. Near the log bridge at the forks, you'll find good campsites, water, and lots of other campers. Do not leave the forks if darkness approaches because the upcoming steep climb through heavy forest offers no good campsites.

You'll climb very sharply through this forest for a mile or so on a clear trail through the trees before reaching a meadowy area; here you'll find more good campsites. The trail is again faint for a stretch as it passes through the grassy area at the margin of the trees, but if you continue up valley, following the main stream, you can't go wrong. Once you reach the dry, open slopes above, the trail becomes wide and clear again, climbing high above the left bank of the stream. The pass is 3.5 uphill miles from the end of the forest, and though at an altitude of 13,945 feet this is a relatively low Andean pass, you'll certainly notice the extra effort it takes to climb in the thin air. At this point you will have gained more than a mile of altitude since leaving the Urubamba valley.

Unless the pass is fog-shrouded and windy, as it often is, you'll have good views back down to the Cusichaca valley and ahead to the Pacamayo valley. In that direction, if the weather is clear, you should be able to trace the upcoming sections of trail as it descends to the Pacamayo and then climbs immediately to the ruins of Runkuracay (three miles away), visible far across the valley as a small, oval structure. From the pass, the initially faint trail descends directly into the valley; do not be confused by side trails turning abruptly to both the left and right just below the pass. You'll soon reach a small spring, and shortly after that the trail will become clear again, descending very steeply and staying well above the stream on its left bank.

The valley floor is a muddy pasture area, but good campsites can be found on the higher, drier ground. The trail is again a bit confusing in the valley floor, easy to lose among the numerous cow paths and stream branches. But if you continue as straight across the valley as possible (don't descend into the thick forest), you'll soon reach the trail that climbs very sharply toward Runkuracay and the second pass. Runkuracay makes a wonderful campsite, with nearby water and flat ground both inside the walls of the ruin and just below it. The little oval building was more than likely a guard and observation post, providing a commanding view of the area below. If you look back toward Dead Woman Pass, you may be able to see how it earned its name—the rocks at the pass form the distinct silhouette of a reclining woman from the vantage point of Runkuracay.

From Runkuracay, the trail continues to climb, often with Inca stonework underfoot, through switchbacks toward the second pass. Hikers shortcutting across these switchbacks have confused the trail in this area, but the main path is relatively clear. You'll walk by two small lakes, and then, after a final steep pitch, reach the pass. The second pass (13,150 feet) makes an excellent rest stop, and on clear days you'll have good views of the glaciated peaks of the Cordillera Vilcabamba.

Below the pass the trail descends rocky slopes, passes to the left of a shallow lake, and then reaches a set of narrow steps leading up a steep, rock slope to the ruins of Sayajmarca (three miles from Runkuracay). If you climb the steps, you'll find that they end at the ruins of a small but complex city perched along a narrow ridge. The site is a wonderful, mysterious place, high and isolated, as the Incas preferred. Be sure to walk through the ruins to the lower tower for a sweeping view of the countryside below and the mountains of the Vilcabamba in the distance. The upper plaza with its walled courtyard overlooking the trail ahead makes an excellent lunch spot. It is possible to camp among the ruins, but water is far below on the main trail.

Beyond Sayajmarca, the trail again enters dense growth. Here you'll find water and campsites. And you'll also find more and more evidence of the work of the Inca road builders. As you climb gradually toward the third pass (much easier than the others), you'll walk over long stretches of Inca paving and pass through a tunnel with carved steps. This is also one of the most beautiful stretches of the entire trail, with wonderful, open views of the surrounding mountains all along the way, culminating at the third pass with your first look down into the deep gorge of the Urubamba River.

Below the pass, you'll find the ruins of the Inca town of Phuyupatamarca (three miles from Sayajmarca). The chief feature of the site is the remarkably preserved series of Inca baths, through which water still runs. From the large, raised platform in the center of the site, you'll have excellent views down into the Urubamba. Above the site are caves which make good shelter in wet weather.

From the ruins, the trail runs alongside the baths and swings to the left. After exiting Phuyupatamarca, the mostly paved trail contours along high above the Urubamba valley. Within a couple of miles, however, you'll reach a powerline; here the trail begins a long and extremely steep descent to the construction site of the new Tourist Hotel (three miles from Phuyupatamarca). The instability of the precipitous hillside has, for the time being anyway, halted work on the building. Exercise caution in crossing the landslide zone near the hotel. If you walk behind the currently abandoned hotel, you'll find a trail that leads to the ruins of Winay Wayna, less than a mile away.

This site is not to be missed. Discovered in 1940, this beautiful little town is hidden by cloud forest and hugs the steep slopes above the Río Urubamba. The upper ruins include a semicircular tower; a trail behind the upper complex leads to a waterfall. Be sure to walk down the stone steps past the series of baths into the lower town. This was the residential district, and the houses are intact except for the wooden roof beams and *ichu* grass thatch. In the lower town you'll also find an observation platform overlooking the river.

From Winay Wayna walk back to the construction area and pick up the main trail again (look for the signpost near the hotel). The trail contours through dense tropical vegetation far above the river, sometimes climbing the steeper stretches on steps carved by the Incas. In several places the trail follows ledges built along cliffs, and in a couple of spots these have collapsed, requiring you to cross them over crude log bridges. Eventually, though, you'll reach Intipunku, the Sun Gate (3.5 miles beyond Winay Wayna), which marks the end of the trail and the entrance to Machu Picchu. Here, hundreds of years ago, tired travelers from the towns of the Urubamba valley would have breathed the same sigh of relief you probably will at having the long walk completed. As you pass through the gate, you'll see the magnificent ruins and the domed peak of Huayna Picchu spread out below you, a sight you'll surely never forget.

Machu Picchu

When Hiram Bingham discovered Machu Picchu on July 24, 1911, local *campesinos* had long been aware of the existence of extensive terraces and buildings on a cloud forest ridge above the Urubamba River. In fact, when Bingham and his party clambered their way through dense foliage to the top of the ridge that day, they found two Quechuas, who had built a hut near the site, happily making their living by growing corn and potatoes on the ancient terraces of the "Lost City." Nevertheless, Bingham's find was astounding, and by the time his native workers had cleared the growth of several centuries from the site, he knew that his discovery was of major importance. One does not have to be an archaeologist to imagine the sense of wonder Bingham and his men experienced as the stunning city slowly emerged from the cloud forest.

Assuming that he had found the last stronghold of the Incas, the lost Vilcabamba of the chronicles where Manco Inca and his followers made their final stand, Bingham proceeded during the excavations of the city to interpret everything he found as proof of his thesis. Since a preponderance of the skeletons found in the city were female (about 80 percent), Bingham interpreted this as proof that Machu Picchu was a religious center, a sanctuary for Inca royalty and the Chosen Women of the Sun after the defeats of Manco Inca in Cuzco and Ollantaytambo. In the final paragraphs of his *Lost City of the Incas,* Bingham paints a sad and lovely picture of these last proud remnants of a grand empire slowly dying out in peace, hidden from the conquistadores by the heights of Machu Picchu.

This explanation of Machu Picchu's place in history has lodged itself in our imaginations. In all likelihood, however, Bingham's attractive version of the city's past is more romantic than actual. Several recent expeditions have gathered convincing evidence that the real Vilcabamba is Espiritu Pampa, the ruins of which lie deeper in the jungle in a region usually closed to visitors without special permission to enter. Ironically, Bingham was also the discoverer of Espiritu Pampa, but he dismissed the find as relatively insignificant.

The discovery of the actual Vilcabamba, however, only deepens the mystery of Machu Picchu. Though many of the important questions concerning the city's purpose and its inhabitants may never be answered conclusively, one can at least speculate with some confidence, based on the fine stonework and elaborate structures of the city's center, that part of Machu Picchu's purpose was surely as both a ceremonial center and a home—or perhaps an important *tambo*—for Inca royalty. But why was this major city and the associated ruins along its primary access road, the Inca Trail, never discovered by the Spanish? In answer to the question, some scholars have concluded that

Machu Picchu

the inhabitants of the entire region—including the sites along the Inca Trail—may have died out or moved away for reasons we'll never know long before the Spanish arrived, making Machu Picchu a city forgotten even by the Incas themselves at the time Pizarro entered Cuzco in 1533.

Whoever they were, the people of Machu Picchu inhabited a largely vertical world, and their city is arguably the most beautifully situated of all ancient sites. The glaciated mountains of the nearby *cordillera* rise high into the sky, and the rapid waters of the Río Urubamba sweep around the ridge of Machu Picchu in a near 180-degree turn far below. Serving to accentuate this verticality, the great dome of Huayna Picchu looms above the lower end of the city. The mists, which often hang about Huayna Picchu, sometimes shrouding the ruins even in the dry season, accentuate both the beauty and the mystery of the city. A large part of Machu Picchu's unique grace, too, comes from the coherence of the city's architecture and the remarkable unity of the man-made and the natural that the Inca planners and builders were able to achieve. The city and its extensive agricultural terraces fit the ridge above the river like an organic part of the landscape.

Standing before Machu Picchu for the first time is a little like running into a celebrity in an airport and being surprised at how much she actually resembles her publicity photos. No matter how much you've anticipated the moment in your imagination, it's impossible for all but the most cynical of travelers to be disappointed in the real thing. Even the small number of extraordinary cynics we've talked to who claim to have been unimpressed with the ruins have an excuse; they had, without exception, simply taken the tourist train out and back in one day, and in doing so were forced to share the site with the scores of tourists who flood the ruins daily from 11 A.M. to 3:30 P.M.

So if you're serious about seeing Machu Picchu under the best of circumstances, we'd strongly recommend spending at least one night there. To accomplish this, you have several options ranging in cost from expensive to dirt cheap. The best choice is the *Hotel Machu Picchu*. Located just outside the entrance to the ruins, this hotel has expensive rooms, expensive meals, and indifferent service; on the other hand, it allows you to avoid the midday crowds from the tourist train, giving you the chance to explore the ruins in relative solitude during the late afternoon and early morning. You can walk right out of the hotel to watch both sunrise and sunset over Machu Picchu, sharing the moment with only a handful of other hotel guests. The hotel is small (only thirty-one rooms) and usually fully booked well in advance, so make reservations as early as possible. Much cheaper accommodations are available in Aguas Calientes, the little town less than a mile upstream from the Machu Picchu train station (an easy walk along the railroad line). There you'll find several very basic and inexpensive hotels; the best of the rather poor lot is the *Hostal Machu Picchu*. From Aguas Calientes you can beat the tourist train crowds to Machu Picchu either by awaking early to walk up to the ruins on the very steep path that shortcuts across the switchbacks of the road (allow a couple of hours to make the climb) or by catching one of the morning's first shuttle buses that travel between the train station and the ruins throughout the day, beginning at about 8 A.M. and ending at around 3:30 P.M. when the last of the tourist train visitors has been taken down the mountain. Camping is also possible in the large field near the train station. To return to Cuzco, buy tickets in advance either for the 4 P.M. tourist train or the 1 P.M. local train.

Unless you walk to Machu Picchu over the Inca Trail, you enter the site at the main gate near the hotel and pass through the Houses of the Guards and into an extensively terraced area, one of the city's agricultural districts. By following the broad path directly through the terraces, you soon reach a series of sixteen enclosed fountains and a group of Machu Picchu's finest structures. Principal of these is the Temple of the Sun, a fine, semicircular, two-story structure displaying excellent stonework. Connected to the temple is the House of the Nusta (princess), and beneath the temple, in a cave under a huge rock, is the Royal Tomb. Here Bingham found several mummies. Across a flight of steps from the Sun Temple is the Royal Sector, presumed to be the residential sector of royalty because of the size of the chambers and the excellent quality of the stonework of the walls and doorways. By the way, the names of the site's buildings and sectors are conventionally those given by Bingham; visitors should know, however, that these designations are to a degree speculative.

Above the Royal Sector, you'll reach a long set of steps and paved paths that lead to a plateau above the agricultural terraces called the Cemetery, so named because Bingham found several burial caves nearby. Here, beside an isolated hut above the terraces, you'll have a magnificent, almost aerial view of the ruins below. Nearby is a large, flat, carved rock, usually referred to as Funeral Rock, allegedly a place where the bodies of the dead were dried in the sun to become mummies. The stone may also have been either a sacrificial altar or a device for astronomical calculations.

Directly below the Royal Sector of the city is a group of structures thought to have been the prisons. There are numerous cells and possibly torture areas that conform to the chroniclers' descriptions of other such places in the Inca empire. Also in this area of the city is the depiction of a large condor carved into the floor of a small plaza. Nearby are numerous small but well-made structures probably used for housing and workshops for the city's many craftsmen.

Back on the broad main path through the site, you'll soon come to the spacious, grassy central plaza. Uphill to the left is the city's religious complex, composed of a small plaza bordered by the Main Temple, the Temple of the Three Windows, and the House of the Priest. Beyond this plaza to the north is one of Machu Picchu's most interesting features, the Intihuatana, a carved stone, which had both religious and astronomical significance. Intihuatanas were apparently a common feature of Inca ceremonial centers. They were used both as

Inca agricultural terraces below Machu Picchu

altars and to chart the progression of the seasons, but the Spaniards, in their attempt to replace worship of the sun with Christianity, destroyed virtually all of them.

Across the main plaza from the religious complex is another group of buildings, including three large, identical structures. This was probably a residential area, though some have postulated that the three identical buildings may have been convents for the Chosen Women.

North of the central plaza is another small plaza surrounded by buildings and a large stone. This was probably a *huaca* of some sort, a minor ceremonial area. Near this spot begins the trail to the top of Huayna Picchu. Unless you suffer from vertigo, be sure to make the climb. The trail ascends *very* steeply and with considerable exposure to the top of the peak, often on narrow steps carved into the rock. Allow an hour for the climb. At the top, views of the ruins, the valley, and the Cordillera Vilcabamba are incredible. A trail down the back (north) side of the peak leads to the Temple of the Moon, a small cave-temple (also reached by a trail that branches off the Huayna Picchu trail a little less than halfway up). Use extreme caution in hiking the Huayna Picchu trails; a fall along one of the exposed sections could be fatal. This three-to-four-hour hike makes an interesting way to spend the middle of the day when the ruins are overrun with train tourists.

The Salkantay Trails

If you fly from Lima to Cuzco, you'll pass directly over (and sometimes, disconcertingly, beside) the high peaks of the Cordillera Vilcabamba, and you'll have an especially good view of the south face of the 20,574-foot Nevado Salkantay. The land below you looks wild and difficult. That it is. But despite how inaccessible the Vilcabamba looks from the air, two fine long-distance trails allow you to walk for days through this spectacular mountain range of glaciated peaks, dense cloud forest, and turbulent rivers, which plunge into the Amazon basin. Along with the mountain scenery, you'll also get a good feel for the lives of the people of the Vilcabamba, for on these trails you'll pass several of the little *estancias* made up of only a handful of thatched houses and llama corrals, which dot the remote valleys of the range. One of these trails skirts Salkantay to the south and west, climbing its flank and then dropping into cloud forest to culminate at Santa Teresa, a stop on the Urubamba valley rail line. The other trail climbs a pass to the south of Salkantay before descending along the mountain's east flank, following the valley of the Río Cusichaca and connecting with the Inca Trail at the village of Huayllabamba (thus offering the possibility of a seven-to-eight-day trek ending at Machu Picchu).

Both trails begin in Mollepata, an isolated village a couple of hours above the main highway between Cuzco and Abancay. Access to Mollepata from Cuzco is, of course, by truck. *Camiónes* leave from Calle Arcopato (a sort of informal collection point for vehicles traveling to the east) in Cuzco early every morning on fairly uncertain schedules. Your best bet is to get to Arcopato no later than 7 A.M. and ask around

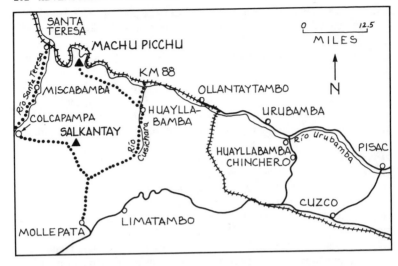

among drivers for trucks to Mollepata. The half-day trip is sure to be crowded and dusty, but it is far from the most uncomfortable truck ride we've encountered in the Andes, and it has the decided advantage of getting you to the trailhead early enough to get in a couple of hours of walking before time to make camp.

Mollepata is a green, rather pretty little town situated well below the 10,000-foot mark (meaning you'll have plenty of climbing to reach the 16,000-foot passes ahead). Here, those who want to hire *arrieros* should have little trouble making arrangements. Trekking agencies in Cuzco will also organize guides and *arrieros* for trips into the Vilcabamba, but their charges will be considerably higher than those you'll be able to arrange on your own. Because both of these walks are fairly long and involve considerable altitude gain, we recommend that all but conditioned, acclimatized, and experienced backpackers make the trip with *arrieros.* Expect cold nights in the vicinities of the high passes. Take along insect repellent for the sometimes buggy cloud forest regions, and be prepared for damp weather even during the dry season if you walk to Santa Teresa on the wet Amazon side of the mountain range. Detailed topo maps of the Vilcabamba are nonexistent; fortunately, though, the trails are relatively clear. The Instituto Geografico Nacional in Lima has only an almost useless 1:200,000 map, which fails to indicate several major trails, rivers, and villages. Even its title is appropriately vague: *Carta de la Region Norte del Cusco.*

Allow plenty of time for either of these treks. Plan on a minimum of five days for the fifty-mile walk to Santa Teresa, and at least four days for the thirty-five-mile walk to Huayllabamba (but remember that from this roadless village you'll either have to walk two to three days on to Machu Picchu or a half-day down to the rail line at km 88).

The two routes leave Mollepata on the same wide, well-used trail, climbing directly toward the mountains to the north. If you begin walking in the afternoon, make camp within a couple of miles of town because the trail passes through a long waterless section beyond this point. Soon the broad path climbs a high ridge, at the top of which a trail branches to the right. This is the main route for both treks. Following it you will soon find yourself high above the Río Blanco, a stream cloudy with white glacier flour. The trail climbs along the left side of this long valley (excellent views of 19,425-foot Nevado Humantay ahead) eventually reaching high, grassy *pampa* and the little stone and thatch *estancia* of Soray (about twelve miles from Mollepata). A short distance above Soray, you'll have your first close-up views of Salkantay with its dazzling snowfields, ice cliffs, and cornices. In this area you'll also find excellent campsites. A mile or so above Soray, at the beginning of a damp meadow, the two routes finally separate.

If you've chosen to walk to Santa Teresa, your route skirts the meadow on its left to climb the pass between Salkantay and Humantay. With its towering rock faces and overhanging glaciers, this pass (only a few feet short of the 16,000-foot mark) is surely one of the most spectacular passes of the Andes. At the pass, this trail turns to the west, descending along an ancient Inca route through wonderful alpine scenery to meet a stream. The trail loses more than a mile of elevation as it descends this stream through increasingly lush vegetation to reach the remote village of Colcapampa (sixteen miles from Soray).

At Colcapampa the trail turns to the northeast, descending through the valley of the Río Santa Teresa. As you work your way down this valley on a clear, well-used trail, you pass the villages of Churubamba, Miscabamba, and Pisanayniyoc, and the cloud forest becomes increasingly dense and junglelike. Waterfalls tumble down the valley walls, and the heavy vegetation along the trail comes to resemble the beautiful dense undergrowth of the Olympic peninsula or the Great Smoky Mountains in the United States. Eventually, the wild growth of the valley's upper reaches gives way to cultivation, and you pass through regions of banana and coffee production.

Finally, the trail reaches the small town of Santa Teresa (twenty miles from Colcapampa). Here you can catch the early morning local train (daily except Sunday) up the Urubamba valley. The train reaches nearby Machu Picchu early enough to give you an hour or two at the ruins before the tourist train from Cuzco arrives (don't leave your pack at the Machu Picchu station; take it up to the site with you and leave it with the guards at the entrance). You can then return to Cuzco on the more comfortable tourist train at 4 P.M. (buy tickets as soon as you arrive at the station).

If at the trail junction above Soray you choose to walk to Huayllabamba, your route follows the right side of the meadow, climbing to the northeast. Eventually, the trail turns more directly east (right), skirts a damp, marshy area, and climbs toward the pass over talus slopes.

From the pass (a little over 16,000 feet), the trail (sometimes a little faint) descends into the valley of the Río Huayllabamba (ten miles from Soray). Follow the left bank of the stream, which becomes for a while an Inca irrigation canal. Beyond the canalized section, cross the bridge to the right bank of the stream, following it past the small Inca ruin of Pampacahuana and on to Huayllabamba (nine miles below the head of the Cusichaca).

From Huayllabamba, you can either turn left (northwest) up the Río Llullucha to follow the Inca Trail to Machu Picchu, or you can continue down the Cusichaca to km 88 at the railway. There you can catch the mid-morning local train for the short ride to Machu Picchu (expect a very crowded ride, though).

The Cordillera Vilcanota

Our first trip to the Cordillera Vilcanota came at the end of a summer-long trip; we were worn out from months of long bus rides, hard walks, and high altitude. We reached Ocongate, a dusty little town on the narrow dirt road to Quincemil and Puerto Maldonado down in the Amazon basin, after an eight-hour ride from Cuzco in a truck filled to overflowing with *campesinos*. We pulled our packs from beneath piles of potatoes and cases of Cuzqueña beer and staggered from the truck feeling dazed and dusty and bone tired. All we wanted were beds, a meal, and a full night's sleep before beginning a trek into the *cordillera* the next morning. We found the beds and the meal, but Ocongate was not the place that night for sleep. A week-long fiesta was approaching its conclusion, and roving bands of musicians and celebrants roamed the dark, nonelectrified streets of the town until dawn playing the stark and beautiful music of their Inca ancestors.

By nine the next morning we had walked down the main road to Tinqui, a little village that serves as the trailhead for the long, high-altitude circumnavigation of Nevado Ausangate. After the previous night's fiesta, Tinqui was a town asleep, not a likely place to find an *arriero* to lead us into the Vilcanota. The only activity was a group of six men sitting in front of a *bodega* drinking beer from large bottles, either to soothe their hangovers from the night before or to prepare early for the continuation of the fiesta later in the evening. We asked them where we might find an *arriero.* One of the six drinkers thrust a warm beer toward us; "Have a cerveza," he said, "No one will go today. It's a fiesta."

He was right. We had to camp at the edge of the village soccer field for another day waiting for the party to end. But when it did and we finally hit the trail, we found that the Vilcanota reimbursed all of the effort and waiting many times over. We were charmed by both the landscape and the people.

The Cordillera Vilcanota is one of Peru's most spectacular but least visited mountain ranges. Less accessible than either the Cordillera Blanca or the Cordillera Vilcabamba, the Vilcanota remains for most travelers simply a distant glimpse of the white, 21,000-foot peak of Nevado Ausangate seen far away on the southern horizon from Cuzco. Though Ausangate dominates the range, peak after peak rises to near

20,000 feet, often crowding the horizon with massive glaciers and rewarding the trekker tenacious enough to travel in the Vilcanota with scenery unsurpassed in the Andes.

Just as fascinating as the mountains, however, are the people of the Vilcanota. Here, Peru's history is visible in other ways than the remains of stone walls, for the *campesinos* of the Vilcanota, among the most traditional of the Peruvian highlanders, carry on their lives in much the same manner that their ancestors did in Inca times. The alpaca herders of the *altiplano* wear the traditional Inca head covering, the *chullo,* and few of them speak anything but Quechua. The women wear dark wool skirts, alpaca shawls, and fringed pancake hats; you'll see them spinning yarn, their spindles whirling in the air like tops, as they walk through the dry hills. Men and women alike travel the difficult trails that connect the scattered villages of the range carrying tiny, efficient bundles of gear—little else besides a blanket, a pot, and a bag of *chuño* and *kamcha*—an outfit light enough to put even the most weight-conscious of backpackers to shame.

Much of the *altiplano* that these people inhabit is above the level of cultivation, but the grassy river valleys between mountains make excellent pasturage for alpaca and llama. Over the centuries these animals and the highlanders who tend them have established a symbiotic relationship. The *campesinos* spend much of their lives caring for their herds, and the animals, in turn, provide them with wool for their fine weavings and with meat for their tables. In addition, in this treeless region, llama dung is a primary fuel source.

Quechua children, Cordillera Vilcanota, Peru

It would, of course, be inaccurate to romanticize the people of the Vilcanota. They live tough lives within close tolerances. The pressure —both economic and cultural—to move to the cities is great, and every year the little mountain *estancias* become more and more abandoned as the highlanders move to urban centers. The educational and medical services available to them, though improved lately, are still minimal by U.S. standards. They work harder to survive than we can imagine. But it would also be inaccurate to underestimate the dignity and pride of these people who continue to live in one of the truly hard, high places of the world.

If you enter the Vilcanota from Ocongate and Tinqui, transportation is difficult at best. Though the road from Cuzco to Urcos is paved, the bulk of the trip is over a rough, twisting, dusty mountain road that makes travel a very slow affair. In Cuzco, you may be told that traffic on the Urcos-to-Quincemil road is one way, alternating directions daily, but we found this was not the case. Though the road is very narrow, traffic was definitely two-way, leading to potentially frightening interludes along the way if your truck happens to be on the outside of the mountain when it encounters another vehicle. Finding a truck going from Cuzco to Ocongate and perhaps on to Tinqui (sometimes called Cooperativo Luaramarca) is to a degree a matter of luck. Large trucks going to Quincemil, passing through Ocongate and Tinqui on the way, leave at very unpredictable intervals from Limacpampa Chica, not far from the Convent of Santo Domingo. The best you can do is to walk down to this little plaza and ask drivers or shopkeepers when trucks are expected to leave. You're a little more likely to find a ride with the smaller trucks that congregate just across the street from Santo Domingo. Go there first thing in the morning, and ask drivers for trucks to Ocongate. Trucks usually leave fairly early, around 8 A.M. or thereabouts, depending on when they collect a full load of passengers and cargo. The ride to Ocongate usually takes around six to eight hours, depending on traffic and the length of the stop in Urcos. Be sure to take a full water bottle and some snacks for this hard all-day trip. Though Ocongate is usually the end of the line for these smaller trucks, drivers will often take hikers on to Tinqui (five miles down the main road) for a small extra charge.

The only hotel and restaurant in Ocongate is the *Alojamento Josmar* on the plaza. This hotel is extremely basic—no electricity, an outhouse for a toilet, a spigot in the courtyard for a washroom—but the rooms are reasonably clean, and the family that runs the place is very friendly. If you choose not to stop in Ocongate, you'll find neither hotels nor restaurants in Tinqui, but hikers are usually welcome to camp on the edges of the soccer field; just be prepared to be the center of attention for the town's children.

Though we usually hike without guides or *arrieros,* the Cordillera Vilcanota is one area where we'd strongly recommend using them since route finding is often difficult there because the valleys of the range are inhabited and trails run everywhere. This confusion is only complicated

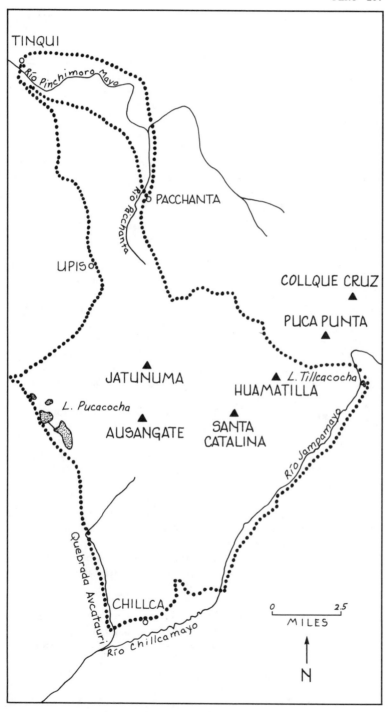

TINQUI

Río Pinchimoro Mayo

Río Pacchanta

PACCHANTA

UPIS

COLLQUE CRUZ ▲

PUCA PUNTA ▲

JATUNUMA ▲

L. Tillcacocha ▲

HUAMATILLA

L. Pucacocha

AUSANGATE ▲

SANTA CATALINA ▲

Río Jamparmayo

Quebrada Avcatauri

CHILLCA

Río Chillcamayo

0   2.5
MILES

↑
N

by the trails made by the thousands of llamas and alpacas that graze the high pastures. Also, hikes in the Vilcanota will take you to very high altitudes and keep you there for days at a time, so even the acclimated can appreciate the luxury of walking without the additional weight of a pack. The cost of an *arriero* is extremely reasonable in Tinqui (about $10 a day for a guide and two pack animals), and under normal, nonfiesta conditions, you should be able to make arrangements within a couple of hours.

The Ausangate Loop Trek

The circuit of Ausangate, which begins and ends in Tinqui without retracing any of the route, is one of the most exciting long-distance treks in the Andes. You'll have excellent views of Ausangate and the subsidiary peaks of the *cordillera*. The hiking is wonderful and includes the crossing of two spectacular passes above glacier level. Campsites along the way are consistently splendid, but your first and last nights on the trail are especially nice because it is possible to camp beside thermal pools hot enough to soak away the dust and soreness of the long climbs. Because this is a high-altitude route, expect very cold nighttime temperatures—the mercury dropped to near 0 degrees Fahrenheit at one of our high camps one night. Since this is a long, high-altitude hike involving much climbing, we recommend it for experienced backpackers only. Most people take about six days for this hike. Try to get the Instituto Geografico Nacional topo sheet "Ocongate" (28–t) if you're in Lima; it accurately covers all of the Ausangate loop as well as the alternate route from Chillca to Pitumarca and the trip from Pitumarca to Laguna Sibinacocha.

From Tinqui, trails forming a virtual maze lead in the direction of Ausangate. One route leaves town on a broad path to the east, staying to the north of the Río Pinchimuro Mayo. Just past Quispirumi, this route turns directly south and soon reaches the Río Pacchanta. Another route leaves Tinqui to the south on a road that begins between the soccer field and a row of buildings. Follow the road that follows the left-hand bank of the Río Pinchimuro Mayo for a half-mile or so until you reach a log bridge crossing to the right bank of the river. After the bridge follow the trail, not the road that climbs above the river, passing by thatch-roofed houses and stone walls. This trail will soon turn toward the east and climb gradually into barren open fields with occasional stone houses visible in the distance. The trail is often really a half-dozen trails that converge and diverge as they work their way across the hills.

About four miles outside Tinqui, with a wide vista of the dry hills and the deeply cut valley of the Pacchanta and Pinchimuro Mayo off to the left, this trail reaches a major junction. Take the left fork at this junction. This trail will take you south into the Pacchanta valley, a beautiful rocky valley with views of Ausangate directly ahead. About six miles from Tinqui, not far from a group of stone houses, you'll reach the hotsprings of Pacchanta, just above the river's right bank. There are good campsites all along the valley, but those near the thermal pools are quite special. Locals use them for soaking, and they've even cut little dammed inlets to allow mixing of the cold river water with the hot spring water to arrive at a comfortable temperature. If you camp here, you'll never forget the experience of watching alpenglow fade over the summit of Ausangate as you luxuriate in the steaming water of the hot spring.

Beyond the springs, the trail continues up the Pacchanta, heading directly toward Ausangate on a clear trail that picks its way through rocks, crossing and recrossing the stream. When you reach the entrance of a broad *quebrada* with a braided stream entering from your left, though, the trail becomes much less apparent. At this point, cross to the right bank of the stream and look for the trail that swings to the left (east), crossing directly in front of Ausangate and passing below a thatch-roofed house. Stay to the right, following the sometimes faint trail as it climbs above the stream and then turns away from it to climb the ridge to your right. Past this ridge, the trail becomes more distinct, but to keep yourself oriented, remember that you are aiming for the obvious notch between Ausangate and Puca Punta. Soon, you'll see a turquoise lake below and to the left of the trail; as you climb, views of the mountains of the Vilcanota become more and more spectacular.

Beyond the lake, the trail climbs through a rocky notch, passing shortly thereafter a small lake off to the left and a llama corral. Eventually (about four miles past the hot springs), you'll climb above the high pastures and into the realm of ice and rock. Here, nearly 300 degrees of the horizon are dominated by glaciated mountains. Ahead, to the left of Ausangate, you'll see the obvious pass, occupied by a big glacier. You don't have to climb the ice and snow, however, because the clear trail climbs through the scree slopes just above the right side of the glacier. If you keep an eye on the high slopes in this area, you might be as lucky as we were and spot a herd of vicuña.

The pass between Ausangate and Puca Punta is the trail's high point, well over 16,000 feet, higher than any U.S. mountain outside Alaska. Unless you've become immune to the power of mountain scenery, you'll certainly be overwhelmed by the glacier below you and the great snowfields of the mountains that fill the sky above. If you look ahead, below the pass, you'll see the little Lagunas Ticllacocha, only an hour of downhill walking away. These lakes (nine miles from Pacchanta hot springs), situated just below glacier level and surrounded by the ragged mountains of the eastern *cordillera,* make as perfect a campsite as you'll ever find. Here you'll probably fall asleep to the sounds of avalanches crackling down the slopes of Collque Cruz and Pico Tres. Since the *lagunas* are only a little short of the 16,000-foot mark, expect very cold temperatures and even snow at this high camp.

From Ticllacocha, the trail descends the Río Jampamayo. After the long climb to the pass, the gentle ramble down the beautiful Jampamayo valley is a welcome relief. The valley floor is green, marshy pasture, and as you work your way through the valley, you're likely to pass hundreds of grazing llamas and alpacas. The main trail begins its descent on the left side of the valley, though a somewhat fainter trail also follows the right bank. If you follow the main trail, make sure to cross over to the right bank before the trail begins to drop into a rocky gorge (about six miles below Ticllacocha). Since the route down the valley is obvious, the only real problem you have to worry about is locating the trail junction at Chillca. This little collection of stone houses and llama corrals is about eight miles below Ticllacocha; watch for it on the right side of the valley.

Here, you have a choice to make. If you want to continue the circuit of Ausangate, your trail turns to the right (northwest) and climbs into the Quebrada Avcatauri. However, if you don't relish the prospect of several more days of high altitude and hard climbs, not to mention the long truck ride back to Cuzco from Ocongate, you have the option of following the main trail, which continues directly down the broad river valley you've been following (after Chillca, the river's name changes to the Chillcamayu). This trail reaches the town of Checacupe on the main Cuzco-to-Puno highway in two fairly easy days of mostly downhill walking. About nine miles below Chillca, the trail reaches the Río Pitumarca, and the valley becomes increasingly inhabited. Below the confluence of the two rivers, the trail swings westward, following the river to reach the town of Pitumarca in about ten miles. From here, you can either try to catch a truck (early morning is your best bet) or walk the five miles down to Checacupe on the main Vilcanota valley highway. In Checacupe you should have no trouble finding a truck or bus traveling back to Cuzco (only three to four hours away over a relatively good road).

If you decide to continue with the Ausangate loop, turn right (north northwest) at Chillca, and follow the trail that ascends the Quebrada Arcatauri along the left bank of the stream. As you climb this narrow canyon, the south face of Ausangate will be directly ahead. Less than a mile above Chillca, the canyon opens into a large field surrounded by talus slopes and the very close-by massif of Ausangate. This field makes an excellent campsite, especially because the very steep climb to the second pass begins immediately above this field.

Two trails begin climbing to the left from the upper edge of this field. The first is a foot trail that climbs virtually straight up toward the pass. The second trail is much gentler to accommodate pack animals but is not really much longer. Horses sensibly refuse to climb the first trail, so if you're traveling with an *arriero,* he'll surely steer you toward the second trail. As you climb toward the pass, look ahead and orient yourself; you're aiming for the notch between glaciated Ausangate on your right and a big barren red mountain, almost Martian-looking, on your left. Near the pass, both ascending trails become pretty vague, but if you don't wander too far off to the left (west), you should reach the pass with no trouble. Here, the trail again exceeds the 16,000-foot level, and the glaciers of Ausangate loom immediately overhead. These high, remote spots are the last refuges not only of the vicuña but also of the *taruka,* the Andean stag, and as we crossed this pass, we noticed two antlered heads of these rare animals peering down on us from a ledge far above the pass.

Beyond the pass, the route is fairly apparent. It descends steeply along talus slopes toward a small lake (good campsite). Just below the lake, the trail reaches an inviting-looking downhill valley, but instead of descending the valley, the trail quickly turns to the right and begins another steep climb on a clear trail. You'll top out of this climb with a view of a lake-strewn valley below you. These are the Lagunas Pucacocha, and there you'll find excellent campsites with wonderful views of the lakes and the heavily glaciated west face of Ausangate.

In the area of the Lagunas (eight miles from Chillca), the trail is often unclear, confused by a multitude of alpaca paths. The main route, however, stays well above the lakes as you descend the left bank of the Quebrada Pucacocha. When you reach the point where the small, aqua-colored Laguna Yanacocha is on your right and a large rock outcrop is on your left, the trail becomes much more obvious. It bears left to work its way through the rocky notch and then descends to a stream that runs into a broad valley to your left. Cross the stream and walk a short distance down its right bank until you reach a side canyon to your right. The trail climbs into this side canyon and along the flank of Ausangate. Near the top of this climb, you'll pass a pond on your right; ahead will be a big gray talus slope. The trail swings to the left, contouring along the talus slope. Soon the trail will begin to descend, bearing to the left into the open rock-strewn valley of the Río Upismayo. At this point all of the serious climbing is behind you.

Like the Jampamayo valley, the attractive green valley of the Upismayo will probably be filled with grazing llamas and alpacas. When you pass a group of llama corrals and large boulders, you are not far from Upis, the thermal pool that most trekkers make their last camp of the trip (about eight miles from Lagunas Pucacocha). From Upis, you'll have a fast nine-mile walk over gently rolling hills back to Tinqui. Below the thermal pools, make sure to cross over to the right side of the valley and pick up the trail there that contours along just above the level of the valley floor. Eventually the landscape opens up into a huge wide marshy valley, which you skirt on the right, passing by stone walls and a small group of thatched houses. The trail, which is quite evident at this point, climbs the low, round ridge just ahead, crossing it into another valley strewn with a half-dozen small ponds and a few houses. You'll be traveling northerly, rambling over the barren hills of the *altiplano,* and an hour or so before the trip's conclusion, you should be able to see far ahead the valley where Tinqui and Ocongate lie. Return transportation from Tinqui or Ocongate to Cuzco is frequent but unpredictable; it would be unusual to have to wait more than two or three hours for a ride though.

The Laguna Sabinacocha Trek

If the Ausangate loop leaves you with a further desire to explore the Vilcanota, another wonderful destination for a week-long trek is the Laguna Sibinacocha. This large and extraordinary lake (almost eight miles long) is situated at an altitude of 15,486 feet and is surrounded by the glaciated, 20,000-foot peaks of the eastern Cordillera Vilcanota. Amazingly, it is frequently visited by flocks of flamingos. The area between the towns of the Vilcanota valley and Sibinacocha is confusingly cut with literally dozens of trails used by alpaca herds and the people of the high valleys, and even well-traveled trails often disappear for long stretches in lush pastures or along rocky slopes. Therefore, route finding is extremely difficult, so we'd strongly recommend hiring an *arriero* to take you on the long trek to the lake.

Because of the multiplicity of trails, there are any number of ways to reach Sibinacocha. One good route to Sibinacocha leaves Pitumarca traveling eastward, soon reaching the Río Pitumarca. This trail climbs along the inhabited river valley until it reaches the confluence of the Coricori and the Yanamayu (about sixteen miles above Pitumarca). Here the trail follows the Yanamayu (the left-hand branch) to the northeast for a couple of miles before turning back to the east. The trail climbs along the Yanamayu for eight miles or so until, at the 15,500-foot level, it reaches a high *puna* dotted with small lakes. The trail passes to the right (south) of Lagunas Aereacocha (about twenty-nine miles from Pitumarca) and Yanacocha (four miles farther on) before finally reaching the southern end of Sibinacocha at the outlet of the Río Cevinamayo. The area around the lake is, like most of the Vilcanota,

On the trail, Cordillera Vilcanota, Peru

crisscrossed with trails, so it is an excellent spot to make day hikes from a base camp. Here again, an *arriero* can help in keeping watch over your camp to prevent pilfering while your group is away hiking.

Sibinacocha can also be reached from Tinqui by walking to the Río Chillcamayu valley. Just above Chillca, a trail turns to the southeast into the Quebrada Misquiunuj, climbs eastward through the Quebrada Lloclla (the continuation of the Misquiunuj) to pass just to the south of Nevado Chuallani and Laguna Negromutayoc, reaching Sibinacocha about twenty miles from Chillca.

6
Bolivia

Compared with Ecuador or even Peru, Bolivia is a raw country, still very much in the process of formation. It is also a difficult country in just about any aspect you care to name—landscape, economy, politics, sociology. It is not an easy land in which to travel, much less to get to know well. The highway system is crude and limited, and only a third of it is paved. Under the best of circumstances getting from point A to point B is difficult—bus and train tickets are almost always in short supply, often necessitating days of waiting. Under less than optimal conditions, travel can become almost impossible—landslides and washouts close roads regularly, and strikes and coups disrupt not only transportation but other basic services at disturbingly frequent intervals. At first glance, the people of Bolivia can seem almost as daunting as the logistics of movement within the country. The Aymara *campesinos* of the *altiplano* often strike the first-time visitor as a stolid, dour people, cheerless as the wind-swept highlands they inhabit.

But for the traveler intent on experiences that are definitely out of the ordinary, Bolivia is worth the effort. The inaccessible landscape that its rough roads cut through is as spectacular as any in the world. And the mountain people—once given a little time to become accustomed to the oddity of an unexpected traveler through their isolated land—can be open, friendly, and helpful.

Geographically, Bolivia is a country delineated by mountains. The relationships between its three regions—the *altiplano,* the Yungas, and the Amazon basin—are defined by the high peaks that partition the country. In Bolivia as elsewhere in the range, the Andes are not a single chain of mountains. Rather, they often form two or three parallel chains that come together at *knudos* (knots), which, as the name implies, are dense and complex groups of mountains. The Cordillera Vilcanota in southern Peru is one such *knudo,* and from it two distinct chains of mountains stretch south to shape the landscape of Bolivia. The western chain, the Cordillera Occidental, forms a natural barrier to the Pacific. The eastern chain, the Cordillera Real, looms over the Amazon basin. From most spots in the northern highlands of Bolivia, the snow mountains of the Cordillera Real rise in stark white contrast against the brown foreground of the *altiplano.* Between Mt. Illampu (20,932 feet) to the north and Mt. Illimani (21,195 feet) to the south, the Cordillera Real (the Royal Range) *averages* over 18,000 feet in height for over 100 miles, making it one of the most impressive collections of mountains in the Andes, if not the world. Six of the *cordillera's* two dozen major peaks exceed 20,000 feet.

The great high-altitude trough that runs between the Cordilleras Occidental and Real is perhaps Bolivia's most characteristic feature. Called the *altiplano,* this high plain is home to more than half of the country's population. It stretches southward for 500 miles and is as much as 80 miles wide. Its elevation varies from 12,000 to 12,500 feet, making it one of the world's highest heavily populated regions. Much of this bleak sun-blasted trough between mountains may have been the basin of an ancient inland sea, of which Lake Titicaca is the remnant. At any rate, beneath the relatively flat surface of the *altiplano* is a great chasm filled with 2,000 to 3,000 feet of sedementation deposited over the millennia by wind and water.

This exceedingly unfruitful-looking land is surprisingly heavily agricultural. Principal crops are, of course, those adapted to harsh high-altitude growing conditions—the *chuño* potato, barley, *quinoa, oca.* Much of the land, too, is used as pasturage for sheep, llamas, and alpaca, the wool from which is an essential element in the *campesino's* effort to piece together a subsistence living in the cold thin air of the *altiplano.*

Sloping off toward the Amazon basin to the east is the fertile Yungas, the local name for a wild cloud forest zone of woody ridges and deep gorges. Here in the lush highland valleys that drain off the moderately heavy rainfall (fifty to seventy inches per year) grow Bolivia's principal cash crops—sugar, bananas, citrus fruits, coca, coffee. To transport these products to market in La Paz, a handful of raw dirt roads pitch headlong from the crest of the Cordillera Real into the increasingly green and dense mountain jungle below. There little *estancias,* fields, and groves cling to the foggy slopes and nestle in the narrow river valleys.

At the base of the Yungas begins the Amazon basin, by far the largest of Bolivia's geographical regions. Though it comprises over half of the country's area, these jungle lowlands are sparsely populated, containing only about 15 percent of the nation's inhabitants, though Bolivia, like Peru and Ecuador, sees its territories in the Amazon basin as the country's primary economic hope for the future.

Bolivia's history as an independent nation is a twisted tale of violence, political instability, and geographic diminuition. The country is now less than half its size at the time of independence in 1825, having lost territory to Peru, Paraguay, Argentina, and Brazil. The most consequential loss, however, was to Chile, to which Bolivia forfeited its access to the Pacific. Even today, 100 years after the war that cost Bolivia its seacoast, you'll see signs in La Paz demanding the return of the long-lost strip of land connecting the country to the sea. Bolivia's territory has been in such a state of flux for so long that even today the exact land area of the country is a matter of some question.

Internally, Bolivia has been no more stable than its borders. Since independence its government has been marked by a succession of military coups. In fact, since World War II, the country has averaged more than a coup per year. For the traveler, though, these coups are of little practical concern; normally, all that is noticeable are unusually large crowds in the plaza and an early curfew.

Ethnographically, Bolivia is the most "Indian" of the Andean countries, with about three-fourths of the population of largely unmixed heritage. The *campesinos* of the northern Bolivian highlands are primarily Aymaras, descendants of the builders of Tihuanaco. These ancient independent people were among the strongest holdouts against the spread of the Inca empire. In fact, so strong was their fight for autonomy that the Incas finally allowed them to keep their language, so while today no one knows the languages of other peoples conquered by the Incas, Aymara is still a living language.

Life has never been easy for the Indians of Bolivia. Their history is one of intense and often brutal exploitation. Under the Spanish they were enslaved and put to work in the country's rich silver mines under conditions that even some Spanish chroniclers found inhuman. Today they are still very much economically exploited by the tiny wealthy percentage of the population that controls the country. The land the Indians inhabit is far from Edenic; wresting a living from it demands work and ingenuity. On cold, cloudy days when the wind scours the *altiplano* and herders wrapped in dark wool ponchos stand bleak guard over flocks of sheep huddled tails to the wind, the lives of the Aymaras seem hard beyond imagining.

But a visit to a high-spirited highland festival such as those held at Copacabana reveals that the Aymaras' way of life, hard as it is, is not without laughter and celebration. The Aymara women add the only spots of brightness to the otherwise drab *altiplano*. Their yellow and magenta skirts flash a welcome bit of color in the brown surroundings (by the way, the headgear favored by the women of the *altiplano* is the rather anachronistic-looking bowler hat, reportedly introduced to Bolivia in the nineteenth century by a British hatmaker stuck with an overstock of bowlers and looking for a new market).

If Bolivia is a difficult country, both for its people and for visitors, it is also a country rich in history, culture, and landscape, a country that will reimburse you in the form of memorable experiences for the extra effort it takes to travel there.

La Paz

Any geographical description of La Paz reads like a litany of "highests"—including the world's highest capital city (12,000 feet—about the altitude of Lhasa in the Tibetan Himalayas) and the world's highest commercial airport (El Alto, 13,400 feet). More interesting is the fact that La Paz is the most "Indian" of the Andean capital cities. Once you leave the modern downtown district, Aymara culture takes over. The streets are often packed with vendors selling everything from dried llama fetuses (to be buried in the foundations of new houses in good-luck ceremonies) to bowler hats. Aymaras in traditional costume mix with city people and crowd the streets of the semilegal black market to shop for hard-to-find imported items. With all its Indian culture on display at every turn, La Paz is perhaps the most interesting of the Andean capital cities in which to wander about either before or after a trip into the mountains.

If you make the hard trip overland to La Paz from Peru, south of Lake Titicaca you'll pass through a landscape stark beyond belief. Virtually unrelieved by any spot of color, the high plains are cold and wind-swept, an unlikely locale for a major city. Even a few miles outside La Paz you'll find few hints that a city with perhaps a million inhabitants (even the best population figures are extremely inexact) lies just ahead. Suddenly the road pitches head over heels into a canyon raw as a fresh wound. Inside, protected from the cold winds that scour the *altiplano* and mercifully nearly 1,000 feet lower in elevation is La Paz.

Like Lima, La Paz is growing explosively under the pressure of country people moving to the city. And as in Lima, many of these newcomers soon find themselves occupying the vast slums that ring the canyon's cold rim and spill out onto the *altiplano* in the direction of El Alto airport. Because of altitude and temperature, La Paz is arranged just the opposite of most any other city you could name—the poor occupy the heights and the wealthy occupy the low areas. In the canyon's floor, far below the rim's slums, is the city's center, a fascinating blend of modern high-rise structures, Spanish architecture, and Indian culture all watched over by snow-capped Mt. Illimani in the distance. Even farther down into the canyon are the fashionable suburbs.

La Paz's main street follows the canyon's floor. Called the Prado, this principal route changes its name from Villazon to 6 de Agosto to 16 de Julio to Santa Cruz as it goes along. On either side of the Prado, a wide boulevard in its central section, the city's secondary streets climb sharply up the canyon walls, making walking about the city a conditioning exercise in itself. But you can hardly get lost in La Paz —walk downhill and you'll eventually reach the Prado.

The governmental center of the city is a few blocks off the Prado at the Plaza Murillo, scene of the political violence that has marked Bolivia's history since independence. In 1946, for example, the country's president was lynched from one of the plaza's lamp posts. Surrounding the plaza are the Presidential Palace (twice burned in revolutions), the National Congress, and the Cathedral. Also of interest is the church and monastery of San Francisco, an ornate colonial structure near the intersection of the Prado and Sagarnaga. Stop outside the church on Saturday mornings for a glimpse of the colorful wedding processions of Aymara couples.

RESOURCES

■ **Hotels** Expect to pay a premium if you want a hotel on or near the Prado. Hotels in the Indian quarter are a much better value and are still within an easy walk of downtown. One of the best of these (and the closest to the Prado) is the moderately priced *Sagarnaga* (on Calle Sagarnaga a few blocks uphill from San Francisco church) where the clean rooms have private baths and hot water. A similar moderately priced hotel is the *Oriental* (858 Illampu). A step down in price is the *Panamericano* (454 Avenida Manco Capac) where tiny rooms have private baths and hot water. One of the best budget hotels in La Paz is the *Residencial Rosario* (704 Illampu), a reasonably clean and pleasant low-end hotel that provides excellent service for its price range (including reliable luggage storage while you're on the trail). The Rosario is often full, in which case budget travelers might try the nearby *Andes* (364 Manco Capac) and *Italia* (303 Manco Capac). It is possible to sample some of the services of the first-class hotels without the expense of staying there. The *Plaza,* for example, allows nonguests to use their pool, sauna, and massage services for a very reasonable fee (an excellent way to soothe trail-sore muscles).

■ **Restaurants** La Paz is an excellent city for settling in and catching up on eating real food after a few days of trail food. Principal of its attractions for meat eaters are the many Argentine-style *parrilladas* where you can order charcoal grilled steaks or the traditional *parrillada* meal, which consists of beef, pork, chicken, sausages, and a variety of organs, often cooked on tableside grills. One of the best of these is the very reasonably priced *Club de la Prensa* (just off the Prado on N. Campero); the main dining room is an open-air garden, so make sure to try the Prensa for lunch on a sunny day. Another excellent *parrillada* is the *Carreta* (32 Calle Batallon Colorados) where the servings are huge. After overdosing on meat, you might want to try the vegetarian restaurant, *El Sol* (222 Calle Nicholas Acosta). Though not cheap, the *Naira* (161 Sagarnaga) is a convenient spot for sampling traditional Andean food. The Naira also offers good folklorico shows of traditional Bolivian music and dancing. For Chinese food, don't miss the *China* (1549 Avenida 16 de Julio). For U.S.-style hamburgers just walk down the Prado and look for the strange imitations of familiar American hamburger chain logos at *Genies* and *Pumperniks.* More interesting and authentic spots for sandwiches are the many *confiterias* (cafés) scattered throughout town. One of the best of these is the *Confiteria Marilyn* (corner of Potosi and Socabaya) where both the sandwiches and meals are filling and very reasonably priced.

■ **Transportation** Offices for Lloyd Aero Boliviana, Eastern, and AeroPeru are all located along the Prado. One recent and very welcome addition to Andean airline routes is Lloyd Aero Boliviana's direct La Paz-to-Cuzco flight. Currently, these flights are scheduled for Tuesdays and Saturdays only.

La Paz's main bus station, the *Terminal Terrestre,* is on Calle Uruguay up from Avenida Montes. Buses for all destinations *except*

Coroico and Copacabana on Lake Titicaca use this station. For Copacabana, try *Transportes Riveros* (660 Avenida Montes), *Expreso Manco Kapac* (506 Calle Tumusla), or *Transtur 2 de Febrero* (Plaza Frente al Cementerio). For Coroico (and Chulumani and Carnavi as well), go to *Flota Yungueña* on Avenida de las Americas in the Villa Fatima section of La Paz (buy tickets early; these buses fill up well in advance). The main train station is just behind the Terminal Terrestre (getting from one to the other, however, requires a long circular walk around them).

The most convenient and certain transportation to almost anywhere within a day's drive of La Paz (including trailheads for the Takesi and Coroico hikes) is provided at a surprisingly reasonable price by the *Centro de Taxis* (corner of Manco Capac and Viacha). Arrange for a driver at least a day in advance. Rates are somewhat flexible, so bargain.

■ **Money Exchange** Convert your traveler's checks or cash to Bolivian pesos at one of the several money exchange offices on the Prado; their rates are usually much better than the banks.

■ **Communications** The central post office is at the corner of Calle Ayacucho and Potosi near the Plaza Murillo. The ENTEL office for long-distance telephone calls is nearby on Ayacucho near Mercado.

■ **Books** The *Amigos del Libro* shop (1430 Calle Mercado) carries a fair selection of books in English.

■ **Tourist Information** The helpful *Dirreccion Nacional de Turismo* is in a kiosk in the center of the Prado (1440 16 de Julio) and can provide basic information on transportation schedules, simple maps of the city, etc. American Express business is handled by *Magri Turismo* (1490 16 de Julio, fifth floor).

■ **Museums** La Paz's most interesting museum is the *Museo Nacional Arqueologico de Tiahuanaco* (90 Calle Tiwanaku), also called the National Museum of Archaeology. As its name implies, the museum is largely devoted to a fine collection of artifacts and displays associated with the ancient city of Tiahuanaco. Other museums of interest include the *Museo Semi-Subterreano* (opposite Miraflores Stadium), an openair display of pre-Inca sculpture, including some monumental pieces from Tiahuanaco. Also worth a visit is the *Museo Nacional de Etnografia y Folklorico* (in a restored colonial house at 916 Calle Ingavi).

■ **Skiing** Another item on the La Paz area's list of "highests" is Chacaltaya, the world's highest lift-served ski area. Don't expect Aspen in the Andes, however. Chacaltaya is very primitive with a spartan restaurant and warming hut and only a crude rope tow to carry skiers to the top of its near-18,000-foot slopes. Chacaltaya is about an hour and a half by car above La Paz over a truly terribly road. Best months for skiing are normally January through May. For information on day tours to the ski area and equipment rentals, contact either the *Club Andino Boliviano* (1473 16 de Julio) or *Crillón Tours* (1223 Avenida Camacho).

■ **Maps** Until recently, if you wanted topo maps of Bolivia, you had to go through the harrowing process of visiting the *Instituto Geografico Militar* (I.G.M.) located in the headquarters of the Bolivian military, an organization understandably not particularly committed to serving the needs of the adventure traveler. Thankfully, that sometimes scary trip is no longer necessary because there is now a comfortingly civilian map office in downtown La Paz (mezzanine level of the Edificio Camara Nacional de Comercio, corner of Colombia and 16 de Julio). Here the staff is friendly and helpful rather than paranoid and threatening. You simply find the quads you want in the sample books and order them from the clerks. Don't wait until the last minute to buy your maps, though; popular quads such as those for Takesi and Coroico are often out of stock, taking a day or two to resupply from the I.G.M. The office is open 9 A.M. to 12:30 P.M. and 3 to 6 P.M. Monday through Friday, 9:30 A.M. to noon on Saturday.

■ **Shopping** For reasonably priced, high-quality handcrafts of all kinds, but particularly weavings, visit the *Artesanias Titicaca* (2320 Avenida Sanchez Lima). For a variety of crafts including leather goods, silver jewelry, and weavings, wander through the numerous shops near the San Francisco church and up Sagarnaga. On Saturdays, don't miss the *Mercado Camacho,* which stretches for blocks along Calle Camacho. The street is full of Aymaras buying and selling produce, meat, household goods, and some craft items. On a narrow cobbled street between Sagarnaga and Illampu you'll find one of the most unusual markets in the Andes—the Witches Market. Here you'll find charms to enhance your love life, improve your earning power, ensure good health, etc. The witches take their business seriously, so if you expect them to talk or sell to you, don't joke around; show a sincere interest.

Muela del Diablo —a Conditioning Walk

The Muela del Diablo (Devil's Molar) is a ragged rock formation outside La Paz. Though not extraordinarily interesting in itself, the Muela makes a good destination for those in need of an acclimatizing, conditioning day hike through the Bolivian countryside. Though the walk itself is not terribly long (eight miles round-trip), arranging transportation to the trailhead can be difficult, so begin early. From downtown take an N microbus (yellow with a Cotacota sign in the window) to Cotacota. The trail—a mule track—starts just across a dry stream bed past the Patio Azul restaurant. The walk to the village below the Muela should take about two to three hours, and nonclimbers can do a bit of scrambling on the lower sections of the outcrop.

Valley of the Moon

As its name suggests, the Valley of the Moon is a barren area of strange rock formations. The gorges and towers of brown-red stone are connected by a maze of paths, so the area makes a good spot for wandering about, picnicking, sunbathing on warm days. It is located further down the canyon from central La Paz. To reach the Valley of the Moon, take the Aranjuez microbus from the Prado. At the end of the line, walk down to the formations (about fifteen minutes).

Zongo Pass

The trip by rough road across Zongo Pass and down into the Yungas is one of the most interesting scenic excursions from La Paz. The road climbs out of La Paz, passes several lakes, including the Zongo reservoir, and finally tops out at the pass between Chacaltayo and Huayna Potosi at over 15,000 feet. Here the mountains of the Cordillera Real rise all around.

There are a couple of ways to make this excursion, both of which are expensive. Perhaps the most interesting way is to rent a four-wheel-drive vehicle in La Paz for a day or two of exploring the area. Check with *Oscar Crespo Maurice Rent-a-Car* (7 Plaza España) for four-wheel-drive rentals. Rates are not terribly high, especially if you share expenses with four or five people. Another alternative is to hire a car and driver for a day from the *Centro de Taxis* (corner of Manco Capac and Viacha).

Tiahuanaco

The ancient ruins of Tiahuanaco, Bolivia's most important archaeological site, lie starkly on the open plains of the *altiplano*. Whether Tiahuanaco was the center of an empire that exerted political control over large areas of the Andes or whether it was the locus of a widespread religious and artistic cult is a matter of some question. At any rate, though, its influence was vast indeed. Traces of Tiahuanaco-style art forms have been found from Ecuador in the north to Argentina and Chile to the south. Yet we know little of the people who constructed Tiahuanaco. Among the earliest of advanced civilizations of the Western hemisphere, the culture that produced these grand constructions and monolithic sculptures may have begun its rise as much as 2,000 years ago and probably reached its peak in about A.D. 600. The site was apparently abandoned while still in the process of construction in about A.D. 900. By the time the first Spanish explorers reached the area, the Aymara Indians, presumably descendants of the Tiahuanaco people, remembered little of the history of the site other than the vague legend that Tiahuanaco had been constructed in a single day.

So impressive are the ruins and so shrouded in mystery are its origins that nineteenth-century explorers of the site claimed it was Atlantis, the point of origination for civilization worldwide. Though the hyperbole of that claim has been well established, the influence of Tiahuanaco culture on later Andean civilizations including the Incas was profound, especially in the area of religious iconography (the sun, the condor, and the puma are central figures of both Tiahuanaco and Inca art) but perhaps also in social and political structure.

The ruins that remain today are primarily those of a great ceremonial center. However, a city of adobe, much less resistant to the passage of the centuries than the sandstone and andesite of the ceremonial structures, may have ringed the site. Though Tiahuanaco is now thirteen miles from Lake Titicaca, there is reason to believe that the lake has receded since the time of its inhabitation and that the city may once have been a port.

The most famous of the remaining features of Tiahuanaco are the Gateway of the Sun, a huge portal carved from a single block of stone. Also impressive are the Kalasasaya palace, a large plazalike enclosure bounded by monoliths, and the huge terraced pyramid of Acapaña.

Most of the tourist agencies in La Paz offer excursions to Tiahuanaco, but if you have a group of three or four, it is just as inexpensive to hire a taxi for the trip and set the itinerary yourself. A cheaper but less certain alternative is to take a bus to the ruins (try Transportes Ingavi, up Calle Manco Capac near the *Cementerio*) and then take your chances on a bus or *colectivo* for the return to La Paz.

Lake Titicaca

Lake Titicaca—at 12,500 feet—holds the distinction of being the world's highest navigable lake. It is 140 miles long and, at its widest point, seventy miles across; the lake covers an area of over 3,000 square miles. Though the old claim that the lake is deep enough to merit the description "bottomless" has been clearly refuted, its greatest depth of nearly 1,500 feet is still remarkable. The lake's waters are not particularly rich in life, but it does produce large trout, which were introduced in the 1930s. Perhaps the most interesting of the lake's inhabitants are the foot-long frogs that flourish in the shallows.

But surpassing the "facts" of Titicaca is its beauty, much of which

Totora reed balsas, Lake Titicaca

lies in the contrast between its dazzling blue water and the bleak landscape of the *altiplano* in which it is set. When you first see the vast blue lake shining in the clear high-altitude sunlight, it is not difficult to understand why Titicaca has held considerable mystical significance to the inhabitants of the *altiplano* since long before the Incas recognized it as the origin of their culture. Traveling around the lake presents the visitor with scene after scene of memorable quality—Aymaras poling their elegant, efficient *totora balsas* (reed boats) through the shallows, herds of llamas and sheep grazing the sparse grass along shore, the white peaks of the Cordillera Real rising beyond the lake to the east.

There are several ways to see the lake. For those short on time and long on pesos, Crillón Tours in La Paz (1223 Avenida Camacho) schedules expensive day trips to Titicaca. These include a private bus to the port of Huatajata where you board a hydrofoil for visits to the Islands of the Sun and Moon before having lunch at Copacabana and then returning to La Paz. It is also possible to travel to Huatajata by public bus and once there arranging with local boatmen for trips across the lake to Suriqui Island, noted for its reed boat builders. For most travelers between Peru and La Paz, though, Copacabana is the most convenient and least expensive town from which to base excursions around and across the lake.

Copacabana

Though neither its Cathedral, its market, or its plaza is particularly interesting, this faded little resort town nevertheless makes a pleasant spot for a visit to Titicaca. The main attraction here is clearly the lake, which sparkles deep blue only a few blocks below the plaza, offering the visitor several good excursions both by boat and by foot. Copacabana is especially interesting to visit during one of its many festivals, the principal of which is held during the first week in August. The normally sleepy town comes alive as *campesinos* pour in from the countryside for days of drinking and celebration. Colorful strings of actual and plastic blossoms decorate trucks and buses that line up outside the Cathedral to wait for the priest to bless their engines with a sprinkle of holy water.

Certainly the most popular excursion from Copacabana is the trip across Lake Titicaca to the sacred Islands of the Sun and Moon. According to one version of Inca history, the sun god, Inti, created the empire's founders, Manco Capac and his sister Mama Occlo, on the Island of the Sun, from which they later traveled north to found Cuzco. On the Island of the Sun you'll find a strange set of steps leading directly into the water, and if you feel like a short walk (two miles round-trip), your boatman will point out the trail to the island's primary ruin, Pilko Caima. The smaller Island of the Moon was apparently devoted to worship of the moon goddess, and there you'll find the ruins of a temple to the moon and a palace for the Chosen Women.

The trip to the islands takes a full day, so it is best to begin as early as possible. Go down to the docks the afternoon before you want to visit the islands to arrange for a boat and set a departure time in advance. Expect to bargain over the trip cost.

Copacabana is also a good base from which to make day hikes into the *altiplano* and around the shores of Lake Titicaca. A short but wonderful late afternoon walk from Copacabana is to climb the nearby steep hill overlooking the lake. From the notch between the hill's two summits you'll have an excellent view of the sun setting over the lake. But the hill is also something of a microcosm of Andean culture. If you climb the lower of the hill's summits, you'll find the ruins of a strategically located Inca outpost. If you climb the higher peak, after walking past the Stations of the Cross, you'll arrive at an impressive Catholic shrine stretched along a narrow rock outcrop overlooking the town, the lake, and the surrounding countryside.

The countryside around Copacabana, especially near the lakeshore on the far side of the shrine hill, is wide open. Numerous trails link the houses and fields of the *campo,* so good lake-view day hikes or running routes of varying lengths are easy to put together. Just set out walking and use the lake to keep your bearings. The unacclimatized should, however, remember that though the crisp air blowing off the lake and the brilliant sun may be invigorating, at an altitude of 12,500 feet, strenuous activity can contribute to *soroche.*

RESOURCES

■ **Hotels** The moderately priced, somewhat faded-looking *Hotel Prefectural* is the best of Copacabana's rather poor selection of hotels only because some of its rooms overlook the lake. If you manage to get a lake-view room, the plain rooms and lack of hot water may not matter. The Prefectural's dining room is the best restaurant in town. The hotel often fills up, so make reservations in La Paz, especially if you plan to arrive on a weekend. The inexpensive *Playa Azul* is Copacabana's second-best hotel. Its cold, spartan rooms have private baths, and the meals (included with the cost of the room) are adequate. Offering similar accommodations are the *La Portenita* (near the plaza) and the *Ambassador* (meals included). For those traveling on very limited budgets, try one of the many dirt cheap *alojamientos* on the side streets between the plaza and the lake.

■ **Restaurants** If your hotel doesn't have a dining room, you'll find Copacabana's restaurants very basic. Try the *Puerta del Sol* on the plaza, *Los Playas* by the lake, or one of the identical little restaurants along the main street between the plaza and the lake.

■ **Transportation** One of Copacabana's attractions is that it makes a convenient stop on the hard overland journey between Puno and La Paz. The Copacabana route is much preferable to the Desaguadero-Guaqui route in scenery and road conditions. All buses leave Copacabana from the plaza. For buses to La Paz via ferry across the Straits of Tiquinia (five to six hours), try to buy tickets as much in advance as possible. Buses to Yunguyo (just across the Peruvian border) with connections to Puno (four to five hours) are less crowded and leave town every half-hour or so; depart early, though, to ensure finding a Puno bus in Yunguyo. For those traveling to Peru, the immigration office is past the Hotel Prefectural. Your bus to Yunguyo should stop here for Bolivian exit stamps. It should also stop a few miles down the road at the Peruvian border were you need a Peruvian entry stamp.

■ **Money Exchange** Cashing traveler's checks in Copacabana can be difficult. If you come from La Paz, change money there. If you come from Peru, change money in Yunguyo.

The La Cumbre-to-Coroico Trek

This exciting hike makes a wonderful introduction to Bolivia for experienced backpackers. It takes you from the windy, cold alpine zone of snow and rock into the steamy, lush jungles of the Yungas where you'll complete the walk among banana groves and tropical birds. From the high point of the walk far above La Cumbre de Yungas Pass (the name means "the crest," and the highway itself reaches an elevation of 15,250 feet), the trail drops nearly 12,000 feet along slopes steep enough to wreak as much physical havoc as a hard climb. The route is an ancient one, predating the Incas, and one long section just above treeline displays some of the best preserved stone paving (12 feet wide) in the Andes. Instituto Geografico Militar topos 5945–II and 6045–III cover most of the walk, though the route is not difficult to follow. The trail is only twenty-eight miles long, but most hikers should allow at least four days for this walk; the jungle sections make for very slow going unless the trail has been recently cleared. Take along insect repellent for the lower sections of the trail, and be prepared for rain at any time of year. A word of caution: when we made this walk, the suspension bridge at Bellavista was in very poor repair and some of the lower sections of trail were in need of clearing; try to check with other hikers for current trail conditions.

The easiest way to reach the trailhead is to take a taxi from the Centro de Taxis. The ride from downtown La Paz will take only an hour and will let you begin your day earlier and with more certainty than if you take a bus or truck. Your driver should take you to La Cumbre Pass on the paved road and then turn off onto the dirt road to drop you off only a mile below the Apacheta Chucura, the high point of the trail near the 16,000-foot mark. Though taxi prices are quite reasonable, a cheaper alternative is to take a bus (8 A.M. daily) from *Flota Yungueña* or *Transportes a las Yungas* in the Villa Fatima section of La Paz; buy tickets in advance. Trucks also leave frequently for the Yungas via La Cumbre from Villa Fatima. You can get to Villa Fatima from downtown by taking a B microbus from Avenida Americas, but these are always packed with riders, so boarding with a backpack is difficult. Taxis from your hotel to Villa Fatima are very cheap and *much* more convenient than the microbuses. From Villa Fatima, buses and trucks leave fairly frequently on the highway that crosses La

Cumbre and descends into the Yungas. As always, arrive very early to ensure finding a ride.

If you take a bus or truck, get out at the road's high point—near a statue of Christ flanked by a big Orange Crush sign. From there turn left off the paved road onto a dirt road going roughly west. Follow this road just beyond where it passes between two small ponds. The road will then swing right (north) toward the pass, an obvious low point along the ridge ahead. Follow the much-used trail up the dark scree slope toward the pass. The mountains of the Cordillera Real form a ragged chain of glaciated peaks all around. At the pass (15,905 feet) is the Apacheta Chucura, one of the largest and perhaps oldest *apachetas* you'll find in the Andes. Here, thousands of travelers over the centuries have left stones to mark the occasion of crossing the pass. Expect very cold weather near the pass. Arrive early for the best chance of good views because clouds usually roll in early in the afternoon.

Below the pass the route is quite clear—a wide graded path in use for centuries. Follow it as it descends sharply into a steep-sided canyon. As it reaches the floor of the *quebrada* of the Río Lama Khuchu, the trail's descent becomes more gradual, passing fields and llama corrals. Near a little *estancia* called Samaña Pamapa (2.5 miles from the *apacheta*), the trail swings to the northeast, continuing to descend gently. The stream through the *quebrada* becomes the Río Phajchiri. Following the clear trail through the lovely canyon, you'll eventually reach the little thatch- and tin-roofed village of Achura (six miles from the pass; the village is occasionally also called Cuchuca). There are plenty of good campsites above the village and a few below it, but don't

An apacheta in the Cordillera Real, Bolivia

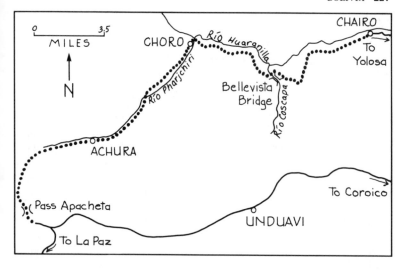

go too far because the stream soon drops into a deep gorge. Supplies are not available in Achura.

Below Achura the trail is truly amazing—a wide, smooth, pre-Inca paved thoroughfare used by the *campesinos* and their livestock. On this paved trail you'll descend for about three miles to treeline. As you descend on the damp, slick trail through the forest, foliage becomes increasingly dense and tropical. There are virtually no campsites between treeline and the village of Choro, four miles ahead, so don't enter the forest late in the afternoon unless you relish the idea of a bivouac in the middle of the trail.

The village of Choro is very nearly the Andean equivalent of a ghost town; only a couple of its thatch houses are occupied. There are, however, excellent campsites in small, grassy fields beside the river. In Choro, cross the river to its right bank over a good suspension bridge (be sure to cross *in* Choro; the dilapidated bridge below the village goes nowhere). Just beyond the bridge, the trail begins to climb steeply, leaving the river far below and swinging to the east. Beyond Choro there are very few campsites—only a few waterless wide spots in the trail suitable for tent pitching, so be sure to fill all water bottles to capacity at one of the many side streams before looking for a campsite.

The long, slow stretch of trail between Choro and trail's end at Chairo (fourteen miles) contours along high above the Río Huarinilla. Over and over the trail dips into dark, heavily jungled coves to cross side streams and then swings out across sunny, exposed hillsides. The trail is often so densely vegetated, it hardly seems like a trail at all. You'll walk for miles and miles with wet leaves slapping your face and thorny limbs scratching your legs. But even though the trail is sometimes virtually invisible, you can hardly get lost because all around you is even denser vegetation. Despite the physical discomfort the trail imposes on walkers, the natural beauty of the Yungas is staggering.

Mist hangs on the green hillsides. Waterfalls splash cool water across the trail. Tropical birds sit in the trees. Swarms of butterflies flicker in the sunlight in clearings.

About seven miles from Choro is the suspension bridge of Bellavista, which crosses a rocky, sheer-sided gorge. Past Bellavista 2.5 miles, you'll reach a house with a gate. From there it is only five miles —including a long, steep descent—to the end of the trail at Chairo.

Chairo is a quiet little end-of-the-road town tucked deep into the gorge of the Huarinilla. A *bodega* in town sells a minimal selection of supplies but does have soft drinks and beer. A truck leaves Chairo most days early in the afternoon. If you miss it, however, you can either camp in a field near the river and wait for the next vehicle, or you can walk the five flat miles out to the main highway (a dirt road) between La Paz and the towns of the Yungas. At the first main intersection after Chairo, turn left; very shortly you'll either have to ford the river or cross a dangerous-looking suspension bridge to make your way up to the highway. There you may be lucky and catch a ride on a truck or bus to Yolosa—four miles to the right along the highway—but don't count on it. Trucks are frequent but mostly filled to overflowing with La Paz-bound goods and passengers.

Yolosa is a strange little truck-stop town, little more than a long line of thatch lean-tos that serve food to the drivers and passengers of cargo trucks making the long, slow trip to La Paz. Small passenger-carrying trucks make the half-hour trip up the mountain to Coroico fairly frequently throughout the day. For those wanting to return directly to La Paz, transportation for the seven-hour trip is much more uncertain. Trucks and buses roar through Yolosa several times an hour, but, again, they're usually filled to capacity. If you do catch a truck back to La Paz, keep your poncho handy—you'll pass beneath a couple of drenching waterfalls along the way.

Coroico

Most people who've just completed the hike will surely want to spend a few days in Coroico, a very pleasant, restful town perched high on the brow of a mountain. There is little to do in Coroico except rest, eat, watch tendrils of cloud move on the green slopes back in the direction of the Río Huarinilla, and sit in the plaza in the evening when the whole town seems to turn out for a stroll.

The best hotel in town is the moderately priced and very nice *Prefectural,* a homey old place that seems more like a *hacienda* than a hotel. The meals in the Prefectural's dining room are the best in town, and the view is lovely; the hotel is often full, but reservations can be made through travel agents in La Paz. The best choice in a budget hotel is the *Hostal Kory* (just off the plaza). Here for a very low charge you'll get an extremely basic room, but the Kory maintains a small, clean swimming pool, and all the rooms open onto balconies with wonderful views of the green hills and the snow-capped mountains through which you walked at the beginning of the La Cumbre trail. For meals, try the restaurant below the Kory for inexpensive steaks, *saltados,* etc. A little shop at the upper end of the plaza sells real coffee, tea, and good homemade cakes and cookies. For something to sip while you enjoy the view from your hotel, walk below the plaza to the convent where the nuns sell wines and liqueurs they make themselves.

The best way to return to La Paz is by the *Flota Yungueña* bus (departures daily at 7 A.M.). The ticket office is just below the plaza on the road back to Yolosa. Tickets for the daily buses back to La Paz are routinely sold out several days in advance, so buy them immediately upon arrival in Coroico.

The Taquesi Trail

The Taquesi trail to Chojlla is perhaps the premier hike in the Andes for those with an interest in pre-Columbian stone paving. The route is an ancient one, certainly predating the Inca period. The wide, paved road would have formed an important link for pre-Columbian peoples between the barren *altiplano* and the fertile Yungas by crossing the Cordillera Real over relatively low passes. Like the La Cumbre-to-Coroico trail, the paving on the Taquesi trail is in a remarkable state of preservation, but it makes up much more of the route—about twelve miles of the route's twenty-five-mile length.

The Taquesi trail is also one of the easier trails in the Andes, one on which even beginners can experience the crossing of a high pass

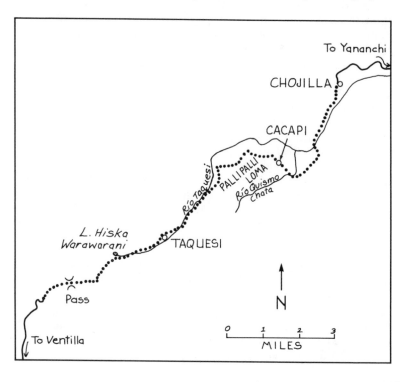

(15,420 feet, but it requires little climbing because it is only a short hike from the trailhead), the day-to-day life in tiny roadless Andean villages, and the descent into the damp, luxuriant cloud forest of the Yungas. For beginners, the Taquesi trail also has the attraction of requiring little effort in route finding—much of the trail, in fact, is twelve feet wide. For those who feel lost without a topo, however, the Instituto Geografico Militar quad 6044–IV covers the entire route. Conditioned, acclimatized hikers can do the walk in two days; others should allow at least three days. Since the trail descends into the Yungas, be prepared for the possibility of rain year-round.

The simplest way to arrange transportation to the trailhead is through the Centro de Taxis where you can hire a car and driver to pick you up at your hotel early in the morning and drop you off at the trailhead just beyond the village of Ventilla—or farther along the rough dirt road toward the first pass if you can talk your driver into going on. For a cheaper, slower alternative, you'll have to take public transportation to Ventilla. Buses leave from the Plaza Belzu early in the morning for the two-hour trip (the tourist information kiosk on the Prado prints up current schedule information for these buses). Alternatively, you can take an N bus from Calle Murillo downtown to the Transito (highway checkpoint) just past Cota-Cota and wait there for a bus or truck. Get there early for the best chance of finding a ride.

If, like most hikers, you begin the trek in Ventilla, walk just beyond the village's center, and look for a narrow dirt road leading up the Palca valley toward the village of Choquekota, about two miles away. Beyond Choquekota, the road continues for about three miles to the San Francisco mine. Shortly before the mine, however, the Taquesi trail branches to the right just past a stream and very quickly begins to climb steeply through switchbacks toward the pass.

Though fairly steep, the climb to the 15,585-foot Taquesi Pass is brief, only a couple of miles, and most of it is over wonderfully preserved paving, probably dating from the Tiahuanaco period. Views from Taquesi Pass are remarkable—on a clear day the snow mountains of the Cordillera Real form a spectacular backdrop, and to the east you look down into the jungle. While at the pass you might toss a stone onto the *apacheta* and look for the nearby abandoned mine shaft.

Beyond the pass, the trail—still wide and paved—descends alongside the Río Taquesi four miles to the village of Taquesi, a wonderful little collection of stone corrals and thatch-roofed huts. There are good campsites in Taquesi as well as at Laguna Lurukeri and Laguna Hiska Warawarani along the way.

From the village, the trail continues to descend, paralleling the river. About a mile below Taquesi, though, the trail crosses the river over a footbridge. Soon you drop into the forests of the Yungas and leave the paved trail behind. This leg of the walk is waterless, so carry full water bottles. After leaving the river, the trail swings around Palli Palli Hill and passes through the village of Kakapi—a collection of houses and an old church about six miles below Taquesi. Shortly, the

Pre-Inca paved trail, Cordillera Real

trail crosses the Río Sochikachi over a footbridge, climbs a small ridge, and then descends to meet and cross the Río Taquesi once more (three miles from Kakapi).

From the footbridge, the trail ascends to the mining town of Chojlla, the end of the hike. At this point you'll have descended almost 9,000 feet since the crossing of Taquesi Pass. The final section of the trail is a rather uninteresting three-mile uphill slog along an aqueduct and past waterworks into the rough, unappealing town.

Getting from Chojlla to La Paz is not usually easy. Buses leave Chojlla daily at 7 A.M. and are often full. Try to buy tickets as soon as you get to town. Trucks also leave for La Paz occasionally; ask around. It is possible to camp near the soccer field in Chojlla while you wait for transportation. A more interesting alternative is to walk an hour or so on to Yanakachi, a much more pleasant town with a small, simple hotel, the *Panorama.* The Chojlla bus to La Paz passes through Yanakachi, and you can catch it there if you buy tickets in Chojlla. Trucks also leave Yanakachi daily for the five-to-seven-hour trip to La Paz. If nothing seems to be moving out of Yanakachi, you could walk half an hour out to the main highway where you'll find lots of truck traffic and should be able to catch a ride over La Cumbre Pass to La Paz.

7
The Amazon Basin

For the visitor, the Amazon basin region of Ecuador, Peru, and Bolivia is a world of surfaces—the dense canopy of trees that looks like a vast green ocean from the air, the slick sheen of flat water moving slowly to the Atlantic, the impenetrable green wall of rain forest rising from the muddy river banks. Those visitors to the Amazon who never see beyond these sometimes bland and monotonous surfaces inevitably leave the jungle with a feeling of vast disappointment. The great living ecosystem of the Amazon basin seems dead to them. They came, as many do, with visions of Tarzan movies dancing in their heads, expecting every tree to be filled with monkeys and toucans, every foot of river to be boiling with vicious piranha, every jungle pool to have its allotted jaguar furtively lapping water. Perhaps somewhere on a remote tributary this Hollywood-sound-stage version of the jungle does exist, but if you come to the Amazon expecting to find it, you're bound to be frustrated and disappointed.

The Amazon does not allow you to penetrate its surfaces effortlessly. You have to work at it. And the difficulties you face are not inconsiderable. Jungle travel is, first of all, expensive. Basic travel services such as hotels and restaurants are noticeably more costly in jungle towns than in mountain towns. And unless you have the equipment, knowledge, and experience to take off safely on your own Huckleberry Finning down the rivers and exploring in the jungle (something no book alone can provide), you're thrown into the expensive hands of guides, jungle lodge operators, and tourist agencies. Even the kinds of exciting trips the inexperienced jungle traveler can safely make on his or her own—for example, day trips in canoes or launches with independent boatmen, jungle camping trips with local guides, long-distance river trips on cargo boats—are often impossible to arrange in advance and subject to frustrating delays. But for those willing to accept these conditions, the Amazon region can be a wonderful travel destination. This chapter makes no attempt to turn you into a seasoned jungle explorer. Rather, it serves to inform you of the kinds of jungle trips that make interesting supplements to a trip to the Andes.

For most people, just pronouncing the word *Amazon* captures something of the essence of adventure. The name—derived from the fierce women warriors Francisco de Orelliana claimed attacked his band of lost explorers on their largely accidental first descent of the river in 1541—is appropriately mythic for a land so rich in mystery. Here, in the strange half-darkness that is daylight under the great rain forest canopy, the impossible can come to seem probable. Even today tales of snakes longer than semitractor-trailer trucks, of lost cities hidden in the jungle, of diamonds as big as a fist filter into the river towns and find believers.

But discounting the mystery and myth of the Amazon for a moment, even to discuss the verifiable "facts" of the basin is of necessity to engage in extremes. For example, though the Nile may or may not be longer (a matter of some disagreement since the source of the Amazon is still open to question; at any rate, both are about 4,000 miles long), the Amazon is by far the greatest river system in the world, containing perhaps 20 percent of the world's fresh river water. The vast quantity of water that flows from the Amazon's 200-mile-wide mouth exceeds the Mississippi's flow more than tenfold and displaces saltwater for 100 miles into the Atlantic. The river's 1,100 tributaries drain an immense basin of 2.7 million square miles, an area equivalent to nearly three-fourths of the United States and almost twice the size of the world's second largest drainage area. Seven of those 1,100 tributaries are over 1,000 miles long in themselves. The best estimate of the number of species of fish inhabiting the river is about 2,000, nearly ten times the number found in the Mississippi; the discovery of new species is a routine matter. All but the largest ocean-going ships can safely navigate well over 2,000 miles up the river to Iquitos.

Another important part of the mystique of the Amazon is in its unusual fauna. Since our exposure to childhood picture books, we've all been familiar with the beautiful jaguar, the awkward-looking tapir, the strange 100-pound rodent capabyra, the giant anaconda, the comic sloth, and the piranha (seldom as vicious in real life as popular myth would have it). They're all there. But don't expect to be overwhelmed with animal life on your visit to the Amazon. To see even a few of the animals of the rain forest, you'll need to get into the jungle, far away from towns and settlements. Even then, you're much more likely to make somewhat less spectacular but still very exciting wildlife observations—the flash of butterfly wings passing through a stray beam of sunlight in the dim rain forest, a playful freshwater dolphin arching and splashing for miles alongside your canoe, a long line of leaf-cutter ants marching across the jungle floor each holding aloft a chunk of foliage, the dark bulk of a caiman submerging in the river's shallows.

But the Amazon is far from an untroubled paradise. Seen by the various economically troubled countries that govern it as their major hope for the future, the Amazon is currently suffering natural resources exploitation not unlike the American West in the late nineteenth and early twentieth centuries. Under this pressure, the unique Amazon ecosystem has proved that its vastness is only matched by its fragility. Today, the rain forest is being cleared for farms and pastureland—some of it for cattle ranches supplying beef to U.S. fast-food chains—at an alarming rate with often disastrous results. When the protective canopy of rain forest is ripped away—just two dozers with a chain stretched between them can clear acres a day—the topsoil often proves thin, easily depleted by crops and easily washed away by the heavy tropical rains. When the soil wears away—often within just a few years—the farmers and ranchers move on to clear more jungle land. What they leave behind is virtual desert, a great patch of muddy infertile subsoil, from which the rain forest cannot regenerate. At the current rate of clearing, the threat of creating the world's largest desert in place of the world's largest forest is real indeed.

Neither have the indigenous people of the Amazon been spared the pressures of development. Since the arrival of Europeans, the history of the native people who over the centuries learned to survive in this difficult land is, like that of the North American Indian, an immensely sad one. What the explorers and developers have wanted from the natives they have taken, killing and enslaving whenever it suited their purposes. And the exploitation has extended well into this century. Indians were taken as slaves as recently as the rubber boom of the late nineteenth and early twentieth centuries. And even today, rumors persist, some of them fairly well documented, of land developers and perhaps governments bombing villages of uncooperative Indians inconveniently located for road construction, oil exploration, or ranching activities. Today, little of the old culture remains, and by the 1990s probably all of the native Amazonians will have been assimilated.

Surprising to most people is the fact that the Amazon is not the place of constant and spectacular danger from animals that its mythologizers have made it out to be. The jaguar, for example, is a shy creature, as wary of you as you are of it, and not a man-eater. Though there are formidable snakes in the Amazon—the extremely deadly fer-de-lance or the anaconda, which can grow to over thirty feet—the jungle floor is not crawling alive with them. We once met a jungle guide with nearly a decade of experience who was quite excited because the day before he had seen his *first* fer-de-lance. Even the notorious piranha is hardly the killer it's usually portrayed to be. First-time visitors to the Amazon are often surprised to see locals swimming in the rivers totally unafraid of suddenly becoming lunch for a school of ravenous fish.

All of which is not to say that the Amazon is totally without danger. Malaria, for example, is a constant threat, and any visitor to the jungle should be very careful to take antimalarial drugs to avoid contracting it (see Chapter 2, "Medical Preparation," for more information). Though piranha are not a constant danger, it is probably a good idea not to swim in rivers because they do harbor numbers of dangerous creatures. Giant catfish weighing several hundred pounds can easily take off a foot. Even more nightmarish is the *candiru* fish. This tiny relative of the catfish likes nothing better than to swim into

THE AMAZON BASIN 235

the anus or urethra. Once inside, it locks itself in place with barbs and must be surgically removed. Be especially careful when stepping out of boats into shallow water; stingrays sometimes lie hidden in the mud and can inflict a painful wound.

Equipment for River/Jungle Travel

The three crucial conditions you'll have to take account of in gathering your equipment for jungle/river travel are insects, heat, and water. For insect problems, of course, simply take plenty of strong insect repellent and buy mosquito coils. The other two conditions are more problematic. In the Amazon, heat is a constant factor; expect daytime highs in the 90-degree-Fahrenheit range, and plan your clothing accordingly, remembering that every clothing choice represents a compromise. Though shorts and short-sleeved shirts may be most comfortable while in towns or on boats, pants and long sleeves provide welcome protection despite their uncomfortable warmth when walking in the jungle or when the mosquitoes and black flies are thick.

Even more difficult to combat is the wetness of the Amazon basin, much of which receives well over 100 inches of rainfall annually. Even in the "dry" season, be prepared for heavy rainfall at any time. Selecting rain gear suitable to Amazon conditions can be a problem. In Amazonian heat and humidity, a waterproof poncho or rain jacket can become a steambath; you become as wet from condensation on the inside as from rainfall on the outside. And we've found "breathable" rain gear made of Gore-Tex or the like to be only marginally more effective than nonbreathable rain gear under these conditions. Though not much help when walking through dense undergrowth, a compact, collapsable umbrella is, we've found, much more functional in towns and on open boats than a poncho.

Foot gear can also be a problem. When walking in the rain forest or on the unpaved streets of raw jungle towns, expect muddy footing. Even well-waterproofed leather boots quickly become waterlogged and take forever to dry out in the humid air. Since trying to keep your feet dry is largely a futile cause in the Amazon anyway, sneakers often make more functional foot gear than boots since they're much easier to wash and quicker to dry out. If you really expect to do some serious slogging through swampy terrain, you can buy rubber overboots in any river town. Perhaps our best advice on coping with the heat and wet of the jungle is to follow the example of Amazon boatmen—wear shorts, T-shirts, and sneakers as much as possible, and get used to staying damp most of the time.

If you plan to do any long-distance travel on river boats, a hammock and mosquito net are essential equipment. These can be purchased at some shops and most markets. While shopping, be sure to check hammocks carefully for size. They're made for short South Americans, not six-foot-tall *Norte Americanos,* so if you're tall, try to find a "double"-sized hammock. Also essential for river boat travel is food. Your passage will usually include meals, but these are normally minimal—pasta, rice, beans, fish, and cooked bananas. Be sure to take along plenty of snacks as well as canned goods to supplement these repetitive meals. Don't forget to take along enough bottled water, soft drinks, and beer to last the trip. Also take iodine water purification tablets; most boats use the river as the primary water source, so the threat of illness is strong unless you limit yourself to bottled drinks and/or carefully treat all water before drinking. Especially on the larger boats traveling the wider tributaries, you'll need binoculars to scan the shores for animal and human activity. On the river, you'll have long days to fill, so be sure to take along plenty of entertainment—books, cards, games, etc.

River Travel

The range of boat travel on the Amazon and its tributaries offers something for every style of travel—everything from luxurious "floating hotels" to rusty old passenger-carrying cargo boats to water logged dugout canoes. The difficulty is finding the kind of river transportation that will provide the kind of jungle experiences you want and that will take you where you want to go when you want to go.

Swinging in a hammock as you float for days on a cargo boat down a big powerful river while the jungle slips by on either bank can be a wonderful experience. It can also become a little frustrating if instead of a comfortable hammock you want close-up views of the rain forest and its animals. Major navigable tributaries like the Ucayali or the Madre de Dios are quite wide, leaving you with primarily long-distance views of the jungle and little chance for a closer look.

To really see the rain forest, you have to get out into it, either on foot or in canoes and small launches on narrow side streams (in our opinion much preferable to walking in the jungle). These narrow streams will put you right into the rain forest. The jungle floor will often be only a few feet away, and the canopy of trees will virtually close over your head. On excursions such as these you'll have the best chances of close-up observation of wildlife.

Arranging such trips is usually not too difficult. If you stay in jungle lodges, they should have guides with canoes and launches readily available. Independent guides are also available in most jungle towns. If you are on your own, ask for guides at the town's tourist office, if there is one. Otherwise you might simply ask your hotel manager for recommendations for guides. If he or she can't help, you should be able to find a boatman for a day trip on side streams if you just wander along the town's waterfront and ask about. Remember to take snacks and plenty of water or bottled drinks on jungle day trips.

If you have time to spare and value leisurely drifting over small boat excursions, a long river trip on cargo boats can be a memorable once-in-a-lifetime experience. And you won't be totally removed from the shore because unless they're fully loaded to begin with, most boats stop over and over at tiny settlements along the route to pick up passengers and cargo, giving you an inside view of life along the river.

The passenger-carrying cargo boats that ply the Amazon and its tributaries are simple two-story craft with the covered upper deck reserved for passengers. Most boats have a half-dozen or so cabins located on the forward end of the passenger deck. For an additional charge you can have one of these tiny, dank cabins with dirty mattresses and holey mosquito netting. If you're equipped for it, though, a more pleasant if less private alternative is to hang your own hammock and mosquito netting with the other passengers in the open, breezy center portion of the deck. Aft, you'll usually find a couple of toilets, a shower, the galley, and, if you're lucky, a snack bar selling beer and soft drinks.

In planning river travel, remember that because currents are usually stronger near the center, downriver boats will bowl down the middle of the river to take advantage of the faster water there, leaving you with only long-distance views of the jungle. Upriver boats, on the other hand, will often hug the banks to avoid fighting the strong current farther out, giving you closer views.

Boat captains are not above a little price gouging with "wealthy" travelers, so before negotiating price, be sure to ask around on the waterfront for the usual cost of passage for your destination.

Jungle Lodges

Particularly in Peru, the jungle lodge business is a booming one. For a price that often approaches $100 per day these operators will transport you to a "remote" jungle lodge and take you to "authentic" Indian villages. It is admittedly an appealing idea, especially if your time in the Amazon is limited. But from the start we must warn that even the better of the jungle lodges are to our minds extremely touristy, and the worst of them are little more than insulting rip-offs designed to bring the traveler and his money to a parting of the ways as quickly and simply as possible. But given the fact that most visitors to the Amazon lack the time and experience to head out into the jungle or onto the waterways alone, the lodges do serve a purpose: they get you out of the muddy river towns and into the rain forest quickly, easily, and safely.

Physically, the several jungle lodges we've seen have been virtually identical—located in a clearing on a backwater tributary, a big open thatch main building that serves as dining room and veranda, a row of clean, simple thatch bungalows for the guests. Mercifully, most lodges lack electricity and do not allow radios, cassette players, or the like. And the food is usually fairly good—fresh-caught fish and local fruits and vegetables.

The problem with many of the lodges, though, is what to *do* while you're there. Lodge operators often seem to see their customers as an extremely lethargic bunch who want to spend most of the day swinging in hammocks on the veranda. For activity, many of them will simply take a gaggle of visitors on the advertised "jungle walk," often just a brief stroll to a faked "Indian village" where day workers in costume put on a show of primitivism as degrading to you as to them. Instead of being exhilarating, such a visit to the jungle can quickly become merely depressing.

Fortunately, some operators do offer more authentic excursions that allow you to move about and actually see some relatively remote sections of the river and jungle in the company of an experienced and knowledgeable guide. If you want to stay in a jungle lodge that provides that kind of value for your money, plan ahead; send away for brochures and comparison-shop the many lodges that advertise their services in the pages of U.S. travel and outdoor magazines. Considering the expense of even a two- or three-day stay at a lodge, a little homework is time well spent. In comparing lodges, try to find out just how "remote" the lodge actually is; many are quite near cities and settlements. Most importantly, find out how ambitious you'll be allowed to get in exploring the jungle. Be especially careful to determine whether the lodge is equipped to arrange individually guided all-day walks and canoe trips for you and your traveling companions. Only on these longer trips can you expect to experience the rain forest even superficially.

River Towns

The river towns of the Amazon's upper tributaries are hardly tourist meccas. You'll find little of luxury or beauty in these muddy, remote population centers. They are for the most part rough, unfinished places, often with a feel of the frontier about them. The principal river ports are bustling towns, full of people and goods on the move. They are towns too busy with their own lives to take much account of the handful of travelers who make their way there, so don't expect very much in the way of tourist services. But if you learn to take them on their own terms, learning to cope with the difficulties of travel and reveling in the strangeness all around you—market stalls selling giant fillets of *piracucu* fish the size of garbage can lids, buzzards sitting on lamp posts after a hard rain spreading their broad wings to dry—then the river towns can be quite exhilarating.

Misahualli

This quiet little river town is only fifteen miles by road from the major jungle town of Tena, the capital of Ecuador's Napo province. Not only does Misahualli make a convenient destination for those descending into the jungle from the popular highland town of Baños (five to seven hours by bus), but it is also a good base of operations for trips into the jungle. There are several tour operators in town who will guide you on single or multiday excursions to visit Indian villages and observe animal and plant life. Tours from Misahualli are considerably less expensive than comparable trips from Peruvian jungle towns.

In Misahualli itself, the handful of hotels are all cheap, basic, and similar, but on the Napo an hour or so by boat below the town are two good and expensive lodge/hotels, the *Jaguar* (near the settlement of Santa Rosa) and the *Anaconda* (on an island in the Napo), both of which will arrange day trips into the jungle for guests.

If you want to go on to Coca from Misahualli, an excellent and relatively easy alternative to a long bus ride is to catch one of the regular passenger canoes that make the seven-hour descent of the Río Napo to Coca. With more than a dozen little settlements along the way, this stretch of river is hardly wilderness, but the trip does provide wonderful scenery and a close look at life along the river. From Coca, daily buses make the return to Quito.

Puerto Francisco de Orellana (Coca)

Located at the confluence of the Coca and Napo rivers, this Ecuadorian town, officially named after the first European to descend the Amazon, is more often called by its older name, Coca, by locals. The town itself is of little interest, just a rough, busy river port and center for oil exploration. Compared with Peruvian and Bolivian jungle towns, however, Coca has the attraction of accessibility—it is fourteen hours by bus from Quito. Accommodations at the few hotels in Coca are similarly simple and inexpensive, but you might give the *Auco* a try first.

One of the most popular all-day excursions from Coca is to hire a motor canoe or launch for the trip down the Napo to Limoncocha, home of a mission and linguistics center. Another interesting trip is to Primavera, about halfway between Coca and Limoncocha. Here you can walk through the jungle to Laguna Taracoa (one mile), camp near the *hacienda* (for a small fee), and hire canoes for further exploration of the jungle.

For those who want the jungle and luxury as well, the Flotel Orellana makes Coca its base port for four-to-five-day trips along the Napo. During the trip the Orellana takes time out for naturalist-led jungle walks, visits to Indian villages, and canoe trips on side streams. Needless to say, all this convenience and luxury (the ship's double- and quadruple-berth cabins even have private baths) does not come cheap. For reservations, contact Metropolitan Touring in Quito (239 Amazonas).

Iquitos

Iquitos, Peru, 2,300 miles from the Amazon's mouth, is the end of the line for large ocean-going ships. Once a lavish center of culture during the grand and brutal rubber boom days of 1880 to 1915, Iquitos is now faded and crumbling, a city waiting for oil exploration to hit pay dirt and bring back its glory days. Even now, though, the city does have a certain decaying charm. The once elegant riverside section of town, the Malecon, is collapsing into the river, but the grand architecture (one of the waterfront buildings was designed by Eiffel) is a concrete reminder of the time when the rubber barons brought the stars of European theater and opera here to the heart of the jungle for performances.

Around town, there are relatively few sights to attract the visitor. You'll probably want to walk through the outdoor market, full of the products of the Amazon. You may also want to have a look at Belén, the exotic-looking slum below Iquitos at the edge of the Amazon. The houses and shops of Belén are built on rafts tethered to pilings. When the river rises—there can be as much as a forty-foot differential in water level—the little town rises with it. And don't neglect to take a walk along the Malecon late in the afternoon to watch the orange and green sunset over the broad Amazon.

The real attraction of Iquitos is obviously the rain forest beyond. But unless you're experienced and equipped for on-your-own jungle travel, Iquitos is an expensive base from which to arrange excursions. Because the area surrounding the city is fairly heavily populated, it is difficult (but not impossible) to arrange interesting day trips with independent boatmen. For really exciting excursions, though, you'll have to get into sparsely inhabited areas, and that will require at least an overnight trip.

There are numerous jungle lodges operating in the Iquitos area, most of which have booking offices in the Plaza de Armas area. Shop carefully before committing yourself to any of these operators, however; some of the Iquitos-based lodges offer the poorest, least interesting services we've seen in Amazonia. One lodge that does seem to satisfy a large portion of its customers is *Explorama*. Don't let the ridiculous name mislead you; Explorama offers some of the most authentic jungle visits available in Iquitos. Their main lodge is about fifty miles from the city, and even more interesting (and more expensive, of course) are the multiday trips they provide to a very rustic smaller lodge up the more remote Río Napo. Explorama is quite good at setting up guided trips

Yagua Indian weaving in traditional costume, Iquitos, Peru

to suit your interests, so you don't have to settle for touristy prepackaged excursions if you don't want to.

For the more adventurous who would like to hike and camp in the jungle, guides are available in Iquitos. Perhaps the most qualified guide in town is Moises Torres Viena, who has taught jungle camping and survival skills to the Peruvian military. As might be expected with this level of expertise, his fees are not cheap, and he expects you to provide food for the trip and your own camping gear. Torres Viena doesn't really have an office, but when not out in the jungle, he is easy to find. He is well known around downtown Iquitos—all we had to do was mention his name to our hotel desk clerk and half an hour later he was waiting in the lobby to discuss setting up an excursion. For suggestions on other jungle guides, check with the Tourist Office (218 Prospero).

For a short, cheap trip from downtown Iquitos to the edge of the jungle, take a bus out to Laguna Quistacocha where a path circling the lake makes a nice afternoon walk and a very good introduction to the rain forest for newcomers. To return to Iquitos, hitch a ride on a truck, or wait for a bus.

If you've just come from the mountains, hotel accommodations in Iquitos will seem quite expensive. For maximum ambience and nice rooms on the high end of our moderate price range, try the *State Tourist Hotel* (a few air-conditioned rooms) on the Malecon overlooking the Amazon. For a nondescript air-conditioned room at similar prices, try the *Safari,* only half a block from the Malecon. One of the better inexpensive hotels in town is the centrally located *Loreto.* The rooms are clean and have private baths; some rooms are air-conditioned, and the others have large fans.

Restaurant meals in Iquitos are also comparatively expensive. For a special meal, be sure to visit *Le Malecon* where the steaks are good but the view of the Amazon at sunset is better. For relatively expensive steaks and Italian food, try *Don Giovanni,* between the plaza and the river. For good Chinese food, go to Plaza 28 de Julio and take your pick of several.

The only ways into or out of Iquitos are by air or by river; the roads venture only a short distance beyond the city. AeroPeru and Faucett schedule at least two flights daily between Iquitos and Lima. Faucett flies between Iquitos and Cuzco on Monday, Wednesday, and Friday. Faucett's Miami-Lima flight stops in Iquitos, so layovers are possible. For long-distance river travel, boats leave frequently for the downriver trip to Leticia, Columbia, where less frequent boats leave for Manaus, Brazil. Upriver boats for Pucallpa and Yurimaguas can be hard to find.

Pucallpa

To our minds, Pucallpa, Peru, is the essence of the jungle town— still a little rough and raw, holding on to the feel of the frontier. Few of its streets are paved, and on a rainy day (in other words, almost every day) a walk through town is a slog through red mud. Buzzards circle darkly over the waterfront and hop tame as pigeons among the shoppers in the market. To sit at Pucallpa's waterfront drinking warm *Amazonia* beer and talking with boatmen in a little thatch lean-to bar knocked together from scrap lumber, while dense rain pelts the gray water of the Río Ucayali and hundreds of tiny frogs hop about the mud at your feet is to feel the Amazon in a way that no $100-a-day jungle lodge can match. And it is just this sort of travel experience that Pucallpa provides at every turn.

Perhaps Pucallpa's primary attraction is Laguna Yarinacocha, once a wide bend in the Ucayali but now an oxbow lake since the river cut a more direct course for itself. Here, only five miles from Pucallpa, you'll find yourself at the edge of the jungle, wonderfully removed from the mud, the grinding trucks, the circling buzzards of downtown. Buses for the lake leave frequently from just below the plaza in Pucallpa. At the lake is the Summer Institute of Linguistics, a group of missionaries devoted to translating the Bible into the languages of the natives. The primary activity at Yarinacocha is to hire a motorized canoe or launch to take you up the lake at least as far as the Shipibo village of San Francisco, a collection of three or four dozen post and thatch houses near the lakeshore. But you might also enjoy having your boatman take you to some of the less visited backwaters of the lake.

As in all jungle towns, decent hotels in Pucallpa are not cheap. The moderate-to-expensive *State Tourist Hotel* is one of the most pleasant places in town, with a nice courtyard and a clean swimming pool that feels wonderful on sticky days. Also good is the moderately priced *Mercedes,* an old, faded, but clean, dry, and very tropical-feeling hotel. If the mud of Pucallpa begins to wear on the nerves, the *Hotel La Cabaña* or the *La Brisa,* both on Yarinacocha, offer relatively expensive but very quiet and pleasant bungalow-style accommodations. Both hotels will help arrange day trips into the jungle for their guests.

Restaurant selection in Pucallpa is limited. In town you'll find several good *chifas,* especially the *Hongkong.* The restaurant connected to the Hotel Mercedes serves adequate *saltados* and steaks, and there are the usual roasted chicken restaurants scattered about. Some of the best restaurants in the Pucallpa area are the several thatch pavillions near the docks at Laguna Yarinacocha. The food is simple (fresh fish, beans and rice, etc.) but good, and the surroundings are pleasant.

Both AeroPeru and Faucett schedule daily flights from Pucallpa to both Lima and Iquitos. Boats make the four-to-seven-day, 550-mile trip downriver from Pucallpa to Iquitos fairly regularly, but of course there are no scheduled departure times. Nothing may be leaving for days at a time. To check on departures, walk out to Puerto La Hoyada, the shanty town port hacked from the jungle on the banks of the Ucayali, and ask around for downriver boats.

Though most visitors to Pucallpa arrive on one of the daily flights from Lima, it is also possible to reach Pucallpa from Lima by road on what is surely one of the great overland journeys anywhere in the world. Transportation on this 500-mile route is varied, often uncertain, and always difficult. But for the hearty, this trip will repay the hardship in exhilarating and varied landscape as it moves from desert coast to high Andes to jungle. Though the trip can be made in one brutal thirty-six-to-forty-eight-hour stretch (TEPSA and Arellano schedule daily departures), the best way is the slow way, using short-haul transportation and extending the trip over five to seven days or more by taking rest stops in the interesting little towns along the way.

The route follows the Central highway as it leaves Lima and quickly climbs into some of the most spectacular Andean scenery Peru has to offer. Early on, the road parallels the Central railway as far as the rather bleak mining town of Oroya. The Central highway then works its way across the 13,000-foot Pampa de Junin to another unappealing mining town, Cerro de Pasco.

Beyond Cerro de Pasco the road loses almost 8,000 feet of elevation in sixty miles to reach the pleasant town of Huanuco, a long day of travel (twelve to fifteen hours) from Lima. Huanuco, with its pretty surrounding countryside and nearby pre-Inca ruins, is something of a resort town and makes a good stopover point. For hotel accommodations, try the moderately priced *State Tourist Hotel* (often full; make reservations in Lima) or the *Hostal Huanuco.*

A short day's travel from Huanuco (four to five hours; departures throughout the day) and well worth a stopover on the way is the town of Tingo Maria, situated in a beautiful cloud forest region and surrounded by coffee, coca, sugarcane, and banana plantations. Here you'll definitely begin to feel the proximity of the jungle in the heavy tropical vegetation that blankets the often-misty hillsides beyond the town. For a good moderately priced hotel, try the *Turista* (outside town); for an inexpensive room, try the *Viena* or the *Royal.*

Beyond Tingo Maria is the last leg of the journey, an all-day ride into the Amazon basin to Pucallpa. On this final day, the highway descends through the green hills, past waterfalls, across the spectacular Boquerón Abad Pass—a naturally formed deep cut through the mountains—and on to Pucallpa on the banks of the Río Ucayali.

Puerto Maldonado

Puerto Maldonado is in a sense a town on the make. It is a rough place that collects the dreamers and misfits who prospect for gold and oil in the remote jungles of southeastern Peru. Situated on the point of land where the Madre de Dios and Tambopata rivers come together, Puerto Maldonado is primarily of interest as a departure point for excursions into the southern jungles, particularly the Tambopata National Wildlife Preserve, about three hours away by boat.

One of the attractions of Puerto Maldonado for the traveler who only wants a quick dip into the jungle to add spice to an otherwise exclusively Andean trip is its proximity to Cuzco. Both AeroPeru and Faucett make the short flight down the eastern slope of the mountains to Puerto Maldonado several times a week (check with a travel agent for current schedules). For those who simply can't get enough of brutal truck rides, it is also possible to travel from Cuzco to Puerto Maldonado overland via Urcos, Ocongate, and Quincemil. Though only about 300 miles long, the trip will probably take two or three days depending on road conditions and the number of flat tires your truck develops. Trucks leave Cuzco fairly often, using the little plaza of Limacpampa Chica as a collection point.

Another part of Puerto Maldonado's attraction is that it is the departure point for two lodges with excellent reputations for providing memorable jungle travel. The *Cuzco Amazonica Lodge* is a couple of hours downriver from Puerto Maldonado, and along with the pleasant thatch-roofed accommodations, it offers interesting jungle hikes and canoe trips on side streams. More unique is the *Explorer's Inn,* located within Peru's Tambopata National Wildlife Preserve. Their jungle day trips are among the most interesting and authentic you'll find. Reservations for these lodges can be made in Cuzco. It is also possible to hire guides in Puerto Maldonado for more independent travel into the Tambopata Preserve and along side streams of the Tambopata and Madre de Dios rivers.

For hotel accommodations in Puerto Maldonado, try the moderately priced *State Tourist Hotel* (often full, so make reservations in advance with Enturperu in Lima or Cuzco). The rooms are nothing special, but the hotel is pleasant primarily for its location on the banks of the Río Tambopata. For inexpensive rooms try the *Moderno* or the *Wilson.*

For those who want to go on to Bolivia and to whom time means nothing, it is possible to travel to the Bolivian river town of Riberalta by boat. This three-to-five-day trip is indeed a spectacular adventure trip through remote jungle, but boats leave Puerto Maldonado for Riberalta very infrequently. You could get lucky and find a boat ready to embark just when you want to leave, but chances are the wait will be long. If you make the trip, be sure to get your exit documentation taken care of before you leave Puerto Maldonado to avoid trouble at the border crossing of Puerto Heath.

Riberalta

Bolivia's most interesting river town is Riberalta, but because of its isolation—there are no roads connecting the town with the highlands of Bolivia—it is probably of interest primarily to those making the trip down the Madre de Dios from Puerto Maldonado. Located at the confluence of the Madre de Dios and the Beni rivers, Riberalta lacks the raw edge that oil and gold seekers sometimes give to a town like Puerto Maldonado. It is still a fairly quiet, agriculture and ranching town, not quite caught up in the hysteria of development that is sweeping the Amazon basin.

To get into the rain forest outside Riberalta, it is not difficult to arrange day trips along small side streams of the Beni or Madre de Dios in motor canoes or launches. You can also rent motor scooters to explore the dirt roads that extend into the jungle, especially toward Lake Tumi Chucua, a lovely spot less than an hour away.

For accommodations in Riberalta, try the moderately priced *Hotel Tropical* (the management is helpful in arranging jungle day trips for guests) or the simple, inexpensive *Riberalta* and *Santa Rita.*

Once in Riberalta, your only way to get to La Paz is by air. There are a handful of outgoing LAB (Lloyd Aero Boliviaro) flights weekly to both La Paz and Cochabamba (Bolivia's third largest city; daily air and rail service from Cochabamba to La Paz).

Appendix I:
SPANISH GLOSSARY

Though it is beyond the scope of this book to provide a complete English-Spanish phrase book for travelers who lack facility in Spanish, the following glossary should, however, help those who have a little knowledge of the language to carry on the basic business of eating, sleeping, and moving about. For more comprehensive language assistance, most bookstores will provide a selection of pocket-sized phrase books to choose from. One especially useful is the Berlitz *Latin-American Spanish* phrase book, which recognizes the sometimes quite different pronunciations and usages of Latin American as opposed to European Spanish. Also useful is the *American Express Spanish* phrase book, which combines a phrase guide and a relatively good Spanish-English dictionary in compact form.

GETTING AROUND

Is there a plane to ——?	Hay un avión a ——?
What time does the flight leave?	A qué hora sale el vuelo?
Where is the train station?	Dónde está el estación ferroviaria?
Is this the train to ——?	Es éste el tren a ——?
I'd like a ticket to ——?	Quiero un boleto a ——?
When is the next bus to ——?	A qué hora es el próximo autobús a ——?
Does this truck go to ——?	Va este camion a ——?
How long does the trip last?	Cuánto dura el viaje?
What is the fare?	Cuánto es la tarifa?

HOTELS

I'd like a single room.	Quisiera una habitación sencilla.
We'd like a double room	Quisiéramos una habitación doble
with two beds.	con dos camas.
with a double bed.	con una cama matrimonial.
with a private bath.	con bano privado.

Is there hot water?	Hay agua caliente?
Is there laundry service?	Hay servicio de lavanderia?
What is the price per night?	Cuál es el precio por noche?
Could I see the room?	Puedo ver la habitación?
The room is too noisy/dark.	El habitación es demasiado ruidosa/oscura.

EATING

I'm hungry.	Tengo hambre.
Is there a restaurant nearby?	Hay un restaurante cerca de aqui?
Is there a menu?	Hay una lista (also carta or menu)?
Do you have ——?	Tiene usted ——?
I'd like ——.	Quisiera ——.

The following vocabulary list should help in decoding the sometimes confusing menus in Andean restaurants.

agua mineral—mineral water

aji de gallina—chicken in a pepper and cheese sauce

ajo—garlic

almuerzo—lunch

anticuchos—beef hearts roasted on skewers

arroz chaufa—fried rice, served in many non-Chinese restaurants in the Andes

asado—roasted

azucar—sugar

buñuelos—doughnuts

cabrito—goat

café—coffee, usually instant

camarónes—shrimp or crayfish

carnero—sheep

carnitas—fried pork

cau-cau—a tripe and potato dish, served over rice

causa—a sort of potato salad

cebiche—raw fish or shellfish marinated in lime juice with onions and peppers

cena—dinner

cerdo—pork

cerveza—beer

chancho—ham

chicha—corn beer

chicharrónes—pork cracklings

choclos—corn on the cob

chorizo—sausage

a la chorrillana—any meat or fish prepared with tomatoes and peppers

chuño—a type of freeze-dried potato

churrasco—any steak with bone in

corazón—heart

cordero—lamb

corvina—sea bass

cuy—guinea pig, usually roasted

desayuno—breakfast

empanadas—meat pies

ensalada—salad

entrada—entrée

escabeche—marinated

estofado—coriander sauce

estofado de carne—meat stew

flan—egg custard

fréjoles—beans, usually served in the form of fréjoles con arroz, beans over rice

fresco—soft drink (Ecuador)
frito—fried
galleta—cookie
gallina/gallo—chicken
gaseosa—soft drink (Peru, Bolivia)
hamburguesa—hamburger
helado—ice cream
al horno—baked
huevos—eggs
humitas—meat and perhaps some vegetables wrapped in corn meal
jamón—ham
jugo—juice
leche—milk
lengua—tongue
lomo—any boneless steak
mani—peanuts
mantequilla—butter
mate de coca—coca leaf tea
a la montado (i.e., *churrasco a la montado*)—meat served with a fried egg and perhaps potatoes and/or rice
mostaza—mustard
ocopa arequipeña—hot sauce served over boiled potatoes
paltas rellenas—stuffed avocados
pan—bread
panqueque—pancake
papas fritas—fried potatoes
parrillada—grilled meat
pato—duck

pavo—turkey
pescado—fish
piquantes—hot sauces
pisco—brandy, excellent in pisco sours
pollo—chicken
pollo a la brasa—grilled chicken
postre—dessert
puerco—pork
rellenos—stuffed
rocotos rellenos—spicy stuffed peppers
saltado—small bits of meat (usually beef) stir-fried with onions, tomatoes, and whatever other vegetables are at hand
salteña—meat and vegetable pastry
sopa—soup, usually clear broth with noodles and perhaps vegetables
sopa a la criolla—meat broth with tomatoes, onion, garlic, and meat, usually beef hearts
tallarines—noodles, as in tallarine saltado, bits of sautéed steak and vegetables over noodles
té—tea
tinto—black coffee
tocino—bacon
torta—cake
tortilla—omelet
trucha—trout
vino—wine

ON THE TRAIL

Where is the trail to ——?   Dónde está el camino a ——?
Where does this trail go?   Adonde va está camino?
How many kilometers is it to ——?   Cuántos kilometros hay a ——?
How far is the next village?   A que distancia está el proximo pueblo?
I'm lost.   Me he perdido.

Where is the nearest water?	Dónde está el proximo agua?
I want to hire an *arriero*.	Quiero emplear un arriero.
What is the cost per day?	Cuál es la cuesta por dia?
How long is the journey?	Cuánto dura el viaje?
May we camp here?	Podemos acampar aqui?

OTHER USEFUL PHRASES

Can I cash a traveler's check?	Puedo cambiar un cheque de viajero?
What is this called?	Cómo se llama esto?
I don't understand.	No comprendo.
Speak more slowly, please.	Habla más despacio, por favor.
May I leave this baggage here?	Podemos dejar esta equipaje aqui?
What's the price?	Cuál es la cuesta?
Where is my luggage?	Dónde está mi equipaje?
Where is there a doctor who speaks English?	Dónde hay un médico que hable inglés?

Appendix II:
QUECHUA GLOSSARY

When the Incas began to gain dominance over the lands that now make up Ecuador, Peru, and Bolivia, they were faced with the very serious problem of trying to govern numerous groups of people who used a number of diverse languages. The administrative solution they arrived at was to make their language—originally probably spoken by only a small group near Cuzco—the official language of the empire. Their solution proved to be remarkably effective, and at the time of the Spanish conquest, Quechua—or perhaps more accurately, *runasimi* (the language of the people)—was spoken from southern Colombia to northern Chile. The Quechua language did not fall with the Inca empire, however. Despite Spanish attempts to discourage its use, Quechua flourished, and today it actually has more native speakers than it did when the last Inca emperor died in 1533. And the *campesinos* are still quite proud of their linguistic heritage; more than once we've heard them argue convincingly that Quechua is more expressive and poetic than Spanish.

Quechua is not, however, an easy language to master. We know because we've been trying for some time with only moderate success. On one trek our guide, who had been patiently teaching us Quechua as we walked, finally threw up his hands in exasperation at our pronunciation. "Speak here," he said, pointing to his throat, "not here," moving his finger to his lips. He very astutely isolated the problem native English speakers have with his glottal-stopped language. But even after you begin to get the feel for the difficult throaty sounds of Quechua, the strange clicks and pops of some words will still cause trouble. The best advice we can give is to spend some time with a Quechua speaker, and try to pick up the nuances of pronunciation as best you can.

You could probably get by on most treks without knowing a word of Quechua, relying on the *campesinos* you meet to be bilingual (most mountain dwellers do know at least some Spanish). But we've found that *campesinos* without exception greatly appreciate even the clumsiest attempts to speak their language and will very patiently try to help you with it—especially if you teach them some English at the same time.

If nothing else, familiarity with a few words of Quechua will make place names more significant for you. For example, if you know that *puka* is red and *pucara* is fortress, then when you visit Pucapucara outside Cuzco, the name will mean much more to you than the awkward mouthful of vowels and consonants would otherwise. If you know that *apu* is master and *rimac* is speaker, the poetry in the name of the roaring Apurimac River becomes evident.

The following very basic guide to Quechua pronunciation and vocabulary should help you get started. One word of caution: the language varies considerably throughout its geographic range. Pronunciation and vocabulary commonly used in the Cuzco region may not be completely understood in, say, Zumbagua, Ecuador. The following guide, though weighted toward the Cuzco region, incorporates Quechua words and expressions from other areas as well.

PRONUNCIATION AND GRAMMAR

Vowels are pronounced as in Spanish, though with somewhat less distinction between *e/i* and *o/u*. Consonants are pronounced as follows:

ch as in chair

h as in here

k as in kelp

kh is an aspirated k sound

l as in land

ll as in llama

m as in mean

n as in nation

ñ as ny

p as in please

ph similar to the *f* in friend

q is pronounced as a fricative; there is no English equivalent, but an exaggerated, explosive pronunciation of the *g* in guitar is close

r as in road

s as in sorrow

sh as in shore

t as in time

th is an aspirated t sound

w as in walk

y as in yellow

Those difficult glottal stop sounds we mentioned earlier are represented in print by apostrophes. In the word *q'enko*, for example, the *q* sound is glottal stopped, meaning that the *q* is pronounced with a closure of the glottis, which produces a slight pause before completing the pronunciation of the word. In Quechua the next-to-last syllable of all words is accented.

Quechua grammar is reasonably simple. Sentence structure seldom varies from the adjective, noun, adverb, verb order. Verb forms are created by adding endings to the root. The infinitive ending is *-y;* thus the infinitive of *puri* (walk) is *puriy.* Present tense verb endings are as follows:

I	-ni	we	-nchis
you	-nki	you	-nkichis
he, she	-an	they	-nku

The past tense is formed simply by injecting *-ra-* between the root and the present tense ending *(I walked* would thus be *purirani).*

Quechua nouns are given endings to indicate their function in the sentence. Though the complexities of noun declension are best learned in a more comprehensive guide to Quechua than ours, observe the nouns in the following Quechua sentence:

Cajamarca-manta San Pablo-man puri-ran.

The endings *-manta* and *-man* indicate, respectively, movement from and toward the noun. A word-for-word translation thus yields:

Cajamarca from San Pablo he/she walked.

Or, more smoothly:

He/she walked from Cajamarca to San Pablo.

The noun ending *-kuna* is used to form plurals. Thus *tumi* (knife) becomes *tumi-kuna* (knives).

A FEW USEFUL PHRASES

At the very least, you should know the Quechua equivalents of "hello." On the trail, passing *campesinos* may greet you with one of several phrases. Still in use is the traditional Inca greeting:

Ama sua, ama llulla, ama quella.   Don't steal, don't lie, don't be lazy.

The usual response is:

Quampas hinallantaq.   To you likewise.

Other greetings include:

Allinllanchu?   How are you?

The response is:

Allinmi.   Fine.

Another greeting is:

Alabado.   Praise God.

The proper response is simply to repeat the word "alabado."

Be sure to know the following words:

ima—what	maikan—which
pi—who	maipi—where

With them you can at least ask basic questions such as:

Ima-tam sutiyki?	What is your name?
Maipi mikuy?	Where is food?
Maipi upyana?	Where is drink?
Maikan ñan ——-man ri-n?	Which trail goes to ——?
Maipi ——-man ñan?	Where is the trail to ——?
Maipi ucu?	Where is water?

Other phrases useful on the trail include the following:

Yaku-nayawackan.	I'm thirsty.
Thantaiki kanchu?	Do you have any bread?

Thantaiki runtu-kuna?   Do you have any eggs?
Imainataq valin? or   How much does it cost?
   Hayka chanin?

VOCABULARY

acka—much, lots
ackaya—to increase
akapa—small
aku—coca cud
aliq—right (direction)
alkila—to hire or rent
almusu—lunch
alqu—dog
añakaw—how pretty!
anca—very
anca caspa—please
ancu—wide
anri *or* ahi—yes
antis—before
apacheta—sacred spot (usually
   a pile of stones, such as a
   pass where traveling
   quechuas deposit their cud of
   coca leaves and toss a few
   eyebrow hairs to the winds,
   thus leaving their fatigue
   behind them)
apu—master
apura—to hurry
apurawman—soon, quickly
ari—yes
asnu—donkey
aswam—more
aw?—isn't that right?
ayca—meat
aylu—community
baka—cow
bentu—wind
bisita—visitor
biyaqi—trip, to travel
bruha—witch
capla—bread
cawpi—middle (as in *cawpi
   nampi*—halfway or *cawpi
   puncaw*—midday)

cay—that
cay-cayta—approximately
caypi—there
cayraq—immediately
chaca—bridge
ciraw—dry season, winter
ciri—cold, to be cold
císi—night
cocha—lake
cula—just one
cumpa—sweater
cun-cunniq—very far away
cunniq—a remote, lonely place
cuy—guinea pig
cuzco—navel
entendi—to understand
fasil—easy
fusfuru—matchstick
gastu—expense, cost
gustawan—I like it
haka—open
hakuwa—let's go!
hanayman—upward
hatun—large, long
hawa runa—stranger
hayka?—how much?
haykap?—when?
hicpa—nearby
huaca—sacred place
huaman—hawk
ici—to walk
icuq—left (direction)
ima—what? (as in *ima ñan?*
   —what road?)
imatataq—why
imayna—how
inti—sun
kabalo—horse
k'aca—beautiful

kamas—later

kanan—now

kanca—market

karga—to carry

karka—dried dung for fuel

karpa—tent

karu—far

kay—this

kaypi—near

ke—that

khatu—market

kila—moon

kosa—good

kusa—thing

lant'a—firewood

lasta—snow or snow mountain

limpu—drinkable water

llacta—town

macay—cave

macu—strong

mana—no

mani—peanut

maipi—where

mayta—whither

maymanta—whence

mayu—river

mikuy—food

mikuy wasi—restaurant

mikuymanta—hungry

muna—want

munani—I want

ñan—path or road

nevado—snow mountain (all *nevados* are *apus*)

nina—fire

pacha—earth

Pacha Mama—Mother Earth

panta—to confuse (as in *panta ñan*—to take the wrong path)

paqarin—tomorrow

pasya—to take a walk

pata—plaza or agricultural terrace

picchu—peak

pucara—fortress

puka—red

puncaw—day

punku—gate, entrance, door

puri—walk, travel

purinkicu—wanderer

pusa—to guide

qan—you

qaqa—cliff

qasi—notch or ravine

qicwa *or* bale—valley

qinti—hummingbird

quena—flute

quilla—moon

qurnada—journey

raymi—festival

ri—to go

riku—to go

rumi—stone

runa—man or person

samapakuna—lodging

sapa—each, every

sara—corn

suti—name

tambo—resting place

tanta—bread

taytalay—thank you

ucu—water

urco—mountain

uru—caterpillars

warmi—woman

wasi—house

wayna—young man (as in *wayna picchu*—young man peak, the peak overlooking Machu Picchu—old man peak)

yacu—water

yupi—trail

Annotated Bibliography

Many travelers to South America wait until they're on their trip to begin to read about where they are. You'll see them sitting looking rather dazed in a café drinking a cup of coffee and trying to read Pablo Neruda's *Heights of Machu Picchu* or Hiram Bingham's *Lost City of the Incas.* However, we've found that a long, physically demanding trip is not really very conducive to serious reading. So unless you have remarkable powers of concentration, plan on doing most of your background reading before you leave home. By doing some reading ahead of time, you'll also be more completely prepared to encounter the Andes, and you'll be at least somewhat familiar with the land, the people, and the history. The following admittedly subjective bibliography includes books that we've found particularly helpful and/or particularly interesting. We've also included a brief discography of a few of the more accessible recordings of traditional Andean music.

Arguedas, José Maria, and Ruth Stephan. *The Singing Mountaineers.* Austin: Univ. of Texas Press, 1957. An enlightening collection of Quechua poetry and songs translated into English—everything from grim Inca war songs that celebrate making drums from the skins of enemies to lovely poems about wandering in the mountains.

Bartle, Jim. *Trails of the Cordilleras Blanca and Huayhuash of Peru.* Lima: Editorial Grafica Pacific Press, 1980. If you plan to spend a long time in the Cordillera Blanca or want to try some trails we don't describe, this book is invaluable. Bartle knows the back country of the Cordillera Blanca as few others do, and he covers in reliable detail virtually every trail in the range. Available in bookstores in Lima, Cuzco, and Huaras.

Bingham, Hiram. *Lost City of the Incas.* London: Travel Book Club, 1952. Though *campesinos* had known of the existence of Machu Picchu for some time, Bingham was the first outsider to discover the city. Despite the fact that archaeological study over the years has disproved many of Bingham's suppositions about Machu Picchu and the ruins nearby, this book is still an interesting account of a fascinating expedition.

Brooks, John, ed. *The South American Handbook.* Bath, England: Trade and Travel Publications. This is the travel guide to end all travel guides. Well over a thousand pages long, it covers everything between the Texas border and Tierra del Fuego at a level of detail that is truly amazing. Its quite extensive lists of hotels and restaurants are updated yearly and are extremely helpful, especially if you're doing a lot of traveling around on your own. With a cover price of thirty dollars, the *Handbook* is a bit of an investment for many travelers.

Crowther, Geoff. *South America on a Shoestring.* South Yarra, Victoria, Australia: Lonely Planet Publications, rev. ed., 1983. Primarily of interest to those who want to know where to find the cheapest hotels and restaurants. Also includes good city maps for many Andean towns.

Frost, Peter. *Exploring Cuzco.* Lima: Editorial Lima, 1980. This useful little book is available at most bookstores in Cuzco and Lima.

Hemming, John. *The Conquest of the Incas.* New York: Harcourt Brace Jovanovich, 1970. This excellent history of the Spanish conquest of the Inca empire should be considered required reading for the thoughtful traveler to the Andes. It is both extremely thorough and quite readable. Besides the account of the conquest itself, Hemming also provides much information on the history, culture, and political organization of the Incas.

————. *Machu Picchu.* New York: Newsweek Books, 1981. A very good brief introduction to the Incas, accompanied by dozens of photographs of Machu Picchu and related subjects.

Jordan, Tanis, and Martin Jordan. *South America River Trips, vol. 2.* Cambridge, Mass.: Bradt Enterprises, 1982. If you're intent on heading off on a trip down an upper tributary of the Amazon on your own (or just daydreaming about it), this book will get you started.

Kelly, Brian, and Mark London. *Amazon.* San Diego: Harcourt Brace Jovanovich, 1983. If you're looking for the romance of the river, this book won't really give it to you. Instead, Kelly and London provide a fascinating, up-to-date, and accurate description of life along the Amazon and the serious threats to this unique ecosystem.

Llosa, Mario Vargas. *The Green House.* New York: Avon Books, 1973.

————. *Aunt Julia and the Scriptwriter.* New York: Avon Books, 1983. These two novels by the famous Peruvian writer (and lately something of a politician) will give you an excellent feel for the Peruvian jungle and Lima, respectively.

Marquez, Gabriel Garcia. *One Hundred Years of Solitude.* New York: Avon Books, 1971. This novel by the Nobel-prize-winning Colombian writer brought Latin American fiction to the attention of the world. Marquez's technique has sometimes been called "magical realism," an attitude that can come in handy for the Andean traveler.

Mason, J. Alden. *The Ancient Civilizations of Peru.* Harmondsworth, England: Penguin, rev. ed., 1968. Though recent archaeological discoveries have somewhat changed the details in the picture of Peru's prehistory, Mason's book still provides a useful and accessible survey of the major Andean civilizations.

Meisch, Lynn. *A Traveler's Guide to El Dorado and the Inca Empire.* New York: Penguin Books, 1980. If you read only one other book on the Andes, make it this one. This marvelous book is not a travel guide in the usual sense; rather, it is much more a cultural introduction to the northern Andes. It is full of very detailed information on markets, fiestas, crafts, food, etc. It is especially essential for those interested in the textiles of the region and for any traveler committed to "low-impact" travel.

Melville, Herman. *The Encantadas.* Numerous editions. Melville's rich, poetic sketches of the Galapagos Islands make an excellent introduction to the area.

Moore, Tui De Roy. *Galapagos: Islands Lost in Time.* New York: Viking, 1980. A wonderful collection of color photographs by a longtime resident of the islands.

Morrison, Tony. *The Andes.* Amsterdam: Time-Life Books, 1975. In his several books on the region, Tony Morrison proves himself one of the most consistently interesting writers on the Andes. This account of trips into the mountains is both informative and atmospheric. The color photography alone will put you in the mood for travel in the Andes.

———. *Land Above the Clouds.* New York: Universe Books, 1974. An interesting survey of Andean wildlife.

———. *Pathways to the Gods.* New York: Harper & Row, 1978. Morrison's clear-headed study of the strange ancient lines still visible at Nazca and elsewhere in the Andes is part travelogue, part archaeology. The account of his attempts to solve the riddle of the lines is as interesting as a good detective novel.

Neruda, Pablo. *The Heights of Machu Picchu,* trans. Nathaniel Tarn. New York: Farrar, Straus & Giroux, 1966. Reading this poem will probably help shape your feeling toward Machu Picchu more than a dozen histories would. Romantics will want to take it along and read it while sitting above the ruins at Inti Punku or Wayna Picchu.

Theroux, Paul. *The Old Patagonia Express.* New York: Pocket Books, 1980. The Andes seem not to have agreed with Theroux, who stays rather cranky throughout his trip. If nothing else, though, this popular account of an epic train journey from Boston to southern Argentina clearly portrays the brutality of long-distance overland travel in South America.

Thornton, Ian. *Darwin's Islands.* Garden City, N.Y.: Natural History Press, 1971. One of the better guides to the natural history of the Galapagos Islands.

Wright, Donald. *Cut Stones and Crossroads.* New York: Viking, 1984. Wright's interesting chronicles of travel in Peru contrast the country's rich past with its current economic and political difficulties.

SOURCES FOR FURTHER INFORMATION

Acosta, Jose de. *The Natural and Moral History of the Indians,* trans. Edward Grimston. London: E. Blout & W. Aspley, 1604.

Ascher, Marcia, and Robert Ascher. *Code of the Quipu.* Ann Arbor: Univ. of Michigan Press, 1981.

Blanco, Hugo. *Land or Death: The Peasant Struggle in Peru.* New York: Pathfinder Press, 1972.

Bradt, George, and Hilary Bradt. *Backpacking and Trekking in Peru and Bolivia.* Boston: Bradt Enterprises, 1975.

———. *Backpacking in Venezuela, Colombia, and Ecuador.* Boston: Bradt Enterprises, 1979.

Cieza de Leon, Pedro de. *The Incas,* trans. Harriet de Onis, ed. Victor von Hagen. Norman: Univ. of Oklahoma Press, 1959.

Cusihuamán, Antonio. *Diccionario Quechua.* Lima: Ministerio de Educación, 1976.

———. *Gramatica Quechua.* Lima: Ministerio de Educación, 1976.

Dorst, Jean. *South America and Central America: A Natural History.* New York: Random House, 1967.

Garcilaso de la Vega, El Inca. *Royal Commentaries of the Incas,* trans. Harold Livermore. Austin: Univ. of Texas Press, 1966.

Goodspeed, Thomas Harper. *Plant Hunters of the Andes.* Berkeley: Univ. of California Press, 1961.

Heath, Donald, and David Reid Williams. *Man at High Altitude.* Edinburgh; N.Y.: Churchill Livingston, 1981.

Kendall, Ann. *Everyday Life of the Incas.* New York: Putnam, 1973.

Kinzl, Hans, and Erwin Schneider. *Cordillera Blanca.* Innsbruck: Universitats Verlag Wagner, 1950.

Kosok, Paul. "The Mysterious Markings of Nazca." *Natural History* 56 (May 1947):200–7.

Matthiessen, Peter. *The Cloud Forest: A Chronicle of the South American Wilderness.* New York: Viking, 1961.

McIntyre, Loren. *The Incredible Incas and Their Timeless Land.* Washington, D.C.: National Geographic Society, 1975.

Reiche, Maria. *Mystery on the Desert.* Lima, 1949.

Ross, E. *Introduction to Ecuador Highland Quichua in Ten Easy Lessons.* Quito: Instituto Linguistico de Verano.

Stevenson, Robert. *Music in Aztec and Inca Territory.* Berkeley: Univ. of California Press, 1968.

Werlich, David P. *Peru: A Short History.* Carbondale: Southern Illinois Univ. Press, 1978.

White, Alan, and Bruce Epler. *The Galapagos Guide.* Quito: Libri Mundi, 1972. Available at Libri Mundi bookstore in Quito or at Galapagos National Park headquarters in Puerto Ayora.

Zuidema, R. T. *The Ceque System of Cusco.* International Archives of Ethnography. Leiden: E. J. Brill, 1964.

DISCOGRAPHY

The Inca Harp. New York: Lyrichord LLST 7359. A beautiful collection of Peruvian harp music.

Kingdom of the Sun. New York: Nonesuch H 72029. An excellent and authentic collection of Peruvian music featuring especially the *quena* (flute) and *antara* (panpipe).

Peru: Music from the Land of Machu Picchu. New York: Lyrichord LLST 7294. Includes a little bit of almost everything you'll hear in the Andes —flutes, harps, guitars, even a brass band.

Urubamba. Burbank, Ca.: Warner Brothers BSK 3553. Paul Simon's production of this recording by the Peruvian quartet, Urubamba, is a little too slick and studied, but the album is still a wonderful evocation of the Andes.

Index

acclimatization, 63, 64, 65
Agoyán falls, 91
Aguas Calientes, 198–99
air travel, 37–38, 46–47; ticket for
   return flight, 22, 47. *See also*
   individual destinations
Alcedo, Volcano, 100
Altar, 92–93
altitude sickness, 63–65
Amanti Island, 168
Amazon basin: Bolivia, 215;
   Ecuador, 71; Peru, 106. *See also*
   Chapter 7
animals, 17–18, 118; in Galapagos
   Islands, 97–98; hazards from,
   53–54
antibiotics, 28–29
Apacheta Chucura, 225, 226
Arequipa, 161–64
arrieros. See guides
Atacames, 95
Ausangate, 208–11; loop trek,
   208–11
autoferro in Ecuador, 93
Ayacucho, 116
Aymara Indians, 216, 217, 220, 221,
   223

backpack, 29–30, 33; on airplanes,
   47
Ballestras, Islas, 158
Baños, 88–90
Baños del Inca, 152
Bartolome Island, 101
beaches: in Ecuador, 94–95; in Peru,
   147–48
beggars, 54
Blanca, Cordillera, 117–44; Grand
   Tour of, 140–41; guides in, 62;
   maps of, 121; travel in, 123–24
boat travel: in Galapagos Islands,
   102–4; on Amazon River, *see* river
   travel; on Lake Titicaca, 167–68,
   223–24
boots, 32
buses, 49, 51. *See also individual*
   destinations

Cabanaconde, 165
Cajamarca, 149–51
Calera, 165
Callao, 107–8
Callejón de Huaylas, 119–20;
   transportation through, 123
cameras, 36, 42, 45
Candelaria, 92
Cantu ruins, 135–36
Carás, 120, 123, 134–36
Carhuáz, 137
Cashapampa, 134, 141
Catac, 127
Cayma, 162
cerebral mountain sickness, 65–66
Chairo, 228
Chala, 161
Chan-Chan ruins, 145–47
Chancos, 140
Chávin culture, 2, 125–27; Chávin
   de Huantar, 125–27, 142, 144;
   other Chávin sites, 152–55
Checacupe, 210
Chetilla, 152, 153, 154
Chilete, 155
Chillca, 210, 213
Chimborazo, 87–88
Chimbote, 122
Chimu culture, 145–47
Chinchero, 187–88
Chivay, 165
chloroquine, 28
Chojlla, 229, 231
Choro, 227
climbing: in Ecuador, 76; of El
   Misti, 165–66; near Ausangate,
   208–9, 210–11; of Mt. Pichincha,
   77–78
clothing, 30–33
Coca, 239
cocaine, 45
coca leaves, 45
Colcabamba, 131, 141
Colcapampa, 203
Colca Valley, 164–65
colectivos, 49–50, 51
Copacabana, 219, 223–25

Cordillera Blanca. *See* Blanca, Cordillera
Coroico, 228–29
Cotacachi, 84
Cotopaxi, 87
Cuenca, 94
Cuicocha, Laguna de, 83–84
Cuismancu culture, 113
Cumbe Mayo, 152–53
Cumbre, La, de Yungas Pass, 225; La Cumbre-to-Coroico Trek, 225–28
currency, 23
Cuzco, 170–78, 201, 206; area excursions, 178–84

Daphne Island, 100
diarrhea, 66–67
Driver's Permit, International, 22
drugs, 45

equipment, 29–37; camping, 33–34; cooking, 34; photographic, 36–37; river travel, 235–36; trekking, 30–37, 124
Esmeraldas, 95
Española Island, 101
Espiritu Pampa, 196
exchange rate, 23

Fansidar, 28
Fernandina Island, 101
festivals (fiestas), 60–61
fishing, deep-sea, 95
Floreana Island, 101
food, trail, 44, 58–60

Galapagos Islands, 95–104; animals in, 97–98. *See also individual islands*
gamma globulin, 27
Genovesa Island, 101
geology, 13–14
Guayaquil, 70–71, 93, 94
guides and *arrieros,* 44, 61–63; in Cordillera Blanca, 124–25, 140; in Cordillera Vilcabamba, 202; in Cordillera Vilcanota, 206–8, 212, 213; for river travel, 236

health problems, 63–69. *See also* medical preparation
hepatitis, 27
hotel accommodations, 54–56. *See also individual locations*

hot water in hotels, 55–56
Huaca Arco Iris ruins, 147
Huaca de la Luna ruins, 147
Huaca del Sol ruins, 147
huacas near Cuzco, 182–84
Huallcacocha, Laguna, 138
Huancayo, 115, 116
Huanchaco, 148
Huanuco, 243
Huarás, 119, 122–25, 127
Huascarán, 118; National Park, 120–21, 125
Huata, 135, 136
Huatajata, 223
Huayllabamba, 193, 202, 203–4
Huayna Picchu, 201
hypothermia, 68–69

Ica, 158–59
Illiniza, 86–87
Iluman, 82
immunization, 26–27
Inca Empire, 3–11, 170–74
Inca ruins. *See* ruins
Inca Trail, 45, 189–99, 201, 204
Ingapirca ruins, 93–94
inoculations, 25–27
Iquitos, 239–41
Isabela Island, 100
Islands of the Sun and Moon ruins, 223

Jampamayo, Río, 209
Jauja, 116
jungle guides, 240–41
jungle lodges, 237–38, 240, 244
jungle travel, 232, 235–38

Kuntur Wasi ruins, 152, 154, 155

Laguna Grande, Cordillera Blanca, 132, 134
Laguna Grande, Paracas Peninsula, 157
Lagunillas, 157
languages, 24–25
La Paz, 216–20; area excursions, 220–22
Latacunga, 85
Lima, 107–13
Limoncocha, 239
Litoral, El, Ecuador, 94–95
Llactapata, 189, 192
Llanganuco-Cashapampa Trek, 128–34

Llanganuco, Lagunas, 128, 130
Llipta, 137, 138

Machu Picchu, 189, 195, 196–201,
    203, 204
mail, 51–52
malaria, 28, 234
maps: Bolivia, 219–20, 225;
    Cordillera Blanca, 121; Ecuador,
    76–77; Inca Trail, 190–91, 192;
    Peru, 111–12; Taquesi trail,
    230
Marcará, 140
Marcawasi, 114–15
medical: preparation, 25–29; kit,
    28–29
medicines, 28–29
Miraflores, 108, 109–10
Misahualli, 238–39
Misti, El, 161, 165–66
Moche culture, 2, 145, 147
Moche, Río, 144–45
Mochican Huacas, 147
Mojanda, Laguna, 84
Mollepata, 201–2
money, 23–24
mountain sickness, 65–66
Muela del Diablo, 220

Napo, Río, 238, 239
Nazca, 159–61; flights over, 160
Negra, Cordillera, 119, 135
Negro, Río, 142, 143–44

Ocongate, 204, 206
Ollantaytambo, 184, 186–87, 189,
    192
Olleros, 143
Olleros-to-Chávin Trek, 142–44
Otavalo, 78–81

Pacchanta valley, 208–9
Pachacámac ruins, 113–14
Palcacocha, Laguna, 142
Pampa San Jose, Nazca, 159–60
Panecillo near Quito, 73–74
Paracas culture, 2
Paracas Peninsula, 156–58
Parón, Laguna, 134–35
Pasaje de Ulta, 137, 139, 141
passport, 21, 22, 41, 42
Peguche, 82
Perolcocha, Laguna, 142
Peru: north coast, 116–17; south
    coast, 155–64

photographic equipment, 36–37
Phuyupatamarca ruins, 195
physical conditioning, 24
Pichincha, Mt., 77–78
Pichinjoto, 187
Pisac, 184–86
Pisco, 158
Pitumarca, 210, 212
Playas, 94–95
polio, 27
Pompey, 139, 141
Portachuelo de Honda, 130, 139–
    40
porters. *See* guides
Primavera, 239
public transportation, 46–51
Pucallpa, 241–43
Puca Punta, 209
Puerto Ayora, 99, 103, 104
Puerto Francisco de Orellana, 239
Puerto Maldonado, 243–44
Puka Pukara ruin, 179, 181–82
pulmonary acute mountain sickness,
    65–66
Puno, 166–70
Punta Llanashallash, 144
Punta Unión, 128, 132, 141
Punta Yanayacu, 141
Puya Raimondi Park, 125

Q'enko huaca, 182–83
Quebrada Cojup, 142
Quebrada Ulta, 136–38, 139
Quebrada Ulta-Honda loop, 136–40
Quechua language, 25, 106. *See also*
    Appendix II
Quechuas, 11–13
Querocicha, Laguna, 127
Quilotoa Crater, 84–86
Quito, 73–77, 78

rabies, 53
railroad travel. *See* trains
rainfall, 38
Real, Cordillera (Bolivia), 215
restaurants, 56–58. *See also*
    individual towns
Riberalta, 244–45
river travel, 235–37
road travel, 48–51
ruins: Inca, 93–94, 151–52, 168,
    172–73, 184–88; Inca, along Inca
    Trail, 192–94; Inca, near Cuzco,
    178–82; pre-Inca, 127–28, 144–47,
    243

Sacsayhuaman ruins, 179–80
Salapunco *huaca,* 183
Salasaca, 90
Salinas, 95
Salkantay, Nevado, 201, 203
San Antonio de Ibarra, 83
San Cristobal Island, 101
San Pablo, Ecuador, 82
San Pablo, Peru, 152, 154, 155
San Pedro de Casta, 114, 115
Santa Cruz Island, 99–100
Santa Eulalia, 114
Santa Fe Island, 100
Santa Rosa, 99
Santa Teresa, 202, 203
Santiago Island, 101
Santo Domingo de los Colorados, 95
Sayajmarca ruins, 194–95
seasons in the Andean countries, 38
Seymour Island, 100
Shilla, 137, 138
Sibinacocha, Laguna, 211–13
sierra (Peru), 105–6
Sillustani ruins, 166
skiing in Bolivia, 219
soroche (altitude sickness), 63–65
Soto Island, 168
South American Explorers Club, 61
South Plaza Island, 100
Spanish language, 24–25
stoves, 34, 44
Student Card, 22

Tambo Machay ruins, 179, 181
Taquesi Pass, 230
Taquesi Trail, 229–31
Taquile Island, 167–68
telegraph service, 52–53
telephone service, 52
tetanus, 27
theft, 41–43
Tiabaya, 162
Tiahuanaco culture, 127
Tiahuanaco ruins, 221–22
Ticlio Pass, 115
Tingo, 162
Tingo Maria, 243
Tinqui, 204, 206, 208, 211, 213
Titicaca, Lake, 166–68, 221, 222–25

Tortuga Reserve, Galapagos, 99, 100
Toro Muerto petroglyphs, 165
Tourist Card, 22
Tungurahua, 91–92
typhoid, 27
trail conditions, 43–45
trains, 48; *autoferro* in Ecuador, 93;
    Tren de la Sierra in Peru, 115–16.
    See also individual destinations
truck, travel by, 50
Trujillo, 144–45, 148–49

Ucayali River, 242
Uros Indians, 166–67
Urubamba, 184, 186–87
Urubamba, Río, 184, 193, 195, 196,
    198
Urubamba Valley, 184

Vaccination, International Certificate
    of, 22, 26
vaccines, 26, 27
Valley of the Moon, 220
Ventanillas de Otuzco, 151–52
Ventilla, 230
Vicos, 140
Vilcabamba, Cordillera, 188–89, 201,
    202
Vilcanota, Cordillera, 204–13
Villa Fatima, 225
visas, 21

water purification, 67–68
weather in the Andean countries,
    38
Willcawain ruins, 127–28
Winay Wayna ruins, 195

Yanahuara, 162
Yanakachi, 231
Yarinacocha, Laguna, 242
yellow fever, 26
Yolosa, 228
Yucay, 186
Yungas, 215, 221, 226, 227–28
Yungay, 119–20, 130

Zongo Pass, 221
Zumbagua, 84–85